FROM INQUIRY TO ACADEMIC WRITING

A Practical Guide

FROM INQUIRY TO ACADEMIC WRITING

A Practical Guide

FOURTH EDITION

for Wayne State University

Stuart Greene
University of Notre Dame

April Lidinsky
Indiana University South Bend

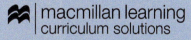

bedford/st.martin's • hayden-mcneil • w.h. freeman • worth publishers

For Bedford/St. Martin's

Vice President, Editorial, Macmillan Learning Humanities: Edwin Hill
Senior Program Director for English: Leasa Burton
Program Manager: John E. Sullivan III
Executive Marketing Manager: Joy Fisher Williams
Director of Content Development: Jane Knetzger
Senior Developmental Editor: Mara Weible
Associate Editor: Stephanie Thomas
Editorial Assistant: Aubrea Bailis
Senior Content Project Manager: Ryan Sullivan
Senior Workflow Project Manager: Lisa McDowell
Production Supervisor: Robert Cherry
Media Project Manager: Rand Thomas
Editorial Services: Lumina Datamatics, Inc.
Composition: Lumina Datamatics, Inc.
Photo Editor: Angela Boehler
Photo Researcher: Richard Fox, Lumina Datamatics, Inc.
Permissions Manager: Kalina Ingham
Senior Art Director: Anna Palchik
Cover Design: William Boardman
Printing and Binding: King Printing Co., Inc.

Copyright © 2018, 2015, 2012, 2008 by Bedford/St. Martin's.

All rights reserved. No part of this book may be reproduced, stored in a retrieval system, or transmitted in any form or by any means, electronic, mechanical, photocopying, recording, or otherwise, except as may be expressly permitted by the applicable copyright statutes or in writing by the Publisher.

Manufactured in the United States of America.

4 5 6 7 8 9 10   23 22 21 20 19

For information, write: Macmillan Learning Curriculum Solutions, 14903 Pilot Drive, Plymouth, MI 48170 (macmillanlearning.com)

ISBN 978-1-319-22307-6   (Wayne State University Edition)

Acknowledgments
Text acknowledgments and copyrights appear at the back of the book on pages 413–15, which constitute an extension of the copyright page. Art acknowledgments and copyrights appear on the same page as the art selections they cover.

Brief Contents

1 Introduction   1
2 Writing Process and the Digital Age 12
3 Analyzing Media 20
4 Voice in Academic and Civic Writing 26
5 Secondary Research Methods and Writing about Research 34
6 Metacognition and Reflection 51
7 From Reading as a Writer to Writing as a Reader   63
8 From Writing Summaries and Paraphrases to Writing Yourself into Academic Conversations   89
9 From Identifying Claims to Analyzing Arguments   112
10 From Identifying Issues to Forming Questions   139
11 From Formulating to Developing a Thesis   166
12 From Synthesis to Researched Argument   190
13 From Ethos to Logos: Appealing to Your Readers   250

Appendix: Citing and Documenting Sources 291

v

Contents

Brief Contents   v
How This Book Supports WPA Outcomes for First-Year Composition   xv
Foreword   xix

1 Introduction   1

Elsa Nilaj, Haley Sharrow, and Leena Ghannam

Why Take a Composition Class?   1

The Writing Process   2
  Asking Questions   2
  Effective Research   3
  Analyzing Media   4
  Peer Review   5
  Revising, Editing, & Publishing   8

Writing Style: How Do I Find Mine?   9

Conclusion   10

2 Writing Process and the Digital Age   12

Nicole L. Wilson

Understanding the Writing Process   12

Consider Ways to Personalize the Writing Process   13

vii

viii   CONTENTS

Prewriting   14
Brainstorming   14
Doing Research   15
Developing an Organizational Pattern   16

(Re)Writing   16
Draft as Necessary   16
Global Revision – Revising   16
Focused Revision – Proofreading   17
Detailed Revision – Editing   17

Digital Ways to Execute the Writing Process   17
Digital Brainstorming Techniques   17
Digital Ways to Do Research   18
Digital Ways to Organize Your Material   18
Digital Ways to Revise   18
Example   19

Further Reading   19

3 Analyzing Media   20
Jared Grogan and Luke Thominet

Introduction   20
Analyzing Images   21
Analyzing Videos   22
Analyzing Interactive Media   23
Works Cited   25

4 Voice in Academic and Civic Writing   26
LaToya Faulk

Defining Voice and Style   26
Style as Identity   29
Style, Home-Based Identity, and Academic Writing   30
Style and Academic Disciplines   31
Works Cited   33

CONTENTS **ix**

5 Secondary Research Methods and Writing about Research 34

Ruth Boeder and Adrienne Jankens

Introduction   34
- Activity 1: Reflective Journaling   36
- Activity 2: Visualizing a Topic   36

Secondary Research Methods and Processes   36
- *Writing Researching Questions   36*
  - Activity 3: Testing the Effectiveness of an I-Search Question   37
- *Turning Research Questions into Search Terms   37*
  - Activity 4: Finding Keywords in a Sentence   38
- *Using Multimodal & Digital Strategies to Keep Track of Research   40*
- *Interacting with Digital Sources   40*
- *Making a Flexible Research Plan   40*
- *Finding Relevant Sources   41*
  - Activity 5: Reflecting on the Types of Sources You Need   42
- *Evaluating Sources   43*
  - Activity 6: The Full CRAAP Test   44

Writing about Your Research Process and Discoveries   45
- *Annotated Bibliographies   45*
- *Research Narratives/The I-Search   45*
- *Integrating Research Results into Your Writing   46*
- *Reporting Information & Synthesizing Sources   46*
- *Citing Sources   48*
  - Activity 7: Citation Information Search   49

Conclusion   50

6 Metacognition and Reflection   51

Adrienne Jankens, Sarah Primeau, Thomas Trimble, Nicole Guinot Varty

Introduction   51

Reflection and Metacognition   52

Purposes of Reflection   53
- *Using Reflection to Plan   53*
- *Using Reflection to Monitor   55*
- *Using Reflection to Evaluate   56*

x CONTENTS

Genres of Reflective Writing   58
Reflective Journals   58
"Talk-Backs"   59
Process Memos   59

Reflecting at the End of the Semester   60

Conclusion   61
■ Sample Journal Prompts   62

Works Cited   62

7 From Reading as a Writer to Writing as a Reader   63

Reading as an Act of Composing: Annotating   63

Reading as a Writer: Analyzing a Text Rhetorically   66
E. D. HIRSCH JR., **Preface to** *Cultural Literacy*   67
Identify the Situation   70
Identify the Writer's Purpose   71
Identify the Writer's Claims   72
Identify the Writer's Audience   72
■ Steps to Analyzing a Text Rhetorically   73
■ A Practice Sequence: Analyzing a Text
Rhetorically   73
EUGENE F. PROVENZO JR., **Hirsch's Desire for a National
Curriculum**   74

Writing as a Reader: Composing a Rhetorical Analysis   76
DAVID TYACK, **Whither History Textbooks?**   77

An Annotated Student Rhetorical Analysis   80
QUENTIN COLLIE, **A Rhetorical Analysis of "Whither History
Textbooks?" (Student Writing)**   81

Writing a Rhetorical Analysis   83
SHERRY TURKLE, **The Flight from Conversation**   84
■ A Practice Sequence: Writing a Rhetorical Analysis   88

8 From Writing Summaries and Paraphrases to Writing Yourself into Academic Conversations   89

Summaries, Paraphrases, and Quotations   89

Writing a Paraphrase   90
■ Steps to Writing a Paraphrase   94
■ A Practice Sequence: Writing a Paraphrase   94

CONTENTS **xi**

Writing a Summary   94

CLIVE THOMPSON, On the New Literacy   *95*
Describe the Key Claims of the Text   97
Select Examples to Illustrate the Author's Argument   99
Present the Gist of the Author's Argument   99
Contextualize What You Summarize   100
- Steps to Writing a Summary   102
- A Practice Sequence: Writing a Summary   102

Writing Yourself into Academic Conversations   102
- Steps to Writing Yourself into an Academic Conversation   104
- A Practice Sequence: Writing Yourself into an Academic Conversation   104

TOM STANDAGE, History Retweets Itself   *105*

9   From Identifying Claims to Analyzing Arguments   112

Identifying Types of Claims   112

DANA RADCLIFFE, Dashed Hopes: Why Aren't Social Media Delivering Democracy?   *113*
Identify Claims of Fact   116
Identify Claims of Value   118
Identify Claims of Policy   118
- Steps to Identifying Claims   120
- A Practice Sequence: Identifying Claims   120

Analyzing Arguments   121
Analyze the Reasons Used to Support a Claim   121
Identify Concessions   124
Identify Counterarguments   125

An Annotated Student Argument   126

MARQUES CAMP, The End of the World May Be Nigh, and It's the Kindle's Fault (Student Writing)   *127*
- Steps to Analyzing an Argument   129
- A Practice Sequence: Analyzing an Argument   130

SUSAN D. BLUM, The United States of (Non)Reading: The End of Civilization or a New Era?   *130*

Analyzing and Comparing Arguments   133

STUART ROJSTACZER, Grade Inflation Gone Wild   *133*

PHIL PRIMACK, Doesn't Anybody Get a C Anymore?   *135*
- A Practice Sequence: Analyzing and Comparing Arguments   137

xii CONTENTS

10 From Identifying Issues to Forming Questions 139

Identifying Issues 140

Draw on Your Personal Experience 141
Identify What Is Open to Dispute 141
Resist Binary Thinking 142
Build on and Extend the Ideas of Others 143
Read to Discover a Writer's Frame 144
Consider the Constraints of the Situation 146
 ■ Steps to Identifying Issues 147

Identifying Issues in an Essay 147

ANNA QUINDLEN, **Doing Nothing Is Something** *148*
 ■ A Practice Sequence: Identifying Issues 150

Formulating Issue-Based Questions 151

Refine Your Topic 153
Explain Your Interest in the Topic 153
Identify an Issue 154
Formulate Your Topic as a Question 154
Acknowledge Your Audience 154
 ■ Steps to Formulating an Issue-Based Question 155
 ■ A Practice Sequence: Formulating an Issue-Based Question 155

An Academic Essay for Analysis 157

WILLIAM DERESIEWICZ, **The End of Solitude** *157*

11 From Formulating to Developing a Thesis 166

Working versus Definitive Theses 167

Developing a Working Thesis: Four Models 168

The Correcting-Misinterpretations Model 168
The Filling-the-Gap Model 169
The Modifying-What-Others-Have-Said Model 170
The Hypothesis-Testing Model 170
 ■ Steps to Formulating a Working Thesis: Four Models 171
 ■ A Practice Sequence: Identifying Types of Theses 171

Establishing a Context for a Thesis 173

An Annotated Student Introduction: Providing a Context for a Thesis 173

CONTENTS **xiii**

COLIN O'NEILL, Money Matters: Framing the College Access Debate (Student Writing) *173*

Establish That the Issue Is Current and Relevant *176*

Briefly Present What Others Have Said *176*

Explain What You See as the Problem *177*

State Your Thesis *178*

■ Steps to Establishing a Context for a Thesis 178

Analyze the Context of a Thesis *179*

KRIS GUTIÉRREZ, *from* Teaching Toward Possibility: Building Cultural Supports for Robust Learning *179*

■ A Practice Sequence: Building a Thesis 183

An Annotated Student Essay: Stating and Supporting a Thesis 184

VERONICA STAFFORD, Texting and Literacy (Student Writing) *185*

12 From Synthesis to Researched Argument 190

Writing a Synthesis 191

PAUL ROGAT LOEB, Making Our Lives Count *191*

ANNE COLBY AND THOMAS EHRLICH, WITH ELIZABETH BEAUMONT AND JASON STEPHENS, Undergraduate Education and the Development of Moral and Civic Responsibility *198*

LAURIE OUELLETTE, Citizen Brand: ABC and the Do Good Turn in US Television *202*

Make Connections among Different Texts *214*

Decide What Those Connections Mean *215*

Formulate the Gist of What You've Read *216*

■ Steps to Writing a Synthesis 220

■ A Practice Sequence: Writing a Synthesis 221

DAN KENNEDY, Political Blogs: Teaching Us Lessons about Community 222

JOHN DICKERSON, Don't Fear Twitter 225

STEVE GROVE, YouTube: The Flattening of Politics 227

Avoiding Plagiarism 231

■ Steps to Avoiding Plagiarism 232

Integrating Quotations into Your Writing 233

Take an Active Stance *233*

Explain the Quotations *234*

Attach Short Quotations to Your Sentences *235*

xiv CONTENTS

■ Steps to Integrating Quotations into Your Writing 237
■ A Practice Sequence: Integrating Quotations 237

An Annotated Student Researched Argument: Synthesizing Sources 237

NANCY PAUL, **A Greener Approach to Groceries: Community-Based Agriculture in LaSalle Square (Student Writing)** 238
■ A Practice Sequence: Thinking about Copyright 249

13 From Ethos to Logos

Appealing to Your Readers 250

Connecting with Readers: A Sample Argument 251

JAMES W. LOEWEN, **The Land of Opportunity** 251

Appealing to Ethos 257

Establish That You Have Good Judgment 258
Convey to Readers That You Are Knowledgeable 259
Show That You Understand the Complexity of a Given Issue 259
■ Steps to Appealing to Ethos 260

Appealing to Pathos 260

Show That You Know What Your Readers Value 261
Use Illustrations and Examples That Appeal to Readers' Emotions 261
Consider How Your Tone May Affect Your Audience 262
■ Steps to Appealing to Pathos 263
■ A Practice Sequence: Appealing to Ethos and Pathos 264

Appealing to Logos: Using Reason and Evidence to Fit the Situation 265

State the Premises of Your Argument 268
Use Credible Evidence 268
Demonstrate That the Conclusion Follows from the Premises 269
■ Steps to Appealing to Logos 270

Recognizing Logical Fallacies 270

Analyzing the Appeals in a Researched Argument 275

MEREDITH MINKLER, **Community-Based Research Partnerships: Challenges and Opportunities** 275
■ A Practice Sequence: Analyzing the Appeals in a Researched Argument 289

Appendix: Citing and Documenting Sources 291

How This Book Supports WPA Outcomes for First-Year Composition

Note: This chart aligns with the latest **WPA Outcomes Statement**, ratified in July 2014.

WPA OUTCOMES	RELEVANT FEATURES OF *FROM INQUIRY TO ACADEMIC WRITING: A PRACTICAL GUIDE*, FOURTH EDITION
Rhetorical Knowledge	
Learn and use key rhetorical concepts through analyzing & composing a variety of texts.	A full range of rhetorical concepts is presented throughout the text. For example, see: <ul><li>the treatment of rhetorical analysis in Chapter 2, "From Reading as a Writer to Writing as a Reader"</li><li>the treatment of argument in Chapter 4, "From Identifying Claims to Analyzing Arguments"</li><li>the treatment of rhetorical appeals in Chapter 9, "From Ethos to Logos"</li></ul>
Gain experience reading and composing in several genres to understand how genre conventions shape and are shaped by readers' and writers' practices and purposes.	A wide range of genres is represented in the text for analysis and composition. <ul><li>See the literacy narratives that conclude Chapter 1 and the Practice Sequence that follows (pp. 19–37).</li><li>Chapter 2 presents rhetorical context as a tool for analysis.</li><li>Throughout the text, all student essays are annotated to indicate particular practices for particular purposes.</li></ul>

xvi HOW THIS BOOK SUPPORTS WPA OUTCOMES FOR FIRST-YEAR COMPOSITION

WPA OUTCOMES	RELEVANT FEATURES OF *FROM INQUIRY TO ACADEMIC WRITING: A PRACTICAL GUIDE*, FOURTH EDITION
Develop facility in responding to a variety of situations and contexts, calling for purposeful shifts in voice, tone, level of formality, design, medium, and/or structure.	Throughout the text, students are instructed to attend to situations and contexts and given strategies for recognizing and responding to them in their composing. For example: • Chapter 6 shows how to establish a context for a thesis. • Chapter 9 shows analysis and modulation of appeals, and Chapter 10 includes examples of visual appeals.
Understand and use a variety of technologies to address a range of audiences.	The range of texts and technologies in the print text and available through LaunchPad help students understand and analyze different technologies they can use in their own composing. • Chapter 10 provides new coverage of visual and multimodal analysis, along with new texts for students to analyze.
Match the capacities of different environments (e.g., print & electronic) to varying rhetorical situations.	The rhetorical and analytical instruction in the text helps students match the capacities of different composing technologies to different rhetorical situations, including words-only and multimodal examples.

Critical Thinking, Reading, and Composing

Use composing and reading for inquiry, learning, thinking, and communicating in various rhetorical contexts.	• Chapter 1 sets the stage for academic writing as a form of inquiry. • Chapters 2–5 show critical reading in action. • Chapters 6 and 8 show how to generate texts and compositions from reading in various rhetorical contexts.
Read a diverse range of texts, attending especially to relationships between assertion and evidence, to patterns of organization, to interplay between verbal and nonverbal elements, and how these features function for different audiences and situations.	• Chapter 4 offers instruction in identifying claims and assertions and relating them to evidence. • Chapter 6 presents thesis statements as ways of developing claims and using evidence depending on the situation. • Chapter 11 shows how to shape a composition via different patterns of organization.
Locate and evaluate primary and secondary research materials, including journal articles, essays, books, databases, & informal Internet sources.	• Chapter 7, "From Finding to Evaluating Sources," presents instruction in locating and evaluating primary and secondary research materials, including journal articles, essays, books, databases, and informal Internet sources. • Chapter 13, "Other Methods of Inquiry," helps students do primary research via interviews and focus groups.

HOW THIS BOOK SUPPORTS WPA OUTCOMES FOR FIRST-YEAR COMPOSITION   **xvii**

WPA OUTCOMES	RELEVANT FEATURES OF *FROM INQUIRY TO ACADEMIC WRITING: A PRACTICAL GUIDE*, FOURTH EDITION
Use strategies—such as interpretation, synthesis, response, critique, and design/redesign—to compose texts that integrate the writer's ideas with those from appropriate sources.	Chapter 8, "From Synthesis to Researched Argument," helps students compose texts that integrate the writer's ideas with those from appropriate sources.
Processes	
Develop a writing project through multiple drafts.	• Chapters 1–13 provide instruction in the various stages of developing writing projects. • Within chapters, the "Practice Sequences" often present compound activities for chapter-specific writing projects, such as comparing arguments in Chapter 4 (pp. 112–13) and developing a synthesis in Chapter 8 (p. 218).
Develop flexible strategies for reading, drafting, reviewing, collaboration, revising, rewriting, rereading, and editing.	• Chapters 2 and 4 offer flexible strategies for rhetorical reading and inventive reading, such as reading to extend the ideas of others. • Chapters 11 and 12 feature concrete strategies on drafting, collaborating, revising, and editing.
Use composing processes and tools as a means to discover and reconsider ideas.	• Throughout the text, the importance of rereading and rewriting to discover and reconsider ideas is emphasized. • Chapter 6 teaches the importance of revising a thesis in light of new evidence.
Experience the collaborative and social aspects of writing processes.	• The habits of mind of academic writing set forth in Chapter 1 emphasize the importance of collaboration and the idea of academic writing as conversation. • Chapter 12, "From Revising to Editing: Working with Peer Groups," presents collaboration and revision as essential components of academic writing.
Learn to give and act on productive feedback to works in progress.	Chapter 12 includes sample documents and worksheets for the various stages of productive feedback readers can give writings.
Adapt composing processes for a variety of technologies and modalities.	Chapter 10's coverage of visual analysis fosters an awareness of how rhetorical concepts function across various technologies and modalities.
Reflect on the development of composing practices and how those practices influence their work.	Practice Sequence assignments often encourage students to reflect on their composing practices and how those practices influence their work.
Knowledge of Conventions	
Develop knowledge of linguistic structures, including grammar, punctuation, and spelling, through practice in composing and revising.	Chapters 11 and 12, on drafting, revising, and editing, help students develop knowledge of linguistic structures, including grammar, punctuation, and spelling.

xviii HOW THIS BOOK SUPPORTS WPA OUTCOMES FOR FIRST-YEAR COMPOSITION

WPA OUTCOMES	RELEVANT FEATURES OF *FROM INQUIRY TO ACADEMIC WRITING: A PRACTICAL GUIDE*, FOURTH EDITION
Understand why genre conventions for structure, paragraphing, tone, and mechanics vary.	The overarching emphasis on rhetorical context and situation in the text fosters critical thinking about genre conventions.
Gain experience negotiating variations in genre conventions.	Critical reading of the variety of formats and genres represented by the multidisciplinary selections in the text imparts experience negotiating variations in genre conventions.
Learn common formats and/or design features for different kinds of texts.	• Annotated texts such as the student essays impart awareness of common formats and/or design features for difference kinds of texts. • The Appendix on documentation styles gives specific instruction in formats and design.
Explore the concepts of intellectual property (such as fair use and copyright) that motivate documentation conventions.	• A "Practice Sequence" in Chapter 8 concerns critical thinking about copyright and intellectual property (p. 246). • The Appendix on documenting sources (specifically MLA and APA formats) raises issues of different documentation conventions.
Practice applying citation conventions systematically in their own work.	The Appendix enables students to apply citation conventions of MLA and APA styles systematically in their own work.

Foreword
Clay Walker and Jeff Pruchnic

The goal of ENG 1020 is to help you begin developing the academic literacy skills needed for success in your college career. These skills include critically reading college-level texts, using a flexible and effective writing process to generate persuasive and analytical arguments, conducting secondary research to develop ideas and your understanding about a topic, and using reflection and metacognition to hone your skills as a writer. Although these learning goals reflect many of the core academic literacy practices required in college programs, students come to ENG 1020 with a range of experiences and attitudes related to reading and writing. While some students feel well equipped for the persuasive and analytical writing tasks of the course, others may feel less certain about their abilities and may dislike writing courses in general because writing has never been their strong suit. Often, students assume that being a good writer is a quality that you are born with—some have it, some don't. However, the opposite is true: writing is a skill that can be taught and learned.

Writing is a practice. While there are concepts that you can learn related to composing texts, developing your ability to write is often more like learning to play a sport or musical instrument. There isn't some mystical "AHA!" moment when it all comes to you. Rather, growth can sometimes be slow, and success depends to some degree on the amount of time and effort you put into practicing your abilities. Anybody can be a good writer given the time and opportunity for sustained effort. This course offers you the opportunity to strengthen and develop your ability to read and write college-level texts at several different levels. Indeed, students are often surprised by the amount of growth they've achieved from the beginning of the semester to the end.

In ENG 1020 you'll apply the Wayne State composition curriculum's core emphases of **discourse community**, **genre**, **rhetorical situation**,

XX FOREWORD

and **metacognition/reflection** to written and multimedia works focused on specific audiences. These audiences may include your classmates, academic and professional audiences of various types, or civic communities you might belong to or wish to influence in a particular way.

- A **discourse community** is a group of people who work together in a social scene (such as a college) toward some shared goal (like education). Often, based on their shared goals, members of a discourse community share expectations about what kinds of writing are "good" or "effective." ENG 1020 prepares you for your entry into the academic discourse community, whose members (largely students and professors) value, among other things, the expression of ideas or arguments based on facts or evidence that are supported by good reasons. Often, students and professors/researchers use secondary research, which is research based on other scholarly books or articles, to develop their own arguments and ideas. To that end, this course also emphasizes the written genres often used in secondary research.

- A **genre** is a type of text used frequently in a social situation to allow various people in that situation to interact together. For instance, a textbook is a classroom genre that allows a teacher to share detailed information related to a course with the students. In ENG 1020, we will focus on a variety of genres critical to secondary research, including the argumentative research essay.

- In order to successfully write in a genre, students must understand its **rhetorical situation**, which broadly refers to the relationship between the audience and the purpose of a text. Understanding the rhetorical situation can help you become a more effective reader and writer. For instance, consider the rhetorical situation of a textbook—a researcher wants to convey information (its purpose) to students (the audience). The textbook achieves these goals by using features like bolded key terms, questions for discussion in class, and examples that illustrate complicated concepts in more detail.

- Finally, students will use **reflection and metacognition** to develop an understanding of their writing practices. Reflection is a technique for looking back at your writing to better understand and analyze what you did and the degree to which your work was successful/not successful. Metacognition, on the other hand, is your ability to think about your thinking. For instance, the more aware you are of how a textbook is structured according to its rhetorical situation, the easier it is for you to critically read and examine its content. Together, reflection and metacognition will allow you to develop your writing practice with more purpose and control.

As with all courses in the Wayne State required writing sequence, mechanical correctness and appropriate academic writing styles are key concerns. However, in ENG 1020, you'll also concentrate specifically on rhetoric (or persuasion) and argument as the major objectives of many important kinds of writing you may be asked to produce. By focusing on rhetoric and audience, assignments in ENG 1020 will require you to do two major types of work. In one type, you'll analyze a particular piece of argumentative discourse to determine how it succeeds (or fails) in appropriately impacting its audience. In another type, you'll develop a persuasive argument based on an extensive secondary research process.

Work in ENG 1020 often takes place through the following key writing tasks, several of which might serve as long-term projects in your 1020 course:

Rhetorical Analysis: Whether we are talking about a recent editorial on a heated political issue, a contemporary car commercial, or the music video for a new hip-hop artist, almost every act of communication can be analyzed as making a particular argument (trying to convince its audience of something) and as focused on moving a specific and identifiable audience. By studying how other authors adapt their argumentative strategies to their specific audiences, you'll learn how you can analyze your own prospective audiences and make the right moves to reach them through written and multimedia discourse.

Research Narrative/I-Search: Using an effective secondary research process is at the core of many college-level writing projects. Writing a research narrative will allow you to develop an awareness of how you move through the secondary research process, from selecting key words to finding and evaluating sources, from drafting research notes to compiling a literature review that summarizes and synthesizes the ideas that emerge from your research.

Researched Arguments: There are writing tasks that will require you to research other scholars' and writers' work in order to cite them as authorities. Other tasks will require you to contextualize your own arguments within the viewpoints of others, and to describe, specifically, whether and how you agree or disagree with prominent perspectives on a particular issue. In researched position papers, you'll execute both of these tasks by demonstrating your knowledge about the practical matters of specific issues as well as current arguments and viewpoints surrounding it. By positioning your own arguments among other viewpoints, you can most effectively convince your audience that your arguments are both fact-based and responsive to the various disagreements surrounding an issue. Your position will likely take the form of one or more modes of argument, including *causal arguments, definition arguments,* and *proposal arguments*.

Causal Arguments: The root causes or probable effects of an event are often highly contested areas in complex social and cultural issues such as the widening gap between upper- and lower-class wages, the cost of tuition, the role of standardized testing in K–12 education, and the widespread immigration of people across borders. The results of a causal analysis/argument for a complex issue often depend on the theoretical or ideological approach that one takes. For instance, analyzing the probable effects of global warming will produce different results when considered from the perspective of how it will affect plants and animals, versus how it will affect coastal cities and infrastructure. When making a cause/effect argument, you must be aware of the theoretical or conceptual lens you use to make your case. Doing so will allow you to position your own analysis/argument in relationship to other positions on the issue.

Definition Arguments: Arguments about *definition* (what a particular term means, or whether or not a particular object or event is captured or referenced by a specific term) are the basis of a surprisingly large amount of disagreements in contemporary political and cultural life. For instance, arguments about the death penalty focus on defining "cruel and unusual punishment." Arguments about marijuana often focus on defining it as a narcotic, a medicine, or simply an inebriating substance like liquor. Similarly, important debates and cultural shifts are often signaled by the changing definition of a particular term (such as "feminism" or "patriotism"). Finally, *complicated definitions*, or terms that require highly specialized explanations, are often problematic when considered from the points of view of multiple audiences. In performing definition arguments, you'll work toward applying definitions to "hard cases," explaining specialized definitions for less-specialized audiences, and arguing why one version of a definition is superior to others for a particular purpose.

Proposal Arguments: Whether we are discussing marriage proposals, grant applications, or ballots promoting a change in existing local or federal laws, proposals are arguments in which an author attempts to convince an audience to perform a particular action or indicate their support for one course of action as opposed to others. In analyzing and crafting your own proposals, you'll learn how to appeal to the common ground you share with an audience, and how to use the common rhetorical features of proposal as a genre. These features include the importance of outlining the positive and negative consequences of undertaking, or not undertaking, an action being proposed. In utilizing these features, you'll master one of the most common genres in argumentative writing as it occurs in academic, civic, and professional realms.

Multimodal Arguments: Many of the arguments we encounter on a regular basis adopt both visual and textual elements to persuade us. Such multimodal arguments are effective in presenting a complex array of facts and data in easily digestible visual presentations, whether through the use of charts and graphs or other means that effectively illustrate the key concepts and arguments presented by the writer.

Reflective Arguments: Throughout the semester, you will be asked to take a critical look at the work you've created or are in the process of creating. Using reflection as a tool in your writing process allows you to better understand and control your own process and to develop an awareness of yourself as a writer. Doing so will allow you to better transfer what you learn in this course to other academic writing situations during your college career.

Through effectively executing assignments and major projects based on these rhetorical tasks, you'll develop the following core competencies:

Reading

- Use reading strategies in order to identify, analyze, evaluate, and respond to arguments, rhetorical elements, and genre conventions in college-level texts and other media.

Writing

- Compose persuasive academic genres, including argument and analysis, using rhetorical and genre awareness.
- Use a flexible writing process that includes brainstorming/inventing ideas, planning, drafting, giving and receiving feedback, revising, editing, and publishing.

Researching

- Use a flexible research process to find, evaluate, and use information from secondary sources to support and formulate new ideas and arguments.

Reflecting

- Use written reflection to plan, monitor, and evaluate one's own learning and writing.

Your work in ENG 1020 will help prepare you for the wide variety of analyses and arguments you will be asked to produce in your academic courses in fields other than English, as well as the various writing tasks you might face at your current job or as a member of various civic communities or groups. ENG 1020 also serves as preparation for your next course in the required Wayne State composition curriculum, whether it be ENG 3010 (Intermediate Writing), ENG 3020 (Community and Writing) or ENG 3050 (Technical Communication I). All of these courses will ask you to take what you've learned in ENG 1020 about audience and genre analysis and use those skills to study the discourse communities associated with your chosen career.

FROM INQUIRY TO ACADEMIC WRITING

A Practical Guide

Introduction

Elsa Nilaj, Haley Sharrow, and Leena Ghannam

At the time of writing this introduction, we are active, full-time scholars at Wayne State University and peer mentors in the Composition Learning Community. As peer mentors, it is not only our job, but also our passion to help students find a love for composition. We strive to push students to engage with their courses by being active participants in an intellectual society who brainstorm and connect with other students about their academic papers and research. As past students and current consultants for students in various writing classes within the Composition Program, we offer a particularly unique and helpful perspective for incoming students to begin their development as writers in a college composition class.

WHY TAKE A COMPOSITION CLASS?

Taking a composition class is an opportunity for you to learn how to be more articulate and creative in your writing. Regardless of your individual academic discipline, writing and reading in complex and informed ways will be essential for approaching numerous forms of media in a myriad of careers. Learning essential writing tools such as an awareness of rhetoric, rhetorical situations, and genre helps you develop your ability to articulate new ideas and persuade people of these ideas more effectively.

Learning how to write also means learning how to think differently, for learning how to write means being able to analyze something with a more informed thought process and perform broader and more effective methods of research. As a result, your own distinct style as a writer will begin to take shape. Your journey in your studies begins to shape the ways in which you explain yourself and the world around you. Forming new pathways of thought and modalities of expression is a constant process. No one is a perfect writer, but one can become better by learning how to develop a piece of writing that is eloquent, structurally sound, and well researched, enabling you to express your ideas in a more complex and comprehensible format.

Working collaboratively with your peers is also an essential aspect of this process. As you approach new crossroads in your individual disciplines, writing classes serve not only as an interdisciplinary expression of your own career paths, but also as a space where you can practice working with people in other departments of the university. Creating large-scale projects and papers can often be intimidating—the support of peers and teachers through collaboration can be a wonderful resource for improving your writing and receiving some advice and catharsis during the writing process. Other students often deal with points of confusion or frustration similar to those you deal with, so working through those difficulties opens up opportunities for a better writing experience altogether. Additionally, peers are able to read and critique your writing, not only helping you get advice and feedback on specific aspects of your writing, but also fostering a safe space around writing with audience comprehension and structure in mind.

In this introduction, we will explore these ideas more thoroughly, working through how to think differently about topics and processes and work with peers and instructors on becoming stronger writers and researchers. In the sections below, we explore asking questions about assignments, choosing research paths, writing and revising projects, engaging in peer review, and developing a writing style.

THE WRITING PROCESS

■ Asking Questions

For composition students, the writing process typically begins when they are introduced to the first project of the class. If you feel confused about an assignment, you may want to address those points of confusion with your professor. It's important to do this at an early stage in the writing process so that you can (1) avoid mistakes before writing, and (2) avoid the procrastination that comes with being too confused and/or too scared to approach your assignment.

Asking questions is a hard thing for most of us to do—we don't want to sound uninformed or ask a dumb or obvious question, but we also don't want to be too specific and risk getting an undetailed or vague answer. Or perhaps we are afraid to ask a professor for clarification, fearing that our writing will be too derivative of their thinking or expectations. So, how do we ask meaningful questions that give us the answers we're looking for? It is important to be informed about the material and to frame a question well, but the answer primarily lies in *not being afraid to ask*.

To gain confidence before asking a question (and make sure your answer doesn't lie in obvious places like assignment sheets or syllabi), be well informed. Before asking questions to your instructor or even peers, you should have read the class material and taken good notes. Reading class materials is always your best bet because you can directly quote or point to a place in the text that you did not understand or with which you had a concern. Class notes are useful because you can use them to refer to class discussions or lectures when asking questions. For example, you might say: "Professor, you mentioned today in class that sometimes articles don't have dates on them. What kinds of problems will this pose when we begin to cite our sources?"

Sometimes asking questions to the instructor may not help you because of the way you *learn*—this is completely *okay*. If you understand topics or concepts better with images, ask the instructor if he or she can provide an example of the work you are trying to produce. If you still feel as if none of these options help you when asking questions, try having *conversations* with your instructor. It's a good idea to have these conversations during class discussions about your topic of concern, during peer review activities, when the class has ended, before class begins, or during office hours. Be sure to bring all the materials you need to explain to your instructor which aspects of writing, reading, or analyzing are causing you trouble.

Asking questions does **NOT** make you an annoyance—college is a place to learn new things, and your professor is there to help you, so never be afraid to ask questions. Additionally, when you invest your time in finding answers to things you may not understand, it is a *great* reflection on you as a student. You will be displaying dedication and hard work, as well as results of improvement! (Not to mention, this will mean instructors will be happy to write recommendations about your engagement and hard work.) Asking questions may feel intimidating or awkward, but the benefits of developing informed writing habits, close relationships with professors, and a more motivated college experience far outweigh those ubiquitous fears.

■ Effective Research

One way to begin your research process is by simply playing around with different databases that the Wayne State University library offers. By doing this, you will understand how the system works (establishing a time period, using advanced searches, etc.) and, most importantly, you will not be as nervous and intimidated when you really begin your research.

Another way you can start your research process is simply by asking a question within the topic that interests you. Many instructors will advise

4   CHAPTER 1 | INTRODUCTION

you to stay away from broad topics; however, one way to do this is by asking broad questions. Begin to read the abstract from each article that catches your interest. Fair warning: when doing research, you will not always get the answer you are looking for. This might feel bad, but it can also be good. It is good because it will give you a chance to think about *why* these articles are not satisfying your question, whether your question was really *asking* something or merely *seeking* a topic, and whether the articles only talk about the topic you're interested in as a tangential or supporting point. These concerns are important to consider so that you can reevaluate the keywords you used in the search engine. As you read abstracts of articles, you should also take note of repetition. If you feel that articles are not satisfying your original question, but they all repeat some kind of word or concept, it is worth recording those repetitions and researching them to see *why* there is a buzz about them. Most likely this will result in exploring your topic further and narrowing down your scope of interest to one specific problem or topic.

Once they feel comfortable enough with their journey through the databases, and they have piled up their articles, one of the most common problems students face (including us) is *how* to read the articles. The best way to start reading an article is by skimming. However, you need to do this *actively*. While skimming, be conscious of the keywords that the author presents in the abstract and throughout the article, and be aware of the headers throughout the article. Make notes in the margins if a new question flourishes in your mind, or if you just want to document an observation that you make while skimming. It's important to do these things while skimming because when you start reading the article, you will have a mental map that can help you decide *where* you want to start reading. You may choose to start in the middle of the article where the author presents their findings, or you may want to start by reading the introduction to see *why* or even *how* the author chose this topic to discuss.

▪ Analyzing Media

In addition to reading scholarly material in your composition class, you may be asked to conduct rhetorical analyses on various kinds of media, and even to think about how you would present your own research in various forms, not only in essays. A rhetorical analysis focuses on understanding how a text makes an argument to its audience using specific textual and rhetorical features. Whether you are asked to analyze an article, a literary work, a film, a music video, or even an advertisement, there are several ways information is being thrown at you, the viewer. As you think and write about different media formats, the essential skill of analysis requires you to parse out all of the different aspects that come together to form the message that the media format is trying to illustrate. The process of learning how to think about media and culture is intrinsically linked with your process of becoming a better writer. The more informed your analysis is, the better and more rounded out your thesis and arguments will be.

In order to filter through important and unimportant information during the research process, a good writer must also be a good reader, as discussed above. Composition classes seek to teach new reading strategy skills, meaning that when you look at a text or any form of media, you will be able to read and respond to it in effective and informed ways. There is a prerequisite to this, however: understanding rhetoric and genre. *Rhetoric* refers to the manner in which ideas are expressed. A *genre* is a text's typical form used frequently in social situations to allow various participants to interact with each other in specific ways. These concepts are essential to developing an analysis because they help define content, purpose, and audience. Without understanding how, why, and for whom a text is written, you may find it difficult to make any assertions or assumptions about the message of the text.

Also, practicing critical reading, which requires you to look into how and why an author chooses to include something in their writing and decipher the metaphors, symbols, and messages in the text, helps you to become a better writer. Through critical reading, you can begin to reverse engineer the way an author thinks. Doing so will help you learn how to think like a writer. Unpacking the structures of a text and understanding its composition will help you think along the writer's train of thought. Eventually, considering rhetorical tools like tone, genre features, and audience appeals will become a natural part of how you write, based on the information you are trying to present.

Responding to texts and arguments of other writers is an essential aspect of analysis, and it will often be featured in the kinds of essays you write as well. For example, traditionally assigned academic essay structures require not only evidence in their body paragraphs, but also interpretation. Learning how to identify what a text is trying to do and why the author is trying to do that will become instrumental in how you choose to respond to it in your essay and develop a thesis based upon that evidence.

■ Peer Review

How can a peer review session help me with my writing?

Looking over the semester schedule for your composition class, you may notice several days marked as "peer review" days. Most often, coming into your first college-level English course after your K–12 education, you may interpret the phrase "peer review day" as a "fun day," or "free for all." At this point in time, it's vital that you forget this correlation because peer review day is one of the most important parts of the writing process during your higher education years. In this English 1020 course and beyond, it is vital for you to gain proper knowledge of how to benefit from this collaborative resource. A peer review day is time allotted for several tasks that will enhance both your writing and the writing of your colleagues. It's an opportunity for you to learn, grow, and develop as a writer and critic.

6   CHAPTER 1 | INTRODUCTION

Wayne State University's Composition Program has built a set of learning outcomes for each student that is attainable by the close of each semester. One of these outcomes emphasizes the importance of developing a flexible writing process that includes receiving and using feedback. Peer reviews are designed to specifically enhance one's ability to further this skill in each of the course learning outcomes. Sometimes these are the hardest days in class because previous experiences haven't prepared you for a collegiate-level review session. In this introduction, you will be prepped with different techniques for being "peer review session ready," so be sure to take notes!

Brainstorming

The first step in successfully preparing yourself for a peer review session is to reflect on the ways you learn best. This is important to determine because visual learners and old fashioned "pencil-paper" learners will brainstorm in different ways.

- For visual learners, it might be most helpful to create concept maps, puzzle pieces, or diagrams to organize your main topic and subtopics. This will allow you to clearly visualize your main points, the smaller details you'd like to include, and how they all fit together.

- For the standard "pencil-paper" kind of student, brainstorming might require nothing more than sitting down in a place that gets your thinking going. Being in an environment that allows your thoughts to flow freely is generally best when you're trying to sort out your thought process on paper, making lists, or freewriting about your ideas.

- If you aren't certain which type of learner you are, or if you're a mix of both, simply start by writing down your thoughts. Then attempt to form a plan of action for how you will approach organizing and writing your piece.

You will find that the more you push your brain to "brainstorm," the easier it will be to start getting the form of your paper in place. Remind yourself that there is nothing neat about starting the writing process. It is essentially trial and error; you'll find one piece of your puzzle appealing, and then realize that it doesn't exactly fit with the rest of what you're striving for. Just cross it out, crumple up the piece of paper, and keep on moving!

Planning & Drafting

Planning is KEY when preparing yourself and your piece of writing for a peer review session. After brainstorming, the very first thing you should do when you're beginning a rough draft is to plan out a schedule for yourself that is attainable and that will match your course calendar. Giving yourself personal goals and having deadlines given to you will help you be successful in your writing process. Stay on top of your homework assignment due dates and pay attention to details when completing assignments. This course is designed to guide you through writing your papers every step of the way.

Use your organization skills and decide how you can best present your information and showcase your ideas to your reader. For each genre you will work through in this class, there are strategies for finding the most effective structure so that your audience can clearly see and follow the ideas you are emphasizing.

Push yourself to formulate a piece with enough content to guide your peers through understanding your ideas during the reviewing process. A rough draft is exactly how it sounds: a rough sketch of what a reader should expect when you're finished with the piece. The last thing you want to do is show up on peer review day with just your header, title, name, date and introduction/thesis in your selected format. At the very least, you should be making detailed notes in an outline that shows each step in your plan of action to complete what should have been a rough draft.

When you're making your way through a rough draft, pay attention to your personal struggles as a writer. If you notice that you begin to struggle with a concept or formatting issue, make note of it in the margins with the comment feature in your word processing software. This will guide your peer review partner(s) to sort out what exactly you want them to focus on. One of the most important parts of preparing for a peer review session is to properly prepare your partner for their time reviewing your draft. Be sure to tell them specific sections in your paper that you want them to spend extra time on. This will ensure the time spent is not time wasted, and it will be better for the learning purposes of both parties.

The final tip for planning and drafting your paper to prepare for a peer review day is to utilize **COLOR**! Color coding each component of your paragraphs is the perfect way to show your peer reviewer what you have included and what you are missing in each part of your paper. You may color code your opening transition statement, your main idea or topic sentence, your claim, the research supporting your claim, analysis of how that piece of research supports your claim, and a closing statement. Think of each paragraph as a sandwich—by color coding your paragraphs, you will more easily see what exactly you're missing.

Feedback

Giving and receiving feedback is essentially what can "make or break" one's writing process. Constructive feedback is needed for success in the composition community. Peer review is set up to allow students to take a break from their own topic and refresh their brain with new ideas. This can help students get their minds back in order for the final stretch of their writing process.

- When giving feedback, pay close attention to the broader scheme of things rather than the standard grammar and spelling errors. Use time efficiently and look at the structure of sentences: Is this a run on? Is this section relevant to the main idea of this paragraph? Does the author have each component in their paragraphs (i.e. can you run through the writing sandwich in your mind to pick out each piece of a functioning paragraph)? Also, be sure to look for the author's notes on their perceived weakness to see if you can suggest anything that might lead them in a strong direction.

- When receiving feedback from your peers, the first thing to remember is that they are giving you feedback to enhance your writing. They are outside readers who can help pick out small details that can largely affect your message. If you have questions on the feedback they provided, don't let it slip under the radar when the clock says it's time to leave. Ask for a method of communication so you can clarify their notes later when you're revising your draft.

After giving and receiving feedback with your peers, step back and reflect on how effective this process was in pointing you in the right direction for the next steps in revision. If you still have unanswered questions about your draft, you can always reach out to the many resources you have available to you: professor's office hours, writing workshops in the UGL, and your peers.

■ Revising, Editing, & Publishing

When you take home your constructive feedback from peer review day, it's important to consider what changes will be appropriate and necessary for your paper. Receiving feedback is nothing more than a tool to help enhance the work you've already put into your piece. Take note of these few reminders:

- Avoid revising your piece all in one sitting; it will be too much and concepts will start to blend together.
- Read your paper slowly and OUT LOUD! This is by far one of the most important tools when revising your work. Reading your paper out loud allows you to catch small flaws in your work that come out differently when you type.
- Don't be afraid to ask another peer to read over any changes you've made. A fresh set of eyes is never a bad thing.
- Track your changes while you edit. This is extremely important because it will allow you to look back and compare any changes made. You can also use this tool in the process of the revising stage if given the option, after submission.

By now, preparing for a peer review should be a piece of cake. You have been provided with all the tools you need to get yourself ready for review day. Take what you've learned and apply it to your own writing in ENG 1020. Remember to always ask questions when you're not certain, and keep in mind that there is most likely no one in the room with a complete, polished "rough" draft. Relax because everything will be just fine. Happy drafting!

WRITING STYLE: HOW DO I FIND MINE?

In English 1020, you will learn the logistics that go into writing a persuasive piece. However, one thing that a lot of students tend to forget is that English 1020 is an opportunity for you to find your voice and style while writing. One of the things that English 1020 focuses on is teaching students how to figure out authors' rhetorical choices so that students understand what the argument and evidence are doing for the audience. Keep in mind that *you* are a part of that audience even though you are mainly using these assigned articles for academic purposes rather than as a source of information on the topic that the author is seeking to shine a light on. Your position as a reader, for any text, is valuable because you have the ability to critique the author's writing. Recognizing what worked, what gripped your attention, or what made you bored is very important because these observations become reflective procedures when you begin to write.

You may or may not know it, but you are developing a certain tone as you begin to write. Tone is important in writing because not only are you personalizing your piece to make it sound like you, but you are also reaching the audience's attention. Here is where your observations as a reader are important: the things you like or dislike in the articles you read will be reflected in your own writing. For example, if you thought that one of the articles had a scientific tone with a lot of jargon that made you bored, chances are you'll make your writing more active and straight to the point so that *your* reader does not feel the same way. Or, it can be the opposite— maybe you thought that an author did not have enough jargon to emphasize the importance of the problem. Therefore, in your writing, you will add more technical or scholarly language to show your understanding of and developing expertise on the topic.

Similarly, you might find your voice through style. Style is the way you choose to structure your writing: paragraphs, sentences, choice of words, and even grammar. Maybe you did not enjoy the length or organization of an article, and you chose to change that in your writing. Deciding how to structure the sentences or sections in your paper shows the reader your logic and thus makes it easier to read your essay or article. Alternatively, if you feel very confident with the voice you have created as a writer, style might be a great way for you to experiment so that your voice is better complimented. Nevertheless, use this class to experiment with titles, headings, and even word choice. Be sure to re-read your drafts aloud and ask yourself if the readers of your essay will enjoy the journey through your persuasive essay (or any other genre of writing you decide to do).

Style and voice are two components that you will have to explore in every English class. Your choices for figuring out how to shape style or voice will be different in each of these classes. The choices you would

10   CHAPTER 1 | INTRODUCTION

potentially make when deciding how to put your voice or style into a piece include the following:

- <u>Disagreeing with your instructors' arguments about a topic.</u> Instructors are always to be respected for the knowledge that they have because they are there to teach you a subject you did not know much about. However, that does not always mean that you *have* to agree with them. Just like you, instructors are always learning new things through new perspectives, so it is your duty as a student to think for yourself. However, your instructors have the expertise to help you figure out what kinds of information and arguments are most important to the rhetorical situation of your writing.

- <u>Choosing topics for research.</u> Choosing topics can be a fun process because it means you get to learn based on the interests you have. However, topics can sometimes have a level of truth that might be dark, controversial, or disturbing. Deciding to have tough conversations about these aspects of topics is part of the journey toward finding your voice not only as a student, but also as a person. Difficult conversations have immense impacts in societies if done with justice and without hesitation, so don't be afraid to bring these conversations into your writing!

- <u>Deciding when to use informal/formal writing.</u> During our academic careers, we have been taught that we need to display a level of professionalism in our writing. Most of us think that this means formal writing. However, this is not always true. How you choose to write depends on how you choose to define words like "professionalism." Professionalism can mean presenting credible information by speaking/writing informally to a certain audience, or it can mean the opposite. Academic writing is all about defining words or concepts on your own terms and presenting how you view them in your writing, while also thinking about how you are responding to the needs and expectations of your academic audience.

Neither style nor voice can be mastered in one semester. However, English 1020 gives you the opportunity to be present as a reader and a writer so that *your* choices are seen in your piece.

CONCLUSION

After reading this introduction from start to finish, you should have the right expectations going into English 1020. Try not to be overwhelmed by the lengthy syllabus you are handed on the first day. Remember that this is an introductory course designed for you to explore your potential and discover your strengths and weaknesses as a student in higher education. This class will give you the opportunity to experiment and learn how to become an informed reader, an effective writer, and an effective

CONCLUSION   11

analyst. Think of this course as your stepping stone to set up a foundation of strong writing skills that you can use for the rest of your scholarly career.

We hope this introduction served our purpose by supplying you with helpful tips and a quick, but thorough, review that will help prepare you for the full semester that lies ahead of you. We wish you the best of luck. May the odds be in your favor!

2

Writing Process and the Digital Age
Nicole L. Wilson

UNDERSTANDING THE WRITING PROCESS

Whether we like it or not, writing is a process, and writing takes time. We can tell ourselves that we do our best work under pressure, or that in the past we have been able to turn in a first draft successfully, but as we continue on our academic path, the reality is that everyone must put effort into writing.

Different teachers and textbooks will break up the writing process differently. Here we will look at three main stages in the writing process: prewriting, writing, and rewriting. It is tempting to skip the first step and just dive into writing, but you will find that some form of prewriting should occur. The more time you spend on the first stage, the less time you will have to spend on the subsequent stages. Different steps in the writing process can fit into the various stages.

When writing studies scholars study the writing process in students, they consistently make two main observations. The first is that no two writers follow the exact same process. For example, a search for "authors' writing process" on YouTube or Dailymotion will reveal several nuanced ways of producing writing. These video interviews demonstrate that instead of following a singularly prescribed method, we all need to interpret the writing process for ourselves and discover how we are the most productive as writers. The second observation is that the more we discover, both about our topics and about ourselves as writers, the more our writing changes. Rather than maintaining a rigid writing process, we must be willing to evaluate regularly how and why we write, as well as to realize that as our knowledge base grows our writing strategies might need to change as well. This change might be a result of feedback we receive from others or from changing academic or professional expectations of our writing. Regardless of why we might want to revisit our writing process, the goal of this section is to explore the fluid possibilities of the traditional writing process.

This section looks at the three main stages of the writing process and labels them as prewriting, writing, and rewriting. However, unlike some linear explanations of the process, this section does not limit the order of the steps. Instead, it asks you to consider that sometimes rewriting occurs simultaneously with writing, as we rewrite sentences before creating new ones, and at other times prewriting is revisited while rewriting because we want to brainstorm ways to flesh out a current section of a paper. The names of these stages follow traditional organizational patterns; however, they do not occur in the same order for most.

CONSIDER WAYS TO PERSONALIZE THE WRITING PROCESS

As you think about how to make the writing process work for you, it is important to reflect on how you have been taught to write in the past. You will want to consider both how you have been taught and different papers you have written. Things to consider as you revise your writing process include the following:

- Which steps in the writing process have different instructors emphasized?
- Which steps in the process do you enjoy the most?
- Which steps do you dread?
- Which steps help you most in defining your ideas for a paper?
- Which steps help you most in organizing your papers?
- Which steps help you most in proofreading and editing effectively?
- Which paper that you have written in the past are you the most proud of?
- What makes you proud of that paper? Was it the grade? Was it the way you wrote it? Was it the way it all came together?
- What types of steps did you take to write that paper?
- What might you have done to make that paper better?
- Have you ever experienced writer's block? What caused it?
- What did you do to overcome writer's block?

Most writers experience some type of writer's block. It is important to consider when you have gotten blocked in the past so that you can take steps to avoid that or plan around it. For example, if you need pressure to write,

14   CHAPTER 2 | WRITING PROCESS AND THE DIGITAL AGE

create a writing group among your peers and give yourselves an earlier deadline to submit drafts of your paper to one another. Or, if you find yourself caught up in fixing mechanical errors, try throwing a towel over your screen so you cannot see what you type. The important thing is to realize that for some, writer's block is part of the process, and we need to be able to plan to work through it rather than be stopped by it.

In your Wayne State courses, you will be expected to reflect on your writing and how the learning objectives for each course have helped you further your skills as a writer. (See the "Foreword" for an explanation of reflection.) Personalizing your writing process and understanding how you write before you start a new project will help you analyze how your writing evolves from course to course.

PREWRITING

The prewriting stage includes all of the activities a writer might complete before actually starting to write. This includes brainstorming, doing research, and developing an organizational pattern for the essay.

■ Brainstorming

Brainstorming can be both formal and informal. We can think about topics while surfing online, driving, or doing mundane tasks around the house. We can also brainstorm with a pad of paper or a word processing program to make writing lists or mind maps as we trace our thoughts from topic to topic. While we brainstorm, we want to consider what we know about our topic as well as what we would like to learn about it. It can be helpful to make visual connections about topics through clustering.

We often think we are finished brainstorming once we have our topic, but that is not the case. Brainstorming can help us develop our sense of the rhetorical situation (purpose, tone, audience, and content) within which we will be writing, as well as the audience/discourse community to which our writing is addressed. (See the "Foreword" for fuller explanations of rhetorical situation and discourse community.) Perhaps more importantly, brainstorming can help us figure out our purpose for writing. Knowing our purpose will also help us determine what types of research we might need. Purpose and audience together help us determine the logos (logic), pathos (emotion), ethos (credibility) ratio that will be needed for an effective paper.

This is also the step in which we will consider the genre of our paper (see the "Foreword" for a fuller explanation of genre). As you pay attention to your audience, you want to pay attention to which genre will be most useful for reaching that audience. You will also want to be aware of how different genres use research. For example, summary papers use only one source, whereas argument papers use multiple sources.

In addition, brainstorming is not simply picking a topic. Brainstorming also involves considering the span of our project. We can begin by asking ourselves a few key questions:

- What is the issue I want to discuss? How can I focus this issue on my community?
- How does a public community define the issue?
- Why is this issue important to my community?
- What problem(s) in my community is (are) caused by this issue?
- How are people working to solve this problem?

Once we have answered these questions, as well as the questions our instructors want us to consider, we are ready to begin our research, when it is required.

■ Doing Research

Research can be one of the most time-intensive parts of the writing process. It is also one activity that writers often try to shortcut as much as possible. But while doing quality research might take you a little time, it will also make for a higher quality paper. If you are unfamiliar with the research process, the WSU library liaison has put together research guides on the library homepage. The guides most suited for English courses can be found at http://guides.lib.wayne.edu/English. There are also additional guides on the library website for other departments and research interests.

The key to effective research is remembering that it is more than typing a few keywords into a search engine and hoping to get lucky and find reliable information about a particular topic. Initial research involves looking for the answers to the questions we asked in our brainstorming session, and advanced research involves investigating the gaps we find in the discourse community. Because research can be time consuming, we must strive to work at it effectively. Therefore, our first responsibility is to pay attention to the requirements for each course and the research that different disciplines require.

While going through the research process, you may also want to conduct your own primary research. Primary research includes interviewing professionals in your field and administering surveys on your research topic. Different courses and instructors have differing requirements for primary research, so you will want to discuss with your instructor appropriate interview subjects and/or survey parameters.

The research process can be daunting. When you first begin doing academic research, it can be helpful to use tools from outside sources in addition to our textbook. The Purdue Online Writing Lab (http://www.owl .english.purdue.edu/owl) offers strategies for selecting, evaluating, analyzing, and organizing your research. It also can be helpful to remember the spiral nature of the writing process. Although you begin doing research to answer your initial questions, research often causes us to ask more questions. We do not want to limit our experiences with research to finding information only. We should use our research to help us define our topic and consider which elements we are interested in exploring further. Research reminds us that the more we learn, the more there is to discover. Therefore, as we progress in our academic studies, we can do initial research to help us determine which direction our in-depth research should take.

■ Developing an Organizational Pattern

Most successful essays, especially those in the humanities, are organized around an issue, a problem, and a solution. It is our job to consider how much time we want to spend on each of these categories. It is also important to consider how the information we have best supports each of the categories. We want to make sure our papers follow a logical pattern as we build our argument. Some writers like to do this with a formal outline. Others like to use a graphic organizer, such as a flow chart or a table. If you are having difficulty considering how your ideas might fit together, you can also use presentation software to help you build your format. For example, the smart art graphics in both Microsoft Word and PowerPoint offer several different organizational patterns that you can use to experiment with your content and decide how it might best flow together.

(RE)WRITING

■ Draft as Necessary

Regardless of how much prewriting we do, in order to receive a grade for our work, we must put something to paper. Anne Lamott talks about writing "shitty first drafts" as a way of motivating us to get something on paper. For the initial drafting period, that is the only goal that we need to have. We just need to start putting our ideas on paper. If we have spent the time asking good research questions and creating a flow chart for our project, we will be able to add detail to that chart. Those details become our first draft. As seen above, the writing stage is the simplest stage of the process. We can maintain its simplicity if we are willing to engage in the rewriting stage, which includes revising, proofreading, and editing.

■ Global Revision - Revising

After writing first drafts, when we initially revise our paper, we know that there are possibly significant changes that need to take place. We are considering whether the way we present our evidence is effective. We are looking for which pieces of research might need to be taken out and which might need to be added. Revision is concerned with issues of content and organization. During this stage of the revision process, it is best to ask questions that address the paper *globally*, or as a whole:

- Does our paper articulate our argument?
- Do we support the argument sufficiently?
- Do we formulate the argument in a way that will be easily understood by our audience?

When we revise, we should go back to our research questions and consider whether those questions are being addressed in our paper. We should also confirm that our paper continually reflects our thesis statement.

■ Focused Revision - Proofreading

When we proofread our paper, we are looking at our tone and presentation. Does our paper flow as well as we would like it to flow? Do we need to add transitions? Will our audience understand how and why we are making the connections we are drawing? Do we make the correct assumptions about the prior knowledge of our audience? Is it clear to our audience what we are asking of them?

■ Detailed Revision - Editing

Editing is when we go over the final details of our paper. This is when we are concerned with grammar. We need to comb over our paper for proper mechanics and formatting issues. We recommend saving this step for last because writers are usually less willing to cut something they spent time editing.

DIGITAL WAYS TO EXECUTE THE WRITING PROCESS

In our culture, we write frequently. We communicate with our friends using social media, and we send text messages rather than calling someone. Since we use technology to write socially, it can sometimes be more comfortable to use technology when writing academically as well. Below are a few tips for using different websites for various steps in the writing process.

■ Digital Brainstorming Techniques

When you have absolutely no topic ideas, use Google's "I'm feeling lucky" feature. It will take you to different topics that are either trendy or artistic, and you could then do your research based on the topic found there. Websites like Google and Wikipedia, or even Pinterest and Tumblr, are great places to find ideas. StumbleUpon and reddit are also good choices for gaining knowledge about a topic because of the ways they are sourced and filtered. In ENG 1020, it will be important for you to find academic sources to further the ideas that you find through these avenues. However, social media can be useful for considering current events or topics of interest to you and your community.

If you have a topic idea, but you are unsure of how to develop that idea, you could also post questions on Facebook or Twitter that invite your community to respond. As you engage in conversation with others, hopefully you will start to shape how you think about your topic. You can ask people if they know about a certain statistic or quote, or you could ask if they find a certain issue problematic or simply normal.

■ Digital Ways to Do Research

As you search for topics, create an account at a digital bookmarking site, such as delicious.com. As you see articles online that relate to your topic or interests, tag them through the site. Using a social bookmarking site, rather than an individual computer's bookmarks, allows you to continually add bookmarks regardless of which device you use or where you study. The tags you develop for your bookmarks will also help you categorize your information so you can narrow the focus of your research.

■ Digital Ways to Organize Your Material

Once you have some ideas and information, use your Wayne email to create a Prezi account. Prezi, or a similar presentation program, allows you to choose a template that follows a particular graphical organization. These templates can give you a frame for understanding your material. While Prezi is typically used for giving presentations, it can allow you to explore different relationships between ideas. It might help you see how things fit together or build upon one another. The advantage of Prezi over Power-Point, again, is that Prezi is not tied to a particular computer and does not require any software. If you do not want to use a template found in a presentation software, you can also use your own personal blog or wiki to freewrite about your ideas and consider how others might tag certain posts.

■ Digital Ways to Revise

Once you have a draft of your paper, it can be helpful to revisit the idea of organization along with flow. One way to check your organization is by using the highlighting feature in a word processing program, such as Google Docs. Pick different colors for various topics or subtopics, then highlight the different subtopics in different colors. Once you finish, look at the color pattern to make sure the paper is organized and flows in a logical manner. Also look for sentences that do not fit within the color scheme and consider cutting those. Highlighting your various points in different colors helps ensure that you have a balanced and well-organized paper. If you find that most of your paper is one color, you might want to consider how to subdivide that particular topic to make sure your paper is accomplishing your purpose.

As you are making revisions and potentially reorganizing material, you can also use the "Track Changes" feature in your word processing program. Doing this allows you to easily undo changes you might not like. Additionally, you can create a "graveyard" file for each paper. As you cut things out of your paper, open up a second document on your computer where you paste all of the information you cut out. Then, if you later decide that you need a particular piece of information, it can be easily restored.

■ Example

In English 1020, I am told to write a proposal about a current problem. Now, my research question will not only consider the "who" and "what" of human trafficking, but it will also ask how the community can prevent trafficking. As I talk to people in my community, I might ask if anyone has ever had a friend who disappeared because of drugs. For my research, I might try to meet with people at Wayne State who are part of the organization Not for Sale and find statistics about trafficking in Detroit.

FURTHER READING

Duckart, Tracy. "Prewriting." The Cache. Humboldt State University, Jan 2012. Web.

Lamott, Anne. *Bird by Bird*. Harpswell: Anchor, 1995. Print.

Perl, Sondra. "The Composing Process of Unskilled College Writers." 1979. *Writing About Writing*. Ed. Elizabeth Wardle and Doug Downs. Boston: Bedford/St. Martin, 2011. Print.

Rose, Mike. "Rigid Rules, Inflexible Plans, and the Stifling of Language: A Cognitivist Analysis of Writer's Block." *College Composition and Communication* 31.4 (1980): 389–401. JSTOR. Web.

3

Analyzing Media
Jared Grogan and Luke Thominet

INTRODUCTION

The purpose of this section is to discuss some of the ways that new media has changed how we read, write, and even think about ourselves as readers and writers. We focus our discussion on how analysis and analytic writing change as we turn our attention to "reading" new media "texts" that include images, video, and interactive multimedia. We define the third type, "interactive media," as media that may include image and video components, but also include a more extensive role for user interaction. Examples of interactive media include interactive television (such as when audiences vote via text message), online forums, video games, interactive advertising, and virtual or augmented reality.

While these three forms of new media are important to both how we communicate and what we value in popular culture, they also play an important role in professional and academic writing today. In the movement from images to videos, and to interactive media, this section discusses interesting similarities and differences in how we read and analyze these digital texts to write about them in meaningful ways. We also offer a basic toolkit for analyzing new media as "multimodal texts," a term that defines any text that integrates written words, static or moving images, and sound.

ANALYZING IMAGES

We can begin with a focus on analyzing static images. It's important first to expand our subject of analysis from photography to static images that literally surround us every day, such as movie posters, street art, billboards, magazine covers, maps, graphs, and charts. Images can be analyzed to explore the important role they play in professional and academic writing, or to examine how they reflect or shape ideas, beliefs, or attitudes in specific communities or popular culture. It is important to know how to analyze images no matter what your field of study. Images are regularly used to convey information, and knowing how to read them can help you both identify the information being conveyed and recognize when it is being misrepresented. In most cases it is important to perform an analysis by considering three approaches: genre analysis, visual analysis, and rhetorical analysis.

You can typically start by identifying the genre (defined in the "Foreword"). Knowing something about genre will help you analyze features of texts, while paying attention to the author's choices and the evolving rhetorical situations. Analyzing the genre of an image requires you to determine the image's genre, and then to describe the genre's established conventions or rules. This will help you and your reader understand the visual choices the artist/author made in creating the image. Knowing the established conventions and rules for creating different types of images, photos, graphics, cartoons, or charts will help you understand the features of the image in relation to the goals of the author, their specific choices in medium, the choices made in the process of composing the image, and the purposes of the image in relation to the expectations of the audience.

Visual analysis generally considers features like arrangement, balance, contrast, emphasis, cropping, size, shape, line, color, and other formal elements of images. Focusing on visual analysis does not mean you are simply focused on "description," as all forms of analysis do require a thesis, or a central point to prove that your analytical approach is supported by the image. Any thesis you may craft will need to be proven by the content of the image you analyze. You can do this by citing the visual details of the object that support the thesis. These details may include the medium, particular techniques (in photography, graphic design, etc.), or composition (the arrangement of elements in the work, the focal point, the use of space, repetition, elements of color, line, perspective, scale, etc.). When performing a visual analysis, you may take ample time to note all of the visual details when you first encounter the image. Then you can begin to search for connections that suggest a theme or an overall organization of the image.

A rhetorical analysis of images considers the features mentioned above, but it also focuses on trying to understand what an image does to persuade a viewer or reader to think or act differently. As you read earlier, we perform rhetorical analyses by examining the rhetorical situation of a text or object, and by thinking about the interactions among an author, their text (the image), and an audience. We then apply rhetorical concepts and principles to try and understand what a text "does rather than what it is" (Corbett). For instance, we can consider how the three appeals (ethos, logos, pathos) are used to explain how an image can prompt viewers to feel emotions or other effects (types of visual pathos); how an image can enhance a logical claim or argument with persuasive visual evidence (types of visual logos); how an image can (mis)represent large amounts of data, be potentially deceptive, or create a bias (all types of visual logos); or how an image can represent and or enhance the "character" or guiding beliefs or ideologies of a person, community, or nation (types of visual ethos).

In ENG 1020, you will likely encounter visual analysis as a means to gain sound practice in applying the basic tools and terms of rhetoric. Analyzing visuals can introduce you to many of the key concepts in rhetoric and also give you an opportunity to demonstrate your ability to think and respond to a given rhetorical situation. (See the "Foreword" for a fuller explanation of rhetorical situation.)

For this assignment, you may be asked to find an example of a persuasive text in the media, something with multimodal components that you think holds some significant persuasive power over an audience. Common choices for analysis in ENG 1020 include the genres of advertising, political campaign advertising, advocacy, public relations documents, popular memes, historic propaganda, graffiti or street art, and recent viral videos. Once you've selected a persuasive image to analyze, you may be asked to focus your analytic writing on the content of the image/object itself (the rhetorical features that produce the impact on an audience), the rhetorical situation (author, audience, context), the discourse communities (defined in "Foreword") involved, and/or the larger trends in the media.

ANALYZING VIDEOS

We can analyze videos as texts in similar ways, by beginning with genre, visual analysis, and rhetorical analysis. However, most attempts to analyze video will also layer one or two new concepts or "tools" that assist in analyzing videos. For instance, James Paul Gee applies the tools of discourse analysis to multimodal texts (texts combining multiple modes of communication, including written, audio, and visual modalities) such as videos. Other theorists will start with rhetorical models for analyzing videos and add concepts from psychology, or critical theories like feminism or Marxism.

Analyzing music videos, for example, can draw on genre, use visual and rhetorical analysis, and make room for other suitable theoretical frames. Past students also seemed particularly amenable to taking on this complex form of analysis with the genre of familiar videos, which they said was interesting. Take for example Kanye West's "We Were Once a Fairytale" (directed by Spike Jonze), in which West shows a distinct awareness of audience and plays on themes of conflict, race, and celebrity that have been integral to his own image in the media. The self-deprecating ethos in the video might challenge you to question the merit of this work, the authenticity of his "cocky" persona, as well as what this does for him in the context of the genre of hip hop and the entertainment industry more generally.

Let's take a look at how this type of analysis might look as a process. When constructing such a rhetorical analysis, you might start with a broad trend in video production or with a particular text. When starting with a text, a brief assessment of the rhetorical situation would lead to more thorough questions about each key component: the author (which often raises the question of the ethos of an artist, as well as more a complex picture of producers and production companies and their motives), the text (the common facets and techniques of music videos, such as the techniques of a short film, the integration a song and imagery, or the promotional qualities or more explicit elements of advertising) and the audience (considering such factors as age, race, and economic status; the values and beliefs appealed to; and the attitudes or ideas reinforced). You could then move on to a close reading of the video, often breaking it down into key segments, stopping frequently at particular frames to think about and/or discuss persuasive facets of imagery, sound, and lyrics, or to think through key rhetorical concepts. You might also move from this kind of content analysis to research into contemporary trends in music video production, with the intent of grounding your findings in the video you've chosen to analyze. This shift from text to trends can support richer analytic work by deepening insights into video, while offering good basic training in research, integrating research into analytic writing, and even grounding research questions.

ANALYZING INTERACTIVE MEDIA

In addition to (or instead of) the other forms discussed above, your instructor may ask you to rhetorically analyze a piece of interactive media. But what exactly do we mean by this term? Actually, we are grouping a rather diverse set of items under this title. Interactive media refers to any work whose content is shaped substantially by user interaction. The most obvious example is that of video games, but other types of interactive media might also be included. For instance, it might benefit you to consider the discussion below when analyzing television shows that rely on viewers (like many reality shows) to vote for an ending (or a winner). You might also consider it in relation to many items on the Internet, in that their networked format is nonlinear (it requires a user to click on a button to show a page, and pages can be viewed in any order or even skipped entirely).

Before turning to more exact theories that could help inform your reading of interactive media, let's explore the interactive qualities of video games in a little more depth. Hopefully this will help you begin to identify some of the difficulties you might face in analyzing this type of media. As an initial example, we will consider Minecraft (we chose this game as an example for two reasons: first because it is one of the most widely discussed games in recent history, and second because it is primarily a single-player game, thereby avoiding further complications of multiple players influencing the game simultaneously). This game is built around the idea of an open-world platform, meaning that the players can move their characters about the game as they please. It is also a sandbox game, which means that players have no specific mission and they can play freely in the game world. When considering the rhetorical intent of such a game, a number of difficulties immediately arise.

First, there is the problem of even identifying precisely what the game is: is it the experience of an individual player or is it the entirety of all possible experiences that the game allows? To make this more concrete, players in Minecraft collect resources and build objects in randomly generated game worlds. One player might start the game in a forest and build a small house and farm. Another player might start in a more mountainous region and build a towering castle. There are also enemies in the game called "creepers." The forest-dwelling farmer might find himself hounded by enemies at night, and will therefore go out and tame wolves to serve as protection. On the other hand, the castle builder might hide away at night and spend his days building higher and higher until he has an intricate spire of a castle. These are two fundamentally different experiences of the same game. Which one do we use when analyzing the rhetoric of the game? Is either sufficient on its own?

While this might seem to be a silly question, it is one that has to be tackled in any analysis of an interactive work. No single experience of the game is going to encapsulate the entirety of what could happen (especially in some more recent games). In fact, in his book *Extra Lives: Why Video Games Matter*, Tom Bissel says that meaning in video games is comparative rather than interpretive (117). By this he means that debates over the meaning of a game could not be settled simply by citing evidence from a playthrough, but rather by comparing and discussing experiences with other players. So the analysis of interactive media fundamentally considers co-creation of the game experience by players.

We also want to briefly address the inherent question of why analyzing interactive media is important. To do this, we turn to the work of James Paul Gee on learning and literacy. One of the fundamental claims of Gee's work is that video games represent highly effective learning technologies, and that the principles that drive these games can also be extended to non-gaming situations. It is well beyond our scope in this section to provide a full explanation of all of Gee's theories (he develops a list of thirty-six separate learning principles in *What Video Games Have to Teach Us About Learning and Literacy*), but we might explore one of his concepts.

For example, in reference to the "Incremental Principle," Gee says, "Learning situations are ordered in the early stages so that earlier cases lead to generalizations that are fruitful for later cases" (225). A clear example of this principle exists in the Legend of Zelda game series. In those games, the player is always given a simple set of weapons at the beginning of the game, and is then introduced to additional weapons and complications as the game continues. Each new weapon likewise is introduced in a dungeon that focuses on fairly straightforward uses of the item. Later, the game requires more complex use of multiple weapons to fully explore dungeons and defeat bosses. The lessons that are learned earlier thus transfer to more complex situations where the knowledge is complicated.

This is also a principle often used in composition classes, where lessons often start by focusing on simple writing moves in order to develop towards more complex writing tasks. For example, a professor might first ask you to write a definition essay to clearly describe something for a particular audience. Those writing moves might also be used in a subsequent proposal essay in which the professor asks you to clearly define a problem before arguing for a solution. In this way, the use of definition becomes complicated by its subordinate relation to a more complex argument.

Moving forward with Gee's work, you might find it useful to explore the full range of his learning principles. If pressed for time, you might look at Gee's article, "Good Video Games and Good Learning," which was published in the Phi Kappa Alpha Forum. In this brief article, Gee reduces his list to fifteen principles and provides a brief explanation of each. If you are using this theory to analyze a game, you might want to consider how the game is setting you up to learn its system. What exactly is it doing to keep you playing? How does it make you better at playing the game?

In ENG 1020, you'll be asked to develop deep critical analyses of nonstandard texts. You will probably be expected to work with the thoughts and theories of others in relation to your analysis of the work. Ultimately, you will be expected to enter into a discourse on this form of media and, at the very least, demonstrate how that discourse might approach the work you are analyzing. While different assignments or even different courses might ask for different levels of analysis, the tools that one uses remain constant.

Let's close here with one last look at why this type of analysis is so important. Many forms of media are becoming increasingly interactive in today's networked society. Analyzing these new types of objects must take into account their interactive functioning to truly grasp how they work. To ignore this is to be blind to much of the rhetoric in modern society. Not only does analyzing interactive media prepare you for looking at complex texts of all sorts during your academic career, but it also prepares you for a world where persuasion is rarely straightforward or passive, and where it is far more likely to ask for and expect your active participation.

WORKS CITED

Bissell, Tom. *Extra Lives: Why Video Games Matter*. New York: Pantheon, 2010. Print.

Gee, James Paul. *What Video Games Have to Teach Us About Learning and Literacy*. Second Edition: Revised and Updated Edition. New York: Macmillan, 2007. Print.

4

Voice in Academic and Civic Writing

LaToya Faulk

DEFINING VOICE AND STYLE

Style consists of both conscious and unconscious decisions writers make about everything from the words they use (diction) and their arrangement in sentences (syntax), to the tone with which they express their point of view and the way they achieve emphasis in a sentence (Butler, 1). In other words, voice (or style) supports the overall purpose of the writing by allowing writers to make choices about how they will deliver a message to an audience.

Often what distinguishes a writer's voice from others' is how they express meaning. Style (or voice) is shaped by context, which refers to the conditions and circumstances that determine the existence of a piece of writing. We each have a range of voices we put on and take off given the occasion and subject matter. Writing in academic and civic communities demands higher concentration, clearer organization of thoughts and ideas, richer and more concise sentence structures, and well-thought-out stylistic approaches. In college writing, stylistic differences are often attributed to the agendas of a discipline, profession, or field of study. Disciplines are types of discourse communities (as discussed in the "Foreword") where groups of individuals communicate in particular genres to achieve a common goal—whether to persuade, entertain or inform.

Although purpose and genre conventions largely affect the range of appropriate styles and tones, skilled writers must be able to think critically about their audience and its relationship to style. (See the "Foreword" for a fuller explanation of genre.) This thinking can be achieved by identifying which stylistic approaches best appeal to your audience. You can do so by conducting research that seeks an awareness of the genre conventions widely consumed and valued by a particular group. Then spend time reflecting on the relationship between genre conventions and the ways in which genre conventions impose a stylistic standard.

Various discourse communities have unique literacy practices used to categorize insiders and outsiders or novices and experts. In looking at stylistic differences within discourse communities, we must first understand that discourse communities can be examined and compared in the same way we learn and examine various languages and identities. In an article by James Gee entitled "Literacy, Discourse, and Linguistics: Introduction," Discourse is referred to as an *identity kit*. This kit comes from culturally acquired instructions on how to act, talk, and write in ways that others within the community acknowledge and reward. Gee outlines four types of discourse communities: primary, secondary, dominant, and non-dominant.

Primary discourse communities "constitute our original home-based sense of identity," while secondary "non-home based social institutions" are communities where we intermingle in the public (485). Secondary discourse communities might include stores, churches, schools, community groups, and state and national businesses. Dominant and non-dominant Discourses make writers aware of how power operates within communities. Although most communities possess a language of insider knowledge crafted through a specific language, style, or expression, this knowledge establishes hierarchies or camaraderie among members. However, dominant discourse communities are often seen as empowering because they have the potential to provide access to economic mobility, prestige, and status (Wardle and Downs ed., 485).

Extending Gee's work, the chart below will help shape an awareness of the variety of stylistic approaches available given the communicative demands of a community. Keep in mind that there are many different styles and voices that can be found in one single piece of writing within a community. Also, new genres and combinations of genre conventions evolve within various communities. In the evolution of new genres, certain stylistic approaches are added, revised, and combined.

	Individual (Primary Discourse Community)	**Social/Civil** (Secondary/Non-Dominant Discourse Community)	**Educational** (Dominant Discourse Community)	**Civic/Professional** (Dominant Discourse Community)
Range of Expression & Literacy Agendas	Home-based language; authentic range of true expression include to share and respond to family, immediate kin, and friends	A language that provides a level of emotional and logistical solidarity with a particular social network (e.g. racial, religious, environmental, or political group; civic organization; Greek life)	Often standardized, non-home based language in which the mastery of a particular or various discourses include obtaining income, status, or social goods (liberating or empowering literacies)	Non-home based language; public voice; sometimes a personal range of expression is mixed with a certain kind of formalized language practice depending on the setting; writing is formalized in a way that meets a common goal
Form	Informal	Formal & Informal	Formal	Formal, Informal, and Causal
English Usage	Personal freedom and comfort (usage of "I"), combination of standard and non-standard English	Structured/Non-structured communication determines when and where standard or non-standard addresses are required	Personal/Self distance in the writing (impersonal tone), precise language, carefully controlled format or organization	Concrete language, some home-based language mixed with standard English
Genres	Facebook posting, Twitter, e-mail (to friend/family member), text messaging (to friend/family member), creating a grocery list, journal writing, special interest magazines, personal essay writing, personal website	Some academic papers, personal essays, some speeches, response papers	Research-based writing or report, persuasive, expository, analytical, professional email, business letter, job application or letter, most academic papers	Political discourse, general interest writing, causal writing, public speeches on social or political issues that affect the community, newsletter or article

STYLE AS IDENTITY

Writing well consists of thinking, feeling and expressing well, of clarity of mind, soul and taste...The style is the man himself. —George-Louis Leclerc de Buffon, *Discourse and Style*

Style is twofold—it is a kind of identity and a rhetorical tool used to formalize communication among a group of individuals for easy consumption of ideas. Often, developing your own unique voice in academic and civic writing comes from evaluating, analyzing, and imitating others in the discourse community. Like speech acquisition, we acquire our own unique voice by mimicking others and acquiring a level of confidence in a voice that is often a collage of other voices we admire, respect, and consider authentic. When we think of 21st century writers like James Baldwin, and his essays, we understand his identity as a unique voice penetrating the pages, making his writing unmistakably his own. Baldwin and many other writers who are widely read and published often discuss their unique style as an attribute related to (1) social issues that matter the most to them, and (2) well-known writers who inspire them in ways that push their style and technique forward. For instance, in an interview with the Paris Review, when asked about how much he read and how it influenced his own writing, Baldwin states, "I read everything. I read my way out of the two libraries in Harlem by the time I was thirteen. One does learn a great deal about writing this way...I'm still learning how to write. I don't know what technique is. All I know is that you have to make the reader see it. This I learned from Dostoyevsky, from Balzac" (Baldwin, par. 15). Making the reader see it depends upon the genre you've been asked to compose and is determined by word choice and arrangement (understanding the types of historical baggage associated with a word), sentence construction (where you place the subject, verb, and object), and often the overall organization of ideas presented in the text.

This leads us to our second understanding of style. As rhetorical tools, stylistic choices are used to conventionalize communication for easy distribution and consumption within a discourse community. In addition to controlling genres, discourse communities share a specific language and style that embed the values and belief systems of that community. Although each member of a community has a personal style and voice, there is also often a shared style or language practice associated with a particular community's norms and habits. Where an understanding of the subject, audience, and purpose for speaking is necessary, let us now turn to the matter of using one's primary discourse to employ a unique style in expository and persuasive writing.

30 CHAPTER 4 | VOICE IN ACADEMIC AND CIVIC WRITING

■ Style, Home-Based Identity, and Academic Writing

> *We affirm the students' right to their own patterns and varieties of language—the dialects of their nurture or whatever dialects in which they find their own identity and style. Language scholars long ago denied that the myth of a standard American dialect has any validity. The claim that any one dialect is unacceptable amounts to an attempt of one social group to exert its dominance over another. Such a claim leads to false advice for speakers and writers, and immoral advice for humans. A nation proud of its diverse heritage and its cultural and racial variety will preserve its heritage of dialects.*
>
> —Excerpt from the 1972 CCCC Students' Right to Their Own Language

The above excerpt from the 1972 CCCC Students' Right to Their Own Language (SRTOL) suggests that students have the right to write in the "dialects of their nurture," or the language codes learned in their home-based communities. Although tension remains regarding the extent to which students are allowed to write in the dialects of their nurture without penalty, composition scholars and writing program administrators such as Elaine Richardson, Arnetha Ball, Ted Lardner, Geneva Smitherman, Peter Elbow, Bonnie Williams, and Staci M. Perryman-Clark have conducted research that focuses on how SRTOL can affirm students' home-based voices when students engage in academic rhetorical situations.

In an article published in 2013 entitled "African American Language, Rhetoric, and Students' Writing: New Direction for SRTOL," Staci Perryman-Clark conducted a case study with three African-American students, investigating the extent to which home-based Englishes, such as AAL (African American Language) or Ebonics, can be used in academic writing to affirm SRTOL. Perryman-Clark claims that students should be able to make strategic choices and explain how various rhetorical situations allow or discourage the usage of non-traditional academic literacy practices like AAL. Further, they should identify and understand certain contexts that require Ebonics vs. Standard English, but also the way writers actually—and quite deliberately—code-switch in written discourse.

More traditional assignments (e.g. argument, analysis, and disciplinary essays with a clear research focus) depend more on abstract writing, active voice, personal distance, and more focus on a higher concentration of knowledge. Whether or not including your home-based language will work within the rhetorical situation of your essay will take some consideration. Understanding your assignment and discussing the genre, purpose, and audience will provide more information on how to make stylistic choices that appeal to the ethos, pathos, and logos of your readers.

Writing assignments that focus on personal literacy practices or popular culture, in which non-traditional academic discourses like AAL are valued, provide opportunities to use or discuss such non-traditional literacy practices. Such assignments may ask you to consider how popular culture and new media use language to persuade specific audiences. For instance, you might analyze the marketing of the 2011 Toyota Sienna minivan, more notably recognized as the "swagger wagon." The commercial uses humor and parodies rap lyrics and AAL as a way to appeal to a younger consumer demographic. This stylistic approach leads viewers to believe that the minivan, often a stigma of middle-aged, suburban, white, American soccer moms, is cool, fun, and perfect for younger new families. The shift in demographic appeal seeks to change the perceptions of the minivan to promote sales among younger car owners. But how many new young families purchased the "swagger wagon"? Was this commercial effective? Does the style of the commercial succeed in fulfilling the intentions of the composers of the commercial?

■ Style and Academic Disciplines

Disciplines shape the style of a writing practice all around. Each discipline has a unique identity kit that often characterizes distinct ways of knowing and communicating (Carter, 2007). As academic writers, we must understand how and why various disciplines communicate knowledge through writing. As we understand how disciplines create meaning through the writing practices valued in that community, we are also able to understand how style and voice are conceptualized through writing in the discipline. In others words, as decision makers seeking to strengthen our ability to make sound judgments on a stylistic approach, we must understand the "intellectual and social conventions of a disciplinary community" (Herrington, 337). These conventions, according to Herrington and other composition scholars, "vary across disciplinary communities and include the kinds of issues the discipline tries to address, the lines of reasoning used to resolve those issues, the social purpose for communicating and a shared assumption about the audience's role and the writer's ethos" (334). To better understand why disciplinary community analysis is so important, you might consider a research paper in a scientific reasoning course that may require you to have introduction, methods, results, analysis, and discussion sections. Early in the composing process, you may need to establish a hypothesis and accumulate evidence related to the hypothesis. These requirements shape the range of style and voice appropriate given the focus of the project.

To conclude, genre conventions help shape our stylistic decisions as writers. Therefore, it is important to learn all you can about the communicative practices of the professional, civic, and academic communities you seek to join or where you already participate. The exercise

32   CHAPTER 4 | VOICE IN ACADEMIC AND CIVIC WRITING

below gives you the opportunity to explore a disciplinary community at Wayne State. Because outcome statements are public and often announce the goals of a particular community, exploring these statements along with asking an expert questions about the discipline's way of approaching style and voice should provide you with flexibility by giving you a range of choices to consider as you communicate in the discipline.

Standard edited English is just one out of several stylistic representations of a linguistic system valued in higher education. It has been my experience that observations and open discussions surrounding style and voice in college often lead writers to questions surrounding who they are and where they might locate a singular authentic style or voice. Identity is multi-layered. We all have multiple forms of language and style because we are all part of numerous discourse communities that have varying communicative practices. When we feel like a stylistic standard "doesn't fit" or just "isn't us," reluctance to put on a voice that feels inauthentic or fake can force us to resist stylistic rules associated with a particular community. This is quite normal, and one way to negotiate this conflict is to first see association within a discourse community as a choice or a kind of liberation. As noted earlier in this section, certain discourse communities allow us access to social, economic, and political goods. These types of communities are seen as liberating because of the human necessity for survival. Second, not being afraid to voice such feelings can lead to experimentation and provocative dialogue with your peers and instructor.

When considering what it means to be a part of several discourse communities, I like to think of it in the same way I think about learning a new language. Do you speak more than one language? Or have you ever tried to learn a new language? For many of us, having to roll new words off of our tongue can feel strange and uncomfortable. You might gain a better insight into the varying ways in which communities shape information if you think of what it takes to learn a new language, such as Spanish or French. Exposure and open access to various languages can be seen as an advantage. For instance, a bilingual writer named Ana Menedéz, in "Bilingual Imagination," contends that learning two languages opened her up to two different worlds and prepared her for adapting to difference and change (24). What we often learn from our awareness of the varying ways in which communities communicate is that there are infinite ways to interpret things.

We must be very observant and analytical of the multiple ways in which the communities where we communicate are similar and different. Moving in and out of varying communities can prompt metacognition and what many scholars call "code-switching." Metacognition is an awareness of how we ourselves make critical rhetorical decisions within various contexts to meet the goals of a community. Code-switching happens when we shift between languages or communicative codes depending on the context. As writers, we must constantly make decisions concerning the effectiveness of our communicative practices. An awareness of where, when, and how communicative codes differ is all part of being a reflective, responsible writer.

WORKS CITED

Bacon, Nora. *The Well-Crafted Sentence (A Writer's Guide to Style)*. New York: Bedford St. Martin, 2013. Print.

Baldwin, James. Interview by Jordan Elgrably. "The Art of Fiction No. 78." *The Paris Review*. 1984: 91. Web.

Beaufort, Ann. *College Writing and Beyond: A Framework University Writing Instruction*. Utah State University Press, 2007. Print.

Butler, Paul. *Style in Rhetoric and Composition: A Critical Sourcebook*. New York: Bedford St. Martin, 2010. Print.

Carter, Michael. "Ways of Knowing, Doing, and Writing in the Disciplines". *College Composition and Communication*. 58:3. (2007):385–418. Print.

Elbow, Peter. *Vernacular Eloquence: What Speech Can Bring to Writing*. Oxford University Press, 2012. Print.

Gee, James. *Social Linguistics and Literacies: Ideology in Discourse*. Routledge, 2011. Print.

Herrington, Anne. "Writing in Academic Settings: A Study of the Contexts for Writing in Two College Chemical Engineering Courses". *Research in the Teaching of English*. 19:4. (1985): 333–359. Print.

Menedéz, Ann. "The Bilingual Imagination." *Poets & Writers*. January/February, 2011. Print.

Wardle, Elizabeth and Downs, Douglas, eds. *Writing about Writing: A College Reader*. New York: Bedford St. Martin, 2011. Print.

"Students' Right to Their Own Language." *College Composition and Communication*. 25: 25, 1974. Print.

5

Secondary Research Methods and Writing about Research

Ruth Boeder and Adrienne Jankens

INTRODUCTION

While we sometimes use research to confirm what we already know, research is most often used in academic settings to answer questions. We call this **inquiry-based research**: posing questions and working to develop conclusions and/or solutions through research. At a **research-intensive university**, like Wayne State, students are expected to be able to develop questions, find and analyze information, and integrate information from relevant sources into their writing in courses across the university.

One of the goals (learning outcomes) of ENG 1020 is for students to use flexible research methods that include finding and evaluating sources to support the development of ideas and arguments. This course will help you develop strategies for the types of **secondary research** that you will conduct for the writing in this class, as well as for the writing you will be asked to do in other contexts. Secondary research means reading documents about a topic or phenomenon, as opposed to **primary research**, which involves directly observing and studying a topic or phenomenon.

It is important to understand that we use research both to figure out what we want to argue *and* to support arguments that we have developed. Reading into a topic can help us identify the **larger conversation** around a topic as well as to locate key **research gaps** or potential problems with the arguments that have been presented. Finding these gaps or issues can help us form research questions. Once we have identified what we want to know, our research process becomes more focused. This focused reading often leads us to continue to revise and refine our ideas and arguments. This section explores these recursive processes that are integral to productive, meaningful, and responsible research.

The **I-Search** project is an example of an inquiry-based research project. In an I-Search, you begin by articulating a question that you want or need to know more about. From there, you explain your prior knowledge on the topic and develop a research plan. As you execute the research plan, you compose a research narrative that describes your search for relevant sources, the information you uncover in those sources, and your reflection on whether and how those sources help you develop conclusions about your research questions. The I-Search concludes with your reflections on the research and writing process, and your thoughts about the topic overall, including any answers, new questions, research gaps, and potential next steps for research that emerge in the process. The point of an I-Search project is to understand that your process of inquiry through research allows you to develop ideas and open new avenues for thought and understanding that weren't available or apparent at the start of your process.

Through the course of your academic writing career, you will likely experience inquiry-based research on a larger scale as well. If you are asked to write an analysis of a book, you will need to learn about the author, the social and/or historical context when the book was published, and what other people have already said about the book's themes and impact. When you are tasked with developing a potential solution to a problem, you will need to learn about the origins of the problem, who is affected by it (and, therefore, who has an interest or stake in solving it), what has already been done to try to fix it, and whether those solutions were successful. Down the line, if you are working on a major research project, such as a master's thesis or doctoral dissertation, you will compose research questions, articulate your methodology, and design research methods for gathering and analyzing data. These kinds of research-based writing begin with asking questions and developing strategies for research and writing, and then moving through the process of evaluating sources, integrating information from sources, analyzing that information, and articulating conclusions.

Throughout this section, we will describe strategies that you can use as you work through the secondary research process. First, we describe secondary research methods and processes that will help you articulate research questions and find and evaluate sources of information. Next, we explain different ways you may be asked to write about your research while you gather ideas. Finally, we discuss how to effectively integrate research into your writing to support arguments and conclusions, looking at ways that you might synthesize information and properly cite sources. Each of these strategies will help you construct your ethos as a researcher and writer.

36   CHAPTER 5 | SECONDARY RESEARCH METHODS

> ### Activity 1: Reflective Journaling
>
> Spend a few minutes writing responses to these questions:
>
> - What do you think your strengths are as a researcher?
> - What do you think your weaknesses are as a researcher?
> - What is one challenge or problem you experienced while you were doing research for a past project? How were you able to overcome or work around it?

> ### Activity 2: Visualizing a Topic
>
> Create a visual map of your research (use a digital mapping tool such as the website bubbl.us, or get out some blank paper and a pen/pencil). Put your research question/main topic in a bubble in the center of the page, using as few words as possible. Add a ring of bubbles surrounding it, listing out as many aspects of the topic as you can, including subtopics and sub-arguments; interested parties, major voices, or authors; history and background; what you already know; and what you still need to know. Add third, fourth, or fifth levels of bubbles as needed. Keep the phrasing of each bubble entry as short as you can. Each of these bubbles could potentially be a useful **keyword**, or a short phrase to use when you search for sources online (either through the library or a web-searching service).

SECONDARY RESEARCH METHODS AND PROCESSES

■ Writing Research Questions

Starting with a strong **research question** is essential for moving forward productively. Simply stated, a research question is the question about your topic that you will explore, finding answers by doing research. You want to begin by clearly and specifically articulating something you want or need to know about. You may also want to do some quick searches in dictionaries or encyclopedias to explore and establish your basic understanding of the topic. Think carefully about the terms you are using in your research question because these terms or keywords sometimes carry certain connotations or might only be understood by a very specialized audience. Sometimes the terms might not be specific enough to give you direction or a sense of purpose for starting your research. You will also want to think about the rhetorical situation for which you are conducting research: how will the research be presented, for what purpose, and to whom? As you find an answer or answers to your research question, those answers will help you form a thesis statement.

SECONDARY RESEARCH METHODS AND PROCESSES   37

Activity 3: Testing the Effectiveness of an I-Search Question

If you are writing an I-Search project for ENG 1020, reflect on the following points to test the effectiveness of your I-Search question:

- Is it written as a question, or set of questions, instead of a statement?
- Do I need to clarify any terms to make my research question understandable to my audience?
- Am I personally invested in exploring this question? Why or how will exploring this question help me? Can I articulate my motivation for asking this question?
- Is my question something I can research using *secondary sources* (documents—typically written ones—that share research results, knowledge, and information from others)? Can it be answered too easily, or do I need a diverse set of sources to understand the answer?
- Is my question specific or concrete enough to explore in 1,500–2,000 words? Or is it too broad or too narrow?

■ Turning Research Questions into Search Terms

Computers are not as intelligent as humans. A search engine, database, or other computer program will look at the precise information—the actual letters and/or characters—that you enter and run that through its pre-defined algorithms (mathematical formulas used to accomplish searches). This means that you need to enter information that matches the kind of information with which the computer program was designed to work.

Some search engines do well with basic questions: ask a smartphone what the weather will be today and it will probably return the correct information. But as questions become more complex, involving more components, computers begin to have a harder time parsing them. Additionally, although the average search engine has been taught to recognize questions-as-questions and to respond with statements, most scholarly databases do not have that capability, and will instead read a question as a statement. When you search academic databases, questions just confuse the databases.

For these reasons, it is important to be able to take your complex research question/s and convert them into simpler keywords. **Keywords** are short phrases, usually one or two words long, that express individual concepts. Your research question may involve several concepts and therefore several keywords that you can use to search scholarly databases. For instance, let's revisit that question about the weather. Perhaps you want to find answers to questions such as "Is our weather average for this time of year? When has it been different? How was it different?" In that case, you might want to search for the words "weather records" or "historical weather" along with the name of a specific town, state, or region. Once you have that data, you can examine it to decide for yourself when the weather was different from or similar to what it is now, and how significant those differences are.

38   CHAPTER 5 | SECONDARY RESEARCH METHODS

RESEARCH QUESTION/TOPIC	KEYWORD IDEAS
How does social media impact our mental health?	social media; web 2.0; specific platform names; mental health; specific mental health issues; relationships; online relationships; self-confidence
Which mass transit options would be most effective in Detroit?	mass transit; public transport/ation; transport/ation systems; urban development; subways; trains; busses; Detroit; urban sprawl; regional transport/ation
How much are Antarctic penguin breeds declining due to global warming?	penguin/s; Antarctica; Antarctic penguins; Antarctic wildlife; penguin breeds; declining population; global warming; climate change

FIGURE 5.1   Research Questions and Keywords

Keywords also are important because they help you stay in control of your search process and results. Taking a moment to convert your question into keywords can help you determine which concepts and ideas in your topic are more important, and which ones are less important. When articles are added to scholarly databases, those databases organize the articles according to their main topics by tagging each article with keywords. This is similar to how a hashtag in a social media post connects that post to others that also use the same hashtag. As you begin reading your search results, you should also pay attention to any keywords you see explicitly identified in your search results. You will want to find the keywords the database is using that most closely match your own expression of the topic. You also should pay attention to any phrases you see repeated in titles or abstracts in your search results. If a particular phrase comes up frequently, you might want to try it out in a search. Below is a chart that lists some research questions and gives examples of keywords that could be used for related searches.

Activity 4: Finding Keywords in a Sentence

Follow the directions in the top row of this grid to help you think of keywords within your research topic/question. An example is provided for you below.

Divide a sheet of paper into three columns. At the top of the first column, write your research topic or question. In the middle column, write only the noun phrases and important verbs from your question. You may also think of some synonyms for these terms. These are your individual, unique ideas for keywords about your topic. At this point, start searching on the library databases using your keywords. As you're searching, record the terminology you spot in the articles' abstracts and subject heading lists. These terms are often standardized within scholarly communities. As you match your terminology to the database terminology, your searching should become easier. As you fill out the chart, reflect on whether your own terms were narrower or broader than those you found in the databases.

COLUMN 1: State your research topic or question	COLUMN 2: List any noun phrases and important verbs from the research question (your keywords)	COLUMN 3: List database keywords from library sources
Ex: How much are Antarctic penguin breeds declining due to global warming?	Ex: penguin/s, Antarctica, Antarctic penguins, Antarctic wildlife, penguin breeds, declining population, global warming, climate change	Ex: Global warming; Ecosystem studies; Models; Marine mammals; Animal populations

As you search, you can use Boolean operators to combine your keywords together. This can make your search more focused and narrow, or more broad and generalized. The most common Boolean operators, which almost every database and search engine will recognize, are the words "and," "or," and "not." Using "and" tells databases to only show you results if they contain both/all the terms listed. Using "or" makes a search broader, telling the search engine to look for several terms and show results that contain any of them. This can be very useful if the term you're searching for has several synonyms. Using "not" limits a search by telling the search engine to not show results containing a certain term. This is useful when you want to see only some elements of a topic and not others, or if you care about some synonyms but the others are irrelevant. The chart below visualizes these operations.

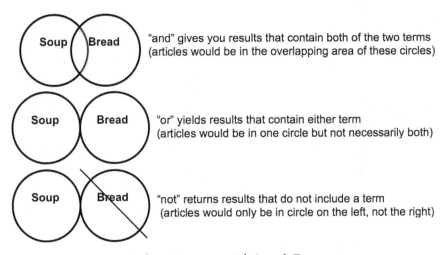

FIGURE 5.2   Using Boolean Operators with Search Terms

■ Using Multimodal & Digital Strategies to Keep Track of Research

Learning how to use various tools to keep track of your research can help you further develop your flexibility in the research and writing process. Because research is recursive (moving from reading, to questions, to finding sources, back to reading, and to synthesis of sources), keeping careful track of the ideas found in the sources you uncover, as well as the ideas you develop from reading, is important. If you do not keep records about what you have found and where you found it, you won't be able to revisit the source again—at least, not without (re)doing a lot of work.

Taking notes or using a research journal to keep track of your searches and progress can save you a lot of time and trouble later on. You could track this information with a paper notebook or binder, a digital note-taking app, or even a voice recorder. Use whatever will be most effective for you. This way, if you find that something hasn't worked out, you can retrace your steps to an idea that may work better. Keeping good records will help you be a flexible researcher.

■ Interacting with Digital Sources

Because your research in ENG 1020 is focused on secondary sources, many of the sources you decide to use will be most readily available to you in digital format. Your experiences working with general Internet search tools such as Google may have led you to some standard practices for keeping track of sites you need to revisit frequently (bookmarking, for example). However, moving into more scholarly research and needing to return to texts to read more deeply for your research project may mean that you need to develop more robust strategies for interacting with these texts.

For example, imagine you are using the library databases as a starting point, and you conduct an advanced search in Academic OneFile. In the advanced search, you have the option to select "full text only" for your results, meaning that the search will only turn up articles with the complete text available for you to read immediately (not all journals will allow their articles to be posted online or included in databases immediately upon publication). Beyond your initial skimming of the text, you will need to make a plan for annotating and taking notes on the source. Will you download the text to annotate on your computer or tablet? Will you print the text to work with, writing your annotations in pen and later transcribing key notes and ideas in a map or online document? You will also want to make a note of which search terms you used to find the items in case you want to look for more pieces like them at a later date.

■ Making a Flexible Research Plan

Sometimes you may find yourself hitting a wall with your research, identifying useful information and narrowing your ideas through an initial search path but needing to know more. When you have tried adjusting your keywords and need to solve your research problem another way, it may make sense to use a library database with another focus. You may also move outside of the library to read online articles on the cultural context surrounding your topic. Additionally, you may spend some time in the works cited or references page of an article to identify other keywords or sources.

Though you will find that your research process continues to develop and change as you discover more through your reading, it is important to begin with a plan for how you will approach your reading and management of sources. Without a plan, you may lose valuable time for reading and writing. Sometimes we describe our experiences with online research as "stumbling around," "falling down a rabbit hole," or even "getting sucked in." But really, even our simple online searches are more purposeful than that. They are grounded in our past conversations and experiences: we know where to look for the things we need and how to phrase even quick Google searches that will get us most efficiently to the information we seek. Over time, each of us has learned when to trust serendipity—when to explore a seemingly coincidental new find to check out its usefulness or accuracy—and when not to because it would take us too far away from our original query. When making a research plan in preparation for a writing project that relies heavily on secondary research, such as the I-Search or the Researched Argument assignments, we can draw from these previous experiences to think about what initial steps and strategies will be most effective. Doing so will allow us more time to explore new ideas along the way without losing sight of our main purpose.

■ Finding Relevant Sources

As you pursue answers to your research question, there may be some obvious places to look for information. But don't be satisfied with only the simple path to your answers: look for the best sources you can find to put together a complete and complex paper.

First, you should be sure to look for a variety of sources that reflect a range of viewpoints on your topic. Different publications are meant for different audiences and therefore have different perspectives on a topic. You may be required to use a certain number of sources that are books or journal articles (more about those to follow). But these aren't the only places to look for information. Depending on your topic and your instructor's requirements, you may also want to consider looking at local or national newspapers or general interest magazines, such as *Time*. These news sources try to meet the needs of a general audience and can sometimes be very useful. You also may want to consider historic or archival sources, which you may be able to see in a special library or museum collection in person, or in a digital collection on an institution's website. Community leaders and organizations sometimes have useful information, and you may be able to use someone's blog entries or look at

42 CHAPTER 5 | SECONDARY RESEARCH METHODS

copies of their newsletter. Within these big categories (academic, general, community) there will still be many individual authors, each with their own unique take on your topic. Think outside the box and always look for the best source for answers to your questions. Consider asking your instructor for suggestions of good places for you to look for information.

Although publications for a general audience and texts written by community members can be very valuable, you will also be expected to use items written for an academic audience. These items, in the form of books and journal articles, are written by professors and researchers who publish the results of their work for an academic audience. Academic audiences often hold very high expectations for the quality of the argument, supporting evidence, and research methodology used in a text. This is why it is common for instructors to require their students to use books and journal articles in their papers. Instructors feel they are acclimating new members of the academic community to the genres of writing common to the group. However, because they have a specialized audience, these books will probably be very different from books you may have read before, which were meant for a general audience. Similarly, a journal article is very different from a newspaper article. Be prepared to spend more time reading these academic sources than you would when reading a fiction book or newspaper article, especially while you are new to the

---

Activity 5: Reflecting on the Types of Sources You Need

Finding relevant sources for your research project is not just about finding sources that relate to your topic. It is also about reflecting on which kinds of sources (books, articles, etc.) will be best for your project and meaningful for your audience. Use the questions below to help you think about the kinds of sources that will work best for your research project:

- Why am I doing this research? Does the rhetorical situation require or necessitate that I use particular kinds of sources? For example, does the assignment description state that I am required to use peer-reviewed scholarly sources? Do articles in the journal I am writing for tend to cite articles from the same journal? Will my audience want to see quantitative data presented visually?

- Is this topic typically discussed in scholarly or popular forums? Is it very specialized, or does it reflect an interest of the general population?

- What kind of audience is implicit in my research question? What kinds of sources will they respect or trust?

- Will having first-person accounts help me build ethos or pathos in my writing? Could I find first-person accounts in newspaper articles, radio stories, or videos?

academic community. As you read more and more of these sources, they will become easier to comprehend and take less time to read.

Chances are that you will feel frustrated at some point (or maybe at multiple points) during your research process. Do not let yourself get discouraged! As you work your way through a problem, you are learning more about your topic. In fact, this is often when experienced writers really get excited about their research, for they enjoy the challenge and feel that this brings out their best or most useful work. Try going back to your search notes or journal to revisit an old idea, or start again with a slightly different approach to the topic. Perhaps give a second look to some sources you had initially dismissed. Maybe talk to your instructor about how to change your topic so it can reflect the sources and information you are finding rather than what you are not finding. Definitely reach out to the university librarians or the writing center for assistance because a fresh pair of eyes can spot ideas and possibilities that you had missed. Overall, stay engaged in the research process and do not give up on it. There will be something for you to learn about and share with your audience in your writing, and you will figure out how to make it work.

■ Evaluating Sources

As you find sources, you will discover that not all of them are good or useful. It is important to be critical of your sources and to hold high standards. Look for items that will be the most helpful in explaining your topic or supporting your argument. Do not just accept the first search results and call it a day! Be rigorous as you examine and read your sources.

There are many things to consider as you decide if a source is worth using for your project, but one tool that may help you is the CRAAP Test. The five letters in the acronym represent five questions or areas you should examine as you consider using an information source:

Currency—How timely is the source?

Relevance—Is the source's topic closely related to your own?

Authority—Who wrote or created the source, and why should you trust them?

Accuracy—Is the source's information correct, as best you can judge?

Purpose—Why does the source exist; could there be an underlying motive or bias?

An expanded version of the CRAAP Test, with additional analytical questions, is provided in *Activity 6*. Remember that this is only a simple tool. If you are doing a project that draws on historical events, you may want to use older sources that could have a very obvious bias, such as the journal of someone who experienced the event you are discussing. There are no "right" or "wrong" answers to the CRAAP Test. Rather, it is meant to help you discover your sources' strengths and weaknesses.

Activity 6: The Full CRAAP Test

Analyze one (or more) of the sources you're considering for your paper by answering the questions listed under each area of the CRAAP test below. Don't just write "yes" or "no"—give a 1–2 sentence explanation of your answer. (Note that some questions are more appropriate for only digital or paper sources.)

Currency: the timeliness of the information

- When was the information published or posted?
- Has the information been revised or updated?
- Does your topic require current information, or will older sources work as well?
- Are any links functional?

Relevance: the importance of the information for your needs

- Does the information relate to your topic or answer your questions?
- Who is the intended audience?
- Is the information at an appropriate level (i.e. not too elementary or advanced for your needs)?
- Have you looked at a variety of sources before deciding to use this one?
- Would you be comfortable citing this source in your research paper?

Authority: the source of the information

- Who is the author/publisher/source/sponsor?
- What are the author's credentials or organizational affiliations?
- Is the author qualified to write on the topic?
- Is there contact information, such as a publisher or email address?
- Does the URL reveal anything about the author or the source? (Examples: .com, .edu, .gov, .org, .net)

Accuracy: the reliability, truthfulness, and correctness of the content

- Where does the information come from?
- Is the information supported by evidence?
- Has the information been reviewed or refereed?
- Can you verify any of the information through another source or from personal knowledge?
- Does the language or tone seem unbiased and free of emotion?
- Are there spelling, grammar, or typographical errors?

*P*urpose: the reason the information exists

- What is the purpose of the information—to inform, teach, sell, entertain, persuade, etc.?
- Do the authors/sponsors make their intentions or purpose clear?
- Is the information fact, opinion, or propaganda?
- Does the point of view appear objective and impartial?
- Are there political, ideological, cultural, religious, institutional, or personal biases?

WRITING ABOUT YOUR RESEARCH PROCESS AND DISCOVERIES

In your writing course, you may be asked to write about your research in several ways. Writing about your research process and the resources you have found can help you think about how to most effectively integrate your research into other kinds of writing, such as a researched argument or an infographic.

■ Annotated Bibliographies

Students are often assigned to write **annotated bibliographies** as part of their research projects. Annotated bibliographies are essentially sets of notes about sources, including a bibliographic entry for the source, a **summary** of the content of the source, and sometimes additional notes about the source. Additional notes may include an *analysis* of the argument or a *discussion* of how that source may be positioned in the research project. Instructors will often specifically ask students to make certain writing moves in the additional notes of an annotated bibliography.

Writing an annotated bibliography can help you with several elements of the research process. First, the task of summarizing sources helps you make sure that you comprehend the content and/or argument of each source. This is achieved through putting the text into your own words and writing a concise summary of the source's content. Second, composing the annotations can help you start to think about how sources fit together in your argument. Which sources convey the same ideas or arguments? How do sources complement each other? Where do authors disagree with one another? These are all things you might think about as you work on deciding which sources you will ultimately use in your research, and on positioning information in your researched writing.

■ Research Narratives/The I-Search

A **research narrative** is a description of the research process and your findings. Sometimes, you may be asked to write a research log or blog about the steps you are taking to find, evaluate, and integrate sources for a research project. This narrative and reflection will help you talk with your classmates and instructor about your research and writing process.

The **I-Search** is a specific kind of research narrative, which includes your motivation for asking the research question, your prior knowledge on the topic, a description of the research process, and reflection on what you find throughout that research process. The I-Search requires you to **monitor** your research strategies and **evaluate** sources of information in the text of the project itself. So while you should make these moves in any research project, you will explicitly write about them in the I-Search.

Because the I-Search essentially tells the story of your research process, you also need to think about which details are important to include in the research narrative. Later, when you **reflect** on your research process, these details can help you remember which strategies you used to learn about your topic, and whether and how those strategies and the sources you uncovered were useful for learning more and/or for crafting an argument. For example, it could be useful to explain the **keywords** you used to search in a database like Academic OneFile, as well as how you narrowed your results once you found a set of potential sources. It could also be useful to explain what you were thinking about when you read through a source, deciding if it was going to be helpful for you or not. The I-Search will document the process for you to reflect on. It will also allow others to understand how you work through research, reading, and writing, and how you came to the conclusions you develop. Thus, it is key to include details beyond the title of the source and its content. Is it important to write about the time of day you did your research or whether or not you were listening to music? Maybe. Is it important to explain what your roommate was eating for breakfast? Maybe not.

■ Integrating Research Results into Your Writing

After you have learned about your topic through the research process, you will need to share your new knowledge with your audience. You have explored the existing conversation about your research question, and now it is your turn to contribute to the conversation. Sometimes you will need to share only your research results, making sure that you report this information accurately, but other times you will use the information you found to support a bigger claim or argument you have created on your own.

■ Reporting Information & Synthesizing Sources

Synthesis writing combines several writers' work by discussing a topic or idea that they all have in common. For example, perhaps you researched the topic of homelessness, and you read two pieces by two authors who propose different methods to decrease homelessness. In a synthesis, you would explain what the two pieces or authors have in common and what is different between them.

Synthesis is at the core of research-based writing. Once you have read your research, you will need to combine the ideas in those pieces to explain to your reader the relationships within the documents and what you saw between them. Perhaps a concept originated with Author A, and then was developed further by Author B. Author C disagrees with B but still agrees with A. Perhaps Author D worked on the same idea as A and B but in a totally different situation or location, so although D presents new knowledge, that author never mentions the previous scholars. Meanwhile, Authors E and F disagree strongly with A and therefore with everything else that all the other authors did, although they only mention A and B.

All of these are common situations that you may have to explain in a research paper by writing a **synthesis** of the sources. This means that as you are reading your research sources, you will have to pay close attention to what the authors are saying so that you can explain those relationships accurately. If the authors refer to each other's work, you will need to explain that. If they don't refer to each other but you see a relationship, either a similarity or a difference, between their work, you'll need to explain that as well.

Sometimes, in other classes, you may be asked to do assignments that do not go very far beyond synthesizing your sources. One common assignment, which you may have already done in high school, is a "research report." This is often similar to an **annotated bibliography**, which was described earlier. Unlike the annotated bibliography, a research report does not include a personal reaction or evaluation of the sources' usefulness for a particular project. Another example of a synthesis-based writing genre is the **literature review**. A literature review pulls together the previous scholarly work on a topic the author is writing about to position the new piece in the ongoing conversation. You may notice a "literature review" section in some of the scholarly articles you read, and you should pay attention to some of the specific writing strategies used there (ex: the transitions and introductory phrases, how sources are organized, how citations are done, etc.). Writing a literature review by itself is also a common assignment for undergraduate students in the sciences and social sciences.

In ENG 1020, though, you'll be going a step beyond simply synthesizing sources. Besides explaining the relationships between your sources, you will also use this knowledge to support your own argument about a topic. As you are presenting your synthesized research and your argument, you will need to think about the specific audience you are addressing. Are you writing for a scholarly audience, such as your instructor, other undergraduates, or academics across the country? Are you writing for a general or popular audience, and you need to be understood by the average person on the street? Are you composing in a textual medium and communicating only through typed words? Or will you have a visual element? Are you also doing a spoken or video presentation? All of these factors can influence which research sources will be the most useful to include in your synthesis and to support your argument.

48 CHAPTER 5 | SECONDARY RESEARCH METHODS

■ Citing Sources

The whole point of research is to learn about what has already been said on a topic and to add your own voice to the conversation. This means that as you are actually composing a paper, presentation, or other document based on your research, you need to make it clear to your own audience or readers which parts and ideas came from you, and which ones are from other authors. You need to acknowledge those other authors and give them credit. In academic work, we call the credit given to other authors a **citation.** As a general practice, citations help your readers know where you found useful information on your topic so they could go back and look at your sources if they were interested. But depending on what sort of audience you are writing for, your individual papers could have very different-looking citations.

Different fields and disciplines have different methods for writing citations because each discipline thinks it is important to share different pieces of information about a source with readers. For instance, if you were writing a paper in a psychology class, you would probably be asked to follow the citation guidelines of the American Psychological Association (APA). In the field of Psychology, scholars publish journal articles pretty frequently, sometimes every year, or even two or three in a year. Therefore, APA citation style includes the year an item was published right after the author's name so the reader will know how recently it was published. On the other hand, scholars in the field of English (and some other humanities fields) do not publish many smaller articles but instead focus on producing one book over the course of several years. Therefore, in the style of the Modern Language Association (MLA)—the style used by English scholars—citations include the title of the work right after the author's name, and the year is pushed further back in the citation. APA and MLA are two of the best-known and most widely used citation styles, but many disciplines have their own specific citation style. Pay close attention to your assignment instructions to see what the citations requirements are, and ask your instructor for clarification and help whenever you feel you need it.

Citation styles have been frequently updated in the last few years to adapt to new web-based publications and information sources, and they will certainly continue to be revised as more new sources come into being. Make sure that you are always using the most current guidelines. Some places you can look for help include the following:

- Published book-length citation or style guides, such as the *MLA Handbook* or the *Publication Manual of the American Psychological Association* (you may be able to find these at the library)

- A website associated with the book, such as style.mla.org or blog.apa-style.org (these often include explanations for rarer or newer kinds of sources that weren't included in the books)

- The WSU campus writing center, located in the undergraduate library (book an appointment on their website, wrtzone.wayne.edu, or maybe attend one of their workshops on citations)

WRITING ABOUT YOUR RESEARCH PROCESS AND DISCOVERIES   49

- The WSU Library's website, especially the Research Guides (may be very helpful for finding resources about a particular discipline's research and citation practices)

- A university-run writing help webpage, such as owl.english.purdue.edu/owl (often has multiple examples all on one page, making it easier to figure out which version best matches your particular source)

- A computerized citation generator, such as EndNote, Zotero, or RefWorks (these are very handy for storing and remembering which sources went with which project—but be careful, because their algorithms for building the citations are not going to be as smart or accurate as your own brain, so you'll need to proofread the automatically-generated citations carefully)

It is up to you to make sure that your citations are done correctly and that you include all of your research sources in your document. The academic community takes citation practice very seriously; it is important to us that we acknowledge the way our work builds on work done by others. By respecting this cultural value and practicing good citations, you will demonstrate your participation and membership in the academic community to your readers.

Activity 7: Citation Information Search

Citations typically contain the following information (though exactly how these elements are combined will vary from one citation style to another):

- The author's name (and sometimes the editor's name for a book that is a collection of smaller pieces, or a sponsoring/publishing organization for a website)

- The title of the piece (if it's an article, book chapter, or single page on a website, you need the name of both that shorter entry and the journal, book, or site itself)

- The publishing information (the issue, volume, and year for an article; the publishing house and year for a book; the date and URL for a website)

For this activity, look through your sources and locate these three categories of information for each one. Record the information on index cards (one card for each source), in a notebook, or in a document on your computer.

CONCLUSION

Your experiences doing research in college courses and for other workplace and personal projects will probably lead you to a few conclusions and insights about your research process as well as your writing process. Most significantly, you will find that research is reiterative and recursive, and that it can take a while to get it done thoroughly. Each time you work on researching a particular question, you may have a refined set of keywords, a new database to dig into, and new sources to read. You will find that your ideas about your topic become more nuanced as you read your sources and your knowledge deepens. You will find that, quite often, the first result is not the best result, and that digging deeper can help you find the really good stuff. Finally, you will learn about the value of time in the research process: the more time you spend reading and reflecting on what you discover, the better chance your ideas will have to change and grow in productive ways.

6

Metacognition and Reflection

Adrienne Jankens, Sarah Primeau, Thomas Trimble, Nicole Guinot Varty

*Throughout your writing courses at Wayne State, you will be asked to engage in various types of **reflective writing** that are designed to help you develop strategies for writing and your overall knowledge about writing. When we reflect on our strategies for writing, we think specifically about our writing process in ways that help us change things that are not working and do things that are working more often and on purpose. In this course, you will use reflection primarily to **plan**, **monitor**, and **evaluate** your learning and writing. This section describes what reflection is, explains various kinds of reflection, and presents several reflective writing assignments that you are likely to encounter in your composition courses at WSU.*

INTRODUCTION

What distinguishes a novice from an expert? Natural talent? Hard work? Good luck? Think of your favorite athlete, musician, actor, or writer. How were they able to make the move from being okay to being really good?

Becoming good at something is a complicated process. One thing that many scholars have observed about experts is that experts seem to be good at *thinking, talking,* and very often *writing* about what they do. As examples, think about interviews with accomplished athletes or musicians that you have seen or read. When asked about their performances, these experts are very good at identifying and describing the specific techniques, strategies, and choices they make as performers. Think of

52 CHAPTER 6 | METACOGNITION AND REFLECTION

a professional baseball pitcher who talks about working to control the specific angle of their arm when throwing. Consider a fashion designer who talks about their choices of color, texture, and line when working on a new design. Experts talk about their work with greater detail and awareness than those whose skills are still developing. The good news is that the ability to think like an expert is not something we're born with. Rather, this kind of thinking can be learned and, more importantly, practiced in ways that can help us become experts at things we want to be good at doing.

Becoming a good writer works much the same way. Contrary to what many people think, being a good writer is not something any of us are born with. But learning how to *think* about writing is one of the most important things we can do to become proficient at writing. In this section, we will talk about how you can use **reflection** to become a better writer.

REFLECTION AND METACOGNITION

We all write in a variety of contexts for a wide range of audiences and purposes. In college, for example, you may write an analysis paper for an English class, a lab report for a Biology class, and a speech for a Business class. As writing teachers, we wish our classes could discuss every context, audience, and type of writing you will encounter here at college, in the workplace, and in your community. But it's not possible to cover that much material in a single college course. As writing teachers, we also know that as students become more experienced writers, they will find it easier to take knowledge from one context and apply it to another.

Reflection, which writing scholar Jennifer Moon defines as a form of thinking dedicated to solving a particular goal or problem, can help students learn how to assess their own development and transfer learning from one situation to a new task. As an example of reflection, think about a runner approaching the starting line of race who thinks, "Keep your head down at the start!" One particular kind of reflection that is important for learning is called **metacognition**, broadly defined as "thinking about thinking." As an example of metacognition, imagine a math student who struggles with story problems thinking, "Why do I find these problems so hard to solve?"

Reflection and metacognition are closely related concepts, so you might think about them as mental processes focused on awareness of the choices you make and the ability to evaluate the effectiveness of your thinking. As an example of reflection in action in a writing class, think about the kinds of questions you might ask yourself while writing the introduction of an assigned essay:

- Does this introduction do a good job of convincing my instructor that I understand the assignment and the concepts she is asking me to write about?
- Is my thesis statement okay, or will I need to come back and revise it after working on the body of the paper?
- Have I explained any concepts or vocabulary that my readers might not be familiar with?

One way that writing instructors help students develop metacognition (i.e. thinking about their choices while writing) is by asking students to *reflect* on their writing in order to notice the choices they made while working on a specific project or to predict how they might use what they have learned in another writing project.

During a writing class, your instructor may ask you to write reflective letters, reflection memos, or journal entries to help you develop the habit of examining your own writing and noticing not just *what* you said, but also *how* you said it and *why* you decided to say it that way. For example, in a particular piece of writing, you may have decided to use certain words or a certain style to meet the expectations of your target audience, like using "Hey guys!" in a group text to your friends. You may have also avoided certain words or a style that you felt did not fit the genre (type of writing) or audience, like "Good day, hearty companions!" Noticing these kinds of choices helps you to develop metacognitive awareness (i.e. awareness of your thinking) and, ultimately, to apply what you know about writing in various college, workplace, and community contexts.

PURPOSES OF REFLECTION

The kinds of reflective writing you'll do in your writing classes here at WSU will often be oriented around three specific purposes: **planning**, **monitoring**, and **evaluating**. Using reflective writing to plan includes writing that describes your understanding of an assignment in your own words, explores previous experiences with similar assignments, or identifies prior knowledge about a topic. Using reflective writing to monitor includes writing that explores what is happening in the middle of drafting or revising processes. Using reflective writing to evaluate includes writing that looks back at drafts to figure out what was successful or not successful in a project.

▪ Using Reflection to Plan

This section will talk about how to use reflection on your prior knowledge to plan your approach to writing tasks. What is **prior knowledge** anyway?

54   CHAPTER 6 | METACOGNITION AND REFLECTION

The quickest way to define **prior knowledge** is "knowledge from before," or knowledge from previous contexts. Another useful (and more fleshed-out) definition of prior knowledge can be found on Carnegie Mellon University's Eberly Center website, which states that prior knowledge in an educational context is "a broad range of pre-existing knowledge, skills, beliefs, and attitudes, which influence how [students] attend, interpret and organize in-coming information." So, according to this definition, you come into this writing class with lots of pre-existing knowledge (stuff you know how to write, what you've written before), skills (tricks and strategies for completing writing tasks), and attitudes (writing is dumb, writing is just too hard, writing is fun, writing is boring). You may not even be totally aware of some of this prior knowledge. This is one area in which reflection is useful.

Knowledge that we have but are not aware of is called **tacit knowledge**. For example, you are not explicitly aware of all of the knowledge you have about driving a car or riding a bike. You may not know how to explain HOW to do it, but *you know how to do it*. You just *drive*. When we reflect on our prior knowledge, we become aware of it in an explicit way—we become conscious of what we know. For instance, if you really thought about it, you could describe step-by-step how to drive a car (first you open the car door, then buckle the seat belt, then put your hands on the wheel, check mirrors, turn ignition, press brake, put car in gear, etc.). Being aware of prior knowledge that you have about writing is a way of taking a tacit process (writing) and making it explicit.

When you're facing a new writing task, it will help to reflect on your prior knowledge about writing to assess what you know and what you'll need to know. The easiest place to start might be with what isn't there. When we don't have prior knowledge about a task or concept, it is termed **absent prior knowledge**. For example, many students might not know what a "white paper" is or how to write one. So, if you were assigned a white paper, you would have absent prior knowledge about this genre of writing and the process of approaching the task. When reflecting on absent prior knowledge as you approach a new writing task, you will want to ask these main questions:

- What do you NOT know?
- What will you need to learn from scratch?

Answering these questions in writing will help you reflect on your absent prior knowledge and engage in **planning reflection**. By knowing what the gaps in your knowledge are, you can plan for accessing the resources you need to accomplish the task. These types of questions give you a place to start working.

The second type of prior knowledge to reflect on is what is there but might not be correct. For example, perhaps you had experiences with five-paragraph essays and had it drilled into your head that the ONLY correct way to write in school is the five-paragraph essay. In college, many instructors will quickly inform you this is not always the case. There are multitudes of academic genres to learn and compose during your college career. So, when you are reflecting on prior knowledge that might need revision, you should ask this main question:

- What do you know that needs to be modified?

Answering this question in writing will help you reflect on the prior knowledge you have that needs to be revised so you can successfully accomplish the writing task.

The third type of prior knowledge to reflect on when facing a new or unfamiliar writing task is the prior knowledge that will readily and helpfully transfer to your current situation. This is knowledge that can be adapted to new situations easily and correctly. For example, if you were trained extensively in correct MLA citation practices, you will be able to use that knowledge in many different college writing tasks. When you are reflecting on prior knowledge that will easily transfer to your current writing task, answer these main questions:

- What do you know and is good-to-go?
- What will be immediately useful here?

Answering these questions in writing will help you reflect on prior knowledge you have that will apply successfully to your current writing task.

As you practice reflecting on your prior knowledge to plan your approaches to writing tasks, it is important to remember that practice makes progress. This type of reflection is a dynamic process that happens over time, so being able to do it "on command" is important! It can give you more control over what you've already learned and what you are currently working on.

In your WSU composition courses, you may do this type of reflection in class, or as homework. You may write reflectively in genres such as reflection journals, KWLs (What do I **k**now? What do I **w**onder? What have I **l**earned?), brainstorming lists, or blogs. As you work on reflection throughout the semester, try to take note of when you reflect on prior knowledge to plan your approach to writing tasks.

■ Using Reflection to Monitor

While learning a new skill, we may have coaches, teachers, family members, and others help "monitor" our progress. A coach may watch you carefully, providing suggestions to improve technique. A teacher may write comments in the margins of your essays (another way to make suggestions for improvement). In a writing course, your instructor and classmates will help you monitor your progress, but it is also important

56   CHAPTER 6 | METACOGNITION AND REFLECTION

for you to develop techniques to monitor your own progress as a writer. Listening to your coaches' and teachers' advice is helpful, but monitoring your own progress is a slightly different process. Monitoring is a "habit of mind" that you can develop during a writing class but continue to use in any future writing situation (*Framework for Success in Postsecondary Writing*, 5).

In your writing class, your instructor may ask you to stop in the middle of a project and reflect. This is an opportunity to **monitor** or do reflection-in-progress. When writing a monitoring reflection, you should answer these main questions:

- How are you engaging with this task?
- What are your goals, and are you making progress toward them?
- What is working? What is frustrating or not working? How can you change your approach so that you are making progress?

Answering these questions in writing can help you usefully monitor your writing process. Sometimes this monitoring work will be done through an assigned process memo or blog post, maybe when you are preparing to submit a draft or after a peer response session.

Developing strategies for doing this monitoring work on your own will help you continue to practice this kind of reflection. In addition to thinking and writing about the questions listed above, you can also monitor your writing by *listening* to it. Reading your draft out loud to yourself can help you hear your writing in a new way and understand differently which writing moves you would like to make next. As you read, take note of things that stand out to you, including the following:

- What sounds brilliant as you read your text? What do you really like?
- What sounds strange? Why? Are there places where you get tripped up as you read?
- How do you feel when you read your draft out loud?
- What would you like to add or change in the sections you have written so far?

Paying attention to your writing through listening to the way the sentences sound can help you think about how someone else will hear or read your text.

▪ Using Reflection to Evaluate

Once you complete a project or a piece of writing, you can look back at what you knew going in and assess how you have added to or revised that knowledge. In other words, you can use reflection to evaluate **what you learned about writing**, and **how your writing itself progressed** over the course of the assignment.

When you have completed a writing task, you can engage in written reflection about your prior knowledge going into that task, and your knowledge coming out of the task, in order to evaluate your learning. This might take the form of a kind of compare/contrast between prior knowledge and present knowledge. The contrast might be between big knowledge gaps (absent prior knowledge): "I didn't know what a white paper was, and now I do." Or the contrast might be more subtle: "at first I just wrote a five-paragraph essay, but when I got feedback on my draft, I realized that my writing could be more complex if I let go of that structure." When writing an evaluating reflection to track your learning, you should answer these main questions:

- What knowledge did you gain in this process?
- How does your current knowledge about writing compare to your knowledge prior to starting this assignment?

Answering these questions in writing can help you not only see what you learned, but also determine if there are any "blind spots" or areas where you still don't really understand. This can help you as you plan the next writing task.

When you finish a writing task, you can use evaluating reflection to gauge how well your writing process worked for you and whether or not your writing progressed. For example, maybe there was something that really got you stuck, such as MLA citations or how to craft a good transition sentence, and you identified it with monitoring reflection. Evaluating reflection is a way to check back with yourself to see how your troubleshooting went and whether or not the methods you chose paid off.

Reflecting to evaluate differs from reflecting to plan or monitor because we have a goal or model in mind that we are using to judge our own writing (Yancey, 50). Additionally, we are judging the effectiveness of our writing and the choices we make as writers. For example, imagine on a very busy day you decide to make a "things to do" list for yourself. As you complete tasks, you cross off or delete things from the list. As you remember new tasks you need to complete, you might add them to your list. Throughout the day, you may be making progress toward completing all the tasks on your list, but simply crossing items off the list is different from *evaluating* your progress. If you were to *evaluate* your progress, you would reflect on your larger goals for the day and decide whether your list of tasks has helped you achieve those goals. Thinking about both the larger goals and the small tasks is important. Similarly, when evaluating a piece of writing, you might think about both your larger goals and the small tasks you completed during the process of writing. When writing an evaluating reflection to see how your writing progressed, you should answer these main questions:

- What worked and what didn't as you wrote this assignment?
- How did your approach to each step of the writing process help or hinder your larger goals for the assignment?

58   CHAPTER 6 | METACOGNITION AND REFLECTION

- How did your approach help or hinder your larger goals for yourself as a writer?

Answering these questions in writing can help you see what you accomplished and what worked for you in your writing process. It can also help you evaluate your progress toward larger writing goals. This kind of written reflection can also help with predicting how to apply current or recent strategies to future writing tasks.

GENRES OF REFLECTIVE WRITING

You may encounter several different kinds of reflective writing in your writing classes and other courses you take here at the university. What follows are descriptions of some of the common forms of reflective writing you'll be asked to do in ENG 1020.

■ Reflective Journals

Many ENG 1020 instructors use some form of writing journal to help students practice using writing to **plan**, **monitor**, and **evaluate** their learning and writing. You will likely have the opportunity to practice all three types of reflection as you compose reflection journals. Journal prompts given to you by your instructor may ask you to write about prior experiences with writing or to think through very specific issues about your writing in terms of particular assignments and tasks. Sometimes, your instructor may collect your journal or individual journal entries to provide feedback. In other situations, your journal will be for your own private use.

One trap of the reflective journal is that students can sometimes think of journal entries as busy work that doesn't really matter when it comes to course grades or becoming a better writer. Reflective writing is certainly additional writing on top of the other drafting and revising you are doing for major projects in a course. It takes time to think about what you have been doing, want to do, or have done, and it takes time to write through those plans, strategies, and evaluations. But think back to the earlier examples of the baseball pitcher and fashion designer. We know that practicing reflection is not just a sign of expertise but a strategy for developing that expertise. In this way, we encourage you to think about the writing you do in your reflective journal as both a discipline and a strategy for getting better. As with most things, what you put into your reflection directly impacts what you get out of it.

The following journal prompts are some of the most commonly used prompts in ENG 1020. For most prompts, students are asked to write for ten to fifteen uninterrupted minutes in a notebook, blog, or digital document.

GENRES OF REFLECTIVE WRITING   **59**

- Describe, in as much detail as you can, your earliest memories of writing. Use these questions to jog your memories: How old were you? Where were you? What kind of technology did you use (cereal, refrigerator magnets, crayons, keyboard, etc.). What kind of reaction did you get from those around you?

- Evaluate your writing process during Project Two from planning and brainstorming, to drafting, revision, and publication. What went well? What did not go well? For which parts of your writing process do you still need good strategies? What do you need to work on moving forward?

■ "Talk-Backs"

A helpful moment to slow down and write through your thoughts is after you read a peer's or teacher's feedback on your writing. Because their feedback is designed to help you think about the next steps you will take in writing, researching, and revising, it is important to revisit your purposes for writing and think about whether and how to take their reactions and suggestions to shape your process and document. Writing scholar Kathleen Blake Yancey describes a kind of reflection-in-action called "talk-backs" in which students identify what the responder has valued in the draft and explain whether they agree or disagree with the responder's reading of the text (38). Writing a "talk-back" is a kind of **monitoring reflection** that can help you think about your writing from another reader's point of view. It can also help you evaluate your draft and plan next steps with some added perspective.

■ Process Memos

A memo is a genre in which the writer identifies and organizes key information that a specific reader needs to understand a larger issue or topic. As you revise and edit a writing project for your class, your instructor might ask you to compose a **process memo** to reflect on the decisions you made throughout your writing process. The purpose of a process memo is twofold: to help you think through what worked and did not work in your writing process (**evaluating reflection**), and to describe your writing process to your instructor so he or she can gain some insight into what was going on behind the scenes of your project. The memo provides key background information to the reader that they would otherwise not have to inform their reading of your project. In a process memo, you might describe the following:

- How and why you selected your topic and purpose
- What brainstorming or prewriting strategies helped you narrow your topic, identify keywords for research, sketch a rough outline, etc.
- What challenges you faced while composing the project, and how you approached solving those issues

60 CHAPTER 6 | METACOGNITION AND REFLECTION

- How you used peer or instructor feedback to help you revise your writing
- How you see your work on the project helping you meet writing or learning goals for the class
- What questions about writing, reading, or research you have moving forward

You might be asked to write through your thoughts about a completed assignment in genres other than memos. Some instructors use letters written to the instructor or future students, while other instructors assign blog posts, handwritten journal prompts, or short in-class writing assignments.

REFLECTING AT THE END OF THE SEMESTER

At the end of a semester, you may be asked to reflect on your work throughout the entire course. In ENG 1020, specifically, students are asked to craft arguments about the degree to which they have accomplished the course learning outcomes through their writing work in the class. This kind of **evaluating reflection** helps both students and teachers assess the learning happening in the course. In a **reflective argument essay**, you will provide evidence of your learning and progress, drawing from the body of informal and formal writing work you have done throughout the semester. To compose this essay, you will use the writing and rhetorical strategies that have been useful for writing other arguments: crafting a claim; identifying the most relevant and persuasive evidence to support that claim; and explaining, analyzing, and evaluating the evidence for your reader. The process memos and other reflections you have written over the course of the semester may help you compose your claims about your progress and learning, and identify relevant evidence to support those claims.

Evaluating reflective writing is important, but it is also complicated. Since the purpose of reflection is often focused on the individual writer, it may not always make sense for instructors to grade reflective writing the way they might grade other kinds of assignments. There are certain kinds of reflective writing assignments, however, such as the reflective argument assignment described in the next section, in which instructors evaluate the quality of reflection when it is used to make arguments and present evidence for readers. In both graded and ungraded situations, self-evaluating your reflective writing is important to help make sure you're maximizing its impact for you as a learner.

When thinking about different levels of reflection that you have engaged in, consider the difference between *description* and *analysis*. To illustrate, here are two contrasting examples, both of which offer the writer's thoughts on their achievement in a rhetorical analysis assignment:

1. *I learned a lot from Project One. In the assignment, we were asked to analyze a magazine article using the concepts of ethos, logos, and pathos. I analyzed the text, and then wrote an outline for my essay before*

starting. I wrote the paper over two days and made sure to proofread it before turning it in. I worked really hard on the assignment, and I must have done well because the instructor gave me an A. I think the important thing to keep in mind when working on a project like this is to follow the directions and make sure there are no errors.

2. *I learned a lot from Project One. In the assignment, we were asked to analyze a magazine article using the concepts of ethos, logos, and pathos. I felt really confident about the assignment because I had a similar project in high school in which we had to analyze a commercial. What made this project challenging was having to pick out specific passages from the text that connected with the different rhetorical concepts. In that way, I now realize I find working with visual arguments like commercials a bit easier than working with written texts. All the same, I feel good about how my project turned out because I was able to move from understanding the article to figuring out how to analyze the writer's strategy of using emotional words like "sacrifice" to make their argument.*

The first example is characterized by descriptions of the writer's actions (e.g. "I *analyzed,*" "I *wrote,*" "I *worked.*"). Those descriptions from the writer's perspective are important, but notice that the second example focuses more on **how the writer feels** (e.g. "I *felt confident*"), **what the writer understands** about their own strengths and weaknesses (e.g. "What made this project challenging"), and **the writer's criteria for positively evaluating their own work** (e.g. "I was able to move from…"). In the second example, the writer moves from simply describing what they did to analyzing what those actions might mean and why they might be important to them as a learner. In the process of analyzing, the writer of the second example demonstrates to their readers both their understanding of the task they're writing about and their capacity to reflect at a fairly deep level. In this way, "reflection" becomes not merely a *task* or a *process* you do, but rather the *subject* of your writing. It gives you a tangible way to focus on specific tasks and processes and what you learn from them.

CONCLUSION

Reflection happens in different ways: by thinking about our plans and strategies, evaluating our work, and by writing through these ideas. Though we do not always reflect through writing reflections, reflective writing is one important way to develop metacognitive practice. You will write reflections in many composition courses to help you develop strong writing, reading, and research practices.

The descriptions of reflective writing in this section are by no means the only ways to think about reflection, but we include them to support your practice with reflective writing. The aim is to develop metacognitive habits for the purposes of growing in writing expertise and becoming independent, flexible writers.

62   CHAPTER 6 | METACOGNITION AND REFLECTION

Sample Journal Prompts

1   Thinking back to your earliest memories of writing, which you wrote about last week, try and create a timeline that represents your changing attitudes about writing throughout your life so far. In your journal entry, try to describe important moments and/or experiences that have shaped your attitudes about writing up through the present day.

2   Describe what you think you learned about writing during Project One. Describe what you learned about your own writing process. Describe what you learned about yourself as a new college student.

3   Now that we're about a month into the semester, describe how things are going with your first semester of college (even if this isn't your first term). What's going well? What's not going well? What's the biggest surprise?

4   In a blog post of 300–400 words, identify and describe the different reading strategies you use to read difficult texts. If you need to use your post to name those strategies for the first time, go ahead and do that.

5   Describe what you've been taught about academic research papers. If you have written an academic research paper, describe the assignment and the paper you wrote. What do you think college instructors expect from such papers? What do you think is difficult about writing research papers?

6   Write a 500-word mini-essay in which you describe how your work in Project Two fulfills the English 1020 course learning outcome about researching.

WORKS CITED

Framework for Success in Postsecondary Writing. Council of Writing Program Administrators, the National Council of Teachers of English, and the National Writing Project, 2011. http://wpacouncil.org/files/framework-for-success-postsecondary-writing.pdf

Moon, Jennifer. *A Handbook of Reflective and Experiential Learning: Theory and Practice*. London: Routledge, 2004. Print.

Yancey, Kathleen Blake. *Reflection in the Writing Classroom*. Logan, UT: Utah State University Press, 1998. Print.

7

From Reading as a Writer to Writing as a Reader

Reading for class and then writing an essay might seem to be separate tasks, but reading is the first step in the writing process. In this chapter we present methods that will help you read more effectively and move from reading to writing your own college essays. These methods will lead you to understand a writer's purpose in responding to a situation, the motivation for asserting a claim in an essay and entering a particular conversation with a particular audience.

Much if not all of the writing you do in college will be based on what you have read. This is the case, for example, when you summarize a philosopher's theory, analyze the significance of an experiment in psychology, or, perhaps, synthesize different and conflicting points of view in making an argument about race and academic achievement in sociology.

As we maintain throughout this book, writing and reading are inextricably linked to each other. Good academic writers are also good critical readers: They leave their mark on what they read, identifying issues, making judgments about the truth of what writers tell them, and evaluating the adequacy of the evidence in support of an argument. This is where writing and inquiry begin: understanding our own position relative to the scholarly conversations we want to enter. Moreover, critical readers try to understand the strategies that writers use to persuade readers to agree with them. At times, these are strategies that we can adapt in advancing our arguments.

READING AS AN ACT OF COMPOSING: ANNOTATING

Leaving your mark on the page—**annotating**—is your first act of composing. When you mark the pages of a text, you are reading critically, engaging with the ideas of others, questioning and testing those ideas, and inquiring

63

64   CHAPTER 7 | FROM READING AS A WRITER TO WRITING AS A READER

into their significance. **Critical reading** is sometimes called *active reading* to distinguish it from memorization, when you just read for the main idea so that you can "spit it back out on a test." When you read actively and critically, you bring your knowledge, experiences, and interests to a text, so that you can respond to the writer, continuing the conversation the writer has begun.

Experienced college readers don't try to memorize a text or assume they must understand it completely before they respond to it. Instead they read strategically, looking for the writer's claims, for the writer's key ideas and terms, and for connections with key ideas and terms in other texts. They also read to discern what conversation the writer has entered, and how the writer's argument is connected to those he or she makes reference to.

When you annotate a text, your notes in the margins might address the following questions:

- What arguments is this author responding to?
- Is the issue relevant or significant?
- How do I know that what the author says is true?
- Is the author's evidence legitimate? Sufficient?
- Can I think of an exception to the author's argument?
- What would the counterarguments be?

Good readers ask the same kinds of questions of every text they read, considering not just *what* a writer says (the content), but *how* he or she says it given the writer's purpose and audience.

The marks you leave on a page might indicate your own ideas and questions, patterns you see emerging, links to other texts, even your gut response to the writer's argument—agreement, dismay, enthusiasm, confusion. They reveal your own thought processes as you read and signal that you are entering the conversation. In effect, they are traces of your own responding voice.

Developing your own system of marking or annotating pages can help you feel confident when you sit down with a new reading for your classes. Based on our students' experiences, we offer this practical tip: Although wide-tipped highlighters have their place in some classes, it is more useful to read with a pen or pencil in your hand, so that you can do more than draw a bar of color through words or sentences you find important. Experienced readers write their responses to a text in the margins, using personal codes (boxing key words, for example), writing out definitions of words they have looked up, drawing lines to connect ideas on facing pages, or writing notes to themselves ("Connect this to Edmundson on consumer culture"; "Hirsch would disagree big time—see his ideas on memorization in primary grades"; "You call THIS evidence?!"). These notes help you get started on your own writing assignments.

Annotating your readings benefits you twice. First, it is easier to participate in class discussions if you have already marked passages that are important, confusing, or linked to specific passages in other texts you have read. It's a sure way to avoid that sinking feeling you get when you return to pages you read the night before but now can't remember at all. Second, by marking key ideas in a text, noting your ideas about them, and making connections to key ideas in other texts, you have begun the process of writing an essay. When you start writing the first draft of your essay, you can quote the passages you have already marked and explain what you find significant about them based on the notes you have already made to yourself. You can make the connections to other texts in the paragraphs of your own essay that you have already begun to make on the pages of your textbook. If you mark your texts effectively, you'll never be at a loss when you sit down to write the first draft of an essay.

Let's take a look at how one of our students marked several paragraphs of Douglas Massey and Nancy Denton's *American Apartheid: Segregation and the Making of the Underclass* (1993). In the excerpt below, the student underlines what she believes is important information and begins to create an outline of the authors' main points.

1. racist attitudes

2. private behaviors

3. & institutional practices lead to ghettos (authors' claim?)

Ghetto = "multistory, high-density housing projects." Post-1950

I remember this happening where I grew up, but I didn't know the government was responsible. Is this what happened in There Are No Children Here?

Authors say situation of "spatial isolation" remains despite court decisions. Does it?

The spatial isolation of black Americans was achieved by a conjunction of <u>racist attitudes</u>, <u>private behaviors</u>, and <u>institutional practices</u> that disenfranchised blacks from urban housing markets and led to the creation of the <u>ghetto</u>. Discrimination in employment exacerbated black poverty and limited the economic potential for integration, and black residential mobility was systematically blocked by pervasive discrimination and white avoidance of neighborhoods containing blacks. <u>The walls of the ghetto were buttressed after 1950</u> by government programs that promoted slum clearance and <u>relocated displaced ghetto residents into multi-story, high-density housing projects</u>.

In theory, this self-reinforcing cycle of prejudice, discrimination, and segregation was broken during the 1960s by a growing rejection of racist sentiments by whites and a series of court decisions and federal laws that banned discrimination in public life. (1) <u>The Civil Rights Act of 1964 outlawed racial discrimination in employment</u>, (2) the <u>Fair Housing Act of 1968 banned discrimination in housing</u>, and (3) the <u>*Gautreaux* and *Shannon* court decisions prohibited public authorities from placing housing projects</u> exclusively in black neighborhoods. Despite these changes, however, the <u>nation's largest black communities remained as segregated as ever in 1980</u>. Indeed, many urban areas displayed a pattern of intense racial isolation that could only be described as <u>hypersegregation</u>.

66   CHAPTER 7 | FROM READING AS A WRITER TO WRITING AS A READER

Subtler racism, not on public record.

Lack of enforcement of Civil Rights Act? Fair Housing Act? Gautreaux and Shannon? Why? Why not?

Although the racial climate of the United States improved outwardly during the 1970s, <u>racism still restricted the residential freedom of black Americans</u>; it just did so in less blatant ways. In the aftermath of the civil rights revolution, few whites voiced openly racist sentiments; realtors no longer refused outright to rent or sell to blacks; and few local governments went on record to oppose public housing projects because they would contain blacks. This lack of overt racism, however, did not mean that prejudice and discrimination had ended.

3

Notice how the student's annotations help her understand the argument the authors make.

1. She numbers the three key factors (racist attitudes, private behaviors, and institutional practices) that influenced the formation of ghettos in the United States.

2. She identifies the situation that motivates the authors' analysis: the extent to which "the spatial isolation of black Americans" still exists despite laws and court decisions designed to end residential segregation.

3. She makes connections to her own experience and to another book she has read.

By understanding the authors' arguments and making these connections, the student begins the writing process. She also sets the stage for her own research, for examining the authors' claim that residential segregation still exists.

READING AS A WRITER: ANALYZING A TEXT RHETORICALLY

When you study how writers influence readers through language, you are analyzing the **rhetoric** (available means of persuasion) of what you read. When you identify a writer's purpose for responding to a situation by composing an essay that puts forth claims meant to sway a particular audience, you are performing a rhetorical analysis. Such an analysis entails identifying the features of an argument to better understand how the argument works to persuade a reader:

- how the writer sees the situation that calls for a response in writing
- the writer's purpose for writing
- intended audience
- kinds of claims
- types of evidence

We discuss each of these elements as we analyze the following preface from E. D. Hirsch's book *Cultural Literacy: What Every American Needs to Know* (1987). Formerly a professor of English, Hirsch has long been interested in educational reform. That interest developed from his (and others') perception that today's students do not know as much as students did in the past. Although Hirsch wrote the book decades ago, many observers still believe that the contemporary problems of illiteracy and poverty can be traced to a lack of cultural literacy.

Read the preface. You may want to mark it with your own questions and responses, and then consider them in light of our analysis (following the preface) of Hirsch's rhetorical situation, purpose, claims, and audience.

E. D. HIRSCH JR.

Preface to *Cultural Literacy*

E. D. Hirsch Jr., a retired English professor, is the author of many acclaimed books, including *The Schools We Need and Why We Don't Have Them* (1996) and *The Knowledge Deficit* (2006). His book *Cultural Literacy* was a best seller in 1987 and had a profound effect on the focus of education in the late 1980s and 1990s.

■ ■ ■

> Rousseau points out the facility with which children lend themselves to our false methods: . . ."The apparent ease with which children learn is their ruin."
>
> —JOHN DEWEY

> There is no matter what children should learn first, any more than what leg you should put into your breeches first. Sir, you may stand disputing which is best to put in first, but in the meantime your backside is bare. Sir, while you stand considering which of two things you should teach your child first, another boy has learn't 'em both.
>
> —SAMUEL JOHNSON

To be culturally literate is to possess the basic information needed to thrive in the modern world. The breadth of that information is great, extending over the major domains of human activity from sports to science. It is by no means confined to "culture" narrowly understood as an acquaintance with the arts. Nor is it confined to one social class. Quite the contrary. Cultural literacy constitutes the only sure avenue of opportunity for disadvantaged children, the only reliable way of combating the social determinism that now condemns them to remain in the same social and educational condition as their parents. That children from poor and illiterate homes tend to remain poor and illiterate is an unacceptable failure of our schools, one which has occurred not because our teachers are inept but chiefly because they are compelled to teach a fragmented curriculum based on faulty educational theories. Some say that our schools by themselves are powerless to change the cycle of poverty and illiteracy. I do not agree. They *can* break the cycle, but only if they themselves break fundamentally with some of the theories and practices that education professors and school administrators have followed over the past fifty years.

Although the chief beneficiaries of the educational reforms advocated in this book will be disadvantaged children, these same reforms will also enhance the literacy of children from middle-class homes. The educational goal advocated is that of mature literacy for *all* our citizens.

The connection between mature literacy and cultural literacy may already be familiar to those who have closely followed recent discussions of education. Shortly after the publication of my essay "Cultural Literacy," Dr. William Bennett, then chairman of the National Endowment for the Humanities and subsequently secretary of education in President Ronald Reagan's second administration, championed its ideas. This endorsement from an influential person of conservative views gave my ideas some currency, but such an endorsement was not likely to recommend the concept to liberal thinkers, and in fact the idea of cultural literacy has been attacked by some liberals on the assumption that I must be advocating a list of great books that every child in the land should be forced to read.

But those who examine the Appendix to this book will be able to judge for themselves how thoroughly mistaken such an assumption is. Very few specific titles appear on the list, and they usually appear as words, not works, because they represent writings that culturally literate people have read about but haven't read. *Das Kapital* is a good example. Cultural literacy is represented not by a *prescriptive* list of books but rather by a *descriptive* list of the information actually possessed by literate Americans. My aim in this book is to contribute to making that information the possession of all Americans.

The importance of such widely shared information can best be understood if I explain briefly how the idea of cultural literacy relates to currently prevailing theories of education. The theories that have dominated American education for the past fifty years stem ultimately from Jean Jacques Rousseau, who believed that we should encourage the natural development of young children and not impose adult ideas upon them before they can truly understand them. Rousseau's conception of education as a process of natural development was an abstract generalization meant to apply to all children in any time or place: to French children of the eighteenth century or to Japanese or American children of the twentieth century. He thought that a child's intellectual and social skills would develop naturally without regard to the specific content of education. His content-neutral conception of educational development has long been triumphant in American schools of education and has long dominated the "developmental," content-neutral curricula of our elementary schools.

In the first decades of this century, Rousseau's ideas powerfully influenced the educational conceptions of John Dewey, the writer who has the most deeply affected modern American educational theory and practice. Dewey's clearest and, in his time, most widely read book on education, *Schools of Tomorrow*, acknowledges Rousseau as the chief source of his educational principles. The first chapter of Dewey's book carries the telling title "Education as Natural Development" and is sprinkled with quotations from Rousseau. In it Dewey strongly seconds Rousseau's opposition to the mere accumulation of information.

> Development emphasizes the need of intimate and extensive personal acquaintance with a small number of typical situations with a view to mastering the way of dealing with the problems of experience, not the piling up of information.

Believing that a few direct experiences would suffice to develop the skills that children require, Dewey assumed that early education need not be tied to specific content. He mistook a half-truth for the whole. He placed too much faith in children's ability to learn general skills from a few typical experiences and too hastily rejected "the piling up of information." Only by piling up specific, communally shared information can children learn to participate in complex cooperative activities with other members of their community.

This old truth, recently rediscovered, requires a countervailing theory of education that once again stresses the importance of specific information in early and late schooling. The corrective theory might be described as an anthropological theory of education, because it is based on the anthropological observation that all human communities are founded upon specific shared information. Americans are different from Germans, who in turn are different from Japanese, because each group possesses specifically different cultural knowledge. In an anthropological perspective, the basic goal of education in a human community is acculturation, the transmission to children of the specific information shared by the adults of the group or polis.

Plato, that other great educational theorist, believed that the specific contents transmitted to children are by far the most important elements of education. In *The Republic* he makes Socrates ask rhetorically, "Shall we carelessly allow children to hear any casual tales which may be devised by casual persons, and to receive into their minds ideas for the most part the very opposite of those which we shall wish them to have when they are grown up?" Plato offered good reasons for being concerned with the specific contents of schooling, one of them ethical: "For great is the issue at stake, greater than appears—whether a person is to be good or bad."

70 CHAPTER 7 | FROM READING AS A WRITER TO WRITING AS A READER

Time has shown that there is much truth in the durable educational   *10*
theories of both Rousseau and Plato. But even the greatest thinkers,
being human, see mainly in one direction at a time, and no thinkers,
however profound, can foresee the future implications of their ideas
when they are translated into social policy. The great test of social
ideas is the crucible of history, which, after a time, usually discloses a
one-sidedness in the best of human generalizations. History, not superior wisdom, shows us that neither the content-neutral curriculum of
Rousseau and Dewey nor the narrowly specified curriculum of Plato is
adequate to the needs of a modern nation.

Plato rightly believed that it is natural for children to learn an adult   *11*
culture, but too confidently assumed that philosophy could devise the
one best culture. (Nonetheless, we should concede to Plato that within
our culture we have an obligation to choose and promote our best traditions.) On the other side, Rousseau and Dewey wrongly believed that
adult culture is "unnatural" to young children. Rousseau, Dewey, and
their present-day disciples have not shown an adequate appreciation of
the need for transmission of specific cultural information.

In contrast to the theories of Plato and Rousseau, an anthropologi-   *12*
cal theory of education accepts the naturalness as well as the relativity
of human cultures. It deems it neither wrong nor unnatural to teach
young children adult information before they fully understand it. The
anthropological view stresses the universal fact that a human group
must have effective communications to function effectively, that effective communications require shared culture, and that shared culture
requires transmission of specific information to children. Literacy, an
essential aim of education in the modern world, is no autonomous,
empty skill but depends upon literate culture. Like any other aspect of
acculturation, literacy requires the early and continued transmission
of specific information. Dewey was deeply mistaken to disdain "accumulating information in the form of symbols." Only by accumulating
shared symbols, and the shared information that the symbols represent, can we learn to communicate effectively with one another in our
national community.

Now let's take a look at the steps for doing a rhetorical analysis.

■ Identify the Situation

The **situation** is what moves a writer to write. To understand what motivated Hirsch to write, we need look no further than the situation he identifies in the first paragraph of the preface: "the social determinism that
now condemns [disadvantaged children] to remain in the same social and

educational condition as their parents." Hirsch wants to make sure his readers are aware of the problem so that they will be motivated to read his argument (and take action). He presents as an urgent problem the situation of disadvantaged children, an indication of what is at stake for the writer and for the readers of the argument. For Hirsch, this situation needs to change.

The urgency of a writer's argument is not always triggered by a single situation; often it is multifaceted. Again in the first paragraph, Hirsch identifies a second concern when he states that poverty and illiteracy reflect "an unacceptable failure of our schools, one which has occurred not because our teachers are inept but chiefly because they are compelled to teach a fragmented curriculum based on faulty educational theories." When he introduces a second problem, Hirsch helps us see the interconnected and complex nature of the situations authors confront in academic writing.

■ Identify the Writer's Purpose

The **purpose** for writing an essay may be to respond to a particular situation; it also can be what a writer is trying to accomplish. Specifically, what does the writer want readers to do? Does the writer want us to think about an issue, to change our opinions? Does the writer want to make us aware of a problem that we may not have recognized? Does the writer advocate for some type of change? Or is some combination of all three at work?

Hirsch's main purpose is to promote educational reforms that will produce a higher degree of literacy for all citizens. He begins his argument with a broad statement about the importance of cultural literacy: "Cultural literacy constitutes the only sure avenue of opportunity for disadvantaged children, the only reliable way of combating the social determinism that now condemns them to remain in the same social and educational condition as their parents" (para. 1). As his argument unfolds, his purpose continues to unfold as well. He identifies the schools as a source of the problem and suggests how they must change to promote literacy:

> Some say that our schools by themselves are powerless to change the cycle of poverty and illiteracy. I do not agree. They *can* break the cycle, but only if they themselves break fundamentally with some of the theories and practices that education professors and school administrators have followed over the past fifty years. (para. 1)

The "educational goal," Hirsch declares at the end of paragraph 2, is "mature literacy for *all* our citizens." To reach that goal, he insists, education must break with the past. In paragraphs 5 through 11, he cites the influence of Jean-Jacques Rousseau, John Dewey, and Plato, tracing what he sees as the educational legacies of the past. Finally, in the last paragraph

72   CHAPTER 7 | FROM READING AS A WRITER TO WRITING AS A READER

of the excerpt, Hirsch describes an "anthropological view, . . . the universal fact that a human group must have effective communications to function effectively, that effective communications require shared culture, and that shared culture requires transmission of specific information to children." It is here, Hirsch argues, in the "transmission of specific information to children," that schools must do a better job.

▪ Identify the Writer's Claims

Claims are assertions that authors must justify and support with evidence and good reasons. The **thesis**, or **main claim**, is the controlling idea that crystallizes a writer's main point, helping readers track the idea as it develops throughout the essay. A writer's purpose clearly influences the way he or she crafts the main claim of an argument, the way he or she presents all assertions and evidence.

Hirsch's main claim is that "cultural literacy constitutes the only sure avenue of opportunity for disadvantaged children, the only reliable way of combating the social determinism that now condemns them to remain in the same social and educational condition as their parents" (para. 1). Notice that his thesis also points to a solution: making cultural literacy the core of public school curricula. Here we distinguish the main claim, or thesis, from the other claims or assertions that Hirsch makes. For example, at the very outset, Hirsch states that "to be culturally literate is to possess the basic information needed to thrive in the modern world." Although this is an assertion that requires support, it is a **minor claim**; it does not shape what Hirsch writes in the remainder of his essay. His main claim, or thesis, is really his call for reform.

▪ Identify the Writer's Audience

A writer's language can help us identify his or her **audience**, the readers whose opinions and actions the writer hopes to influence or change. In Hirsch's text, words and phrases like *social determinism*, *cycle of poverty and illiteracy*, *educational reforms*, *prescriptive*, and *anthropological* indicate that Hirsch believes his audience is well educated. References to Plato, Socrates, Rousseau, and Dewey also indicate the level of knowledge Hirsch expects of his readers.

Finally, the way the preface unfolds suggests that Hirsch is writing for an audience that is familiar with a certain **genre**, or type, of writing: the formal argument. Notice how the author begins with a statement of the situation and then asserts his position. The very fact that he includes a preface speaks to the formality of his argument. Hirsch's language, his references, and the structure of the document all suggest that he is very much in conversation with people who are experienced and well-educated readers.

More specifically, the audience Hirsch invokes is made up of people who are concerned about illiteracy in the United States and the kind of social determinism that appears to condemn the educationally disadvantaged to poverty. Hirsch also acknowledges directly "those who have closely followed recent discussions of education," including the conservative William Bennett and liberal thinkers who might be provoked by Bennett's advocacy of Hirsch's ideas (para. 3). Moreover, Hirsch appears to assume that his readers have achieved "mature literacy," even if they are not actually "culturally literate." He is writing for an audience that not only is well educated but also is deeply interested in issues of education as they relate to social policy.

Steps to Analyzing a Text Rhetorically

1 **Identify the situation.** What motivates the writer to write?

2 **Identify the writer's purpose.** What does the writer want readers to do or think about?

3 **Identify the writer's claims.** What is the writer's main claim? What minor claims does he or she make?

4 **Identify the writer's audience.** What do you know about the writer's audience? What does the writer's language imply about the readers? What about the writer's references? The structure of the essay?

Hirsch's writings on cultural literacy have inspired and provoked many responses to the conversation he initiated decades ago. Eugene F. Provenzo's book *Critical Literacy: What Every American Needs to Know*, published in 2005, is a fairly recent one. Provenzo examines the source of Hirsch's ideas, his critiques of scholars like John Dewey, the extent to which Hirsch's argument is based on sound research, and the implications of Hirsch's notion of cultural literacy for teaching and learning. Despite its age, Hirsch's book remains relevant in discussions about the purpose of education, demonstrating how certain works become touchstones and the ways academic and cultural conversations can be sustained over time.

A Practice Sequence: Analyzing a Text Rhetorically

To practice the strategies of rhetorical analysis, read "Hirsch's Desire for a National Curriculum," an excerpt from Eugene F. Provenzo's book, using these questions as a guide:

- What motivates Provenzo as a writer?
- What does he want readers to think about?

74 CHAPTER 7 | FROM READING AS A WRITER TO WRITING AS A READER

- What is Provenzo's main point?
- Given the language Provenzo uses, who do you think his main audience is?

EUGENE F. PROVENZO JR.

Hirsch's Desire for a National Curriculum

Eugene F. Provenzo Jr. is a professor in the Department of Teaching and Learning in the School of Education at the University of Miami in Coral Gables, Florida. His career as a researcher has been interdisciplinary in nature. Throughout his work, his primary focus has been on education as a social and cultural phenomenon. One of his prime concerns has been the role of the teacher in American society. He is also interested in the impact of computers on contemporary children, education, and culture. He is author or coauthor of numerous books, including *Teaching, Learning, and Schooling: A Twenty-First Century Perspective* (2001); *Internet and Online Research for Teachers* (Third Edition, 2004); and *Observing in Schools: A Guide for Students in Teacher Education* (2005).

■ ■ ■

To a large extent, Hirsch, in his efforts as an educational reformer, wants to establish a national curriculum.

> Our elementary schools are not only dominated by the content-neutral ideas of Rousseau and Dewey, they are also governed by approximately sixteen thousand independent school districts. We have viewed this dispersion of educational authority as an insurmountable obstacle to altering the fragmentation of the school curriculum even when we have questioned that fragmentation. We have permitted school policies that have shrunk the body of information that Americans share and these policies have caused our national literacy to decline.

This is an interesting argument when interpreted in a conservative political context. While calling for greater local control, Hirsch and other conservatives call for a curriculum that is controlled not at the state and local level, but at the national level by the federal government.

Putting contradictions like this aside, the question arises as to whether or not Hirsch even has a viable curriculum. In an early review of Hirsch's *Cultural Literacy*, Hazel Whitman Hertzberg criticized the book and its list of 5,000 things every American needs to know for its fragmentation. As she explained:

> Hirsch's remedy for curricular fragmentation looks suspiciously like more fragmentation. Outside of the dubious claim that his list represents what literate people know, there is nothing that holds it together besides its arrangement in alphabetical order. Subject-matter organization is ignored. It is not hard to imagine how Hirsch's proposal would have been greeted by educational neoconservatives had it been made by one of those professors of education who he charges are responsible for the current state of cultural illiteracy.

Hertzberg wonders what Hirsch's "hodgepodge of miscellaneous, arbitrary, and often trivial information" would look like if it were put into a coherent curriculum.

In 1988 Hirsch did in fact establish the Core Knowledge Foundation, *3* which had as its purpose the design of a national curriculum. Called the "Core Knowledge Sequence," the sequence offered a curriculum in six content areas: history, geography, mathematics, science, language arts, and fine arts. Hirsch's curriculum was intended to represent approximately half of the total curriculum for K–6 schools. Subsequent curriculum revisions include a curriculum for grades seven and eight as well as one at the preschool level.

Several hundred schools across the United States currently use *4* Hirsch's model. A national conference is held each year, which draws several thousand people. In books like *What Your First Grader Needs to Know* (1991) as well as *A First Dictionary of Cultural Literacy: What Our Children Need to Know* (1989) and *The Dictionary of Cultural Literacy* (1993), along with the Core Knowledge Sequence, one finds a fairly conservative but generally useful curriculum that conforms to much of the content already found in local school systems around the country.

Hirsch seems not to recognize that there indeed is a national curricu- *5* lum, one whose standards are set by local communities through their acceptance and rejection of textbooks and by national accreditation groups ranging from the National Council of Teachers of Mathematics to the National Council for Social Studies Teachers and the National Council of Teachers of English. One need only look at standards in different subject areas in school districts across the country to realize the extent to which there is indeed a national curriculum.

Whether the current curriculum in use in the schools across the *6* country is adequate is of course open to debate. Creating any curriculum is by definition a deeply political act, and is, or should be, subject to considerable negotiation and discussion at any level. But to act as though there is not a de facto national curriculum is simply inaccurate. First graders in most school districts across the country learn about the weather and the seasons, along with more basic skills like adding and subtracting. Students do not learn to divide before they learn how to add or multiply. Local and state history is almost universally introduced for the first time in either third or fourth grade. It is reintroduced in most states at the seventh or eighth grade levels. Algebra is typically taught in the ninth grade. Traditions, developmental patterns of students, textbook content, and national subject standards combine to create a fairly uniform national curriculum.

Hirsch's complaint that there is no national curriculum is not 7 motivated by a desire to establish one but rather a desire to establish a curriculum that reflects his cultural and ideological orientation. It is a sophisticated assault on more inclusive and diverse models of curriculum and culture—one that represents a major battle in the culture wars of the last twenty years in the United States.

WRITING AS A READER: COMPOSING A RHETORICAL ANALYSIS

One of our favorite exercises is to ask students to choose a single paragraph or a brief section from a text they have read and to write a rhetorical analysis. We first ask our students to identify the writer's key claims and ideas to orient them to the main points they want to make in their analysis. We then ask our students to consider such features as the situation that calls for a response in writing and the writer's purpose, intended audience, kinds of claims, and types of evidence. In their rhetorical analyses, we encourage our students to analyze the ways writers develop their ideas and the extent to which these strategies succeed. That is, we ask our students to consider how writers express their ideas, develop their points of view, respond to a given situation, and use evidence to persuade readers. Once you are able to identify *how* writers make arguments, look critically at what works and what doesn't in making a persuasive argument; then you will be able to make use of their strategies in your own writing.

For example, one of our students wrote a rhetorical analysis of an excerpt from David Tyack's book on education, *Seeking Common Ground: Public Schools in a Diverse Society* (2004). In his book, Tyack examines the extent to which the purpose of education in American schools has developed out of and reflected the political, economic, and moral concerns of the nation. His analysis begins with the emergence of public schools in the nineteenth century and demonstrates a sense of continuity in twenty-first-century education, particularly in light of contemporary debates around national standards, teacher evaluation, social justice, equity, civic engagement, and the common good. This continuity is best represented in the quest for a common denominator of political and moral truths, often evidenced in textbooks that point to the progress of history and American democracy, the focus on great men who understood the grandeur of America's destiny, and the importance of individual character in building a strong nation founded on shared values. For Tyack, history textbooks have served as a significant source of civic education — that is, "what adults thought children should learn about the past" — and assimilation. However, the search for common values in official histories (what he calls "stone monuments") has not been without dissent, given their focus on white, male, Protestant ideology. Tyack also writes about the ways in which educators have dealt with questions of social and educational diversity, particularly race, immigration and ethnicity, and gender; efforts to establish models of educational governance to meet the needs of a pluralistic society; and the implications of opening public education to a free market.

Note that in the following passage, Tyack assesses the state of American history textbooks by citing a number of writers, sometimes generally and at other times more specifically, to address ways to solve the problems he identifies (for example, Patricia Nelson Limerick's proposal for a "pluralistic model of history").

As you read the Tyack passage, take notes on the rhetorical situation, purpose, main claim, audience, and language. You may want to underline passages or circle words and phrases where the writer makes the following points explicit:

- the situation that motivates his writing,
- the purpose of his analysis and argument,
- his main claim or thesis, and
- who he believes his audience is.

DAVID TYACK

Whither History Textbooks?

David Tyack was the Vida Jacks Professor of Education and Professor of History, Emeritus, at Stanford University. In addition to writing *Seeking Common Ground*, he authored *The One Best System: A History of American Urban Education* (1974) and coauthored *Tinkering Toward Utopia: A Century of Public School Reform* (1997), *Law and the Shaping of Public Education, 1785–1954* (1991), *Learning Together: A History of Coeducation in American Public Schools* (1992), and *Public Schools in Hard Times: The Great Depression and Recent Years* (1984).

78   CHAPTER 7 | FROM READING AS A WRITER TO WRITING AS A READER

A history textbook today is hardly the republican catechism that Noah Webster appended to his famous speller. It is more like pieces of a sprawling novel with diverse characters and fascinating subplots waiting for an author to weave them into a broader narrative. Now a noisy confusion reigns about what stories the textbooks should tell. Special-interest groups of the right and left pressure publishers to include or drop topics, especially in big states such as California or Texas. Worries abound about old truths betrayed and new truths ignored. Many groups want to vet or veto what children learn, and it is unclear what roles teachers, parents, ethnic groups, religious activists, historians, and others should play. Tempers rise. In New York debates over a multicultural curriculum, Catherine Cornbleth and Dexter Waugh observed, "both sides engaged in a rhetoric of crisis, doom, and salvation."

In the United States, unlike most other nations, private agencies—publishing companies—create and sell textbooks. Thus commerce plays an important part in deciding which historical truths shall be official. To be sure, public agencies usually decide which textbooks to adopt (about half of the states delegate text adoption to local districts, and the rest use some form of state adoption). For all the conventionality of the product, the actual production and sale of textbooks is still a risky business. It's very expensive to create and print textbooks, and the market (the various agencies that actually decide which to adopt) is somewhat unpredictable. In addition, at any time some citizens are likely to protest whatever messages the texts send. Textbook adoption can be a free-for-all.

Thus it is not surprising that textbooks still beget textbooks. To control risk, companies find it wise to copy successes. Old icons (Washington) remain, but publishers respond to new demands by multiplying new state-approved truths. It has been easier to add those ubiquitous sidebars to the master narrative than to rethink it, easier to incorporate new content into a safe and profitable formula than to create new accounts. American history textbooks are enormous—888 pages, on average—in part because publishers seek to neutralize or anticipate criticisms by adding topics. The result is often not comprehensive coverage but a bloated book devoid of style or coherence.

The traditional American fear of centralized power, salient today in debates over national standards and tests, has resulted in a strange patchwork of agencies and associations—textbook companies, state and local governments, lobby groups of many persuasions, individuals who want to play Grand Inquisitor—to choose and monitor the public truths taught in the texts. One of the most rapid ways of changing what students learn in American schools is to transform the textbooks, but the present Rube Goldberg system of creating and selecting textbooks makes such a change very difficult (though fine history textbooks have on occasion appeared).

What are some strategies to cope with the cross-cutting demands on history textbooks? Three possible ones are these: muddling through with modest improvements; turning over the task of writing textbooks to experts; or devising texts that depart from the model of state-approved truths and embrace instead the taking of multiple perspectives. Each of these has some advantages and faults that are worth contemplating.

Muddling through may seem sensible to people who believe that there is a vast gap between superheated policy talk about the defects of textbooks and the everyday reality teachers face in classrooms. Is all the debate over bad textbooks a dust-devil masquerading as a tornado? For many teachers, the big challenge is to prepare students for high-stakes tests they must take for graduation, and textbooks are a key resource in that task.

Teachers tend to find the status quo in textbooks more bearable than do the critics. When a sample of classroom teachers was asked their opinion of the textbooks they used, they generally said that the books are good and getting better. Teachers rely heavily on textbooks in their instruction, employing them for about 70 percent of class time.

A commonsense argument for muddling through, with gradual improvement of textbooks, is that pedagogical reforms rarely work well if they are imposed on teachers. Study after study has shown that teachers tend to avoid controversy in teaching American history (indeed, being "nonpartisan" is still judged a virtue, as it was in the past). And parents and school board members, like teachers, have their own ideas about what is "real history." Too sharp a turn in the historical highway might topple reform. So some teachers argue that the best way to improve education is to keep the old icons and welcome the newcomers in the textbooks. And hope that the students in fact *do read* the textbooks! Common sense—that's the way to cope amid all the confusion.

An alternate approach to reform of textbooks is to set good state or local standards for history courses and turn the writing of textbooks over to experts—an approach used in many nations and sometimes advocated in the United States today. Muddling through just maintains the status quo and guarantees incoherence in textbooks and hence in learning. In the current politics and commerce of text publishing, "truth" becomes whatever the special interests (left or right) pressure textbook companies to say. Current textbooks are often victims of commercial timidity, veto groups, and elephantiasis (888 pages!).

What is missing, proponents of this view argue, is a clear set of national standards about what students should know and a vivid and cogent text that engages students in learning. Those who call for expertise suggest that history is too important *not* to be left to the historians.

But this response to the faults of history texts presents its own problems. Calling in the experts doesn't eliminate disputes; PhDs love to differ among themselves. Teachers are adept at sabotaging reforms dropped on them from above. And amid all the commercialism and special interests now rife in the process of selecting textbooks, the public still deserves some say in deciding what American students learn about the past, expert or not. *11*

Patricia Nelson Limerick, professor of history at the University of Colorado, suggests a pluralistic model of history that contrasts with both muddling through and textbooks by experts. She recently suggested that the Little Bighorn Battlefield, where Sioux and Cheyenne fought George Armstrong Custer, needed not two monuments, one in honor of the Indians and one to recognize Custer and his soldiers, but "a different kind of memorial—one in which no point of view dominates." She imagines visitors walking among memorials to the warriors and Custer, but also to the enlisted men dragooned into the slaughter, to Custer's widow, to the families of the white soldiers, and to the children and wives of the Indian warriors. *12*

Such perspective-taking lies at the core of historical understanding of a socially diverse nation. Pluralistic history can enhance ethnic self-respect and empathy for other groups. Parallel to the monuments Limerick proposes, texts for a pluralistic civic education might have not one master narrative but several, capturing separate identities and experiences. *13*

But the history of Americans in their separate groups would be partial without looking as well at their lives in interaction. Our society is pluralistic in character, and so should be the history we teach to young citizens. But alongside that *pluribus* citizens have also sought an *unum*, a set of shared political aspirations and institutions. One reason there have been so many textbook wars is that group after group has, in turn, sought to become part of a common story told about our past. The *unum* and the *pluribus* have been in inescapable tension, constantly evolving as Americans struggled to find common ground and to respect their differences. *14*

AN ANNOTATED STUDENT RHETORICAL ANALYSIS

Now read our student's rhetorical analysis about David Tyack's discussion of history textbooks in "Whither History Textbooks?" We have annotated the student's analysis to point out how he identifies the author's situation, purpose, argument, and audience.

AN ANNOTATED STUDENT RHETORICAL ANALYSIS   **81**

Collie 1

Quentin Collie

A Rhetorical Analysis of
"Whither History Textbooks?"

The student provides an overview of the author's argument.

In my analysis, I will focus on "Whither History Textbooks?" which serves as a conclusion to David Tyack's chapter on American history textbooks in his book *Seeking Common Ground*. In this section, Tyack explains the state of history textbooks in American schools today, the causes and influences that result in what he sees as a problem with trying to cover too many topics without much depth, and possible ways in which history textbooks can be changed and improved. In advocating for a pluralistic account of history, Tyack use specific words and phrases that convey his impatience with American history textbooks and presents a number of options to make his discussion appear fair.

The student explains the author's argument in more detail and, specifically, the source of what the author sees as a problem in teaching history. This is the situation that calls for some response in writing: that textbooks have become "heavy" and "boring." The student then describes three possible approaches that the author takes to address the problem he identifies in teaching history in school.

Tyack points out that today's textbooks are, for the most part, bulky and disjointed. Many storylines and historic figures are pieced together without any all-encompassing narrative flow or style. Textbooks have come to take this form because of two significant influences. On one hand, nearly every interest group argues for certain events, figures, or issues to be included in the history curriculum. On the other hand, in a more economical sense, textbooks that present the traditional and generic American narrative have been the most successful. As a result, textbook authors and producers attempt to intersperse the variety of new pieces into the original American narrative. This results in the heavy and boring textbooks that students use in the classroom today. Tyack offers three possibilities for how to navigate through the demands and difficulties involved in history textbook production: continuing the use of current textbooks with moderate additions and improvements, delegating the writing of textbooks to experts, and embracing a new style of textbook which emphasizes the multiple perspectives of Americans.

In this particular section of the book, Tyack's purpose seems to be a call for change. In describing the current types of textbooks, he implies his personal stance through his word choice. Tyack's use of vivid imagery throughout this part of his book allows him to delve into the textbook problem by appealing to the emotions of

1

2

3

82   CHAPTER 7 | FROM READING AS A WRITER TO WRITING AS A READER

Collie 2

The student underscores the author's purpose. He then shows how language reflects the author's point of view. In addition, the student helps us see that the situation the author responds to is not only about how textbooks are written, but how educators choose to adopt textbooks.

the reader. For instance, Tyack explains that the average American history textbook is 888 pages long and laments this length as the reason that most of today's history books are "bloated" and "devoid of style or coherence" (para. 3). He also alludes to anarchy when he claims that "textbook adoption can be a free-for-all" (para. 2), establishing his skeptical perspective on the decision processes of textbook writers as well as of those who buy them. Another way Tyack explains his views on the methodology behind buying and selling textbooks is through an allusion to a "Rube Goldberg system" (para. 4) in his description of how textbooks are created and sold. This reference implies that our current method has become unnecessarily complex and has rendered making changes in history textbooks difficult or impossible.

He points out the author's strategy for developing the argument, one that forces knowledgeable readers to draw their own conclusions.

Tyack does not advocate for just any change, but, rather, a particular change and ideal type of textbook. He does not make an outright statement of support for a particular plan. Instead, he presents an examination of possibilities that leads the audience to decide which one option is superior. The possibilities include using the same format with slight changes, having experts write the textbooks, and departing from the regular model of textbooks to include new truths and multiple perspectives. He makes a point to state that each option has both pros and cons to be considered.

4

The student points to the author's concession that not everyone agrees that the quality of textbook writing is a problem. The student again demonstrates how word choice conveys an author's point of view and that the author does not find this first solution tenable.

Tyack writes that teachers, in general, do not have a large problem with the current types of textbooks, and pedagogical reforms rarely work if imposed on teachers. This evidence argues in favor of using the same types of textbooks. The discussion of this particular option, however, ends with its success resting on a "hope that the students in fact *do read* the textbooks!" (para. 8). This statement carries a tone of sarcasm, leaving the reader with a feeling that Tyack believes that students will not read this type of textbook, so this particular plan of action is not likely to improve the schools. In addition, Tyack's exact phrasing for this possibility is "muddling through with modest improvements" (para. 5). From word choice alone, the reader can see that Tyack discredits this idea. The verb *muddle* is associated with things being confused, messed up, and unclear, so his choice of this word implies that he thinks using the current format for textbooks results in teachers and students having

5

WRITING A RHETORICAL ANALYSIS   **83**

Collie 3

a confused and incorrect view of American history. Eventually, he concludes that "muddling through just maintains the status quo and guarantees incoherence in textbooks and hence learning" (para. 9).

He presents the author's second possible solution to the problem but explains why the author is not sympathetic to that position.

His next suggested approach is using textbooks written by experts. This option could set clear national standards about what students should be learning about history by those most informed. This option, however, also has its faults as Tyack argues that the experts differ in their opinions. Furthermore, the public does deserve some input about material to be taught to its children, which this option would take away.

Although it would seem that the author lets readers draw their own conclusions, the student explains how Tyack uses research to give credence to this last solution to the problem.

Tyack's final option is "a pluralistic model of history that contrasts with both muddling through and textbooks by experts" (para. 12). Tyack argues that "such perspective-taking lies at the core of historical understanding of a socially diverse nation. Pluralistic history can enhance ethnic self-respect and empathy for other groups" (para. 13). Tyack supports this point of view with quotations from a professor of history, which gives credibility to this option. In addition, Tyack does not discuss any possible difficulties in pursuing this type of textbook, even though he stated earlier that each option has both benefits and faults. In this, Tyack appears to be considering multiple possibilities for textbook reform, but, at the same time, he dismisses two of the options and advocates for a particular course of action through his writing strategy.

WRITING A RHETORICAL ANALYSIS

By now you should have a strong sense of what is involved in rhetorical analysis. You should be ready to take the next steps: performing a rhetorical analysis of your own and then sharing your analysis and the strategies you've learned with your classmates.

Read the next text, "The Flight from Conversation" by Sherry Turkle, annotating it to help you identify her situation, purpose, thesis, and audience. As you read, also make a separate set of annotations—possibly with a different color pen or pencil, circled, or keyed with asterisks—in which you comment on or evaluate the effectiveness of her essay. What do you like or dislike about it? Why? Does Turkle persuade you to accept her point of view? What impressions do you have of her as a person? Would you like to be in a conversation with her?

SHERRY TURKLE

The Flight from Conversation

Sherry Turkle—the Abby Rockefeller Mauzé Professor of the Social Studies of Science and Technology in the Program in Science, Technology, and Society at the Massachusetts Institute of Technology—is a licensed clinical psychologist with a joint doctorate in sociology and personality psychology from Harvard University. Director of the MIT Initiative on Technology and Self, she is the author or editor of many books, including *The Second Self: Computers and the Human Spirit* (1984), *Life on the Screen: Identity in the Age of the Internet* (1995), *Simulation and Its Discontents* (2009), and *Alone Together: Why We Expect More from Technology and Less from Each Other* (2011). "The Flight from Conversation" appeared in the April 12, 2012, issue of *The New York Times Magazine*.

■ ■ ■

We live in a technological universe in which we are always communicating. And yet we have sacrificed conversation for mere connection. 1

At home, families sit together, texting and reading e-mail. At work executives text during board meetings. We text (and shop and go on Facebook) during classes and when we're on dates. My students tell me about an important new skill: It involves maintaining eye contact with someone while you text someone else; it's hard, but it can be done. 2

Over the past fifteen years, I've studied technologies of mobile connection and talked to hundreds of people of all ages and circumstances about their plugged-in lives. I've learned that the little devices most of us carry around are so powerful that they change not only what we do, but also who we are. 3

We've become accustomed to a new way of being "alone together." Technology-enabled, we are able to be with one another, and also elsewhere, connected to wherever we want to be. We want to customize our lives. We want to move in and out of where we are because the thing we value most is control over where we focus our attention. We have gotten used to the idea of being in a tribe of one, loyal to our own party. 4

Our colleagues want to go to that board meeting but pay attention only to what interests them. To some this seems like a good idea, but we can end up hiding from one another, even as we are constantly connected to one another. 5

A businessman laments that he no longer has colleagues at work. He doesn't stop by to talk; he doesn't call. He says that he doesn't want to interrupt them. He says they're "too busy on their e-mail." But then he pauses and corrects himself. "I'm not telling the truth. I'm the one who 6 doesn't want to be interrupted. I think I should. But I'd rather just do things on my BlackBerry."

A 16-year-old boy who relies on texting for almost everything says 7 almost wistfully, "Someday, someday, but certainly not now, I'd like to learn how to have a conversation."

In today's workplace, young people who have grown up fearing con- 8 versation show up on the job wearing earphones. Walking through a college library or the campus of a high-tech start-up, one sees the same thing: We are together, but each of us is in our own bubble, furiously connected to keyboards and tiny touch screens. A senior partner at a Boston law firm describes a scene in his office. Young associates lay out their suite of technologies: laptops, iPods, and multiple phones. And then they put their earphones on. "Big ones. Like pilots. They turn their desks into cockpits." With the young lawyers in their cockpits, the office is quiet, a quiet that does not ask to be broken.

In the silence of connection, people are comforted by being in touch 9 with a lot of people — carefully kept at bay. We can't get enough of one another if we can use technology to keep one another at distances we can control: not too close, not too far, just right. I think of it as a Goldilocks effect.

Texting and e-mail and posting let us present the self we want to be. 10 This means we can edit. And if we wish to, we can delete. Or retouch: the voice, the flesh, the face, the body. Not too much, not too little — just right.

Human relationships are rich; they're messy and demanding. We 11 have learned the habit of cleaning them up with technology. And the move from conversation to connection is part of this. But it's a process in which we shortchange ourselves. Worse, it seems that over time we stop caring, we forget that there is a difference.

We are tempted to think that our little "sips" of online connec- 12 tion add up to a big gulp of real conversation. But they don't. E-mail, Twitter, Facebook, all of these have their places — in politics, commerce, romance, and friendship. But no matter how valuable, they do not substitute for conversation.

Connecting in sips may work for gathering discrete bits of informa- 13 tion or for saying, "I am thinking about you." Or even for saying, "I love you." But connecting in sips doesn't work as well when it comes to understanding and knowing one another. In conversation we tend to one another. (The word itself is kinetic; it's derived from words that mean to move, together.) We can attend to tone and nuance. In conversation, we are called upon to see things from another's point of view.

Face-to-face conversation unfolds slowly. It teaches patience. When 14 we communicate on our digital devices, we learn different habits. As we ramp up the volume and velocity of online connections, we start to expect faster answers. To get these, we ask one another simpler questions; we dumb down our communications, even on the most important matters. It is as though we have all put ourselves on cable news. Shakespeare might have said, "We are consum'd with that which we were nourish'd by."

And we use conversation with others to learn to converse with our- *15* selves. So our flight from conversation can mean diminished chances to learn skills of self-reflection. These days, social media continually asks us what's "on our mind," but we have little motivation to say something truly self-reflective. Self-reflection in conversation requires trust. It's hard to do anything with 3,000 Facebook friends except connect.

As we get used to being shortchanged on conversation and to getting *16* by with less, we seem almost willing to dispense with people altogether. Serious people muse about the future of computer programs as psychiatrists. A high school sophomore confides to me that he wishes he could talk to an artificial intelligence program instead of his dad about dating; he says the AI would have so much more in its database. Indeed, many people tell me they hope that as Siri, the digital assistant on Apple's iPhone, becomes more advanced, "she" will be more and more like a best friend—one who will listen when others won't.

During the years I have spent researching people and their relation- *17* ships with technology, I have often heard the sentiment "No one is listening to me." I believe this feeling helps explain why it is so appealing to have a Facebook page or a Twitter feed—each provides so many automatic listeners. And it helps explain why—against all reason—so many of us are willing to talk to machines that seem to care about us. Researchers around the world are busy inventing sociable robots, designed to be companions to the elderly, to children, to all of us.

One of the most haunting experiences during my research came *18* when I brought one of these robots, designed in the shape of a baby seal, to an elder-care facility, and an older woman began to talk to it about the loss of her child. The robot seemed to be looking into her eyes. It seemed to be following the conversation. The woman was comforted.

And so many people found this amazing. Like the sophomore who *19* wants advice about dating from artificial intelligence and those who look forward to computer psychiatry, this enthusiasm speaks to how much we have confused conversation with connection and collectively seem to have embraced a new kind of delusion that accepts the simulation of compassion as sufficient unto the day. And why would we want to talk about love and loss with a machine that has no experience of the arc of human life? Have we so lost confidence that we will be there for one another?

We expect more from technology and less from one another, and *20* seem increasingly drawn to technologies that provide the illusion of companionship without the demands of relationship. Always-on/always-on-you devices provide three powerful fantasies: that we will always be heard; that we can put our attention wherever we want it to be; and that we never have to be alone. Indeed our new devices have turned being alone into a problem that can be solved.

When people are alone, even for a few moments, they fidget and reach for a device. Here connection works like a symptom, not a cure, and our constant, reflexive impulse to connect shapes a new way of being. *21*

Think of it as "I share, therefore I am." We use technology to define ourselves by sharing our thoughts and feelings as we're having them. We used to think, "I have a feeling; I want to make a call." Now our impulse is, "I want to have a feeling; I need to send a text." *22*

So, in order to feel more, and to feel more like ourselves, we connect. But in our rush to connect, we flee from solitude, our ability to be separate and gather ourselves. Lacking the capacity for solitude, we turn to other people but don't experience them as they are. It is as though we use them, need them as spare parts to support our increasingly fragile selves. *23*

We think constant connection will make us feel less lonely. The opposite is true. If we are unable to be alone, we are far more likely to be lonely. If we don't teach our children to be alone, they will know only how to be lonely. *24*

I am a partisan for conversation. To make room for it, I see some first, deliberate steps. At home, we can create sacred spaces: the kitchen, the dining room. We can make our cars "device-free zones." We can demonstrate the value of conversation to our children. And we can do the same thing at work. There we are so busy communicating that we often don't have time to talk to one another about what really matters. Employees asked for casual Fridays; perhaps managers should introduce conversational Thursdays. Most of all, we need to remember—in between texts and e-mails and Facebook posts—to listen to one another, even to the boring bits, because it is often in unedited moments, moments in which we hesitate and stutter and go silent, that we reveal ourselves to one another. *25*

I spend the summers at a cottage on Cape Cod, and for decades I walked the same dunes that Thoreau once walked. Not too long ago, people walked with their heads up, looking at the water, the sky, the sand and at one another, talking. Now they often walk with their heads down, typing. Even when they are with friends, partners, children, everyone is on their own devices. *26*

So I say, look up, look at one another, and let's start the conversation. *27*

CHAPTER 7 | FROM READING AS A WRITER TO WRITING AS A READER

A Practice Sequence: Writing a Rhetorical Analysis

1 Write a brief rhetorical analysis of Sherry Turkle's essay, referring to your notes and citing passages where she indicates her situation, purpose, main claim, and audience.

2 An option for group work: As a class, divide into three or more groups. Groups should answer the following questions in response to Turkle's essay:

Group 1: Identify the situation(s) motivating Turkle to write. Then evaluate: How well does her argument function as a conversation with other authors who have written on the same topic?

Group 2: Analyze the audience's identity, perspectives, and conventional expectations. Then evaluate: How well does the argument function as a conversation with the audience?

Group 3: Analyze the writer's purpose. Then evaluate: Do you believe Turkle achieves her purpose in this essay? Why or why not?

Then, as a class, share your observations:

- To what extent does the author's ability as a conversationalist — that is, her ability to enter into a conversation with other authors and her audience — affect your evaluation of whether she achieves her purpose in this essay?

- If you were to meet this writer, what suggestions or advice would you give her for making her argument more persuasive?

8

From Writing Summaries and Paraphrases to Writing Yourself into Academic Conversations

Reading like a writer and writing like a reader help you understand how texts work rhetorically. When you start to use those texts to build your own arguments, there are certain strategies for working with the words and ideas of others that you will have to learn. Often you can quote the words of an author directly; but just as often you will restate (paraphrase) and condense (summarize) the arguments of others to educate your reader about the issues in a particular academic conversation. Indeed, many academic essays begin with a **literature review**—a roundup that summarizes important arguments and perspectives in such a conversation—as a prelude to the writer setting forth his or her own arguments on an issue. In this chapter, we will present methods of paraphrase and summary. Learning to paraphrase and summarize helps you understand texts and convey that understanding to other participants in the conversation.

SUMMARIES, PARAPHRASES, AND QUOTATIONS

In contrast to quotations, which involve using another writer's exact words, paraphrases and summaries are both restatements of another writer's ideas in your own words, but they differ in length and scope:

- A paraphrase is frequently about the same length as the original passage.

90 CHAPTER 8 | SUMMARIES, PARAPHRASES, AND ACADEMIC CONVERSATIONS

- A summary generally condenses a significantly longer text, conveying the argument not only of a few sentences but also of entire paragraphs, essays, or books.

In your own writing, you might paraphrase a few sentences or even a few paragraphs, but you certainly would not paraphrase a whole essay (much less a whole book). In constructing your arguments, however, you will often have to summarize the main points of the lengthy texts with which you are in conversation.

Both paraphrasing and summarizing are means to inquiry. That is, the act of recasting someone else's words or ideas into your own language, to suit your argument and reach your readers, forces you to think critically: What does this passage really mean? What is most important about it for my argument? How can I best present it to my readers? It requires making choices, not least of which is determining the best way to present the information—through paraphrase, summary, or direct quotation. In general, the following rules apply:

- *Paraphrase* when all the information in the passage is important, but the language is not key to your discussion, or if it may be difficult for your readers to understand.
- *Summarize* when you need to present only the key ideas of a passage (or an essay or a book) to advance your argument.
- *Quote* when the passage is so effective—so clear, so concise, so authoritative, so memorable—that you would be hard-pressed to improve on it.

WRITING A PARAPHRASE

A **paraphrase** is a restatement of all the information in a passage in your own words, using your own sentence structure and composed with your own audience in mind to advance your argument.

- When you paraphrase a passage, start by identifying key words and phrases, and think of other ways to state them. You may have to reread what led up to the passage to remind yourself of the context. For example, did the writer define terms earlier that he or she uses in the passage and now expects you to know?
- Continue by experimenting with word order and sentence structure, combining and recombining phrases to convey what the writer says without replicating his or her style. As you consider how best to state the writer's idea in your own words, you should come to a much better understanding of what the writer is saying. By thinking critically, then, you are clarifying the passage for yourself as much as for your readers.

WRITING A PARAPHRASE 91

Let's look at a paraphrase of a passage from science fiction writer and scholar James Gunn's essay "Harry Potter as Schooldays Novel"*:

ORIGINAL PASSAGE

The situation and portrayal of Harry as an ordinary child with an extraordinary talent make him interesting. He elicits our sympathy at every turn. He plays a Cinderella-like role as the abused child of mean-spirited foster parents who favor other, less-worthy children, and also fits another fantasy role, that of changeling. Millions of children have nursed the notion that they cannot be the offspring of such unremarkable parents; in the Harry Potter books, the metaphor is often literal truth.

PARAPHRASE

According to James Gunn, the circumstances and depiction of Harry Potter as a normal boy with special abilities captivate us by playing on our empathy. Gunn observes that, like Cinderella, Harry is scorned by his guardians, who treat him far worse than they treat his less-admirable peers. And like another fairy-tale figure, the changeling, Harry embodies the fantasies of children who refuse to believe that they were born of their undistinguished parents (146).

In this paraphrase, the writer uses his own words to express key terms (*circumstances and depiction* for "situation and portrayal," *guardians* for "foster parents") and rearranges the structure of the original sentences. But the paraphrase is about the same length as the original and says essentially the same things as Gunn's original.

Now, compare the paraphrase with this summary:

SUMMARY

James Gunn observes that Harry Potter's character is compelling because readers empathize with Harry's fairy tale–like plight as an orphan whose gifts are ignored by his foster parents (146).

The summary condenses the passage, conveying Gunn's main point without restating the details. Notice how both the paraphrase and the summary indicate that the ideas are James Gunn's, not the writer's — "According to James Gunn," "James Gunn observes" — and signal, with page references, where Gunn's ideas end. *It is essential that you acknowledge your sources*, a subject we come back to in our discussion of plagiarism on page 231. The

---

*Gunn's essay appears in *Mapping the World of Harry Potter: An Unauthorized Exploration of the Bestselling Fantasy Series of All Time*, edited by Mercedes Lackey (Dallas: BenBella, 2006).

CHAPTER 8 | SUMMARIES, PARAPHRASES, AND ACADEMIC CONVERSATIONS

point we want to make here is that borrowing from the work of others is not always intentional. Many students stumble into plagiarism, especially when they are attempting to paraphrase. Remember that it's not enough to change the words in a paraphrase; you must also change the structure of the sentences and cite your source.

You may be wondering: "If paraphrasing is so tricky, why bother? What does it add? I can see how the summary of Gunn's paragraph presents information more concisely and efficiently than the original, but the paraphrase doesn't seem to be all that different from the source and doesn't seem to add anything to it. Why not simply quote the original or summarize it?"

Good questions. The answer is that you paraphrase when the ideas in a passage are important but the language is not key to your discussion or it may be difficult for readers to understand. When academics write for their peers, they draw on the specialized vocabulary of their disciplines to make their arguments. By paraphrasing, you may be helping your readers, providing a translation of sorts for those who do not speak the language.

Consider this paragraph by George Lipsitz from his academic book *Time Passages: Collective Memory and American Popular Culture* (1990), and compare the paraphrase that follows it:

ORIGINAL PASSAGE

The transformations in behavior and collective memory fueled by the contradictions of the nineteenth century have passed through three major stages in the United States. The first involved the establishment and codification of commercialized leisure from the invention of the telegraph to the 1890s. The second involved the transition from Victorian to consumer-hedonist values between 1890 and 1945. The third and most important stage, from World War II to the present, involved extraordinary expansion in both the distribution of consumer purchasing power and in both the reach and scope of electronic mass media. The dislocations of urban renewal, suburbanization, and deindustrialization accelerated the demise of tradition in America, while the worldwide pace of change undermined stability elsewhere. The period from World War II to the present marks the final triumph of commercialized leisure, and with it an augmented crisis over the loss of connection to the past.

PARAPHRASE

Historian George Lipsitz argues that Americans' sense of the past is rooted in cultural changes dating from the 1800s and has evolved through three stages. In the first stage, technological innovations of the nineteenth century gave

WRITING A PARAPHRASE **93**

> rise to widespread commercial entertainment. In the second stage, dating
> from the 1890s to about 1945, attitudes toward the consumption of goods and
> services changed. Since 1945, in the third stage, increased consumer spending
> and the growth of the mass media have led to a crisis in which Americans find
> themselves cut off from their traditions and the memories that give meaning
> to them (12).

Notice that the paraphrase is not a word-for-word translation of the original. Instead, the writer has made choices that resulted in a slightly briefer and more accessible restatement of Lipsitz's thinking. (Although this paraphrase is shorter than the original passage, a paraphrase can also be a little longer than the original if extra words are needed to help readers understand the original.)

Notice too that several specialized terms and phrases from the original passage—the "codification of commercialized leisure," "the transition from Victorian to consumer-hedonist values," "the dislocations of urban renewal, suburbanization, and deindustrialization"—have disappeared. The writer not only looked up these terms and phrases in the dictionary but also reread the several pages that preceded the original passage to understand what Lipsitz meant by them.

The paraphrase is not meant to be an improvement on the original passage—in fact, historians would most likely prefer what Lipsitz wrote—but it may help readers who do not share Lipsitz's expertise understand his point without distorting his argument.

Now compare this summary to the paraphrase:

SUMMARY

> Historian George Lipsitz argues that technological, social, and economic changes
> dating from the nineteenth century have culminated in what he calls a "crisis over
> the loss of connection to the past," in which Americans find themselves cut off from
> the memories of their traditions (12).

Which is better, the paraphrase or the summary? Neither is better or worse in and of itself. Their correctness and appropriateness depend on how the restatements are used in a given argument. That is, the decision to paraphrase or summarize depends entirely on the information you need to convey. Would the details in the paraphrase strengthen your argument? Or is a summary sufficient? In this case, if you plan to focus your argument on the causes of America's loss of cultural memory (the rise of commercial entertainment, changes in spending habits, globalization), then a paraphrase might be more helpful. But if you plan to define *loss of cultural memory*, then a summary may provide enough context for the next stage of your argument.

94 CHAPTER 8 | SUMMARIES, PARAPHRASES, AND ACADEMIC CONVERSATIONS

Steps to Writing a Paraphrase

1 **Decide whether to paraphrase.** If your readers don't need all the information in the passage, consider summarizing it or presenting the key points as part of a summary of a longer passage. If a passage is clear, concise, and memorable as originally written, consider quoting instead of paraphrasing. Otherwise, and especially if the original was written for an academic audience, you may want to paraphrase the original to make its substance more accessible to your readers.

2 **Understand the passage.** Start by identifying key words, phrases, and ideas. If necessary, reread the pages leading up to the passage, to place it in context.

3 **Draft your paraphrase.** Replace key words and phrases with synonyms and alternative phrases (possibly gleaned from the context provided by the surrounding text). Experiment with word order and sentence structure until the paraphrase captures your understanding of the passage, in your own language, for your readers.

4 **Acknowledge your source.** Protect yourself from a charge of plagiarism and give credit for ideas you borrow.

A Practice Sequence: Writing a Paraphrase

1 In one of the sources you've located in your research, find a sentence of some length and complexity, and paraphrase it. Share the original and your paraphrase of it with a classmate, and discuss the effectiveness of your restatement. Is the meaning clear to your reader? Is the paraphrase written in your own language, using your own sentence structure?

2 Repeat the activity using a short paragraph from the same source. You and your classmate may want to attempt to paraphrase the same paragraph and then compare results. What differences do you detect?

WRITING A SUMMARY

As you have seen, a **summary** condenses a body of information, presenting the key ideas and acknowledging the source. A common activity or assignment in a composition class is to *summarize* a text. You may be asked to read a text, reduce it to its main points, and convey them, without any details or examples, in a written summary. The goal of this assignment is to sharpen your reading and thinking skills as you learn to distinguish between main ideas and supporting details. Being able to distill information in this manner is crucial to critical thinking.

However, summarizing is not an active way to make an argument. While summaries do provide a common ground of information for your readers, you must shape that information to support the purposes of your researched argument with details that clarify, illustrate, or support their main ideas for your readers.

We suggest a method of summarizing that involves

1. describing the author's key claims,

2. selecting examples to illustrate the author's argument,

3. presenting the gist of the author's argument, and

4. contextualizing what you summarize.

We demonstrate these steps for writing a summary following Clive Thompson's article "On the New Literacy."

CLIVE THOMPSON

On the New Literacy

A print journalist at *New York Magazine*, Clive Thompson started his blog, Collision Detection, in September 2002, when he was beginning his year as a Knight Fellow in Science Journalism at MIT. Collision Detection has become one of the most well-regarded blogs on technology and culture. The blog receives approximately 3,000 to 4,000 hits a day. His piece on literacy appeared in *Wired* magazine in 2009.

As the school year begins, be ready to hear pundits fretting once again about how kids today can't write—and technology is to blame. Facebook encourages narcissistic blabbering, video and PowerPoint have replaced carefully crafted essays, and texting has dehydrated language into "bleak, bald, sad shorthand" (as University College of London English professor John Sutherland has moaned). An age of illiteracy is at hand, right?

Andrea Lunsford isn't so sure. Lunsford is a professor of writing and rhetoric at Stanford University, where she has organized a mammoth project called the Stanford Study of Writing to scrutinize college students' prose. From 2001 to 2006, she collected 14,672 student writing samples—everything from in-class assignments, formal essays, and

96 CHAPTER 8 | SUMMARIES, PARAPHRASES, AND ACADEMIC CONVERSATIONS

journal entries to e-mails, blog posts, and chat sessions. Her conclusions are stirring.

"I think we're in the midst of a literacy revolution the likes of which we haven't seen since Greek civilization," she says. For Lunsford, technology isn't killing our ability to write. It's reviving it—and pushing our literacy in bold new directions.   3

The first thing she found is that young people today write far more than any generation before them. That's because so much socializing takes place online, and it almost always involves text. Of all the writing that the Stanford students did, a stunning 38 percent of it took place out of the classroom—life writing, as Lunsford calls it. Those Twitter updates and lists of 25 things about yourself add up.   4

It's almost hard to remember how big a paradigm shift this is. Before the Internet came along, most Americans never wrote anything, ever, that wasn't a school assignment. Unless they got a job that required producing text (like in law, advertising, or media), they'd leave school and virtually never construct a paragraph again.   5

But is this explosion of prose good, on a technical level? Yes. Lunsford's team found that the students were remarkably adept at what rhetoricians call *kairos*—assessing their audience and adapting their tone and technique to best get their point across. The modern world of online writing, particularly in chat and on discussion threads, is conversational and public, which makes it closer to the Greek tradition of argument than the asynchronous letter and essay writing of 50 years ago.   6

The fact that students today almost always write for an audience (something virtually no one in my generation did) gives them a different sense of what constitutes good writing. In interviews, they defined good prose as something that had an effect on the world. For them, writing is about persuading and organizing and debating, even if it's over something as quotidian as what movie to go see. The Stanford students were almost always less enthusiastic about their in-class writing because it had no audience but the professor: It didn't serve any purpose other than to get them a grade. As for those texting short-forms and smileys defiling *serious* academic writing? Another myth. When Lunsford examined the work of first-year students, she didn't find a single example of texting speak in an academic paper.   7

Of course, good teaching is always going to be crucial, as is the mastering of formal academic prose. But it's also becoming clear that online media are pushing literacy into cool directions. The brevity of texting and status updating teaches young people to deploy haiku-like concision. At the same time, the proliferation of new forms of online pop-cultural exegesis—from sprawling TV-show recaps to 15,000-word videogame walkthroughs—has given them a chance to write enormously long and complex pieces of prose, often while working collaboratively with others.   8

> We think of writing as either good or bad. What today's young people know is that knowing who you're writing for and why you're writing might be the most crucial factor of all.
>
> 9

■ Describe the Key Claims of the Text

As you read through a text with the purpose of summarizing it, you want to identify how the writer develops his or her argument. You can do this by what we call "chunking," grouping related material together into the argument's key claims. Here are two strategies to try.

Notice how paragraphs begin and end.   Often, focusing on the first and last sentences of paragraphs will alert you to the shape and direction of an author's argument. It is especially helpful if the paragraphs are lengthy and full of supporting information, as much academic writing is.

Because of his particular journalistic forum, *Wired* magazine, the paragraphs Thompson writes are generally rather short, but it's still worth taking a closer look at the first and last sentences of his opening paragraphs:

> *Paragraph 1:* As the school year begins, be ready to hear pundits fretting once again about how kids today can't write—and technology is to blame. Facebook encourages narcissistic blabbering, video and PowerPoint have replaced carefully crafted essays, and texting has dehydrated language into "bleak, bald, sad shorthand" (as University College of London English professor John Sutherland has moaned). An age of illiteracy is at hand, right?
>
> *Paragraph 2:* Andrea Lunsford isn't so sure. Lunsford is a professor of writing and rhetoric at Stanford University, where she has organized a mammoth project called the Stanford Study of Writing to scrutinize college students' prose. From 2001 to 2006, she collected 14,672 student writing samples—everything from in-class assignments, formal essays, and journal entries to e-mails, blog posts, and chat sessions. Her conclusions are stirring.

Right away you can see that Thompson has introduced a topic in each paragraph—pundits' criticism of students' use of electronic media in the first, and a national study designed to examine students' literacy in the second—and has indicated a connection between them. In fact, Thompson is explicit in doing so. He asks a question at the end of the first paragraph and then raises doubts as to the legitimacy of critics' denunciation of young people's reliance on blogs and posts to communicate. How will Thompson elaborate on this connection? What major points does he develop?

98   CHAPTER 8 | SUMMARIES, PARAPHRASES, AND ACADEMIC CONVERSATIONS

Notice the author's point of view and use of transitions.   Another strategy for identifying major points is to pay attention to descriptive words and transitions. For example, Thompson uses a rhetorical question ("An age of illiteracy is at hand, right?") and then offers a tentative answer ("Andrea Lunsford isn't so sure") that places some doubt in readers' minds.

Notice, too, the words that Thompson uses to characterize the argument in the first paragraph, which he appears to challenge in the second paragraph. Specifically, he describes these critics as "pundits," a word that traditionally refers to an expert or knowledgeable individual. However, the notion of a pundit, someone who often appears on popular talk shows, has also been used negatively. Thompson's description of pundits "fretting," wringing their hands in worry that literacy levels are declining, underscores this negative association of what it means to be a pundit. Finally, Thompson indicates that he does not identify with those who describe students as engaging in "narcissistic blabbering." This is clear when he characterizes the professor as having "moaned."

Once you identify an author's point of view, you will start noticing contrasts and oppositions in the argument—instances where the words are less positive, or neutral, or even negative—which are often signaled by how the writer uses transitions.

For example, Thompson begins with his own concession to critics' arguments when he acknowledges in paragraph 8 that educators should expect students to "[master] formal academic prose." However, he follows this concession with the transition word "but" to signal his own stance in the debate he frames in the first two paragraphs: "online media are pushing literacy into cool directions." Thompson also recognizes that students who write on blogs tend to write short, abbreviated texts. Still, he qualifies his concern with another transition, "at the same time." This transition serves to introduce Thompson's strongest claim: New media have given students "a chance to write enormously long and complex pieces of prose, often while working collaboratively with others."

These strategies can help you recognize the main points of an essay and explain them in a few sentences. For example, you could describe Thompson's key claims in this way:

1. Electronic media give students opportunities to write more than in previous generations, and students have learned to adapt what they are writing in order to have some tangible effect on what people think and how they act.

2. Arguably, reliance on blogging and posting on Twitter and Facebook can foster some bad habits in writing.

3. But at least one major study demonstrates that the benefits of using the new media outweigh the disadvantages. This study indicates that students write lengthy, complex pieces that contribute to creating significant social networks and collaborations.

■ Select Examples to Illustrate the Author's Argument

A summary should be succinct, which means you should limit the number of examples or illustrations you use. As you distill the major points of the argument, try to choose one or two examples to illustrate each major point. Here are the examples (in italics) you might use to support Thompson's main points:

1. Electronic media give students opportunities to write more than in previous generations, and students have learned to adapt what they are writing in order to have some tangible effect on what people think and how they act. *Examples from the Stanford study: Students "defined good prose as something that had an effect on the world. For them, writing is about persuading and organizing and debating"* (para. 7).

2. Arguably, reliance on blogging and posting on Twitter and Facebook can foster some bad habits in writing. *Examples of these bad habits include critics' charges of "narcissistic blabbering," "bleak, bald, sad shorthand," and "dehydrated language"* (para. 1). *Thompson's description of texting's "haiku-like concision"* (para. 8) *seems to combine praise (haiku can be wonderful poetry) with criticism (it can be obscure and unintelligible).*

3. But at least one major study demonstrates that the benefits of using the new media outweigh the disadvantages. *Examples include Thompson's point that the writing in the new media constitutes a "paradigm shift"* (para. 5). *Andrea Lunsford observes that students are "remarkably adept at what rhetoricians call* kairos—*assessing their audience and adapting their tone and technique to best get their point across"* (para. 6).

A single concrete example may be sufficient to clarify the point you want to make about an author's argument. Throughout the essay, Thompson derives examples from the Stanford study to support his argument in the final two paragraphs. The most concrete, specific example of how the new media benefit students as writers appears in paragraph 6, where the primary research of the Stanford study describes students' acquisition of important rhetorical skills of developing writing that is opportune (*kairos*) and purposeful. This one example may be sufficient for the purposes of summarizing Thompson's essay.

■ Present the Gist of the Author's Argument

When you present the **gist** of an argument, you are expressing the author's central idea in a sentence or two. The gist is not quite the same thing as the author's thesis statement. Instead, it is your formulation of the author's main idea, composed for the needs of your own argument.

Thompson's observations in paragraph 8 represent his thesis: "But it's also becoming clear that online media are pushing literacy into cool directions. . . . [T]he proliferation of new forms of online pop-cultural exegesis—from sprawling TV-show recaps to 15,000-word videogame walkthroughs—has given [students] a chance to write enormously long and complex pieces of prose, often while working collaboratively with others." In this paragraph, Thompson clearly expresses his central ideas in two sentences, while also conceding some of the critics' concerns. However, in formulating the gist of his argument, you want to do more than paraphrase Thompson. You want to use his position to support your own. For example, suppose you want to qualify the disapproval that some educators have expressed in drawing their conclusions about the new media. You would want to mention Thompson's own concessions when you describe the gist of his argument:

GIST

In his essay "On the New Literacy," Clive Thompson, while acknowledging some academic criticism of new media, argues that these media give students opportunities to write more than in previous generations and that students have learned to adapt what they are writing in order to have some tangible effect on what people think and how they act.

Notice that this gist could not have been written based only on Thompson's thesis statement. It reflects knowledge of Thompson's major points, his examples, and his concessions.

■ Contextualize What You Summarize

Your summary should help readers understand the context of the conversation:

- Who is the author?
- What is the author's expertise?
- What is the title of the work?
- Where did the work appear?
- What was the occasion of the work's publication? What prompted the author to write the work?
- What are the issues?
- Who else is taking part in the conversation, and what are their perspectives on the issues?

Again, because a summary must be concise, you must make decisions about how much of the conversation your readers need to know. If your assignment is to practice summarizing, it may be sufficient to include only information about the author and the source. However, if you are using the summary to build your own argument, you may need to provide more context. Your practice summary of Thompson's essay should mention that

Key Claim(s)	Examples	Gist	Context
1. Electronic media prompt more student writing than ever before, and students use their writing to make a difference.	The Stanford study: Students "defined good prose as something that had an effect on the world" (para. 7).	In his essay "On the New Literacy," Clive Thompson, while acknowledging some academic criticism of new media, argues that these media give students opportunities to write more than in previous generations and that students have learned to adapt what they are writing in order to have some tangible effect on what people think and how they act.	Thompson is a journalist who has written widely on issues in higher education. His essay "On the New Literacy" appeared in *Wired* in August 2009 (http://www.wired.com/techbiz/people/magazine/17-09/st_thompson). Under consideration is the debate that he frames in his opening paragraphs.
2. Arguably, reliance on blogging and posting can foster some bad writing habits.	Complaints of "bleak, bald, sad shorthand" and "narcissistic blabbering" (para. 1); texting can be obscure.		
3. But one major study shows the benefits of new media on student writing.	A "paradigm shift" (para. 5) to fluency in multiple formats and skill in assessing and persuading audiences.		

FIGURE 8.1 Worksheet for Writing a Summary

he is a journalist and should cite the title of and page references to his essay. You also may want to include information about Thompson's audience, publication information, and what led to the work's publication. Was it published in response to another essay or book, or to commemorate an important event?

We compiled our notes on Thompson's essay (key claims, examples, gist, context) in a worksheet (Figure 8.1). All of our notes in the worksheet constitute a type of prewriting, our preparation for writing the summary. Creating a worksheet like this can help you track your thoughts as you plan to write a summary.

Here is our summary of Thompson's essay:

The gist of Thompson's argument.

This concession helps to balance enthusiasm based on a single study.

Thompson's main point with example.

In his essay "On the New Literacy," Clive Thompson, while acknowledging some academic criticism of new media, argues that these media give students opportunities to write more than in previous generations and that students have learned to adapt what they are writing in order to have some tangible effect on what people think and how they act. Arguably, reliance on blogging and posting on Twitter and Facebook can foster some bad habits in writing. But at least one major study demonstrates that the benefits of using the new media outweigh the disadvantages. Students write lengthy, complex pieces that contribute to creating significant social networks and collaborations.

102   CHAPTER 8 | SUMMARIES, PARAPHRASES, AND ACADEMIC CONVERSATIONS

Steps to Writing a Summary

1 **Describe the key claims of the text.** To understand the shape and direction of the argument, study how paragraphs begin and end, and pay attention to the author's point of view and use of transitions. Then combine what you have learned into a few sentences describing the key claims.

2 **Select examples to illustrate the author's argument.** Find one or two examples to support each key claim. You may need only one example when you write your summary.

3 **Present the gist of the author's argument.** Describe the author's central idea in your own language with an eye to where you expect your argument to go.

4 **Contextualize what you summarize.** Cue your readers into the conversation. Who is the author? Where and when did the text appear? Why did the author write? Who else is in the conversation?

A Practice Sequence: Writing a Summary

1 Summarize a text that you have been studying for research or for one of your other classes. You may want to limit yourself to an excerpt of just a few paragraphs or a few pages. Follow the four steps we've described, using a summary worksheet for notes, and write a summary of the text. Then share the excerpt and your summary of it with two of your peers. Be prepared to justify your choices in composing the summary. Do your peers agree that your summary captures what is important in the original?

2 With a classmate, choose a brief text of about three pages. Each of you should use the method we describe above to write a summary of the text. Exchange your summaries and worksheets, and discuss the effectiveness of your summaries. Each of you should be prepared to discuss your choice of key claims and examples and your wording of the gist. Did you set forth the context effectively?

WRITING YOURSELF INTO ACADEMIC CONVERSATIONS

In her essay "The Flight from Conversation" (see p. 84), Sherry Turkle reflects upon her research on mobile technology and what she sees as the unfortunate trend toward "sacrificing conversation for mere connection."

You are probably familiar with the experience of walking into a coffee shop or the library on campus and seeing friends sitting across from one another but engaged with laptops or phones instead of with each other. "Alone together," as Turkle puts it, and she laments the "diminished chances to learn skills of self-reflection," a habit of mind that we agree is vital to academic writing and thinking. Thus, she blames technology that encourages broad and shallow connection without real face-to-face engagement. But as we also suggest, much academic conversation occurs on the page and screen, involving the exchange of ideas through writing. The philosopher Kenneth Burke uses this metaphor of an ongoing parlor conversation to capture the spirit of academic writing:

> Imagine that you enter a parlor. You come late. When you arrive, others have long preceded you, and they are engaged in a heated discussion, a discussion too heated for them to pause and tell you exactly what it is about. In fact, the discussion had already begun long before any of them got there, so that no one present is qualified to retrace for you all the steps that had gone before. You listen for a while, until you decide that you have caught the tenor of the argument; then you put in your oar. Someone answers; you answer him; another comes to your defense; another aligns himself against you, to either the embarrassment or gratification of your opponent, depending upon the quality of your ally's assistance. However, the discussion is interminable. The hour grows late, you must depart. And you do depart, with the discussion still vigorously in progress.*

Now that you have learned some important skills of rhetorical analysis and summary, then, it is important to think about ways to write yourself into academic conversations. Doing so will depend on three strategies:

- which previously stated arguments you share;
- which previously stated argument you want to refute; and
- what new opinions and supporting information you are going to bring to the conversation.

You may, for example, affirm others for raising important issues about the environment, employment opportunities, or the tendency of new technologies to limit community building and democratic deliberation. Then again, as you consider the arguments of others, you may feel that they have not given sufficient thought or emphasis to ideas that you think are important. In the end, you can write yourself into the conversation by explaining that writers have ignored a related issue entirely. So you are looking for gaps in others' arguments—something we discuss in more detail in the chapters that follow—an opening that provides an opportunity to provide a unique perspective in the conversation of ideas.

---

*Kenneth Burke, *The Philosophy of Literary Form* (Berkeley: University of California Press, 1941, pp. 110–11).

104   CHAPTER 8 | SUMMARIES, PARAPHRASES, AND ACADEMIC CONVERSATIONS

Steps to Writing Yourself into an Academic Conversation

- **Retrace the conversation**, including the relevance of the topic and situation, for readers by briefly discussing an author's key claims and ideas. This discussion can be as brief as a sentence or two and include a quotation for each author you cite.

- **Respond to the ideas of others** by helping readers understand the context in which another's claims make sense. "I get this if I see it this way."

- **Discuss possible implications** by putting problems aside and asking, "Do their claims make sense?"

- **Introduce conflicting points of view** and raise possible criticisms to indicate something the authors whose ideas you discuss may have overlooked.

- **Formulate your own claim** to assert what you think.

- **Ensure that your own purpose as a writer is clear to readers.**

A Practice Sequence: Writing Yourself into an Academic Conversation

1   We would like you to read an excerpt from Tom Standage's book *Writing on the Wall*, follow the steps to writing yourself into the conversation, and write a short, one-page argument. In doing so, retrace the conversation by explaining Standage's argument in ways that demonstrate your understanding of it. In turn, formulate your own position by explaining whether you believe that Standage has represented the issue well. Is there an opening in his argument that enables you to offer a perspective that he has perhaps ignored or overlooked?

2   An option for group work:
- As a group, discuss Sherry Turkle's argument in Chapter 7 that mobile technology has led to sacrificing conversation for mere connection—that we are "alone together." List the reasons why her argument makes sense and reasons why your group might take issue with her perspective. What do you feel she might have ignored or overlooked?

- Next, compare Turkle's argument with Standage's point of view in which he challenges Turkle's assertion that new technologies encourage "flight from conversation."

- Finally, each member of the group should write an argument that takes into account the conversation that Turkle and Standage have initiated with their efforts to make sense of how mobile technology has affected our lives.

TOM STANDAGE

History Retweets Itself

A writer and journalist from England with a degree from Oxford University, Tom Standage has published six books, including *The Victorian Internet* and *Writing on the Wall*, from which the excerpt that follows is taken. He has published articles on science, technology, and business in the *New York Times*, *Wired*, and the *Daily Telegraph*. He has also worked as a science and technology writer for the *Guardian* and deputy editor at *The Economist*.

■ ■ ■

1   Social media, whether in the form of the printing press or the Internet, can be a force for freedom and openness, simply because oppressive regimes often rely on manipulating their citizens' view of the world, and a more open media environment makes that harder to accomplish. But the other side of the scales is not empty; this benefit must be weighed against the fact that social media can make repression easier, too. As Morozov notes, the Internet "penetrates and reshapes all walks of political life, not just the ones conducive to democratization." Anyone who hopes that the Internet will spread Western-style liberal democracy must bear in mind that the same digital tools have also been embraced by campaigners with very different aims, such as Hezbollah in Lebanon and ultra-right-wing nationalist groups in Russia. The test case in this argument is China, which now has more Internet users than any other country—more than in North America and Europe combined. Weibo and other online forums have given Chinese Internet users unprecedented freedom to express their views. Yet the swift and ruthless censoring of blog posts and weibo messages criticizing senior officials or calling for real-world demonstrations shows that widespread Internet adoption need not necessarily threaten the regime. Indeed, the ability to monitor the Internet may make it easier for the government to keep the lid on dissent.

2   A rather more mundane but widely expressed concern about social media is that the ease with which anyone can now publish his or her views online, whether on Twitter, on blogs, or in comment threads, has led to a coarsening of public discourse. Racism, sexism, bigotry, incivility, and ignorance abound in many online discussion forums. Twitter allows anyone to send threats or abuse directly to other users. No wonder the Internet is often likened to a sewer by politicians, clergymen, and newspaper columnists.

3   Yet the history of media shows that this is just the modern incarnation of the timeless complaint of the intellectual elite, every time

106 CHAPTER 8 | SUMMARIES, PARAPHRASES, AND ACADEMIC CONVERSATIONS

technology makes publishing easier, that the wrong sort of people will use it to publish the wrong sorts of things. In the early sixteenth century, Erasmus complained that printers "fill the world with pamphlets and books that are foolish, ignorant, malignant, libelous, mad, impious and subversive; and such is the flood that even things that might have done some good lose all their goodness." Worse, these "swarms of new books" were "hurtful to scholarship" because they lured readers away from the classics, which is what Erasmus felt people ought to have been reading.

Printers had, however, quickly realized that there was a far larger *4* audience, and more money to be made, printing pamphlets and contemporary works rather than new editions of classical works. Similarly, in England, the Worshipful Company of Stationers bemoaned the explosion of unlicensed pamphlets that appeared after the collapse of press controls in 1641, complaining that "every ignorant person that takes advantage of a loose presse may publish the fancies of every idle brain as so manyfestly appeareth by the swarmes of scandalous and irksome pamphletts that are cryed about the streetes." The Company was hoping to be granted a renewed monopoly on printing, which had previously allowed it to control what was printed, and therefore what people read. Its grumbling is not dissimilar to that of professional journalists bemoaning the rise of pajama-clad bloggers, invading their turf and challenging the status quo.

Those in authority always squawk, it seems, when access to publishing is broadened. Greater freedom of expression, as John Milton noted in *Areopagitica*, means that bad ideas will proliferate as well as good ones, but it also means that bad ideas are more likely to be challenged. Better to provide an outlet for bigotry and prejudice, so they can be argued against and addressed, than to pretend that such views, and the people who hold them, do not exist. In a world where almost anyone can publish his or her views, the alternative, which is to restrict freedom of expression, is surely worse. As Milton's contemporary Henry Robinson put it in 1644, "It were better that many false doctrines were published, especially with a good intention and out of weaknesse only, than that one sound truth should be forcibly smothered or wilfully concealed; and by the incongruities and absurdities which accompany erroneous and unsound doctrines, the truth appears still more glorious, and wins others to the love thereof." One man's coarsening of discourse is another man's democratization of publishing. The genie is out of the bottle. Let truth and falsehood grapple!

Whatever you think about the standards of online discussions, there *6* is no doubt that people are spending a lot of time engaging in them. This raises another concern: that social media is a distracting waste of time that diverts people from more worthwhile pursuits, such as work and study. Surveys carried out in 2009 found that more than half of British and American companies had banned workers from using Twitter, Facebook, and other social sites. Many employers also block access to LinkedIn, a social-networking site for business users, because they worry that it allows employees to spend their time networking and advertising themselves to other potential employers. Simply put, companies readily equate social networking with social notworking.

This too is a familiar worry. Coffeehouses, the social-media platforms of their day, inspired similar reactions in the seventeenth century. They were denounced in the 1670s as "a vast loss of time grown out of a pure novelty" and "great enemies to diligence and industry." But the mixing of people and ideas that occurred in coffeehouses, where patrons from many walks of life would gather to discuss the latest pamphlets, led to innovations in science, commerce, and finance. By providing an environment in which unexpected connections could be made, coffeehouses proved to be hotbeds of collaborative innovation.

Similarly, a growing number of companies have concluded that social networking does have a role to play in the workplace, if done in the right way. They have set up "enterprise social networks," which create a private, Facebook-like social network to facilitate communication among employees and, in some cases, with workers at client and supplier companies, too. This sort of approach seems to have several benefits: its similarity to Facebook means little or no training is required; sharing documents and communicating via discussion threads is more efficient than using e-mail; it is easier to discover employees' hidden knowledge and talents; and it makes it easier for far-flung teams to collaborate.

A study by McKinsey and Company, a management consulting firm, found that the use of social networking within companies could increase the productivity of skilled knowledge workers by 20 to 25 percent and that the adoption of the technology in four industries (consumer goods, financial services, professional services, and advanced manufacturing) could create economic benefits worth between $900 billion and $1.3 trillion a year. Such predictions should always be taken with a very large dose of salt, but McKinsey found that 70 percent of companies were already using social technologies to some extent; and more than 90 percent said they were already benefitting as a result. Far from being a waste of time, then, Facebook-like social networks may in fact be the future of business software.

Even if it has value in the office, however, is there a danger that social media is harming our personal lives? Some observers worry that social media is in fact antisocial, because it encourages people to commune with people they barely know online to the detriment of real-life relationships with family and friends. "Does virtual intimacy degrade our

108   CHAPTER 8 | SUMMARIES, PARAPHRASES, AND ACADEMIC CONVERSATIONS

experience of the other kind and, indeed, of all encounters, of any kind?" writes Sherry Turkle, an academic at MIT, in her book *Alone Together*. She worries that "relentless connection leads to a new solitude. We turn to new technology to fill the void, but as technology ramps up, our emotional lives ramp down." Similarly, William Powers, author of *Hamlet's BlackBerry*, laments the way that his family would rather chat with their online friends than with each other. "The digital crowd has a way of elbowing its way into everything, to the point where a family can't sit in a room together for half an hour without somebody, or everybody, peeling off," he writes. His proposed solution: an "Unplugged Sunday" when the use of computers and smartphones is banned.

It is clear that the desire to be connected to one's distant friends, *11* using whatever technology is available, is timeless. Cicero particularly valued the way letters connected him to his friends in the months after the death of his beloved daughter Tullia in 45 B.C. And he relished the contact his daily letters with his friend Atticus provided, even when they contained little information. "Write to me . . . every day," he wrote to Atticus. "When you have nothing to say, why, say just that!" Concerns about unhealthy dependence on new media technologies also have a long history: recall Plato's objections to writing in the *Phaedrus*, and Seneca's derision of his fellow Romans as they rushed to the docks to get their mail. By the seventeenth century, satirists were lampooning news junkies and the hunger with which they sought out the latest corantos.

From Roman letter-writers to manuscript poetry-sharing networks *12* to news-sharing clergymen in the American colonies, the exchange of media has long been used to reinforce social connections. The same is true today. Zeynep Tufekci, a media theorist at Princeton University, suggests that the popularity of social media stems from its ability to reconnect people in a world of suburbanization, long working hours, and families scattered around the globe by migration. Social media, she argues, is also a welcome antidote to the lonely, one-way medium of television. People who use social media can stay in contact with people they would otherwise lose touch with and make contact with like-minded individuals they might otherwise have never met. "Social media is enhancing human connectivity as people can converse in ways that were once not possible," Tufekci argues. A study published in 2011 by researchers at the University of Pennsylvania concluded that "it is incorrect to maintain that the Internet benefits distant relationships at the expense of local ties. The Internet affords personal connections at extreme distances but also provides the opportunity for new and supplemental local interaction." Another analysis, conducted in 2009 by researchers at the University of Toronto and involving four thousand Canadians, found that 35 percent felt that technology made them feel closer and more connected to other family members, and only 7 percent said that technology made them feel less connected. Tellingly, 51% of respondents said it made no difference, which suggests that many people no longer make a distinction between online and offline worlds, but regard them as an integrated whole.

New technologies are often regarded with suspicion. Turkle worries about the "flight from conversation," citing teenagers who would rather send a text than make a phone call. And on Unplugged Sunday, Powers and his family engage in communal pursuits that include watching television together. It seems odd to venerate the older technologies of the telephone and the television, though, given that they were once condemned for being anti-social in the same way social media is denounced today. ("Does the telephone make men more active or more lazy? Does it break up home life and the old practice of visiting friends?" asked a survey carried out in San Francisco in 1926.) There is always an adjustment period when new technologies appear, as societies work out the appropriate etiquette for their use and technologies are modified in response. During this transitional phase, which takes years or even decades, technologies are often criticized for disrupting existing ways of doing things. But the technology that is demonized today may end up being regarded as wholesome and traditional tomorrow, by which time another apparently dangerous new invention will be causing the same concerns. *13*

What clues can history provide about the future evolution of social media? Even though Facebook, Twitter, and other social platforms provide a way for people to share information by sharing along social connections, they still resemble old-fashioned media companies such as newspapers and broadcasters in two ways: they are centralized (even though the distribution of information is carried out by the users, rather than the platform owners) and they rely on advertising for the majority of their revenue. Centralization grants enormous power to the owners of social platforms, giving them the ability to suspend or delete users' accounts and censor information if they choose to do so— or are compelled to do so by governments. Relying on advertising revenue, meanwhile, means platform owners must keep both advertisers and users happy, even though their interests do not always align. As they try to keep users within the bounds of their particular platforms, to maximize their audience for advertising, the companies that operate social networks have started to impose restrictions on what their customers can do and on how easily information can be moved from one social platform to another. In their early days, it makes sense for new social platforms to be as open as possible, to attract a large number of users. Having done so, however, such platforms often try to fence their users into "walled gardens" as they start trying to make money. *14*

The contrast between big social platforms on the one hand, and e-mail and the web on the other, is striking. Both e-mail and web *15* publishing work in an entirely open, decentralized way. The servers that store and deliver e-mail and the programs used to read and write messages are all expected to work seamlessly with each other, and for the most part they do. The same is true of web servers, which store and deliver pages, and the web browsers used to display pages and navigate between them. Anyone who wants to set up a new e-mail or web server can add it to the Internet's existing ecosystem of such servers. If you are setting up a new blog or website, there are also plenty of companies to choose from who will host it for you, and you can move from one to another if you are unsatisfied with their service. None of this is true for social networking, however, which takes place inside huge, proprietary silos owned by private companies. Moving your photos, your list of friends, or your archive of posts from one service to another is difficult at best, and impossible at worst. It may be that healthy competition among those companies, and a reluctance to alienate their hundreds of millions of users by becoming too closed, will enable the big social platforms to continue in this semi-open state for many years to come.

But another possibility is that today's social platforms represent a *16* transitional stage, like AOL and CompuServe in the 1990s. They were proprietary, centralized services that introduced millions of people to the wonders of the Internet, but they were eventually swept aside by the open web. Similarly, perhaps the core features of social networking and social media—maintaining lists of friends, and exchanging information with them—will move to an open, decentralized model. Such a model is possible for e-mail and web publishing because of the existence of agreed technical standards on how e-mail messages and web pages ought to be encoded and transmitted. Several such standards have already been proposed for decentralized or distributed social networks, though none has yet gained much traction. There will be technical difficulties synchronizing friend lists, maintaining privacy and security, and delivering updates quickly across millions of users, all of which give centralized social networks a clear advantage at the moment. But every time a major social network is involved in a privacy violation, an unpopular change in the terms of service, or a spat over censorship, a few more adventurous users decide to give one of the various decentralized social networks a try. "I think it's important to design new systems that work in a distributed way," says Tim Berners-Lee. "We must make systems in which people can collaborate together, but do it in a way that's decentralized, so it's not based on one central hub."

A decentralized social platform could be based around personal *17* silos of data over which users would have direct control. This approach would also address concerns that the new online public sphere that has been brought into being by social media is largely in the hands of private companies who are beholden to advertisers and shareholders rather than users. But there is another way for Facebook, Twitter, and other platforms to make themselves more accountable to users and less dependent on advertisers: to start charging users for some or all services. Many Internet services operate on a model in which a small percentage of paying customers subsidize a much larger number of nonpaying users. Social platforms could charge for things such as providing detailed analytics to commercial users of their platforms, more customization options for user profiles, or an advertising-free service. App.net, a subscription-funded Twitter-like service launched in September 2012, prides itself on being an "ad-free social network" that is based on "selling our product, not our users." This ensures, the company says, that its financial incentives are aligned with those of its members. Whether or not its particular model proves to have broad appeal, the future of social media is likely to see new models based on decentralized architectures and paying customers being added to the mix.

But whatever form social media takes in the future, one thing is clear: it is not going away. As this book has argued, social media is not new. It has been around for centuries. Today, blogs are the new pamphlets. Microblogs and online social networks are the new coffeehouses. Media-sharing sites are the new commonplace books. They are all shared, social platforms that enable ideas to travel from one person to another, rippling through networks of people connected by social bonds, rather than having to squeeze through the privileged bottleneck of broadcast media. The rebirth of social media in the Internet age represents a profound shift—and a return, in many respects, to the way things used to be.

9

From Identifying Claims to Analyzing Arguments

A **claim** is an assertion of fact or belief that needs to be supported with **evidence**—the information that backs up a claim. A main claim, or **thesis**, summarizes the writer's position on a situation and answers the question(s) the writer addresses. It also encompasses the minor claims, along with their supporting evidence, that the writer makes throughout the argument.

As readers, we need to identify a writer's main claim, or thesis, because it helps us organize our own understanding of the writer's argument. It acts as a signpost that tells us, "This is what the essay is about," "This is what I want you to pay attention to," and "This is how I want you to think, change, or act."

When you evaluate a claim, whether it is an argument's main claim or a minor claim, it is helpful to identify the type of claim it is: a claim of fact, a claim of value, or a claim of policy. You also need to evaluate the reasons for the claim and the evidence that supports it. Because academic argument should acknowledge multiple points of view, you should also be prepared to identify what, if any, concessions a writer offers his or her readers, and what counterarguments he or she anticipates from others in the conversation.

IDENTIFYING TYPES OF CLAIMS

To illustrate how to identify a writer's claims, let's take a look at a text written by an educator in the field of business ethics, Dana Radcliffe, that examines the relationship between social media and democracy.

112

The text is followed by our analysis of the types of claims (fact, value, and policy) and then, in the next section, of the nature of arguments (use of evidence, concessions, and counterarguments) the author presents.

DANA RADCLIFFE

Dashed Hopes: Why Aren't Social Media Delivering Democracy?

Dana Radcliffe has taught business ethics at the Samuel Curtis Johnson Graduate School of Management at Cornell University since 2000. As an adjunct at Syracuse University, he teaches ethics courses in the Maxwell School of Citizenship and Public Affairs and the College of Engineering and Computer Science. As a blogger for the *Huffington Post*, he has written about ethics in business, politics, and public policy. Professor Radcliffe earned a PhD from Syracuse University, an MBA from the University of California, Los Angeles, an MPhil in philosophy from Yale University, and a BA in philosophy from Fort Hays State University. This essay is a version of remarks presented to a session of the Pacific Council on International Policy, October 10, 2015. It follows up on his 2011 blog post "Can Social Media Undermine Democracy?"

■ ■ ■

Four years ago, in the months following the Arab Spring,[1] hopes ran high that the growing use of social media would bring a flowering of democracy throughout the world. Facebook and Twitter had helped dissidents drive tyrants from power in Tunisia, Egypt, and Libya. In established democracies, citizens' groups—most notably, the Tea Party in the U.S.—were influencing politics by leveraging social media. Indeed, a *Forbes* cover story on the power of social media concluded that "the world is becoming more democratic and reflective of the will of ordinary people."

Sadly, such optimism proved ill-founded. Now, in 2015, popular government seems to be receding globally. With the qualified exception of Tunisia, the Arab Spring did not transform dictatorships into democracies, and democratic governments seem unable to find consensus solutions to many pressing policy questions. What happened? Why haven't social media made the world more democratic?

In seeking an answer, we can begin with [the] nature of democracy itself. Because a country's citizens have competing interests and values, their effectively governing themselves through elections of leaders

[1] *Editor's note:* Arab Spring was a revolutionary wave of demonstrations, protests, and civil wars that began on December 17, 2010. Most insurgencies occurred in Syria, Libya, and Yemen, with uprisings in other countries, including Saudi Arabia, Iraq, Algeria, Kuwait, and Morocco.

and other democratic processes requires *deliberation*. It requires that citizens and their representatives discuss and debate what the government should or should not do, defending their views by appealing to shared principles and purposes. As one scholar, Daniel Gayo-Avello, recently observed, "Deliberation is crucial in modern democracy . . . Proper democratic deliberation assumes that citizens are equal participants, opposing viewpoints are not only accepted but encouraged, and that the main goal is to achieve 'rationally motivated consensus.'" Political philosophers Amy Gutmann and Dennis Thompson, in their influential *Democracy and Disagreement* (Belknap, 1996), point out that "the demand for deliberation has been a familiar theme in the American constitutional tradition. It is integral to the ideal of republican government as the founders understood it. James Madison judged the design of political institutions in part by how well they furthered deliberation."

To be sure, "deliberative democracy" is an ideal to which existing democratic systems only roughly approximate. Nevertheless, the concept provides a plausible standard for evaluating democracies. Moreover, it reminds us that the health of a democracy depends in large part on its fostering deliberation that leads to policies whose legitimacy most citizens accept. Hence, the impact of social media on democratic deliberation may help explain why they have not brought about a new global era of democracy. *4*

The issue here is the political power of social media, and it entails three key questions: What power do they confer? Who possesses that power? How do those who have the power use it? *5*

First, the power of social media is evident. Functionally, it is the ability to communicate, instantaneously, with a large number of people. Politically, it is the power to inform or misinform, to engage or manipulate, to mobilize or control. In general, it is the power to affect, directly and on a vast scale, the political beliefs and actions of citizens. *6*

Second, when the government controls social media, this power is in its hands. When the government does not control social media, its political power belongs to citizens who can access them and is exercised by groups of like-minded individuals who use them to organize and coordinate political activities. *7*

Third, as for how the political power of social media is wielded by those who possess them, recent history gives us some salient examples: *8*

- Protesters using them in organizing mass demonstrations against oppressive governments during the Arab Spring;
- the Chinese government's allowing critics of public officials and policies to "vent" online but tightly censoring calls for collective action;

- the Russian government's employing its immense digital propaganda machine to convince many Europeans that the CIA shot down the Malaysian airliner over Ukraine;
- the Islamic State's utilizing social media to recruit disaffected Muslim youths from around the world;
- in 2008, the Obama campaign's innovative application of social media to raise record amounts of money from small donors and customize its messages to different demographics;
- the use of social media by an impassioned minority of Americans angry at "big government" to form and advance the Tea Party movement.

In all these cases, social media were—or are—used as *political weapons*. Of course, I am not implying moral equivalence in these examples. My point is that the political power of social media has been used most effectively in *adversarial* contexts—in circumstances of *struggle* or *competition*. In those cases, the regime, organization, or group holding the power uses it against individuals, groups, or institutions whose interests or goals conflict with theirs. Consequently, whether they are revolutionaries, totalitarian governments, candidates for office, or special interests, political partisans using social media as tactical weapons are not concerned about *deliberation*. 9

Who, then, cares about promoting democratic deliberation? It is citizens and leaders who understand that democratic processes necessitate deliberative disagreement and, in the legislative process, negotiation and compromise. However, when these advocates of democracy look to social media to establish and strengthen democratic processes, they encounter a basic problem: social media appear unsuited to serve as forums of political deliberation. Research into online behavior suggests several reasons: 10

- Users tend not to seek opportunities to engage in serious political dialogue with people whose views differ from their own. Rather, as social media expert Curtis Hougland notes, "people choose to reinforce their existing political opinions through their actions online."
- A recent Pew Research Center report offers evidence that people are much less willing to post their political views on social media when they believe their followers would disagree with them.
- Daniel Gayo-Avello has found that "when political discussions occur they are not rational and democratic deliberations . . . [because] political information in social media generally lacks quality and strong arguments, is usually incoherent and highly opinionated."

To these I would add some intuitions of mine: *11*

- When people who have strong political opinions avoid engaging opponents in reasoned debate but have them bolstered by social media followers, they tend to become more rigid in those views—and so, are even less interested in democratic deliberation.

- As a result, political partisans connected through social media tend to oppose legislative compromises on their pet issues, demanding that elected representatives they support "stand on principle," regardless of political realities or the common good.

- Finally, perhaps because using social media is, physically, a solitary activity, it tends not to cultivate civic virtues—such as respect for opponents—that Gutmann and Thompson argue are critical to democratic deliberation.

In short, with regard to political discussion, current use of social   *12*
media favors affinity over engagement, expression over debate, silence over disagreement, dogmatism over compromise, and—toward opponents—disdain over respect. This, I believe, is largely why we have so far been unable to move beyond the use of social media as political weapons to make them instruments of deliberative democracy.

■ Identify Claims of Fact

Claims of fact are assertions (or arguments) that seek to define or classify something or establish *that a problem or condition has existed, exists, or will exist*. Claims of fact are made by individuals who believe that something is true; but claims are never simply facts, and some claims are more objective, and so easier to verify, than others.

For example, "It's raining in Portland today" is a "factual" claim of fact; it's easily verified. But consider the argument some make that the steel and automotive industries in the United States have depleted our natural resources and left us at a crisis point. This is an assertion that a condition exists. A careful reader must examine the basis for this kind of claim: Are we truly facing a crisis? And if so, are the steel and automotive industries truly responsible? A number of politicians counter this claim of fact by insisting that if the government were to harness the vast natural resources in Alaska, there would be no "crisis." This is also a claim of fact, in this case an assertion that a condition will exist in the future. Again, it is based on evidence, evidence gathered from various sources that indicates sufficient resources in Alaska to keep up with our increasing demands for resources and to allay a potential crisis.

Our point is that most claims of fact are debatable and challenge us to provide evidence to verify our arguments. They may be based on factual information, but they are not necessarily true. Most claims of fact present **interpretations** of evidence derived from **inferences**. That is, a writer will examine evidence (for example, about the quantity of natural resources in Alaska and the rate that industries harness those resources and process them into goods), draw a conclusion based on reasoning (an inference), and offer an explanation based on that conclusion (an interpretation).

So, for example, an academic writer will study the evidence on the quantity of natural resources in Alaska and the rate that industries harness those resources and process them into goods; only after the writer makes an informed decision on whether Alaska's resources are sufficient to keep pace with the demand for them will he or she take a position on the issue.

Claims that seek to define or classify are also claims of fact. For example, researchers have sought to define a range of behaviors such as autism that actually resist simple definition. After all, autism exists along a behavioral spectrum attributed variably to genetics and environment. Psychologists have indeed tried to define autism using a diagnostic tool to characterize behaviors associated with communication and social interaction. However, definitions of autism have changed over time, reflecting changing criteria for assessing human behavior and the perspective one takes. So do we in fact have a "crisis" in the over diagnosis of autistic behaviors as some have claimed? For that matter, who gets to decide what counts as a crisis?

Let's now come to Radcliffe's claim of fact that social media services have not fulfilled the promise of fostering a more democratic world, nor have they promoted (as the *Forbes* article asserts) "the will of ordinary people." Despite a few exceptions in which social media services have empowered democratic change, Radcliffe's review of the global political climate forces readers to reconsider claims that connect social media and the growth of democracy. Do social media services actually have a causal relationship with the Arab Spring—the wave of insurrections across the Middle East that triggered subsequent shifts to democracy? Radcliffe takes issue with this apparently factual **causal claim**. But the careful reader will want to see how Radcliffe goes about challenging others' claims to support his own claim of fact that "such optimism proved ill-founded." Note how he asks questions to propel his argument ("What happened? Why haven't social media made the world more democratic?") and provides a claim of definition. Radcliffe's **definitional claim** serves as an important rhetorical strategy for making an argument about what democracy is and the conditions that exist to support democratic principles. After all, how can others maintain that social media services such as Twitter and Facebook foster the spread of democracy if they have not defined a key term like "democracy"? This is especially true if a primary component of democracy is what Radcliffe describes as a "deliberative process."

We invite you to examine Radcliffe's primary claim and the evidence he uses to challenge a prevailing argument in the media and to support his own view that a true democracy "requires that citizens and their representatives discuss and debate what the government should or should not do, defending their views by appealing to shared principles and purposes." Does he convincingly present his argument that others overstate the effect of social media because, at least implicitly, they fail to adequately define democracy and the democratic process? That is, do you accept his definition as the standard—or at least a plausible standard rooted in a **factual claim**—upon which to measure others' arguments? Do social media services confer power? If so, who uses such power, and how do they use it? Finally, to what extent do social media services act as adequate forums for deliberation?

▪ Identify Claims of Value

A claim of fact is different from a **claim of value**, which *expresses an evaluation of a problem or condition that has existed, exists, or will exist*. Is a condition good or bad? Is it important or inconsequential?

For example, an argument that developing the wilderness in Alaska would irreversibly mar the beauty of the land indicates that the writer values the beauty of the land over the possible benefits of development. A claim of value presents a judgment, which is sometimes signaled by a value-laden word like *ugly*, *beautiful*, or *immoral*, but may also be conveyed more subtly by the writer's tone and attitude.

Radcliffe makes a claim of value when he concludes by stating "with regard to political discussion, current use of social media favors affinity over engagement, expression over debate, silence over disagreement, dogmatism over compromise, and—toward opponents—disdain over respect." This statement follows from Radcliffe's initial observation that use of social media does not support the "reflective . . . will of ordinary people," and from the evidence presents that social media services can be detrimental to the will of people when controlled by oppressive leaders. He writes, "When people who have strong political opinions avoid engaging opponents in reasoned debate but have them bolstered by social media followers, they tend to become more rigid in those views. . . . As a result, political partisans connected through social media tend to oppose legislative compromises on their pet issues . . . regardless of political realities or the common good." Radcliffe underscores these observations in the final paragraph: "This, I believe, is largely why we have so far been unable to move beyond the use of social media as political weapons to make them instruments of deliberative democracy." This may seem like a claim of fact, but Radcliffe's claim is based on interpretation of the evidence he presents and the definition he establishes as the standard on which to judge whether a country is democratic. Whether you are persuaded by Radcliffe's claim depends on the evidence and reasons he uses for support. We discuss the nature of evidence and what constitutes "good" reasons later in this chapter.

▪ Identify Claims of Policy

A **claim of policy** is an argument for what should be the case, *that a condition should exist*. It is a call for change or a solution to a problem.

Two recent controversies on college campuses center on claims of policy. One has activists arguing that universities and colleges should have a policy that all workers on campus earn a living wage. The other has activists arguing that universities and colleges should have a policy that prevents them from investing in countries where the government ignores human rights. Claims of policy are often signaled by words like *should* and *must*: "For public universities to live up to their democratic mission, they *must* provide all their workers with a living wage."

In "Ten Ways Social Media Can Improve Campaign Engagement and Reinvigorate American Democracy," political scientist Darrell West describes how social media can "reinvigorate American democracy." West develops an argument that echoes Dana Radcliffe's claim that social media services do not foster or promote democratic practices, much less the kind of civic engagement that others (such as the author of the *Forbes* article Radcliffe cites) suggest. Although West makes a **claim of fact** when he observes that "Despite social networking's track record for generating democratic engagement . . . it has proven difficult to sustain political interest and activism online over time and move electronic engagement from campaigns to governance," he is most concerned with fostering policies that increase interest in the political process.

West describes a meeting of experts at the Brookings Institute, where participants share ways to encourage grassroots efforts to create change and govern at local, state, and national levels. One participant, political consultant Mindy Finn, argues that political advocacy "should take advantage of [social] networks to set the agenda and drive civic discussions," explaining that advocacy should "involve everything from the questions that get asked during debates to the manner in which journalists cover the election." Finn appears less interested in the deliberative process that preoccupies Radcliffe and embraces the role that social media can play in motivating citizenship and engagement. Another participant, professor of government Diana Owens, suggests that universities "[should] take on the responsibility as a matter of policy to increase civic education for political action." A policy claim points readers to a set of actions they can take in the future, and West's participants all declare policies they would like to see pursued.

Not all writers make their claims as explicitly as these authors do, and it is possible that claims of fact may seem like interpretive claims, as they are based on the inferences we draw from evidence. Thus, it is the writer's task to make a distinction between a claim of fact and interpretation with sufficient evidence. But you should be able to identify the different types of claims. Moreover, you should keep in mind what the situation is and what kind of argument can best address what you see as a problem. Ask yourself: Does the situation involve a question of fact? Does the situation involve a question of value? Does the situation require a change in policy? Or is some combination at work?

120 CHAPTER 9 | FROM IDENTIFYING CLAIMS TO ANALYZING ARGUMENTS

Steps to Identifying Claims

1 **Ask:** Does the argument assert that a problem or condition has existed, exists, or will exist? Does the argument seek to establish that a definition is true and can serve as a standard for making relevant judgments? Does the argument ask you to accept the premise that one thing has caused another? If so, it's claim of fact.

2 **Ask:** Does the argument express an evaluation of a problem or condition that has existed, exists, or will exist? If so, it's a claim of value.

3 **Ask:** Does the argument call for change, and is it directed at some future action? If so, it's a claim of policy.

A Practice Sequence: Identifying Claims

What follows is a series of claims. Identify each one as a claim of fact, value, or policy. Be prepared to justify your categorizations.

1 Taxing the use of fossil fuels will end the energy crisis.

2 We should reform the welfare system to ensure that people who receive support from the government also work.

3 Images of violence in the media create a culture of violence in schools.

4 The increase in homelessness is a deplorable situation that contradicts the whole idea of democracy.

5 Distributing property taxes more equitably is the one sure way to end poverty and illiteracy.

6 Individual votes don't really count.

7 Despite the 20 percent increase in the number of females in the workforce over the past forty years, women are still not treated equitably.

8 Affirmative action is a policy that has outlived its usefulness.

9 There are a disproportionate number of black males in American prisons.

10 The media are biased, which means we cannot count on newspapers or television news for the truth.

ANALYZING ARGUMENTS

Analyzing an argument involves identifying the writer's main and minor claims and then examining (1) the reasons and evidence given in support of each claim, (2) the writer's concessions, and (3) the writer's attempts to handle counterarguments.

■ Analyze the Reasons Used to Support a Claim

Stating a claim is one thing; supporting that claim is another. As a critical reader, you need to evaluate whether a writer has provided *good reasons* to support his or her position. Specifically, you will need to decide whether the support for a claim is recent, relevant, reliable, and accurate. As a writer, you will need to use the same criteria when you support your claims.

Is the source recent? Knowledgeable readers of your written arguments not only will be aware of classic studies that you should cite as "intellectual touchstones"; they will also expect you to cite recent evidence, evidence published within five years of when you are writing.

Of course, older research can be valuable. For example, in a paper about molecular biology, you might very well cite James Watson and Francis Crick's groundbreaking 1953 study in which they describe the structure of DNA. That study is an intellectual touchstone that changed the life sciences in a fundamental way.

Or if you were writing about educational reform, you might very well mention E. D. Hirsch's 1987 book *Cultural Literacy*. Hirsch's book did not change the way people think about curricular reform as profoundly as Watson and Crick's study changed the way scientists think about biology, but his term *cultural literacy* continues to serve as useful shorthand for a particular way of thinking about curricular reform that remains influential to this day.

Although citing Hirsch is an effective way to suggest you have studied the history of an educational problem, it will not convince your readers that there is a crisis in education today. To establish that, you would need to use as evidence studies published over the past few years to show, for example, that there has been a steady decline in test scores since Hirsch wrote his book. And you would need to support your claim that curricular reform is the one sure way to bring an end to illiteracy and poverty with data that are much more current than those available to Hirsch in the 1980s. No one would accept the judgment that our schools are in crisis if your most recent citation is decades old.

Is the source relevant? Evidence that is relevant must have real bearing on your issue. It also depends greatly on what your readers expect. For example, suppose two of your friends complain that they were unable to sell their condominiums for the price they asked. You can claim there is a crisis in the housing market, but your argument won't convince most readers if your only evidence is personal anecdote.

Such *anecdotal evidence* may alert you to a possible topic and help you connect with your readers, but you will need to test the **relevance** of your friends' experience—Is it pertinent? Is it typical of a larger situation or condition?—if you want your readers to take your argument seriously. For example, you might scan real estate listings to see what the asking prices are for properties comparable to your friends' properties. By comparing listings, you are defining the grounds for your argument. If your friends are disappointed that their one-bedroom condominiums sold for less than a three-bedroom condominium with deeded parking in the same neighborhood, it may well be that their expectations were too high.

In other words, if you aren't comparing like things, your argument is going to be seriously flawed. If your friends' definition of what constitutes a "reasonable price" differs dramatically from everyone else's, their experience is probably irrelevant to the larger question of whether the local housing market is depressed.

Is the source reliable? You also need to evaluate whether the data you use to support your argument are reliable. After all, some researchers present findings based on a very small sample of people that can also be rather selective.

For example, a researcher might argue that 67 percent of the people he cited believe that school and residential integration are important concerns. But how many people did this person interview? More important, who responded to the researcher's questions? A reliable claim cannot be based on a few of the researcher's friends.

Let's return to the real estate example. You have confirmed that your friends listed their condominiums at prices that were not out of line with the market. Now what? You need to seek out reliable sources to continue testing your argument. For example, you might search the real estate or business section of your local newspaper to see if there are any recent stories about a softening of the market; and you might talk with several local real estate agents to get their opinions on the subject.

In consulting local newspapers and local agents, you are looking for **authoritative sources** against which to test your anecdotal evidence—the confirmation of experts who report on, study, evaluate, and have an informed opinion on local real estate. Local real estate agents are a source of **expert testimony**, firsthand confirmation of the information you have discovered. You would probably not want to rely on the testimony of a single real estate agent, who may have a bias; instead, talk with several agents to see if a consensus emerges.

Is the source accurate? To determine the accuracy of a study that you want to use to support your argument, you have to do a little digging to find out who else has made a similar claim. For instance, if you want to cite authoritative research that compares the dropout rate for white students with the rate for students of color, you could look at research conducted by the Civil Rights Project. Of course, you don't need to stop your search there. You could also check the resources available through the National Center for Education Statistics. You want to show your readers that you have done a relatively thorough search to make your argument as persuasive as possible.

The accuracy of **statistics**—factual information presented numerically or graphically (for example, in a pie or bar chart)—is difficult to verify. To a certain extent, then, their veracity has to be taken on faith. Often the best you can do is assure yourself that the source of your statistical information is authoritative and reliable—government and major research universities generally are "safe" sources—and that whoever is interpreting the statistical information is not distorting it.

Returning again to our real estate example, let's say you've read a newspaper article that cites statistical information about the condition of the local real estate market (for example, the average price of property and volume of sales this year in comparison to last year). Presumably the author of the article is an expert, but he or she may be interpreting rather than simply reporting on the statistics.

To reassure yourself one way or the other, you may want to check the sources of the author's statistics—go right to your source's sources—which a responsible author will cite. That will allow you to look over the raw data and come to your own conclusions. A further step you could take would be to discuss the article with other experts—local real estate agents—to find out what they think of the article and the information it presents.

Now, let's go back to Dana Radcliffe's essay. How does he develop his assertion that social media services do not foster democratic principles of deliberation or help participants engage in serious dialogue about views different from their own? For that matter, how does Radcliffe arrive at the conclusion—or claim—that "social media appear unsuited to serve as forums of political deliberation?" Radcliffe first establishes what he sees as a plausible standard for defining deliberation as a key principle underlying a democratic society. He bolsters his argument by citing two well-known political philosophers, Amy Gutmann and Dennis Thompson, whose influential *Democracy and Disagreement* (Belknap, 1996) he quotes: "They point out that the demand for deliberation has been a familiar theme in the American constitutional tradition. It is integral to the ideal of republican government as the founders understood it. James Madison judged the design of political institutions in part by how well they furthered deliberation." Importantly, Gutmann and Thompson cite former president and founding father James Madison to identify deliberation as a significant component of democracy and a standard with which to measure the extent to which a society promotes democratic principles.

Radcliffe then makes a series of observations about events that have occurred across the world since the Arab Spring. He points out that the Chinese government seems to allow "critics of public officials and policies to 'vent' online but tightly censors calls for collective action." He also suggests that the Islamic State uses "social media to recruit disaffected Muslim youths from around the world," and as you will note, he uses additional examples to illustrate the extent to which social media services have been "used as *political weapons*." As readers, we may take for granted that Radcliffe's observations are based in "fact," but Radcliffe does not actually cite sources of his "data" to show that "the regime, organization, or group holding the power uses it against individuals, groups, or institutions whose interests or goals conflict with theirs." You would be right to question the basis of such a claim.

In advancing his claim that social media does not support democratic engagement, Radcliffe relies on authoritative sources to explain the behavior of those who use social media. He cites a recent Pew Research Center report, which "offers evidence that people are much less willing to post their political views on social media when they believe their followers would disagree with them." The Pew Research Center describes itself as a "nonpartisan, non-advocacy group" whose aim is to stimulate citizen involvement in community issues and conduct research on public opinion on social and political issues. Radcliffe also cites Daniel Gayo-Avello, who concludes that "when political discussions occur they are not rational and democratic deliberations . . . [because] political information in social media generally lacks quality and strong arguments [and] is usually incoherent and highly opinionated." A professor of computer science at the University of Oviedo in Spain who conducts social media research, Gayo-Avello serves as a credible source of data to support Radcliffe's claim. However, as critical readers, we should inquire into the nature of authors' claims, the source of evidence, and the accuracy of the information authors rely on to advance their claims.

■ Identify Concessions

Part of the strategy of developing a main claim supported with good reasons is to offer a **concession**, an acknowledgment that readers may not agree with every point the writer is making. A concession is a writer's way of saying, "Okay, I can see that there may be another way of looking at the issue or another way to interpret the evidence used to support the argument I am making."

For instance, you may not want your energy costs to go up, but after examining the reasons why it may be necessary to increase taxes on gasoline—to lower usage and conserve fossil fuels—you might concede that a tax increase on gasoline could be useful. The willingness to make concessions is valued in academic writing because it acknowledges both complexity and the importance of multiple perspectives. It also acknowledges the fact that information can always be interpreted in different ways.

Dana Radcliffe makes a concession when he acknowledges that not every reader will define democracy as he does, with an emphasis on deliberation. "Who, then, cares about promoting democratic deliberation?" He maintains that much is at stake for readers who identify with the value he attaches to deliberation as a core principle of democracy: "It is citizens and leaders who understand that democratic processes necessitate deliberative disagreement and, in the legislative process, negotiation and compromise."

Often a writer will signal concessions with phrases like the following:

- "It is true that . . ."
- "I agree with X that Y is an important factor to consider."
- "Some studies have convincingly shown that . . ."

Generally, the writer will then go on to address the concession, explaining how it needs to be modified or abandoned in the light of new evidence or the writer's perspective on the issue.

■ Identify Counterarguments

As the term suggests, a **counterargument** is an argument raised in response to another argument. You want to be aware of and acknowledge what your readers may object to in your argument. Anticipating readers' objections is an important part of developing a conversational argument.

For example, if you were arguing in support of universal health care, you would have to acknowledge that the approach departs dramatically from the traditional role the federal government has played in providing health insurance. That is, most people's access to health insurance has depended on their individual ability to afford and purchase this kind of insurance. You would have to anticipate how readers would respond to your proposal, especially readers who do not feel that the federal government should ever play a role in what has typically been an individual responsibility.

Anticipating readers' objections demonstrates that you understand the complexity of the issue and are willing at least to entertain different and conflicting opinions.

In Dana Radcliffe's essay on social media and democracy, he implicitly concedes that not all readers will care about promoting deliberative democracy; he acknowledges a possible counterargument by citing a *Forbes* article, the author of which contends that "the world is becoming more democratic and reflective of the will of ordinary people." Of course, this is the point that Radcliffe takes issue with, one that clearly resonates for others. Radcliffe remains mindful of critical readers when he reiterates the counterargument that challenges his very definition of whether a nation promotes democracy. "To be sure, 'deliberative democracy' is an ideal to which existing democratic systems only roughly approximate. Nevertheless, the concept provides a plausible standard for evaluating democracies." That is, he recognizes that his definition is the "ideal" and that few governments in practice actually reflect this ideal. But he is invested in such an idea and returns to his original premise: "Nevertheless, the concept provides a plausible standard for evaluating democracies. Moreover, it reminds us that the health of a democracy depends in large part on its fostering deliberation that leads to policies whose legitimacy most citizens accept."

In an argument that is more conversational than confrontational, writers establish areas of common ground, both to convey different views that are understood and to acknowledge the conditions under which those different views are valid. Writers do this by making concessions and anticipating and responding to counterarguments.

This conversational approach is what many people call a **Rogerian approach to argument**, based on psychologist Carl Rogers's approach to psychotherapy. The objective of a Rogerian strategy is to reduce listeners' sense of threat so that they are open to alternatives. For academic writers, it involves four steps:

1. Conveying to readers that their different views are understood.
2. Acknowledging conditions under which readers' views are valid.
3. Helping readers see that the writer shares common ground with them.
4. Creating mutually acceptable solutions to agreed-on problems.

The structure of an argument, according to the Rogerian approach, grows out of the give-and-take of conversation between two people and the topic under discussion. In a written conversation, the give-and-take of face-to-face conversation takes the form of anticipating readers' counterarguments and uses language that is both empathetic and respectful, to put the readers at ease.

AN ANNOTATED STUDENT ARGUMENT

We have annotated the following essay to show the variety of claims the student writer uses, as well as some of the other argumentative moves he performs. The assignment was to write an argument out of personal experience and observation about the cultural impact of a technological innovation. Marques Camp chose to write about the Kindle, an electronic reading device developed by the online retailer Amazon that allows users to download books for a fee. The user cannot share the download electronically with other users. Camp touches on a number of issues reflected in his claims.

As you read the essay, imagine how you would respond to his various claims. Which do you agree with, which do you disagree with, and why? What evidence would you present to support or counter his claims? Do you detect a main claim? Do you think his overall essay develops and supports it?

AN ANNOTATED STUDENT ARGUMENT   **127**

Camp 1

Marques Camp
Professor Fells
English 1020
January 28, 20 —
The End of the World May Be Nigh, and It's the Kindle's Fault

"Libraries will in the end become cities."
— Gottfried Wilhelm Leibniz, German polymath

The student presents a claim of fact that others have made.

The future of written human history will come, as they will have us believe, in the form of the Amazon Kindle and its millions of titles, ready to change the way people read, ready to revolutionize the way people see the world.

He lays the basis for a counterargument by questioning whether this is a real threat at all, citing some technological precedents.

The Kindle is a signpost for our times, a major checkpoint in our long and adventurous journey from the world of printed paper to the twenty-first-century world of digitalization. We first saw this paradigm shift with newspapers, where weekly columns were taken over by daily blog posts, where 48-point sans-serif headlines transformed into 12-point Web links. We then moved on into television, where Must-See TV was replaced with On-Demand TV, where consumers no longer sat around in the living room with their families during prime time but rather watched the latest episode of their favorite show commercial-free from the comfortable and convenient confines of their laptop, able to fast-forward, rewind, and pause with a delightful and devilish sense of programming omnipotence. We are now seeing it, slowly but surely, slay the giant that we never thought could be slain: the world of books.

In this paragraph, he makes a claim of fact about unequal access to technological innovation and offers a concession to what many see as the value of the Kindle.

Contrary to popular belief, easier access to a wider quantity of literature is not a universal revolution. The Kindle speaks to the world that measures quantity by the number of cable television channels it has, speed by the connectivity of its wireless networks, and distance by the number of miles a family travels for vacation. Yes, the Kindle is the new paradigm for universal access and literary connectivity. But it is much like a college degree in the sense that it is merely a gateway to a wealth of opportunity. The problem, however, is gaining access to this gateway in the first place.

1

2

3

128   CHAPTER 9 | FROM IDENTIFYING CLAIMS TO ANALYZING ARGUMENTS

Camp 2

He supports his claim of fact with evidence based on experience: that sharing books provides something technology cannot offer.

Books often pass from hand to hand, from friend to friend, from generation to generation, many times with the mutual understanding that remuneration is not necessary — merely the promise of hope that the new reader is as touched and enlightened by the book as the previous one. This transfer serves more than a utilitarian function; symbolically, it represents the passage of hope, of knowledge, of responsibility.

Evidence from observation: not everyone has access to new technologies, but people will always have access to books.

The book, in many cases, represents the only sort of hope for the poorest among us, the great equalizer in a world full of financial and intellectual capital and highly concentrated access to this capital. The wonderful quality of the book is that its intellectual value is very rarely proportional to its financial value; people often consider their most valuable book to be one they happened to pick up one day for free.

An evaluative claim — that the widening gap between rich and poor is danger-ous — adds another layer to the argument.

The proliferation of the Kindle technology, however, will result in a wider disconnect between the elite and the non-elite — as the old saying goes, the rich will get richer and the poor will get poorer. Unfortunately for the poor, this is no financial disconnect — this is a widening of the gap in the world of ideas. And this is, perhaps, the most dangerous gap of all.

A further evaluative claim — that new tech-nological devices offer little hope to "victims" of illiteracy — is followed by a claim of fact that books inspire people to create change in the world.

The Kindle Revolution, ironically, may end up contributing to the very disease that is antithetical to its implied function: illiteracy. Make no mistake, the Kindle was not designed with the poor in mind. For those in most need of the printed word, for those who are the most vulnerable victims of the illiteracy threat, the pricey Kindle offers little in the way of hope. One book for a poor person is all he or she needs to be inspired and change the world; with the Kindle, that one book is consolidated and digitized, transformed from a tangible piece of hope and the future into a mere collection of words in the theoretically infinite dimension of cyberspace. A "book" on the Kindle is a book wedged among many other books, separated by nothing more than title, devoid of essence, devoid of uniqueness, devoid of personality, devoid of its unique position in space — precisely what makes a book a "book," as opposed to a mere collection of words. It is no longer singular, no longer serendipitous, no longer distinguishable.

The e-book cannot, like a bound book, pass through multiple hands and eventually settle itself on the right person, ready

4

5

6

7

8

AN ANNOTATED STUDENT ARGUMENT **129**

Camp 3

An evaluative claim in which the author observes that technology can make reading passive. Then a claim of fact: that the experience of reading can be transformative.

to be unleashed as a tool to change the world. Due to the restrictions on sharing and reselling e-books with the Kindle, the very nature of reading books transforms from highly communal to individualistic, from highly active to somewhat passive. The Kindle will lead to the mystification of books, wherein they become less unique capsules of thoughts and ideas and experiences and more utility-oriented modes of information-giving. What many Kindle advocates fail to realize is that oftentimes, the transformative quality of books resides less in the actual words comprising the book and more in the actual experience of reading.

The student offers a final evaluative claim, observing that the Kindle threatens to mask the relationship between ideas and the world.

His concluding claim falls just short of making a proposal — but he does suggest that those in positions of power must ensure the proliferation of books.

There is also something to be said for the utter corporeality of books that lies at the heart of Leibniz's metaphor. Libraries are physical testaments to all that we have learned and recorded during human history. The sheer size of libraries and the sheer number of volumes residing in them tell us, in a spatial sense, of all the theoretical knowledge we have accumulated in the course of our existence, and all the power we have to further shape and define the world we live in. The Kindle and other digital literary technologies are threatening the very connection between the world of ideas and the material world, threatening to take our literal measures of progress and hide them away in the vast database of words and ideas, available only to those with money to spare and a credit card for further purchases.

9

If libraries will indeed become cities, then we need to carefully begin to lay the foundations, book on top of book on top of book, and we are going to have to ensure that we have enough manpower to do it.

10

Steps to Analyzing an Argument

1 **Identify the type of claim.** Is it a claim of fact? Value? Policy?

2 **Analyze the reasons used to support the claim.** Are they recent? Relevant? Reliable? Accurate?

3 **Identify concessions.** Is there another argument that even the author acknowledges is legitimate?

4 **Identify counterarguments.** What arguments contradict or challenge the author's position?

130 CHAPTER 9 | FROM IDENTIFYING CLAIMS TO ANALYZING ARGUMENTS

A Practice Sequence: Analyzing an Argument

Use the criteria in the "Steps to Analyzing an Argument" box to analyze the following blog post by Susan D. Blum. What types of claim does she advance? What seems to be her main claim? Do you find her reasons recent, relevant, reliable, and accurate? What sort of concessions does she make? What counterarguments would you raise?

SUSAN D. BLUM

The United States of (Non)Reading: The End of Civilization or a New Era?

Susan D. Blum is a professor of anthropology at the University of Notre Dame whose wide areas of professional interest and expertise include Asian studies and education. She has written or edited many publications, including *Portraits of "Primitives": Ordering Human Kinds in the Chinese Nation* (2001), *My Word! Plagiarism and College Culture* (2009), and *Making Sense of Language: Readings in Culture and Communication* (2009; 2013). She also writes the Learning versus Schooling blog for the *Huffington Post*, where this essay was posted on October 8, 2013.

■ ■ ■

Just the other day one of my undergraduate assistants reported a friend's boast that he had not read anything for school since fifth grade. A student at an excellent university, successful, "clever," "smart," he can write papers, take exams, participate in class or online discussions. Why would he have to read?

Students sometimes don't buy the class books. Professors are shocked. 2

Several years ago a student told me that she regarded all assigned 3 reading as "recommended," even if the professors labeled it "required." Were professors so dumb that they didn't know that?

The idea of assigned reading, as the core activity of college students, 4 is old. Students don't see it as central; faculty do.

And though I used to, and sometimes still do, spend a lot of energy 5 lamenting this, by taking a broader view of the nature of reading and writing, I have come to understand it and even to some extent accept it.

Student avoidance of reading is not an entirely new problem. When 6 I was in graduate school, in the 1980s, one of my most indelible memories was of a new classmate, straight out of a first-rate college, complaining in our anthropology theory class that we had to keep finding out what other people thought. When was it time for us to convey our viewpoints? Why all that reading?

Some college course evaluations ask students what percentage of the reading they did. Some report they did as much as 90 percent. Some as little as 25 percent.

In a systematic study of college students' reading, Kylie Baier and four colleagues reported that students mostly (40 percent) read for exams. Almost 19 percent don't read for class. In terms of time, 94 percent of students spend less than two hours on any given reading for class; 62 percent spend less than an hour. Thirty-two percent believe they could get an A without reading; 89 percent believe they could get at least a C.

Among many other educational crises, there is a perceived crisis given that "students are increasingly reading less and less."

When faculty enter new institutions, they often ask colleagues: How much reading should I assign? Some departments offer guidelines about the number of pages: Assign twenty-five pages for each meeting of first-year classes, but no more than one hundred pages a week for any course. This has always struck me as strange, given that a page of a novel and a page of a double-column textbook have completely different amounts of text, and take different kinds of attention and time. In response to this faculty challenge, Steve Volk—named the Carnegie Professor of the Year in 2011, so he knows something about teaching—wrote on the Web site of Oberlin College's Center for Teaching Innovation and Excellence that there is no magic formula for numbers of pages. He suggests instead that faculty consider "What do you want the reading to do?"

But it is not only college teachers who worry about how much people are reading. There is a widespread belief that Americans in general read less and less. This perception builds on public conversations about the lack of reading. In 2007 a National Endowment for the Arts study concluded that adults' reading habits were in severe decline. Only 57 percent of adults read a book voluntarily in 2002, down from 61 percent in 1992.

This was supposed to have all sorts of terrible consequences: educational, of course, but also economic, social, moral, you name it.

Reversing the cup-half-empty conclusion, a 2013 study showed that more than half read books for pleasure—just not what the NEA defines (or would if the Government were functioning) as "literature."

And the Pew interpretation was that if reading for work and school is added to "voluntary reading," then almost all people read "books" at some point during the year: 79 percent of 18 to 24 year-olds, and 90 percent of 16 to 17 year-olds.

It is undeniable that people are reading (looking at) writing all the time. It may not be in physical books, however. And just this week, *USA Today* argued that digital devices increase book reading (on the devices). 15

David Carr wrote in 2008 about the decline in attention—not only in our students. Attention spans, focus, mindfulness . . . all these are shrinking. Technology plays a role in this, as many of us spend much of our lives looking at short items. *The Onion*, the humor website, puts most of its efforts into its headlines. Blogs should be at most one thousand words, but three hundred is better. (This one is too long.) 16

So if students are sipping text constantly on their devices, and suddenly they are asked to consume what sounds like an insurmountable mountain of pages in some other form—and for what!?—they are likely to avoid it entirely. 17

"Flipping the classroom" has attempted to seek some kind of accountability from students for their reading, so that they have to engage in one way or another with their material prior to assembling for the precious moment of face-to-face interaction. This requires reading—but reading with a goal. Students often like to do that, as a kind of scavenger hunt for what is useful and important. Just having them read for background ideas seems to be fading. 18

Actually, I have stopped worrying constantly about this. Students are reading. The public is reading. They may not sit for hours, still and attentive, and focus on one item. They may confuse their facts. They may miss a complex argument. 19

Don't misunderstand. I worship reading. When I travel for three days, in addition to all my devices I bring six books and five (print) magazines. Yet I cannot concentrate the way I used to. So those less devoted. . . . Should we cut them off from the world, isolate them in soundproof rooms with no WiFi, and force them to read a book? 20

Writing has evolved, and will evolve. And with it reading changes. From clay tablets designed to record debts to bronze proclamations of kings and emperors, from bamboo strips recording rituals to complex philosophical arguments on paper, from paintings for the royal afterlife to paperback novels, from stone tablets proclaiming a new moral code to infinitesimal elements on a shiny handheld device—from its origins, writing has transformed, and will continue to change. It is not entirely that the medium is the message, but the medium affects the message. Since humans are the ones doing the writing, we get the writing that suits our purposes. 21

We are all getting a front-row seat to a sudden change in medium, and therefore in writing and reading. What a quick and shocking ride this is! 22

Read all about it! 23

ANALYZING AND COMPARING ARGUMENTS

As an academic writer, you will often need to compare disparate claims and evidence from multiple arguments addressing the same topic. Rarely, however, will those arguments be simplistic pro/con pairs meant to represent two opposing sides to an issue. Certainly the news media thrive on such black-and-white conflict, but academic writers seek greater complexity and do not expect to find simple answers. Analyzing and comparing essays on the same topic or issue will often reveal the ways writers work with similar evidence to come up with different, and not necessarily opposed, arguments.

The next two selections are arguments about grade inflation. Both are brief, and we recommend you read through them as a prelude to the activity in analyzing and comparing arguments that follows them. As you read, try to note their claims, the reasons used to support them, concessions, and counterarguments.

STUART ROJSTACZER

Grade Inflation Gone Wild

A former professor of geophysics at Duke University with a PhD in applied earth sciences, Stuart Rojstaczer has written or coauthored many geological studies in his career as a scientist. He has also published a book, *Gone for Good: Tales of University Life after the Golden Age* (1999), and numerous articles on higher education and grading. He is the creator of gradeinflation.com, where he posts a variety of charts and graphs chronicling his data about grade inflation. This op-ed piece appeared in the *Christian Science Monitor* on March 24, 2009.

■ ■ ■

About six years ago, I was sitting in the student union of a small liberal arts college when I saw a graph on the cover of the student newspaper that showed the history of grades given at that institution in the past 30 years.

Grades were up. Way up.

I'm a scientist by training and I love numbers. So when I looked at that graph, I wondered, "How many colleges and universities have data like this that I can find?" The answer is that a lot of schools have data like this hidden somewhere. Back then, I found more than 80 colleges and universities with data on grades, mostly by poking around the Web. Then I created a website (gradeinflation.com) so that others could find this data. I learned that grades started to shoot up nationwide in the 1960s, leveled off in the 1970s, and then started rising again in the 1980s. Private schools had much higher grades than public schools, but virtually everyone was experiencing grade inflation.

What about today?

Grades continue to go up regardless of the quality of education. At a time when many are raising questions about the quality of U.S. higher education, the average GPA at public schools is 3.0, with many flagship state schools having average GPAs higher than 3.2. At a private college, the average is now 3.3. At some schools, it tops 3.5 and even 3.6. "A" is average at those schools! At elite Brown University, two-thirds of all letter grades given are now A's.

These changes in grading have had a profound influence on college life and learning. When students walk into a classroom knowing that they can go through the motions and get a B+ or better, that's what they tend to do, give minimal effort. Our college classrooms are filled with students who do not prepare for class. Many study less than 10 hours a week—that's less than half the hours they spent studying 40 years ago. Paradoxically, students are spending more and more money for an education that seems to deliver less and less content.

With so few hours filled with learning, boredom sets in and students have to find something to pass the time. Instead of learning, they drink. A recent survey of more than 30,000 first-year students across the country showed that nearly half were spending more hours drinking than they were studying. If we continue along this path, we'll end up with a generation of poorly educated college graduates who have used their four years principally to develop an addiction to alcohol.

There are many who say that grade inflation is a complicated issue with no easy fix. But there are solutions. At about the same time that I started to collect data on rising grades, Princeton University began to actually do something about its grade-inflation problem. Its guidelines have the effect of now limiting A's on average to 35 percent of students in a class. Those guidelines have worked. Grades are going back down at Princeton and academic rigor is making a comeback. A similar successful effort has taken place at Wellesley College in Massachusetts. And through a concerted effort on the part of faculty and leadership, grades at Reed College in Oregon have stayed essentially constant for 20 years.

Princeton, Wellesley, and Reed provide evidence that the effort to keep grade inflation in check is not impossible. This effort takes two major steps. First, school officials must admit that there is a problem. Then they must implement policies or guidelines that truly restore excellence.

I asked Dean Nancy Malkiel at Princeton why so few schools seem to be following Princeton's lead. "Because it's hard work," she answered.

"Because you have to persuade the faculty that it's important to do the work."

Making a switch will take hard work, but the effort is worthwhile. The alternative is a student body that barely studies and drinks out of boredom. That's not acceptable. Colleges and universities must roll up their sleeves, bring down inflated grades, and encourage real learning. It's not an impossible task. There are successful examples that can be followed. I'm looking forward to the day when we can return to being proud of the education that our nation's colleges and universities provide.

PHIL PRIMACK

Doesn't Anybody Get a C Anymore?

Phil Primack is a journalist, editor, and policy analyst who teaches journalism at Tufts University, where he is a senior fellow at the Jonathan M. Tisch College of Citizenship and Public Service. His articles have appeared in many regional and national publications, including the *New York Times*, the *Boston Globe*, and *Columbia Journalism Review*. The following piece appeared in the *Boston Globe* on October 5, 2008.

■ ■ ■

The student deserved a B-minus. Maybe even a C-plus, I had decided. One paper was especially weak; another was late. But then I began to rationalize. The student had been generally prepared and contributed to class discussion, so I relented and gave what I thought was a very generous B. At least I wouldn't get a complaint about this grade, I figured. Then came the e-mail.

Why such a "low grade," the indignant student wrote.

"Low grade"? Back when I attended Tufts in the late 1960s, a B in certain courses was something I could only dream about. But grade inflation, the steady rise in grade point averages that began in the 1960s, now leaves many students regarding even the once-acceptable B—which has always stood for "good"—as a transcript wrecker, and a C—that is, "average"—as unmitigated disaster. More and more academic leaders may lament grade inflation, but precious few have been willing to act against it, leaving their professors all alone in the minefield between giving marks that reflect true merit and facing the wrath of students for whom entitlement begins with the letter A.

Grade inflation "is a huge problem," says former U.S. senator Hank Brown, who tried to make it a priority issue as president of the

University of Colorado in 2006. "Under the current system at a lot of schools, there is no way to recognize the difference between an outstanding job and a good job. Grade inflation hides laziness on the part of the students, and as long as it exists, even faculty who want to do a good job [in grading] don't feel they can."

That's because many professors fear that "tough grading" will trigger poor student evaluations or worse, which in turn can jeopardize the academic career track. "In my early years, students would say they liked my class, but the grades were low and the work level high," says retired Duke University professor Stuart Rojstaczer. "I had to get with the program and reduce my own expectations of workload and increase grades in order to have students leave my class with a positive impression to give to other students so they would attend [next year]. I was teaching worse, but the student response was much more positive."

Harvard University is the poster campus for academic prestige—and for grade inflation, even though some of its top officials have warned about grade creep. About 15 percent of Harvard students got a B-plus or better in 1950, according to one study. In 2007, more than half of all Harvard grades were in the A range. Harvard declined to release more current data or officially comment for this article. At the University of Massachusetts at Amherst, the average GPA in 2007 was 3.19 (on a four-point scale), up from 3.02 a decade earlier. That "modest increase" simply reflects better students, UMass spokesman Ed Blaguszewski says in an e-mail. "Since our students have been increasingly well-prepared . . . it makes sense that their UMass grades have crept up. Essentially, the profile of the population has changed over time, so we don't consider this to be grade inflation."

That's certainly the most common argument to explain away grade inflation—smarter students naturally get higher grades. But is it that simple? Privately, many faculty members and administrators say colleges are unwilling to challenge and possibly offend students and their hovering, tuition-paying parents with some tough grade love. And without institutional backing, individual faculty members simply yield to whining students.

But not everywhere. The most cited—and extreme—case of taking on grade inflation is at Princeton University, which in 2004 directed that A's account for less than 35 percent of undergraduate course grades. From 2004 to 2007, A's (A-plus, A, A-minus) accounted for 40.6 percent of undergraduate course grades, down from 47 percent in the period 2001 to 2004.

Closer to home, Wellesley College calls for the average grade in basic undergraduate courses to be no higher than a B-plus (3.33 GPA). "It's not that we're trying to get grades down, but we're trying to get grades to mean something," says associate dean of the college Adele Wolfson, who teaches chemistry. Wellesley's GPA, which stood at 3.47 in 2002 and was 3.4 when the policy was implemented two years later, fell to 3.3 this year, mainly because of more B grades and fewer A's. "The A has really become the mark of excellence," she says, "which is what it should be."

The problem, says Rojstaczer, is that such policies are the exceptions, and that grade inflation will be reduced only through consistent prodding and action by top officials. "In truth, some university leaders are embarrassed that grading is so lax, but they are loath to make any changes," he says in an e-mail. "Grade inflation in academia is like the alcoholic brother you pretend is doing just fine. When someone calls your brother a drunk, you get angry and defend him, although privately you worry. That's where we are with grade inflation: public denial and private concern."

10

A Practice Sequence: Analyzing and Comparing Arguments

1 To practice these strategies, first break up into small groups to discuss four different concerns surrounding grade inflation:

> *Group 1:* Define what you think grade inflation is.

> *Group 2:* Discuss whether you think grade inflation is a problem at the university or college you attend. What evidence can you provide to suggest that it is or is not a problem?

> *Group 3:* Why should students or faculty be concerned with grade inflation? What's at stake?

> *Group 4:* How would you respond if the administration at your university or college decided to limit the number of A's that faculty could give students?

Reassemble as a class and briefly report on the discussions.

2 Analyze Stuart Rojstaczer's argument in "Grade Inflation Gone Wild," addressing the following questions:

- What evidence does Rojstaczer use to indicate that there is a problem?

- How would you characterize this evidence (for example, scientific, anecdotal), and to what extent are you persuaded by the evidence he provides to suggest that grade inflation has a profound effect on "life and learning"?

- To what extent does he persuade you that a change in policy is necessary or that such a change would make a difference?

138   CHAPTER 9 | FROM IDENTIFYING CLAIMS TO ANALYZING ARGUMENTS

3 Now compare Phil Primack's and Stuart Rojstaczer's strategies for developing an argument.

- How does Primack establish that there is a problem? To what extent is his approach as persuasive as Rojstaczer's?
- What strategies would you identify in either argument as strategies that you might employ to develop your own argument?
- To what extent are you persuaded by the counterargument that Primack introduces?
- What do you think Primack wants you to do or think about in his analysis?
- In the end, does Primack add anything to your understanding of the problem of whether your college or university should introduce a policy to limit grade inflation?

4 As an alternative assignment, write a three-page essay in which you compare the arguments student Marques Camp and Professor Susan D. Blum make about the state of reading today. Consider their main claims and how they support them. Explain which argument you find more persuasive, and why. Feel free to draw on your own experience and make use of personal anecdotes to make your case.

10

From Identifying Issues to Forming Questions

Remember that inquiry is central to the process of composing. As you move from reading texts to writing them, you will discover that writing grows out of answering these questions:

- What are the concerns of the authors I've been reading?
- What situations motivate them to write?
- What frames or contexts do these writers use to construct their arguments?
- What is my argument in response to their writing?
- What is at stake in my argument?
- Who will be interested in reading what I have to say?
- How can I connect with both sympathetic and antagonistic readers?
- What kinds of evidence will persuade my readers?
- What objections are they likely to raise?

To answer these questions, you must read in the role of writer, with an eye toward

- *identifying an issue* (an idea or a statement that is open to dispute) that compels you to respond in writing,
- *understanding the situation* (the factors that give rise to the issue and shape your response), and
- *formulating a question* (what you intend to answer in response to the issue).

139

140 CHAPTER 10 | FROM IDENTIFYING ISSUES TO FORMING QUESTIONS

TABLE 10.1   A Series of Situations with Related Issues and Questions

SITUATION	ISSUE	QUESTION
Different state legislatures are passing legislation to prevent Spanish-speaking students from using their own language in schools.	Most research on learning contradicts the idea that students should be prevented from using their own language in the process of learning a new language.	Under what conditions should students be allowed to use their own language while they learn English?
A manufacturing company has plans to move to your city with the promise of creating new jobs in a period of high unemployment.	You feel that this company will compromise the quality of life for the surrounding community because the manufacturing process will pollute the air.	What would persuade the city to prevent this company from moving in, even though the company will provide much-needed jobs?
Your school has made an agreement with a local company to supply vending machines that sell drinks and food. The school plans to use its share of the profits to improve the library and purchase a new scoreboard for the football field.	You see that the school has much to gain from this arrangement, but you also know that obesity is a growing problem at the school.	Is there another way for the school to generate needed revenue without putting students' health at risk?
An increasing number of homeless people are seeking shelter on your college campus.	Campus security has stepped up its efforts to remove the homeless, even though the shelters off campus are overcrowded.	How can you persuade the school to shelter the homeless and to provide funds to support the needs of the homeless in your city?

In Table 10.1, we identify a series of situations and one of the issues and questions that derive from each of them. Notice that the question you ask defines the area of inquiry as you read; it also can help you formulate your working thesis, the statement that answers your question. (We say more about developing a thesis in Chapter 11.) In this chapter, in addition to further discussing the importance of situation, we look at how you can identify issues and formulate questions to guide your reading and writing.

IDENTIFYING ISSUES

In this section we present several steps to identifying an issue. You don't have to follow them in this particular order, and you may find yourself going back and forth among them as you try to bring an issue into focus.

Keep in mind that issues do not simply exist in the world well formed. Instead, writers construct what they see as issues from the situations they observe. For example, consider legislation to limit downloads from the Internet. If such legislation conflicts with your own practices and sense of freedom, you may have begun to identify an issue: the clash of values over what constitutes fair use and what does not. Be aware that others may not understand your issue and that in your writing you will have to explain carefully what is at stake.

■ Draw on Your Personal Experience

You may have been taught that formal writing is objective, that you must keep a dispassionate distance from your subject, and that you should not use *I* in a college-level paper. The fact is, however, that our personal experiences influence how we read, what we pay attention to, and what inferences we draw. It makes sense, then, to begin with you—where you are and what you think and believe.

We all use personal experience to make arguments in our everyday lives. In an academic context, the challenge is to use personal experience to argue a point, to illustrate something, or to illuminate a connection between theories and the sense we make of our daily experience. You don't want simply to tell your story. You want your story to strengthen your argument.

For example, in *Cultural Literacy*, E. D. Hirsch personalizes his interest in reversing the cycle of illiteracy in America's cities. To establish the nature of the problem in the situation he describes, he cites research showing that student performance on standardized tests in the United States is falling. But he also reflects on his own teaching in the 1970s, when he first perceived "the widening knowledge gap [that] caused me to recognize the connection between specific background knowledge and mature literacy." And he injects anecdotal evidence from conversations with his son, a teacher. Those stories heighten readers' awareness that school-aged children do not know much about literature, history, or government. (For example, his son mentions a student who challenged his claim that Latin is a "dead language" by demanding, "What do they speak in Latin America?")

Hirsch's use of his son's testimony makes him vulnerable to criticism, as readers might question whether Hirsch can legitimately use his son's experience to make generalizations about education. But in fact, Hirsch is using personal testimony—his own and his son's—to augment and put a human face on the research he cites. He presents his issue, that schools must teach cultural literacy, both as something personal and as something with which we should all be concerned. The personal note helps readers see Hirsch as someone who has long been concerned with education and who has even raised a son who is an educator.

■ Identify What Is Open to Dispute

An issue is something that is open to dispute. Sometimes the way to clarify an issue is to think of it as a *fundamental tension* between two or more conflicting points of view. If you can identify conflicting points of view, an issue may become clear.

142 CHAPTER 10 | FROM IDENTIFYING ISSUES TO FORMING QUESTIONS

Consider E. D. Hirsch, who believes that the best approach to educational reform is to change the curriculum in schools. His position: A curriculum based on cultural literacy is the one sure way to reverse the cycle of poverty and illiteracy in urban areas.

What is the issue? Hirsch's issue emerges in the presence of an alternative position. Jonathan Kozol, a social activist who has written extensively about educational reform, believes that policymakers need to address reform by providing the necessary resources that all students need to learn. Kozol points out that students in many inner-city schools are reading outdated textbooks and that the dilapidated conditions in these schools—windows that won't close, for example—make it impossible for students to learn.

In tension are two different views of the reform that can reverse illiteracy: Hirsch's view that educational reform should occur through curricular changes, and Kozol's view that educational reform demands socioeconomic resources.

■ Resist Binary Thinking

As you begin to define what is at issue, try to tease out complexities that may not be immediately apparent. That is, try to resist the either/or mindset that signals binary thinking.

If you considered only what Hirsch and Kozol have to say, it would be easy to characterize the problems facing our schools as either curricular or socioeconomic. But it may be that the real issue combines these arguments with a third or even a fourth, that neither curricular nor socioeconomic changes by themselves can resolve the problems with American schools.

After reading essays by both Hirsch and Kozol, one of our students pointed out that both Hirsch's focus on curriculum and Kozol's socioeconomic focus ignore another concern. She went on to describe her school experience in racial terms. In the excerpt below, notice how this writer uses personal experience (in a new school, she is not treated as she had expected to be treated) to formulate an issue.

> Moving from Colorado Springs to Tallahassee, I was immediately struck by the differences apparent in local home life, school life, and community unity, or lack thereof. Ripped from my sheltered world at a small Catholic school characterized by racial harmony, I was thrown into a large public school where outward prejudice from classmates and teachers and "race wars" were common and tolerated. . . .
>
> In a school where students and teachers had free rein to abuse anyone different from them, I was constantly abused. As the only black student in English honors, I was commonly belittled in front of my "peers" by my teacher. If I developed courage enough to ask a question, I was always answered with the use of improper grammar and such words as "ain't" as my teacher attempted to simplify the material to "my level" and to give me what he called "a little learning." After discussing several

> subjects, he often turned to me, singling me out of a sea of white faces, and asked, "Do *you* understand, Mila?" When asking my opinion of a subject, he frequently questioned, "What do *your* people think about this?" Although he insisted on including such readings as Martin Luther King's "I Have a Dream" speech in the curriculum, the speech's themes of tolerance and equity did not accompany his lesson.

Through her reading, this student discovered that few prominent scholars have confronted the issue of racism in schools directly. Although she grants that curricular reform and increased funding may be necessary to improve education, she argues that scholars also need to address race in their studies of teaching and learning.

Our point is that issues may be more complex than you first think they are. For this student, the issue wasn't one of two positions—reform the curriculum or provide more funding. Instead, it combined a number of different positions, including race ("prejudice" and "race wars") and the relationship between student and teacher ("Do *you* understand, Mila?") in a classroom.

In this passage, the writer uses her experience to challenge binary thinking. Like the student writer, you should examine issues from different perspectives, avoiding either/or propositions that oversimplify the world.

■ Build on and Extend the Ideas of Others

Academic writing builds on and extends the ideas of others. As an academic writer, you will find that by extending other people's ideas, you will extend your own. You may begin in a familiar place, but as you read more and pursue connections to other readings, you may well end up at an unexpected destination.

For example, one of our students was troubled when he read Melissa Stormont-Spurgin's description of homeless children. The student uses details from her work (giving credit, of course) in his own:

> The children . . . went to school after less than three hours of sleep. They wore the same wrinkled clothes that they had worn the day before. What will their teachers think when they fall asleep in class? How will they get food for lunch? What will their peers think? What could these homeless children talk about with their peers? They have had to grow up too fast. Their worries are not the same as other children's worries. They are worried about their next meal and where they will seek shelter. Their needs, however, are the same. They need a home and all of the securities that come with it. They also need an education (Stormont-Spurgin 156).

Initially the student was troubled by his own access to quality schools, and the contrast between his life and the lives of the children Stormont-Spurgin describes. Initially, then, his issue was the fundamental tension between his own privileged status, something he had taken for granted, and the struggle that homeless children face every day.

144 CHAPTER 10 | FROM IDENTIFYING ISSUES TO FORMING QUESTIONS

However, as he read further and grew to understand homelessness as a concern in a number of studies, he connected his personal response to a larger conversation about democracy, fairness, and education:

> Melissa Stormont-Spurgin, an author of several articles on educational studies, addresses a very real and important, yet avoided issue in education today. Statistics show that a very high percentage of children who are born into homeless families will remain homeless, or in poverty, for the rest of their lives. How can this be, if everyone actually does have the same educational opportunities? There must be significant educational disadvantages for children without homes. In a democratic society, I feel that we must pay close attention to these disadvantages and do everything in our power to replace them with equality.

Ultimately, the student refined his sense of what was at issue: *Although all people should have access to public education in a democratic society, not everyone has the opportunity to attend quality schools in order to achieve personal success.* In turn, his definition of the issue began to shape his argument:

> Parents, teachers, homeless shelters, and the citizens of the United States who fund [homeless] shelters must address the educational needs of homeless children, while steering them away from any more financial or psychological struggles. Without this emphasis on education, the current trend upward in the number of homeless families will inevitably continue in the future of American society.

The student shifted away from a personal issue—the difference between his status and that of homeless children—to an issue of clashing values: the principle of egalitarian democracy on the one hand and the reality of citizens in a democracy living in abject poverty on the other. When he started to read about homeless children, he could not have made the claim he ends up making, that policymakers must make education a basic human right.

This student offers us an important lesson about the role of inquiry and the value of resisting easy answers. He has built on and extended his own ideas—and the ideas of others—after repeating the process of reading, raising questions, writing, and seeing problems a number of times.

■ Read to Discover a Writer's Frame

A more specialized strategy of building on and extending the ideas of others involves reading to discover a writer's **frame**, the perspective through which a writer presents his or her arguments. Writers want us to see the world a certain way, so they frame their arguments much the same way photographers and artists frame their pictures.

For example, if you were to take a picture of friends in front of the football stadium on campus, you would focus on what you would most like to remember—your friends' faces—blurring the images of the people walking behind your friends. Setting up the picture, or framing it, might require using light and shade to make some details stand out more than others. Writers do the same with language.

E. D. Hirsch uses the concept of *cultural literacy* to frame his argument for curricular reform. For Hirsch, the term is a benchmark, a standard: People who are culturally literate are familiar with the body of information that every educated citizen should know. Hirsch's implication, of course, is that people who are not culturally literate are not well educated. But that is not necessarily true. In fact, a number of educators insist that literacy is simply a means to an end—reading to complete an assignment, for example, or to understand the ramifications of a decision—not an end in itself. By defining and using *cultural literacy* as the goal of education, Hirsch is framing his argument; he is bringing his ideas into focus.

When writers use framing strategies, they also call attention to the specific conversations that set up the situation for their arguments. Framing often entails quoting specific theories and ideas from other authors and then using those quotations as a perspective, or lens, through which to examine other material. In his memoir *Hunger of Memory: The Education of Richard Rodriguez* (1982), Richard Rodriguez uses this method to examine his situation as a nonnative speaker of English desperate to enter the mainstream culture, even if it means sacrificing his identity as the son of Mexican immigrants. Reflecting on his life as a student, Rodriguez comes across Richard Hoggart's book *The Uses of Literacy* (1957). Hoggart's description of "the scholarship boy" presents a lens through which Rodriguez can see his own experience. Hoggart writes:

> With his family, the boy has the intense pleasure of intimacy, the family's consolation in feeling public alienation. Lavish emotions texture home life. *Then*, at school, the instruction bids him to trust lonely reason primarily. Immediate needs set the pace of his parents' lives. From his mother and father the boy learns to trust spontaneity and nonrational ways of knowing. *Then*, at school, there is mental calm. Teachers emphasize the value of a reflectiveness that opens a space between thinking and immediate action.
>
> Years of schooling must pass before the boy will be able to sketch the cultural differences in his day as abstractly as this. But he senses those differences early. Perhaps as early as the night he brings home an assignment from school and finds the house too noisy for study. He has to be more and more alone, if he is going to "get on." He will have, probably unconsciously, to oppose the ethos of the hearth, the intense gregariousness of the working-class family group. . . . The boy has to cut himself off mentally, so as to do his homework, as well as he can.

Here is Rodriguez's response to Hoggart's description of the scholarship boy:

> For weeks I read, speed-read, books by modern educational theorists, only to find infrequent and slight mention of students like me. . . . Then one day, leafing through Richard Hoggart's *The Uses of Literacy,* I found, in his description of the scholarship boy, myself. For the first time I realized that

146   CHAPTER 10 | FROM IDENTIFYING ISSUES TO FORMING QUESTIONS

there were other students like me, and so I was able to frame the meaning of my academic success, its consequent price—the loss.

Notice how Rodriguez introduces ideas from Hoggart "to frame" his own ideas: "I found, in his description of the scholarship boy, myself. For the first time I realized that there were other students like me, and so I was able to frame the meaning of my academic success, its consequent price—the loss." Hoggart's scholarship boy enables Rodriguez to revisit his own experience with a new perspective. Hoggart's words and idea advance Rodriguez's understanding of the problem he identifies in his life: his inability to find solace at home and within his working-class roots. Hoggart's description of the scholarship boy's moving between cultural extremes—spontaneity at home and reflection at school—helps Rodriguez bring his own youthful discontent into focus.

Rodriguez's response to Hoggart's text shows how another writer's lens can help frame an issue. If you were using Hoggart's term *scholarship boy* as a lens through which to clarify an issue in education, you might ask how the term illuminates new aspects of another writer's examples or your own. And then you might ask, "To what extent does Hirsch's cultural literacy throw a more positive light on what Rodriguez and Hoggart describe?" or "How do my experiences challenge, extend, or complicate the scholarship-boy concept?"

■ Consider the Constraints of the Situation

In identifying an issue, you have to understand the situation that gives rise to the issue, including the contexts in which it is raised and debated. One of the contexts is the *audience*. In thinking about your issue, you must consider the extent to which your potential readers are involved in the dialogue you want to enter, and what they know and need to know. In a sense, audience functions as both context and **constraint**, a factor that narrows the choices you can make in responding to an issue. An understanding of your potential readers will help you choose the depth of your discussion; it will also determine the kind of evidence you can present and the language you can use.

Another constraint on your response to an issue is the form that response takes. For example, if you decide to make an issue of government-imposed limits on what you can download from the Internet, your response in writing might take the form of an editorial or a letter to a legislator. In this situation, length is an obvious constraint: Newspapers limit the word count of editorials, and the best letters to legislators tend to be brief and very selective about the evidence they cite. A few personal examples and a few statistics may be all you can include to support your claim about the issue. By contrast, if you were making your case in an academic journal, a very different set of constraints would apply. You would have more space for illustrations and support, for example.

Finally, the situation itself can function as a major constraint. For instance, suppose your topic is the decline of educational standards. It's difficult to imagine any writer making the case for accelerating that decline, or any audience being receptive to the idea that a decline in standards is a good thing.

Steps to Identifying Issues

1. **Draw on your personal experience.** Start with your own sense of what's important, what puzzles you, or what you are curious about. Then build your argument by moving on to other sources to support your point of view.

2. **Identify what is open to dispute.** Identify a phenomenon or some idea in a written argument that challenges what you think or believe.

3. **Resist binary thinking.** Think about the issue from multiple perspectives.

4. **Build on and extend the ideas of others.** As you read, be open to new ways of looking at the issue. The issue you finally write about may be very different from what you set out to write about.

5. **Read to discover a writer's frame.** What theories or ideas shape the writer's focus? How can these theories or ideas help you frame your argument?

6. **Consider the constraints of the situation.** Craft your argument to meet the needs of and constraints imposed by your audience and form.

IDENTIFYING ISSUES IN AN ESSAY

In the following editorial, published in 2002 in *Newsweek*, writer Anna Quindlen addresses her concern that middle-class parents overschedule their children's lives. She calls attention to the ways leisure time helped her develop as a writer and urges parents to consider the extent to which children's creativity depends on having some downtime. They don't always have to have their time scheduled. As you read Quindlen's "Doing Nothing Is Something," note what words and phrases Quindlen uses to identify the situation and to indicate who her audience is. Identify her main claim as one of fact, value, or policy. Finally, answer the questions that follow the selection to see if you can discern how she locates, defines, and advances her issue.

ANNA QUINDLEN

Doing Nothing Is Something

Anna Quindlen is a best-selling author of novels and children's books, but she is perhaps most widely known for her nonfiction and commentary on current events and contemporary life. She won a Pulitzer Prize in 1992 for her "Public and Private" column in the *New York Times*, and for ten years wrote a biweekly column for *Newsweek*. Some of her novels are *Object Lessons* (1991), *Blessings* (2002), and *Every Last One* (2010). Her nonfiction works and collections include *Living Out Loud* (1988), *Thinking Out Loud* (1994), *Loud and Clear* (2004), and *Good Dog. Stay.* (2007).

■ ■ ■

1 Summer is coming soon. I can feel it in the softening of the air, but I can see it, too, in the textbooks on my children's desks. The number of uncut pages at the back grows smaller and smaller. The loose-leaf is ragged at the edges, the binder plastic ripped at the corners. An old remembered glee rises inside me. Summer is coming. Uniform skirts in mothballs. Pencils with their points left broken. Open windows. Day trips to the beach. Pickup games.

2 Hanging out. How boring it was.

3 Of course, it was the making of me, as a human being and a writer. Downtime is where we become ourselves, looking into the middle distance, kicking at the curb, lying on the grass, or sitting on the stoop and staring at the tedious blue of the summer sky. I don't believe you can write poetry, or compose music, or become an actor without downtime, and plenty of it, a hiatus that passes for boredom but is really the quiet moving of the wheels inside that fuel creativity.

4 And that, to me, is one of the saddest things about the lives of American children today. Soccer leagues, acting classes, tutors—the calendar of the average middle-class kid is so over the top that soon Palm handhelds will be sold in Toys "R" Us. Our children are as overscheduled as we are, and that is saying something.

5 This has become so bad that parents have arranged to schedule times for unscheduled time. Earlier this year the privileged suburb of Ridgewood, New Jersey, announced a Family Night, when there would be no homework, no athletic practices, and no after-school events. This was terribly exciting until I realized that this was not one night a week, but one single night. There is even a free-time movement, and Web site: familylife1st.org. Among the frequently asked questions provided online: "What would families do with family time if they took it back?"

6 Let me make a suggestion for the kids involved: How about nothing? It is not simply that it is pathetic to consider the lives of children who don't have a moment between piano and dance and homework to talk about their day or just search for split ends, an enormously satisfying

leisure-time activity of my youth. There is also ample psychological research suggesting that what we might call "doing nothing" is when human beings actually do their best thinking, and when creativity comes to call. Perhaps we are creating an entire generation of people whose ability to think outside the box, as the current parlance of business has it, is being systematically stunted by scheduling.

A study by the University of Michigan quantified the downtime *7* deficit; in the last twenty years American kids have lost about four unstructured hours a week. There has even arisen a global Right to Play movement: in the Third World it is often about child labor, but in the United States it is about the sheer labor of being a perpetually busy child. In Omaha, Nebraska, a group of parents recently lobbied for additional recess. Hooray, and yikes.

How did this happen? Adults did it. There is a culture of adult distrust *8* that suggests that a kid who is not playing softball or attending science-enrichment programs — or both — is huffing or boosting cars: If kids are left alone, they will not stare into the middle distance and consider the meaning of life and how come your nose in pictures never looks the way you think it should, but instead will get into trouble. There is also the culture of cutthroat and unquestioning competition that leads even the parents of preschoolers to gab about prestigious colleges without a trace of irony: This suggests that any class in which you do not enroll your first grader will put him at a disadvantage in, say, law school.

Finally, there is a culture of workplace presence (as opposed to *9* productivity). Try as we might to suggest that all these enrichment activities are for the good of the kid, there is ample evidence that they are really for the convenience of parents with way too little leisure time of their own. Stories about the resignation of presidential aide Karen Hughes unfailingly reported her dedication to family time by noting that she arranged to get home at 5:30 one night a week to have dinner with her son. If one weekday dinner out of five is considered laudable, what does that say about what's become commonplace?

Summer is coming. It used to be a time apart for kids, a respite from *10* the clock and the copybook, the organized day. Every once in a while, either guilty or overwhelmed or tired of listening to me keen about my monumental boredom, my mother would send me to some rinky-dink park program that consisted almost entirely of three-legged races and making things out of Popsicle sticks. Now, instead, there are music camps, sports camps, fat camps, probably thin camps. I mourn hanging out in the backyard. I mourn playing Wiffle ball in the street without a sponsor and matching shirts. I mourn drawing in the dirt with a stick.

Maybe that kind of summer is gone for good. Maybe this is the leading *11* edge of a new way of living that not only has no room for contemplation but is contemptuous of it. But if downtime cannot be squeezed during the school year into the life of frantic and often joyless activity with

150   CHAPTER 10 | FROM IDENTIFYING ISSUES TO FORMING QUESTIONS

which our children are saddled while their parents pursue frantic and often joyless activity of their own, what about summer? Do most adults really want to stand in line for Space Mountain or sit in traffic to get to a shore house that doesn't have enough saucepans? Might it be even more enriching for their children to stay at home and do nothing? For those who say they will only watch TV or play on the computer, a piece of technical advice: The cable box can be unhooked, the modem removed. Perhaps it is not too late for American kids to be given the gift of enforced boredom for at least a week or two, staring into space, bored out of their gourds, exploring the inside of their own heads. "To contemplate is to toil, to think is to do," said Victor Hugo. "Go outside and play," said Prudence Quindlen. Both of them were right.

Reading as a Writer

1. What evidence of Quindlen's personal responses and experiences can you identify?
2. What phenomenon has prompted her to reflect on what she thinks and believes? How has she made it into an issue?
3. Where does she indicate that she has considered the issue from multiple perspectives and is placing her ideas in conversation with those of others?
4. What sort of lens does she seem to be using to frame her argument?
5. What constraints (such as the format of an editorial) seem to be in play in the essay?

A Practice Sequence: Identifying Issues

This sequence of activities will give you practice in identifying and clarifying issues based on your own choice of reading and collaboration with your classmates.

1   Draw on your personal experience. Reflect on your own responses to what you have been reading in this class or in other classes, or issues that writers have posed in the media. What concerns you most? Choose a story that supports or challenges the claims people are making in what you have read or listened to. What questions do you have? Make some notes in response to these questions, explaining your personal stake in the issues and questions you formulate.

2   Identify what is open to dispute. Take what you have written and formulate your ideas as an issue, using the structure we used in our example of Hirsch's and Kozol's competing arguments:

- Part 1: Your view of a given topic
- Part 2: At least one view that is in tension with your own

If you need to, read further to understand what others have to say about this issue.

3 Resist binary thinking. Share your statement of the issue with one or more peers and ask them if they see other ways to formulate the issue that you may not have thought about. What objections, if any, do they make to your statement in part 1? Write these objections down in part 2 so that you begin to look at the issue from multiple perspectives.

4 Build on and extend the ideas of others. Now that you have formulated an issue from different perspectives, explaining your personal stake in the issue, connect what you think to a broader conversation in what you are reading. Then try making a claim using this structure: "Although some people would argue _____, I think that _____."

5 Read to discover a writer's frame. As an experiment in trying out multiple perspectives, revise the claim you make in exercise 4 by introducing the frame, or lens, through which you want readers to understand your argument. You can employ the same sentence structure. For example, here is a claim framed in terms of race: "Although people should have access to public education, recent policies have worsened racial inequalities in public schools." In contrast, here is a claim that focuses on economics: "Although people should have access to public education, the unequal distribution of tax money has created what some would call an 'economy of education.'" The lens may come from reading you have done in other courses or from conversations with your classmates, and you may want to attribute the lens to a particular author or classmate: "Although some people would argue_____, I use E. D. Hirsch's notion of cultural literacy to show_____."

6 Consider the constraints of the situation. Building on these exercises, develop an argument in the form of an editorial for your local newspaper. This means that you will need to limit your argument to about 250 words. You also will need to consider the extent to which your potential readers are involved in the conversation. What do they know? What do they need to know? What kind of evidence do you need to use to persuade readers?

FORMULATING ISSUE-BASED QUESTIONS

As we have said, when you identify an issue, you need to understand it in the context of its situation. Ideally, the situation and the issue will be both relevant and recent, making the task of connecting to your audience that much easier when you write about the issue. For example, the student writer who was concerned about long-standing issues of homelessness and lack of educational opportunity connected to his readers by citing recent statistics and giving the problem of homelessness a face: "The children . . . went to school after less than three hours of sleep. They wore the same wrinkled clothes that they had worn the day before." If your issue does not immediately fulfill the criteria of relevance and timeliness, you need to take that into consideration as you continue your reading and research on the issue. Ask yourself, "What is on people's minds these days?" "What do they need to know about?" Think about why the issue matters to you, and imagine why it might matter to others. By the time you write, you should be prepared to make the issue relevant for your readers.

In addition to understanding the situation and defining the issue that you feel is most relevant and timely, you can formulate an issue-based question that can help you think through what you might be interested in writing about. This question should be specific enough to guide inquiry into what others have written. An issue-based question can also help you accomplish the following:

- clarify what you know about the issue and what you still need to know;

- guide your inquiry with a clear focus;

- organize your inquiry around a specific issue;

- develop an argument (rather than simply collecting information) by asking *How?*, *Why?*, *Should?*, or *To what extent is this true (or not true)?*;

- consider who your audience is;

- determine what resources you have, so that you can ask a question that you will be able to answer with the resources available to you.

A good question develops out of an issue, some fundamental tension that you identify within a conversation. In "Doing Nothing Is Something," Anna Quindlen identifies a problem that middle-class parents need to know about: that overscheduling their children's lives may limit their children's potential for developing their creativity. As she explores the reasons why children do not have sufficient downtime, she raises a question that encourages parents to consider what would happen if they gave their children time to do nothing: "Might it be even more enriching for their children to stay at home and do nothing?" (para. 11). Through identifying what is at issue, you should begin to understand for whom it is an issue—for whom you are answering the question. In turn, the answer to your question will help you craft your thesis.

In the following section, we trace the steps one of our students took to formulate an issue-based question on the broad topic of language diversity. Although we present the steps in sequence, be aware that they are guidelines only: The steps often overlap, and there is a good deal of room for rethinking and refining along the way.

FORMULATING ISSUE-BASED QUESTIONS   **153**

■ Refine Your Topic

Generally speaking, a **topic** is the subject you want to write about. For example, homelessness, tests, and violence are all topics. So are urban homelessness, standardized tests, and video game violence. And so are homelessness in New York City, aptitude tests versus achievement tests, and mayhem in the video game *Grand Theft Auto*. As our list suggests, even a specific topic needs refining into an issue before it can be explored effectively in writing.

The topic our student wanted to focus on was language diversity, a subject her linguistics class had been discussing. She was fascinated by the extraordinary range of languages spoken in the United States, not just by immigrant groups but by native speakers whose dialects and varieties of English are considered nonstandard. She herself had relatives for whom English was not a first language. She began refining her topic by putting her thoughts into words:

> I want to describe the experience of being raised in a home where non–Standard English is spoken.
>
> I'd like to know the benefits and liabilities of growing up bilingual.
>
> I am curious to know what it's like to live in a community of nonnative speakers of English while trying to make a living in a country where the dominant language is English.

Although she had yet to identify an issue, her attempts to articulate what interested her about the topic were moving her toward the situation of people in the United States who don't speak Standard English or don't have English as their first language.

■ Explain Your Interest in the Topic

At this point, the student encountered E. D. Hirsch's *Cultural Literacy* in her reading, which had both a provocative and a clarifying effect on her thinking. She began to build on and extend Hirsch's ideas. Reacting to Hirsch's assumption that students should acquire the same base of knowledge and write in Standard Written English, her first, somewhat mischievous thought was, "I wonder what Hirsch would think about cultural literacy being taught in a bilingual classroom?" But then her thinking took another turn, and she began to contemplate the effect of Hirsch's cultural-literacy agenda on speakers whose English is not standard or for whom English is not a first language. She used a demographic fact that she had learned in her linguistics class in her explanation of her interest in the topic: "I'm curious about the consequences of limiting language diversity when the presence of ethnic minorities in our educational system is growing."

■ Identify an Issue

The more she thought about Hirsch's ideas, and the more she read about language diversity, the more concerned our student grew. It seemed to her that Hirsch's interest in producing students who all share the same base of knowledge and all write in Standard Written English was in tension with her sense that this kind of approach places a burden on people whose first language is not English. That tension clarified the issue for her. In identifying the issue, she wrote:

> Hirsch's book actually sets some priorities, most notably through his list of words and phrases that form the foundations of what it means to be "American." However, this list certainly overlooks several crucial influences in American culture. Most oversights generally come at the expense of the minority populations.

These two concerns—with inclusion and with exclusion—helped focus the student's inquiry.

■ Formulate Your Topic as a Question

To further define her inquiry, the student formulated her topic as a question that pointed toward an argument: "To what extent can E. D. Hirsch's notion of 'cultural literacy' coexist with our country's principles of democracy and inclusion?" Notice that her choice of the phrase *To what extent* implies that both goals do not go hand in hand. If she had asked, "Can common culture coexist with pluralism?" her phrasing would imply that a yes or no answer would suffice, possibly foreclosing avenues of inquiry and certainly ignoring the complexity of the issue.

Instead, despite her misgivings about the implications of Hirsch's agenda, the student suspended judgment, opening the way to genuine inquiry. She acknowledged the usefulness and value of sharing a common language and conceded that Hirsch's points were well taken. She wrote:

> Some sort of unification is necessary. Language, . . . on the most fundamental level of human interaction, demands some compromise and chosen guidelines. . . . How can we learn from one another if we cannot even say hello to each other?

Suspending judgment led her to recognize the complexity of the issue, and her willingness to examine the issue from different perspectives indicated the empathy that is a central component of developing a conversational argument.

■ Acknowledge Your Audience

This student's question ("To what extent can E. D. Hirsch's notion of 'cultural literacy' coexist with our country's principles of democracy and inclusion?") also acknowledged an audience. By invoking cultural literacy, she assumed an audience of readers who are familiar with Hirsch's ideas, probably including policymakers and educational administrators. In gesturing toward democracy, she cast her net very wide: Most Americans probably admire the "principles of democracy." But in specifying inclusion as a democratic principle, she wisely linked all Americans who believe in democratic principles, including the parents of schoolchildren, with all people who have reason to feel excluded by Hirsch's ideas, especially non-native speakers of English, among them immigrants from Mexico and speakers of African American Vernacular English. Thus, this student was acknowledging an audience of policymakers, administrators, parents (both mainstream and marginalized), and those who knew about and perhaps supported cultural literacy.

Steps to Formulating an Issue-Based Question

1 **Refine your topic.** Examine your topic from different perspectives. For example, what are the causes of homelessness? What are its consequences?

2 **Explain your interest in the topic.** Explore the source of your interest in this topic and what you want to learn.

3 **Identify an issue.** Determine what is open to dispute.

4 **Formulate your topic as a question.** Use your question to focus your inquiry.

5 **Acknowledge your audience.** Reflect on what readers may know about the issue, why they may be interested, and what you would like to teach them.

A Practice Sequence: Formulating an Issue-Based Question

As you start developing your own issue-based question, it might be useful to practice a five-step process that begins with a topic, a word or phrase that describes the focus of your interests. Here, apply the process to the one-word topic *homelessness*.

1 Expand your topic into a phrase. "I am interested in the *consequences* of homelessness," "I want to *describe* what it means to be homeless," or "I am interested in discussing the *cause* of homelessness."

2 Explain your interest in this topic. "I am interested in the consequences of homelessness because homelessness challenges democratic principles of fairness."

3 Identify an issue. "The persistence of homelessness contradicts my belief in social justice."

4 Formulate your topic as a question. "To what extent can we allow homelessness to persist in a democratic nation that prides itself on providing equal opportunity to all?"

5 Acknowledge your audience. "I am interested in the consequences of homelessness because I want people who believe in democracy to understand that we need to work harder to make sure that everyone has access to food, shelter, and employment."

The answer to the question you formulate in step 4 should lead to an assertion, your main claim, or *thesis*. For example, you could state your main claim this way: "Although homelessness persists as a widespread problem in our nation, we must develop policies that eliminate homelessness, ensuring that everyone has access to food, shelter, and employment. This is especially important in a democracy that embraces social justice and equality."

The thesis introduces a problem and makes an assertion that you will need to support: "We must develop policies that eliminate homelessness, ensuring that everyone has access to food, shelter, and employment." What is at issue? Not everyone would agree that policies must be implemented to solve the problem. In fact, many would argue that homelessness is an individual problem, that individuals must take responsibility for lifting themselves out of poverty, homelessness, and unemployment. Of course, you would need to read quite a bit to reach this final stage of formulating your thesis.

Try using the five-step process we describe above to formulate your own topic as a question, or try formulating the following topics as questions:

- violence in video games
- recycling
- the popularity of a cultural phenomenon (a book, a film, a performer, an icon)
- standardized tests
- professional sports injuries
- town-gown relationships
- media representation and gender
- government and religion
- vegetarianism

AN ACADEMIC ESSAY FOR ANALYSIS

The following essay by William Deresiewicz provides an intriguing academic extension of the topic that Anna Quindlen writes about (p. 148): the need for the young to have solitary, unscheduled time. His essay illustrates many of the strategies we have discussed thus far: raising questions, stating a thesis by placing an argument in the stream of a broader conversation, using evidence to support his claims. As you read Deresiewicz's essay, you might use the following questions as a guide:

- What is Deresiewicz's thesis? Would you characterize his claim as one of fact? Value?
- What types of evidence does he use to support his claim?
- What do Deresiewicz's vocabulary and citations indicate about his target audience?
- What does Deresiewicz want his readers to do or think about?

WILLIAM DERESIEWICZ

The End of Solitude

William Deresiewicz taught English at Yale University from 1998 to 2008. He is now a contributing writer at *The Nation* and was nominated for a 2009 National Magazine Award for his reviews and criticism. His essay "The End of Solitude" appeared in *The Chronicle of Higher Education* in January 2009 and represents one of many debates about literacy that scholars have waged concerning the benefits and limits of new technologies. Deresiewicz observes that technology fulfills a human impulse to be known, to be connected with others. Posting on social media enables us to be visible and helps validate who we are as individuals. However, he worries that this instinct to be connected also has an adverse effect: We lose a sense of solitude and the space he believes we all need to have in order to understand who we are, what we believe, and what we value. He worries, too, that a new generation does not see the point of solitude because so many young people equate solitude with loneliness.

■ ■ ■

What does the contemporary self want? The camera has created a culture of celebrity; the computer is creating a culture of connectivity. As the two technologies converge — broadband tipping the Web from text to image, social-networking sites spreading the mesh of interconnection ever wider — the two cultures betray a common impulse. Celebrity and connectivity are both ways of becoming known. This is what the contemporary self wants. It wants to be recognized, wants to be connected: It wants to be visible. If not to the millions, on *Survivor* or *Oprah*, then to the hundreds, on Twitter or Facebook. This is the quality that validates us, this is how we become real to ourselves—by being seen by others. The great contemporary terror is anonymity. If Lionel Trilling was right, if the property that grounded the self, in Romanticism, was sincerity, and in modernism it was authenticity, then in postmodernism it is visibility.

So we live exclusively in relation to others, and what disappears from our lives is solitude. Technology is taking away our privacy and our concentration, but it is also taking away our ability to be alone. Though I shouldn't say taking away. We are doing this to ourselves; we are discarding these riches as fast as we can. I was told by one of her older relatives that a teenager I know had sent 3,000 text messages one recent month. That's 100 a day, or about one every 10 waking minutes, morning, noon, and night, weekdays and weekends, class time, lunch time, homework time, and toothbrushing time. So on average, she's never alone for more than 10 minutes at once. Which means, she's never alone. *2*

I once asked my students about the place that solitude has in their lives. One of them admitted that she finds the prospect of being alone so unsettling that she'll sit with a friend even when she has a paper to write. Another said, why would anyone want to be alone? *3*

To that remarkable question, history offers a number of answers. Man may be a social animal, but solitude has traditionally been a societal value. In particular, the act of being alone has been understood as an essential dimension of religious experience, albeit one restricted to a self-selected few. Through the solitude of rare spirits, the collective renews its relationship with divinity. The prophet and the hermit, the sadhu and the yogi, pursue their vision quests, invite their trances, in desert or forest or cave. For the still, small voice speaks only in silence. Social life is a bustle of petty concerns, a jostle of quotidian interests, and religious institutions are no exception. You cannot hear God when people are chattering at you, and the divine word, their pretensions notwithstanding, demurs at descending on the monarch and the priest. Communal experience is the human norm, but the solitary encounter with God is the egregious act that refreshes that norm. (Egregious, for no man is a prophet in his own land. Tiresias was reviled before he was vindicated, Teresa interrogated before she was canonized.) Religious solitude is a kind of self-correcting social mechanism, a way of burning out the underbrush of moral habit and spiritual custom. The seer returns with new tablets or new dances, his face bright with the old truth. *4*

Like other religious values, solitude was democratized by the Reformation and secularized by Romanticism. In Marilynne Robinson's interpretation, Calvinism created the modern self by focusing the soul inward, leaving it to encounter God, like a prophet of old, in "profound isolation." To her enumeration of Calvin, Marguerite de Navarre, and *5*

Milton as pioneering early-modern selves we can add Montaigne, Hamlet, and even Don Quixote. The last figure alerts us to reading's essential role in this transformation, the printing press serving an analogous function in the sixteenth and subsequent centuries to that of television and the Internet in our own. Reading, as Robinson puts it, "is an act of great inwardness and subjectivity." "The soul encountered itself in response to a text, first Genesis or Matthew and then *Paradise Lost* or *Leaves of Grass*." With Protestantism and printing, the quest for the divine voice became available to, even incumbent upon, everyone.

But it is with Romanticism that solitude achieved its greatest cultural salience, becoming both literal and literary. Protestant solitude is still only figurative. Rousseau and Wordsworth made it physical. The self was now encountered not in God but in Nature, and to encounter Nature one had to go to it. And go to it with a special sensibility: The poet displaced the saint as social seer and cultural model. But because Romanticism also inherited the eighteenth-century idea of social sympathy, Romantic solitude existed in a dialectical relationship with sociability—if less for Rousseau and still less for Thoreau, the most famous solitary of all, then certainly for Wordsworth, Melville, Whitman, and many others. For Emerson, "the soul environs itself with friends, that it may enter into a grander self-acquaintance or solitude; and it goes alone, for a season, that it may exalt its conversation or society." The Romantic practice of solitude is neatly captured by Trilling's "sincerity": the belief that the self is validated by a congruity of public appearance and private essence, one that stabilizes its relationship with both itself and others. Especially, as Emerson suggests, one beloved other. Hence the famous Romantic friendship pairs: Goethe and Schiller, Wordsworth and Coleridge, Hawthorne and Melville.

Modernism decoupled this dialectic. Its notion of solitude was harsher, more adversarial, more isolating. As a model of the self and its interactions, Hume's social sympathy gave way to Pater's thick wall of personality and Freud's narcissism—the sense that the soul, self-enclosed and inaccessible to others, can't choose but be alone. With exceptions, like Woolf, the modernists fought shy of friendship. Joyce and Proust disparaged it; D. H. Lawrence was wary of it; the modernist friendship pairs—Conrad and Ford, Eliot and Pound, Hemingway and Fitzgerald—were altogether cooler than their Romantic counterparts. The world was now understood as an assault on the self, and with good reason.

The Romantic ideal of solitude developed in part as a reaction to the emergence of the modern city. In modernism, the city is not only more menacing than ever, it has become inescapable, a labyrinth: Eliot's London, Joyce's Dublin. The mob, the human mass, presses in. Hell is other people. The soul is forced back into itself—hence

160 CHAPTER 10 | FROM IDENTIFYING ISSUES TO FORMING QUESTIONS

the development of a more austere, more embattled form of self-validation, Trilling's "authenticity," where the essential relationship is only with oneself. (Just as there are few good friendships in modernism, so are there few good marriages.) Solitude becomes, more than ever, the arena of heroic self-discovery, a voyage through interior realms made vast and terrifying by Nietzschean and Freudian insights. To achieve authenticity is to look upon these visions without flinching; Trilling's exemplar here is Kurtz. Protestant self-examination becomes Freudian analysis, and the culture hero, once a prophet of God and then a poet of Nature, is now a novelist of self—a Dostoyevsky, a Joyce, a Proust.

But we no longer live in the modernist city, and our great fear is not submersion by the mass but isolation from the herd. Urbanization gave way to suburbanization, and with it the universal threat of loneliness. What technologies of transportation exacerbated—we could live farther and farther apart—technologies of communication redressed—we could bring ourselves closer and closer together. Or at least, so we have imagined. The first of these technologies, the first simulacrum of proximity, was the telephone. "Reach out and touch someone." But through the 1970s and 1980s, our isolation grew. Suburbs, sprawling ever farther, became exurbs. Families grew smaller or splintered apart, mothers left the home to work. The electronic hearth became the television in every room. Even in childhood, certainly in adolescence, we were each trapped inside our own cocoon. Soaring crime rates, and even more sharply escalating rates of moral panic, pulled children off the streets. The idea that you could go outside and run around the neighborhood with your friends, once unquestionable, has now become unthinkable. The child who grew up between the world wars as part of an extended family within a tight-knit urban community became the grandparent of a kid who sat alone in front of a big television, in a big house, on a big lot. We were lost in space. *9*

Under those circumstances, the Internet arrived as an incalculable blessing. We should never forget that. It has allowed isolated people to communicate with one another and marginalized people to find one another. The busy parent can stay in touch with far-flung friends. The gay teenager no longer has to feel like a freak. But as the Internet's dimensionality has grown, it has quickly become too much of a good thing. Ten years ago we were writing e-mail messages on desktop computers and transmitting them over dial-up connections. Now we are sending text messages on our cell phones, posting pictures on our Facebook pages, and following complete strangers on Twitter. A constant stream of mediated contact, virtual, notional, or simulated, keeps us wired in to the electronic hive—though contact, or at least two-way contact, seems increasingly beside the point. The goal now, *10* it seems, is simply to become known, to turn oneself into a sort of miniature celebrity. How many friends do I have on Facebook? How many people are reading my blog? How many Google hits does my name generate? Visibility secures our self-esteem, becoming a substitute, twice removed, for genuine connection. Not long ago, it was easy to feel lonely. Now, it is impossible to be alone.

As a result, we are losing both sides of the Romantic dialectic. *11* What does friendship mean when you have 532 "friends"? How does it enhance my sense of closeness when my Facebook News Feed tells me that Sally Smith (whom I haven't seen since high school, and wasn't all that friendly with even then) "is making coffee and staring off into space"? My students told me they have little time for intimacy. And of course, they have no time at all for solitude.

But at least friendship, if not intimacy, is still something they want. *12* As jarring as the new dispensation may be for people in their 30s and 40s, the real problem is that it has become completely natural for people in their teens and 20s. Young people today seem to have no desire for solitude, have never heard of it, can't imagine why it would be worth having. In fact, their use of technology—or to be fair, our use of technology—seems to involve a constant effort to stave off the possibility of solitude, a continuous attempt, as we sit alone at our computers, to maintain the imaginative presence of others. As long ago as 1952, Trilling wrote about "the modern fear of being cut off from the social group even for a moment." Now we have equipped ourselves with the means to prevent that fear from ever being realized. Which does not mean that we have put it to rest. Quite the contrary. Remember my student, who couldn't even write a paper by herself. The more we keep aloneness at bay, the less are we able to deal with it and the more terrifying it gets.

There is an analogy, it seems to me, with the previous generation's *13* experience of boredom. The two emotions, loneliness and boredom, are closely allied. They are also both characteristically modern. The *Oxford English Dictionary*'s earliest citations of either word, at least in the contemporary sense, date from the nineteenth century. Suburbanization, by eliminating the stimulation as well as the sociability of urban or traditional village life, exacerbated the tendency to both. But the great age of boredom, I believe, came in with television, precisely because television was designed to palliate that feeling. Boredom is not a necessary consequence of having nothing to do, it is only the negative experience of that state. Television, by obviating the need to learn how to make use of one's lack of occupation, precludes one from ever discovering how to enjoy it. In fact, it renders that condition fearsome, its prospect intolerable. You are terrified of being bored—so you turn on the television.

162 CHAPTER 10 | FROM IDENTIFYING ISSUES TO FORMING QUESTIONS

I speak from experience. I grew up in the 1960s and 1970s, the *14* age of television. I was trained to be bored; boredom was cultivated within me like a precious crop. (It has been said that consumer society wants to condition us to feel bored, since boredom creates a market for stimulation.) It took me years to discover—and my nervous system will never fully adjust to this idea; I still have to fight against boredom, am permanently damaged in this respect—that having nothing to do doesn't have to be a bad thing. The alternative to boredom is what Whitman called idleness: a passive receptivity to the world.

So it is with the current generation's experience of being alone. *15* That is precisely the recognition implicit in the idea of solitude, which is to loneliness what idleness is to boredom. Loneliness is not the absence of company, it is grief over that absence. The lost sheep is lonely; the shepherd is not lonely. But the Internet is as powerful a machine for the production of loneliness as television is for the manufacture of boredom. If six hours of television a day creates the aptitude for boredom, the inability to sit still, a hundred text messages a day creates the aptitude for loneliness, the inability to be by yourself. Some degree of boredom and loneliness is to be expected, especially among young people, given the way our human environment has been attenuated. But technology amplifies those tendencies. You could call your schoolmates when I was a teenager, but you couldn't call them 100 times a day. You could get together with your friends when I was in college, but you couldn't always get together with them when you wanted to, for the simple reason that you couldn't always find them. If boredom is the great emotion of the TV generation, loneliness is the great emotion of the Web generation. We lost the ability to be still, our capacity for idleness. They have lost the ability to be alone, their capacity for solitude.

And losing solitude, what have they lost? First, the propensity for *16* introspection, that examination of the self that the Puritans, and the Romantics, and the modernists (and Socrates, for that matter) placed at the center of spiritual life—of wisdom, of conduct. Thoreau called it fishing "in the Walden Pond of [our] own natures," "bait[ing our] hooks with darkness." Lost, too, is the related propensity for sustained reading. The Internet brought text back into a televisual world, but it brought it back on terms dictated by that world—that is, by its remapping of our attention spans. Reading now means skipping and skimming; five minutes on the same Web page is considered an eternity. This is not reading as Marilynne Robinson described it: the encounter with a second self in the silence of mental solitude.

But we no longer believe in the solitary mind. If the Romantics had *17* Hume and the modernists had Freud, the current psychological model—

and this should come as no surprise — is that of the networked or social mind. Evolutionary psychology tells us that our brains developed to interpret complex social signals. According to David Brooks, that reliable index of the social-scientific zeitgeist, cognitive scientists tell us that "our decision-making is powerfully influenced by social context"; neuroscientists, that we have "permeable minds" that function in part through a process of "deep imitation"; psychologists, that "we are organized by our attachments"; sociologists, that our behavior is affected by "the power of social networks." The ultimate implication is that there is no mental space that is not social (contemporary social science dovetailing here with postmodern critical theory). One of the most striking things about the way young people relate to one another today is that they no longer seem to believe in the existence of Thoreau's "darkness."

The MySpace page, with its shrieking typography and clamorous imagery, has replaced the journal and the letter as a way of creating and communicating one's sense of self. The suggestion is not only that such communication is to be made to the world at large rather than to oneself or one's intimates, or graphically rather than verbally, or performatively rather than narratively or analytically, but also that it can be made completely. Today's young people seem to feel that they can make themselves fully known to one another. They seem to lack a sense of their own depths, and of the value of keeping them hidden. *18*

If they didn't, they would understand that solitude enables us to secure the integrity of the self as well as to explore it. Few have shown this more beautifully than Woolf. In the middle of *Mrs. Dalloway*, between her navigation of the streets and her orchestration of the party, between the urban jostle and the social bustle, Clarissa goes up, "like a nun withdrawing," to her attic room. Like a nun: She returns to a state that she herself thinks of as a kind of virginity. This does not mean she's a prude. Virginity is classically the outward sign of spiritual inviolability, of a self untouched by the world, a soul that has preserved its integrity by refusing to descend into the chaos and self-division of sexual and social relations. It is the mark of the saint and the monk, of Hippolytus and Antigone and Joan of Arc. Solitude is both the social image of that state and the means by which we can approximate it. And the supreme image in *Mrs. Dalloway* of the dignity of solitude itself is the old woman whom Clarissa catches sight of through her window. "Here was one room," she thinks, "there another." We are not merely social beings. We are each also separate, each solitary, each alone in our own room, each miraculously our unique selves and mysteriously enclosed in that selfhood. *19*

To remember this, to hold oneself apart from society, is to begin to think one's way beyond it. Solitude, Emerson said, "is to genius *20* the stern friend." "He who should inspire and lead his race must be defended from traveling with the souls of other men, from living, breathing, reading, and writing in the daily, time-worn yoke of their opinions." One must protect oneself from the momentum of intellectual and moral consensus—especially, Emerson added, during youth. "God is alone," Thoreau said, "but the Devil, he is far from being alone; he sees a great deal of company; he is legion." The university was to be praised, Emerson believed, if only because it provided its charges with "a separate chamber and fire"—the physical space of solitude. Today, of course, universities do everything they can to keep their students from being alone, lest they perpetrate self-destructive acts, and also, perhaps, unfashionable thoughts. But no real excellence, personal or social, artistic, philosophical, scientific, or moral, can arise without solitude. "The saint and poet seek privacy," Emerson said, "to ends the most public and universal." We are back to the seer, seeking signposts for the future in splendid isolation.

Solitude isn't easy, and isn't for everyone. It has undoubtedly never been the province of more than a few. "I believe," Thoreau said, "that men are generally still a little afraid of the dark." Teresa and Tiresias will always be the exceptions, or to speak in more relevant terms, the young people—and they still exist—who prefer to loaf and invite their soul, who step to the beat of a different drummer. But if solitude disappears as a social value and social idea, will even the exceptions remain possible? Still, one is powerless to reverse the drift of the culture. One can only save oneself—and whatever else happens, one can still always do that. But it takes a willingness to be unpopular. *21*

The last thing to say about solitude is that it isn't very polite. Thoreau knew that the "doubleness" that solitude cultivates, the ability to stand back and observe life dispassionately, is apt to make us a little unpleasant to our fellows, to say nothing of the offense implicit in avoiding their company. But then, he didn't worry overmuch about being genial. He didn't even like having to talk to people three times a day, at meals; one can only imagine what he would have made of text-messaging. We, however, have made of geniality—the weak smile, the polite interest, the fake invitation—a cardinal virtue. Friendship may be slipping from our grasp, but our friendliness is universal. Not for nothing does "gregarious" mean "part of the herd." But Thoreau understood that securing one's self-possession was worth a few wounded feelings. He may have put his neighbors off, but at least he was sure of himself. Those who would find solitude must not be afraid to stand alone. *22*

AN ACADEMIC ESSAY FOR ANALYSIS   **165**

Writing as a Reader

1. Recast Deresiewicz's essay as Anna Quindlen might in her *Newsweek* column. Obviously, her *Newsweek* column is much shorter (an important constraint). She also writes for a more general audience than Deresiewicz, and her tone is quite different. To strengthen your sense of her approach, you may want to browse some of Quindlen's other essays in editions of *Newsweek* or in some of her essay collections listed in the headnote on page 148.

2. Recast Deresiewicz's essay in terms of a writer you read regularly—for example, a columnist in your local newspaper or a blogger in some online venue. Use your imagination. What is the audience, and how will you have to present the issue to engage and persuade them?

11

From Formulating to Developing a Thesis

Academic writing explores complex issues that grow out of relevant, timely conversations in which something is at stake. An academic writer reads as a writer to understand the issues, situations, and questions that lead other writers to make claims. Readers expect academic writers to take a clear, specific, logical stand on an issue, and they evaluate how writers support their claims and anticipate counterarguments. The logical stand is the **thesis**, an assertion that academic writers make at the beginning of what they write and then support with evidence throughout their essay. The illustrations and examples that a writer includes must relate to and support the thesis. Thus, a thesis encompasses all of the information writers use to further their arguments; it is not simply a single assertion at the beginning of an essay.

One of our students aptly described the thesis using the metaphor of a shish kebab: The thesis runs through every paragraph, holding the paragraphs together, just as a skewer runs through and holds the ingredients of a shish kebab together. Moreover, the thesis serves as a signpost throughout an essay, reminding readers what the argument is and why the writer has included evidence—examples, illustrations, quotations—relevant to that argument.

An academic thesis

- makes an assertion that is clearly defined, focused, and supported.
- reflects an awareness of the conversation from which the writer has taken up the issue.
- is placed at the beginning of the essay.

166

- runs through every paragraph like the skewer in a shish kebab.
- acknowledges points of view that differ from the writer's own, reflecting the complexity of the issue.
- demonstrates an awareness of the readers' assumptions and anticipates possible counterarguments.
- conveys a significant fresh perspective.

It is a myth that writers first come up with a thesis and then write their essays. The reality is that writers use issue-based questions to read, learn, and develop a thesis throughout the process of writing. Through revising and discussing their ideas, writers hone their thesis, making sure that it threads through every paragraph of the final draft. The position writers ultimately take in writing—their thesis—comes at the end of the writing process, after not one draft but many.

WORKING VERSUS DEFINITIVE THESES

Writers are continually challenged by the need to establish their purpose and to make a clear and specific assertion of it. To reach that assertion, you must first engage in a prolonged process of inquiry, aided by a well-formulated question. The question serves as a tool for inquiry that will help you formulate your **working thesis**, your first attempt at an assertion of your position. A working thesis is valuable in the early stages of writing because it helps you read selectively, in the same way that your issue-based question guides your inquiry. Reading raises questions, helping you see what you know and need to know, and challenging you to read on.

Never accept your working thesis as your final position. Instead, continue testing your assertion as you read and write, and modify your working thesis as necessary. A more definitive thesis will come once you are satisfied that you have examined the issue from multiple perspectives.

For example, one of our students wanted to study representations of femininity in the media. In particular, she focused on why the Barbie doll has become an icon of femininity despite what many cultural critics consider Barbie's "outrageous and ultimately unattainable physical characteristics." Our student's working thesis suggested she would develop an argument about the need for change:

> The harmful implications of ongoing exposure to these unattainable ideals, such as low self-esteem, eating disorders, unhealthy body image, and acceptance of violence, make urgent the need for change.

The student assumed that her research would lead her to argue that Barbie's unattainable proportions have a damaging effect on women's self-image and that something needs to be done about it. However, as she read scholarly research to support her tentative thesis, she realized that a more compelling project would be less Barbie-centric. Instead, she chose to examine the broader phenomenon of how the idea of femininity is created and reinforced by society. That is, her personal interest in Barbie was supplanted by her discoveries about cultural norms of beauty and the power they have to influence self-perception and behavior. In her final draft, this was her definitive thesis:

> Although evidence may be provided to argue that gender is an innate characteristic, I will show that it is actually the result of one's actions, which are then labeled *masculine* or *feminine* according to society's definitions of ideal gender. Furthermore, I will discuss the communication of such definitions through the media, specifically in music videos, on TV, and in magazines, and the harmful implications of being exposed to these ideals.

Instead of arguing for change, the student chose to show her readers how they were being manipulated, leaving it to them to decide what actions they might want to take.

DEVELOPING A WORKING THESIS: FOUR MODELS

What are some ways to develop a working thesis? We suggest four models that may help you organize the information you gather in response to the question guiding your inquiry.

■ The Correcting-Misinterpretations Model

This model is used to correct writers whose arguments you believe have misconstrued one or more important aspects of an issue. The thesis typically takes the form of a factual claim. Consider this example and the words we have underlined:

> <u>Although scholars have addressed curriculum</u> to explain low achievement in schools, <u>they have failed to fully appreciate the impact of limited resources</u> to fund up-to-date textbooks, quality teachers, and computers. Therefore, reform in schools must focus on economic need as well as curriculum.

The clause beginning with "Although" lays out the assumption that many scholars make, that curriculum explains low educational achievement; the clause beginning with "they have failed" identifies the error those scholars have made by ignoring the economic reasons for low achievement in schools. Notice that the structure of the sentence reinforces the author's position. He explains what he sees as the faulty assumption in a subordinate clause and reserves the main clause for his own position. The two clauses indicate that different authors hold conflicting opinions. Note that the writer could have used a phrase such as "they [scholars] have *understated* the impact of limited resources" as a way to reframe

DEVELOPING A WORKING THESIS: FOUR MODELS **169**

the problem in his thesis. In crafting your thesis, choose words that signal to readers that you are correcting others' ideas, or even misinterpretations, without being dismissive. One more thing: Although it is a common myth that a thesis can be phrased in a single sentence (a legacy of the five-paragraph theme, we suspect), this example shows that a thesis can be written in two (or more) sentences.

■ The Filling-the-Gap Model

The gap model points to what other writers may have overlooked or ignored in discussing a given issue. The gap model typically makes a claim of value. Consider this student's argument that discussions of cultural diversity in the United States are often framed in terms of black and white. Our underlining indicates the gap the writer has identified:

> If America is truly a "melting pot" of cultures, as it is often called, then <u>why is it that stories and events seem only to be in black and white? Why is it that when history courses are taught about the period of the civil rights movement, only the memoirs of African Americans are read</u>, like those of Melba Pattillo Beals and Ida Mae Holland? Where are <u>the works of Maxine Hong Kingston</u>, who tells the story of alienation and segregation in schools through the eyes of a Chinese child? African Americans were denied the right to vote, and many other citizenship rights; but Chinese Americans were denied even the opportunity to become citizens. I am not diminishing the issue of discrimination against African Americans, or belittling the struggles they went through. <u>I simply want to call attention to discrimination against other minority groups and their often-overlooked struggles to achieve equality.</u>

In the student's thesis, the gap in people's knowledge stems from their limited understanding of history. They need to understand that many minority groups were denied their rights.

A variation on the gap model also occurs when a writer suggests that although something might appear to be the case, a closer look reveals something different. For example: "Although it would *appear* that women have achieved equality in the workplace, their paychecks suggest that this is not true."

One of our students examined two poems by the same author that appeared to contradict each other. She noticed a gap others had not seen:

> In both "The Albatross" and "Beauty," Charles Baudelaire chooses to explore the plight of the poet. Interestingly, despite their common author, the two poems' portrayals of the poet's struggles appear contradictory. "The Albatross" seems to give a somewhat sympathetic glimpse into the exile of the poet — the "winged voyager" so awkward in the ordinary world. "Beauty" takes what appears to be a less forgiving stance: The poet here is docile, simply a mirror. Although both pieces depict the poet's struggles, a closer examination demonstrates how the portrayals differ.

170 CHAPTER 11 | FROM FORMULATING TO DEVELOPING A THESIS

In stating her thesis, the student indicates that although readers might expect Baudelaire's images of poets to be similar, a closer examination of his words would prove them wrong.

■ The Modifying-What-Others-Have-Said Model

The modification model of thesis writing assumes that mutual understanding is possible. For example, in proposing a change in policy, one student asserts:

> Although scholars have claimed that the only sure way to reverse the cycle of homelessness in America is to provide an adequate education, we need to build on this work, providing school-to-work programs that ensure graduates have access to employment.

Here the writer seeks to modify other writers' claims, suggesting that education alone does not solve the problem of homelessness. The challenge he sets for himself is to understand the complexity of the problem by building on and extending the ideas of others. In effect, he is in a constructive conversation with those whose work he wants to build on, helping readers see that he shares common ground with the other writers and that he hopes to find a mutually acceptable solution to the agreed-on problem.

■ The Hypothesis-Testing Model

The hypothesis-testing model begins with the assumption that writers may have good reasons for supporting their arguments, but that there are also a number of legitimate reasons that explain why something is, or is not, the case. The questions motivating your research will often lead you to a number of possible answers, but none are necessarily more correct than others. That is, the evidence is based on a hypothesis that researchers will continue to test by examining individual cases through an inductive method until the evidence refutes that hypothesis.

For example, over the last decade, researchers have generated a number of hypotheses to explain the causes of climate change. Some have argued that climate change, or global warming, can be explained by natural causes, that change is a cyclical process. Those who adopt such a view might use evidence to demonstrate that oceans produce heat and that change can be attributed to a steady increase in heat production over time. Others have persuasively shown that humans have caused global warming by burning fossil fuels that increase the amount of carbon in the air, which creates what scientists call the "greenhouse effect." Each assertion is based on a set of inferences from observation and the data available to test each hypothesis. Moreover, the truth value of any assertion is based on the probability that global warming can be attributed to any one cause or explanation.

The hypothesis-testing model assumes that the questions you raise will likely lead you to multiple answers that compete for your attention. The following is one way to formulate such an argument in which you examine rival hypotheses before coming to a conclusion.

> Some people explain *this* by suggesting *that*, but a close analysis of the problem reveals several compelling, but competing explanations.

You may not find a definitive explanation, so you will need to sort through the evidence you find, develop an argument, and acknowledge the reasonable counterarguments that critical readers will raise. In the end, you are not really proving that something is the case, such as the causes of global warming, but you are helping readers understand what you see as the best case given the available evidence.

Steps to Formulating a Working Thesis: Four Models

1 **Misinterpretations model:** "Although many scholars have argued about A and B, a careful examination suggests C."

2 **Gap model:** "Although scholars have noted A and B, they have missed the importance of C."

3 **Modification model:** "Although I agree with the A and B ideas of other writers, it is important to extend/refine/limit their ideas with C."

4 **Hypothesis-testing model:** "Some people explain A by suggesting B, but a close analysis of the problem reveals the possibility of several competing/complementary explanations such as C, D, and E."

A Practice Sequence: Identifying Types of Theses

Below is a series of working theses. Read each one and then identify the model—misinterpretations, gap, modification, or hypothesis-testing—that it represents.

1 A number of studies indicate that violence on television has a detrimental effect on adolescent behavior. However, few researchers have examined key environmental factors like peer

pressure, music, and home life. In fact, I would argue that many researchers have oversimplified the problem.

2 Although research indicates that an increasing number of African American and Hispanic students are dropping out of high school, researchers have failed to fully grasp the reasons why this has occurred.

3 I want to argue that studies supporting single-sex education are relatively sound. However, we don't really know the long-term effects of single-sex education, particularly on young women's career paths.

4 Although recent studies of voting patterns in the United States indicate that young people between the ages of 18 and 24 are apathetic, I want to suggest that not all of the reasons these studies provide are valid.

5 Indeed, it's not surprising that students are majoring in fields that will enable them to get a job after graduation. But students may not be as pragmatic as we think. Many students choose majors because they feel that learning is an important end in itself.

6 Some reformers have assumed that increasing competition will force public schools to improve the quality of education, but it seems that a number of recent initiatives can be used to explain why students have begun to flourish in math and reading, particularly in the primary grades.

7 It is clear that cities need to clean up the dilapidated housing projects that were built over half a century ago; but few, if any, studies have examined the effects of doing so on the life chances of those people who are being displaced.

8 In addition to its efforts to advance the cause of social justice in the new global economy, the university must make a commitment to ending poverty on the edge of campus.

9 Although the writer offers evidence to explain the sources of illiteracy in America, he overstates his case when he ignores other factors, among them history, culture, and economic well-being. Therefore, I will argue that we place the discussion in a broader context.

10 More and more policymakers argue that English should be the national language in the United States. Although I agree that English is important, we should not limit people's right to maintain their own linguistic and cultural identity.

ESTABLISHING A CONTEXT FOR A THESIS

In addition to defining the purpose and focus of an essay, a thesis must set up a **context** for the writer's claim. The process of establishing a background for understanding an issue typically involves four steps:

1. Establish that the topic of conversation, the issue, is current and relevant—that it is on people's minds or should be.

2. Briefly summarize what others have said to show that you are familiar with the topic or issue.

3. Explain what you see as the problem—a misinterpretation, a gap, or a modification that needs to be made in how others have addressed the topic or issue—perhaps by raising the questions you believe need to be answered.

4. State your thesis, suggesting that your view on the issue may present readers with something new to think about as it builds on and extends what others have argued.

You need not follow these steps in this order as long as your readers come away from the first part of your essay knowing why you are discussing a given issue and what your argument is.

AN ANNOTATED STUDENT INTRODUCTION: PROVIDING A CONTEXT FOR A THESIS

We trace these four steps below in our analysis of the opening paragraphs of a student's essay. Motivating his argument is his sense that contemporary writers and educators may not fully grasp the issues that limit the opportunities for low-income youth to attend college. His own family struggled financially, and he argues that a fuller appreciation of the problem can help educators partner with families to advise youth in more informed ways.

O'Neill 1

Colin O'Neill

Money Matters:

Framing the College Access Debate

The student establishes the timeliness and relevance of an issue that challenges widely held assumptions about the value of attending college.

College is expensive. And with prices continuing to rise each year, there are those who are beginning to question whether or not college is a worthy investment. In a recent *Newsweek* article, journalist Megan McArdle (2012) asserts that the process of obtaining a college degree has morphed into a "national neurosis"

1

O'Neill 2

and calls upon Americans to question whether college is necessary for lifelong success. McArdle joins a chorus of voices calling upon a reevaluation of the current educational pipeline at a time when the number of American students who are ill-prepared to face the rigors of a college curriculum has increased. Some writers suggest that a renaissance of vocational education may, in fact, begin to compensate for the disparate nature of American education. Based on research conducted by Bozick and DeLuca (2011), it is clear that these opinions are grounded in reality.

He begins to summarize what others have said to demonstrate his familiarity with the conversation in popular media and scholarship.

Of nearly 3,000 surveyed "college non-enrollees," roughly 50 percent attributed their withdrawal from the education system to either the high cost of college education or the desire to look for work and embark along their chosen career path. However, for those like me, who believe strongly that higher education is a right that ought to be available to all students, McArdle's and others' assertions add to the list of physical and social barriers that keep students of poorer backgrounds from pursuing their educational aspirations. The ability to pay for college may not be the only consideration keeping students from exploring higher education. Instead, researchers have overlooked the extent to which knowledge (or the lack of it) of college costs and awareness of different financing options (such as grants, scholarships, and loans) may preemptively alter the way in which children envision themselves within the college experience.

The student identifies what he sees as a problem signaled by words like "however," "overlooked," and "instead" and begins to formulate his own argument.

He points out a misconception that he wants to correct.

In many cities where the median household income often hovers slightly above $30,000, college is, according to some educators, a pipedream to which nearly every family aspires, but most are not convinced this goal will ever become a reality (United States Census Bureau). Indeed, with the average cost of a college education rising to upwards of $20,000, it is unclear whether this dream will, in fact, come true. Although parents have a strong desire to send their kids to college, the financial numbers do not seem to add up. While educators have tended to leave parents responsible for educating their children on the financial realities of higher education, researchers such as Elliot, Sherraden, Johnson, and Guo (2010) make the case that awareness of college costs makes its way into the worldview of students as young as second grade. In light of this work, it becomes important to note that the large price tag of a college

The student cites research to further define the problem and show that he is aware of the very real barriers that affect college access for low-income youth.

O'Neill 3

He uses research to understand further a problem that others may have overlooked or ignored.

degree may have implications that spread far beyond a particular family's capacity to fund their children's education. As the recent research of Bozick and DeLuca (2011) suggests, the cost of college is changing and challenging the way students begin to examine the purpose and necessity of college education. College costs are diminishing one's access to college in more ways than restricting their ability to foot the bill. For low-income students and their families, for whom every day is filled with financial burdens of all sorts, high college costs are changing the way they perceive college as an institution.

4

The correlation between the college choice process and students' perceptions of the cost of higher education is not an unexamined phenomenon. Many researchers have looked at the ways in which the cost of a college education affects the ways low-income students begin to foster a relationship with the college system. The existing body of research, however, has tended to focus solely on high school students, students who are mere months away from beginning the college search process. According to Cabrera and La Nasa (2000), the college choice process actually begins much earlier, commencing between the time a child enters middle school and embarks upon his or her high school journey. It is this process that ultimately dictates the level of college access a particular student does or does not have. Therefore, my study will focus primarily on what Cabrera and La Nasa (2000) termed the "predisposition" stage. Between grades seven and nine, predisposition draws upon parental encouragement, socioeconomic status, and "information about college." Along the trajectory set in place by Cabrera and La Nasa (2000), these factors have a profound influence on the search and choice stages of the college-access process. Recognizing the interrelational nature of these different stages, that is, both how they are different and how each one builds upon the other, is key to navigating the ill-defined nature of the pre-collegiate experience.

Citing a key study, the student underscores a gap in the research, again signaled by "however."

He adopts a frame through which to think about the issue and narrow his focus.

He begins to offer a solution to a problem researchers have not fully appreciated.

5

Given the findings of prior research, it is important to push back the discussion about college affordability and college access to examine how the notion of cost impacts the fragile, emerging relationship that middle school students are just beginning to develop. To recognize how students begin to understand college

176 CHAPTER 11 | FROM FORMULATING TO DEVELOPING A THESIS

O'Neill 4

The student explains that the purpose of his research is to fill the gap he identifies above and correct a misunderstanding.

and develop college aspirations, then, I conducted interviews with middle school children to assess how early awareness of college costs plays a role in shaping families' decisions about the need, desire for, and accessibility of higher education. By doing so, I have tried to fill a gap left behind by previous research and add to the wider discussion of college affordability and its overall impact on college access amongst students of all ages. Although educators may argue that American education ought to revert to an old, draconian system of vocational education, preparing low-income students to enter technical fields, I argue that it is important to create programs that encourage parents, teachers, and students to think early about the costs of college and the possibilities that exist to help children pursue a college degree.

Here he makes a policy-related claim that challenges a conflicting point of view.

■ Establish That the Issue Is Current and Relevant

Ideally, you should convey to readers that the issue you are discussing is both current (what's on people's minds) and relevant (of sufficient importance to have generated some discussion and written conversation). In the first two sentences of the first paragraph, O'Neill explains that the increase in college costs has not only become a focus of national attention, evidenced in the *Newsweek* article he cites, but has motivated writers to question whether the cost to low-income families is a worthwhile investment. In the next sentence, he explains that the author of this article, Megan McArdle, is not alone in challenging some widely held assumptions about the value of attending college. In fact, O'Neill indicates that McArdle "joins a chorus of voices calling upon a reevaluation of the current educational pipeline at a time when the number of American students who are ill-prepared to face the rigors of a college curriculum has increased." Thus, O'Neill demonstrates that the issue he focuses on is part of a lively conversation and debate that has captured the imagination of many writers at the time he was writing about college access.

■ Briefly Present What Others Have Said

It is important to introduce who has said what in the conversation you are entering. After all, you are joining that conversation to make your contribution, and those who are in that conversation expect you to have done your homework and acknowledge those who have already made important contributions.

AN ANNOTATED STUDENT INTRODUCTION: PROVIDING A CONTEXT FOR A THESIS **177**

In the first few sentences of his introduction, O'Neill sets the stage for his review of research by citing McArdle's *Newsweek* article. Although he takes issue with McArdle, he is careful to explain her argument. In addition, he refers to research in the final sentence of the first paragraph to suggest the extent to which her argument may be "grounded in reality." Indeed, in the second paragraph, he cites a study that reports on the significant number of students surveyed who dropped out of college, nearly half attributing their decision to the high costs of pursuing a college degree. However, O'Neill, who makes clear that he believes everyone has a "right" to an education, uses his review to reframe the issue, calling attention to the way McArdle and others have "overlooked the extent to which knowledge (or the lack of it) of college costs and awareness of different financing options (such as grants, scholarships, and loans) may preemptively alter the way in which children envision themselves within the college experience." In turn, O'Neill highlights research that focuses on parents' and children's perceptions of college access as a way to challenge those writers who call for a "reevaluation of the current educational pipeline."

By pointing out what journalists and researchers may have overlooked in discussing the college-going prospects of low-income youth, O'Neill is doing more than listing the sources he has read. He is establishing that a problem, or issue, exists. Moreover, his review gives readers intellectual touchstones, the scholars (e.g., Cabrera and La Nasa [2000]) who need to be cited in any academic conversation about college access. A review is not a catchall for anyone writing on a topic. Instead it should represent a writer's choice of the most relevant participants in the conversation. O'Neill's choice of sources and his presentation of them convey that he is knowledgeable about his subject. (Of course, it is his readers' responsibility to read further to determine whether he has reviewed the most relevant work and has presented the ideas of others accurately. If he has, readers will trust him, whether or not they end up agreeing with him on the issue.)

■ Explain What You See as the Problem

If a review indicates a problem, as O'Neill's review does, the problem can often be couched in terms of the models we discussed earlier: misinterpretations, gaps, modification, or hypothesis testing. In paragraph 4, O'Neill identifies what he sees as a gap in how journalists and researchers approach the cost of attending college and the question of "whether college is necessary to lifelong success." He suggests that such a view is the consequence of a gap in knowledge (notice our underlining):

> The existing body of research, however, has tended to focus solely on high school students, students who are mere months away from beginning the college search process. According to Cabrera and La Nasa (2000), the college choice process actually begins much earlier, commencing between the time a child enters middle school and embarks upon his or her high school journey.

While O'Neill acknowledges the value of others' writing, his review of research culminates with his assertion that it is important to understand the problem of college costs with greater depth and precision. After all, researchers and journalists have overlooked or ignored important sources of information. At stake for O'Neill is that limiting low-income youth's access to higher education challenges a more equitable view that all children deserve a chance to have a successful life. Moreover, at the end of paragraph 3, he shifts the burden from parents, alone, to educators who clearly influence the "way students begin to examine the purpose and necessity of college education."

■ State Your Thesis

An effective thesis statement helps readers see the reasoning behind a writer's claim; it also signals what readers should look for in the remainder of the essay. O'Neill closes paragraph 5 with a statement that speaks to both the purpose and the substance of what he writes:

> Although educators may argue that American education ought to revert to an old, draconian system of vocational education, preparing low-income students to enter technical fields, I argue that it is important to create programs that encourage parents, teachers, and students to think early about the costs of college and the possibilities that exist to help children pursue a college degree.

In your own writing, you can make use of the strategies that O'Neill uses in his essay. Words like *although*, *however*, *but*, *instead*, and *yet* can set up the problem you identify. Here is a variation on what O'Neill writes: "One might argue that vocational programs may provide a reasonable alternative to meeting the needs of low-income students for whom college seems unaffordable and out of reach; however [but, yet], such an approach ignores the range of possibilities that exist for changing policies to ensure that all children have access to a college education."

Steps to Establishing a Context for a Thesis

1 **Establish that the issue is current and relevant.** Point out the extent to which others have recognized the problem, issue, or question that you are writing about.

2 **Briefly present what others have said.** Explain how others have addressed the problem, issue, or question you are focusing on.

3 **Explain what you see as the problem.** Identify what is open to dispute.

4 **State your thesis.** Help readers see your purpose and how you intend to achieve it — by correcting a misconception, filling a gap, modifying a claim others have accepted, or stating an hypothesis.

AN ANNOTATED STUDENT INTRODUCTION: PROVIDING A CONTEXT FOR A THESIS   **179**

▪ Analyze the Context of a Thesis

In "Teaching Toward Possibility," educator Kris Gutiérrez argues that teaching should focus on student learning and provide students with multiple tools from different disciplines to ensure that students engage in what she describes as "deep learning." She also explains that culture plays a key role in learning, particularly for students from nondominant groups. However, she reframes the notion of culture as a set of practices, as a verb, which she distinguishes from inert conceptions of culture based on individuals' membership in a particular ethnic community. Her essay, published in 2011, is addressed to educators, teachers, and policy makers. As you read the following excerpt, you may feel puzzled by some of Gutiérrez's vocabulary and perhaps even excluded from the conversation at times. Our purpose in reprinting this excerpt is to show through our annotations how Gutiérrez has applied the strategies we have been discussing in this chapter. As you read, make your own annotations, and then try to answer the questions—which may involve careful rereading—that we pose after the selection. In particular, watch for signpost words or phrases that signal the ideas the writer is challenging.

KRIS GUTIÉRREZ

From Teaching Toward Possibility: Building Cultural Supports for Robust Learning

The author establishes the relevance and timeliness of the issue.

This is particularly relevant for an audience of teachers who want to know how to motivate students whose backgrounds they may be unfamiliar with.

Consider the potential learning power of a unit on environmental inequities or environment racism for middle or high school students in which students are provided the opportunity to examine the issue deeply and broadly. We did just this over a number of years in rigorous summer programs for high school students from migrant farm worker backgrounds. Students learned environmental science, learned traditional information about the environment, learned about the history of the area of study, as well as the history of environmental issues in their local and immediate communities. This way of learning required interdisciplinary reading, including reading across genres, points of view, and across historical time and space. These learning practices enticed students to want to learn more, to research, and to make connections across relevant ideas and their varied meanings within and across academic

1

and home communities. In short, instruction was coherent, historicized, textured, layered, and deeply supported in ways that allowed students to access and engage with rigorous texts and high status knowledge, as well as work in and through the contradictions and tensions inherent in knowledge production and authentic science/learning issues.

Gutiérrez further establishes the relevance of teaching non-dominant students and seeks to correct a misconception about the nature of teaching, learning, and culture.

In the following section, I draw on the case of teaching science to migrant students mentioned above to elaborate a challenge to reductive approaches to teaching and learning that offer the "quick-fix" and provide "off the shelf" solutions to education; that is, those relying on silver bullet solutions to solve complex educational problems or using theory and research uncritically or without sufficient understanding because it is fashionable to do so. One such quick-fix approach is found in learning styles approaches to learning, particularly cultural learning styles conceptions in which regularities in cultural communities are characterized as static and unchanging and general traits of individuals are attributable categorically to ethnic group membership.

She cites her own work to support her argument and then reviews relevant studies to challenge approaches to teaching and learning that fail to conceptualize the notion of culture adequately.

In my work (Gutiérrez, 2002; Gutiérrez & Rogoff, 2003), I have argued the importance of moving beyond such narrow assumptions of cultural communities by focusing both on regularity and variance in a community's practices (as well as those of individuals). Employing a cultural-historical-activity theoretical approach to learning and development (Cole & Engeström, 2003; Engeström, 1987; Leontiev, 1981) is one productive means toward challenging static and ahistorical understandings of cultural communities and their practices, as this view focuses attention on variations in individual and group histories of engagement in cultural practices. Variations, then, are best understood as proclivities of people who have particular histories of engagement with specific cultural activities, not as traits of individuals or collections of individuals. In other words, individual and group experience in activities—not their traits—become the focus.

Gutiérrez reframes the way educators should view culture, and this new frame is the lens through which she develops her argument.

AN ANNOTATED STUDENT INTRODUCTION: PROVIDING A CONTEXT FOR A THESIS   181

Through this new conception of culture, Gutiérrez defines what she sees as a gap in what educators know and need to know. She attributes this gap to what educators have ignored and cites additional research to make her point.

Within this view, it becomes easier to understand the limitations of learning styles approaches in which individuals from one group might be characterized as "holistic learners"—where individuals from another group may be characterized as learning analytically or individuals may be divided into cooperative versus individualist learners on the basis of membership in a particular cultural group. Such methods ignore or minimize variation and focus on perceived or over-generalized regularities. Further, learning styles pedagogical practices have been used to distinguish the learning styles of "minority" group members and to explain "minority" student failure (see Foley, 1997; Kavale & Forness, 1987; Irvine & York, 1995 for reviews). Of consequence, addressing learning styles as traits linked to membership in cultural communities also seems to be a common way to prepare teachers about diversity (Guild, 1994; Matthews, 1991). Understandably, teaching to a difference that can be labeled (e.g., learning modalities) may be appealing to teachers who have limited resources, support, or training to meet the challenges of new student populations. However, attribution of learning style or difference based on group membership can serve to buttress persistent deficit model orientations to teaching students from nondominant communities; without acknowledging both the regularity and variance makes it harder to understand the relation of individual learning and the practices of cultural communities, which in turn can hinder effective assistance to student learning (Gutiérrez & Rogoff, 2003).

Her use of "however" distinguishes what she sees as a prevailing school of thought and what she believes should be the case. Educators' misconceptions about culture are the source of the problem she identifies.

Gutiérrez reaffirms the issue between two competing ideas.

The key issue here is that learning styles approaches are grounded in reductive notions of culture that conflate race/ethnicity with culture—a practice that often leads to one-size-fits-all approaches and understandings of the learning process of students from non-dominant communities. Consider familiar statements such as "My Latino students learn this way" or "I need to teach to the cultural background of my African American students" and even, "Asian students

182   CHAPTER 11 | FROM FORMULATING TO DEVELOPING A THESIS

The lens of culture that she has adopted helps us understand the nature of the misconception that she identifies and solve a problem in educating students from non-dominant groups. This last sentence is her main claim.

are good at math." Such generalizations are based on the assumption that people hold uniform cultural practices based on their membership in a particular community. Culture from this perspective is something you can observe from people's phenotype, physical characteristics, national origin, or language. Culture, then, is best considered a verb or said differently, culture is better understood as people's practices or how people live culturally (Moll, 1998). This more dynamic and instrumental role of culture should help us avoid the tendency to conflate culture with race and ethnicity and assumptions about people's cultural practices.

To avoid conflating race/ethnicity with culture, I often remind researchers and educators to invoke the "100-percent Piñata rule"—that is, 100-percent of Mexicans do not hit piñatas 100-percent of the time. While piñatas may in fact be a prevalent cultural artifact in many Mexican and Mexican-descent communities (and now across many household and communities in the Southwest), we would not make generalizations about their use and would expect variation in piñata practices, their meaning, value,

She restates her claim about culture.

and use. Thus, while cultural artifacts mediate human activity, they have varying functions in use and in practice, just as there is regularity and variance in any cultural community and its practices.

Reading as a Writer

1. What specific places can you point to in the selection that illustrate what is at issue for Gutiérrez?

2. How does she use her review to set up her argument?

3. What specific words and phrases does she use to establish what she sees as the problem? Is she correcting misinterpretations, filling a gap, or modifying what others have said?

4. What would you say is Gutiérrez's thesis? What specifics can you point to in the text to support your answer?

5. What would you say are the arguments Gutiérrez wants you to avoid? Again, what specific details can you point to in the text to support your answer?

AN ANNOTATED STUDENT INTRODUCTION: PROVIDING A CONTEXT FOR A THESIS   183

A Practice Sequence: Building a Thesis

We would like you to practice some of the strategies we have covered in this chapter. If you have already started working on an essay, exercises 1 through 4 present an opportunity to take stock of your progress, a chance to sort through what you've discovered, identify what you still need to discover, and move toward refining your thesis. Jot down your answer to each of the questions below and make lists of what you know and what you need to learn.

1   Have you established that your issue is current and relevant, that it is or should be on people's minds? What information would you need to do so?

2   Can you summarize briefly what others have said in the past to show that you are familiar with how others have addressed the issue? List some of the key texts you have read and the key points they make.

3   Have you identified any misunderstandings or gaps in how others have addressed the issue? Describe them. Do you have any ideas or information that would address these misunderstandings or help fill these gaps? Where might you find the information you need? Can you think of any sources you should reread to learn more? (For example, have you looked at the works cited or bibliographies in the texts you've already read?)

4   At this point, what is your take on the issue? Try drafting a working thesis statement that will present readers with something new to think about, building on and extending what others have argued. In drafting your thesis statement, try out the models discussed in this chapter and see if one is an especially good fit:

- *Misinterpretations model:* "Although many scholars have argued about A and B, a careful examination suggests C."
- *Gap model:* "Although scholars have noted A and B, they have missed the importance of C."
- *Modification model:* "Although I agree with A and B ideas of other writers, it is important to extend/refine/limit their ideas with C."
- *Hypothesis-testing model:* "Some people explain A by suggesting B, but a close analysis of the problem reveals the possibility of several competing/complementary explanations such as C, D, and E."

184   CHAPTER 11 | FROM FORMULATING TO DEVELOPING A THESIS

5   If you haven't chosen a topic yet, try a group exercise. Sit down with a few of your classmates and choose one of the following topics to brainstorm about as a group. Choose a topic that everyone in the group finds interesting, and work through exercises 1 through 4 in this practice sequence. Here are some suggestions:

- the moral obligation to vote
- the causes or consequences of poverty
- the limits of academic freedom
- equity in education
- the popularity of _____
- gender stereotypes in the media
- linguistic diversity
- the uses of a liberal education
- journalism and truth
- government access to personal information

AN ANNOTATED STUDENT ESSAY: STATING AND SUPPORTING A THESIS

We have annotated the following student essay to illustrate the strategies we have discussed in this chapter for stating a thesis that responds to a relevant, timely problem in a given context. The assignment was to write an argument focusing on literacy, based on research. Veronica Stafford chose to write about her peers' habit of texting and the ways in which this type of social interaction affects their intellectual development. Stafford develops a thesis that provides a corrective to a misconception that she sees in the ongoing conversations about texting. Her approach is a variation on the strategy in which writers correct a misinterpretation. In turn, you will see that she makes claims of fact and evaluation in making an argument for changing her peers' penchant for texting.

As you read the essay, reflect on your own experiences: Do you think the issue she raises is both timely and relevant? How well do you think she places her ideas in conversation with others? How would you respond to her various claims? Which do you agree with and disagree with, and why? What evidence would you present to support or counter her claims? Do you think she offers a reasonable corrective to what she believes is a misconception about texting?

AN ANNOTATED STUDENT ESSAY: STATING AND SUPPORTING A THESIS   185

Stafford 1

Veronica Stafford
Professor Wilson
English 1102
April 20 —

Texting and Literacy

As students walk to class each day, most do not notice
the other people around them. Rather than talking with others,
they are texting their friends in the next building, in their dorm,
or back home. Although social networking is the most common
use for text messages, they are not used solely for socializing.
While texting is a quick and easy way to keep up with friends,
it threatens other aspects of our lives. When students spend
time texting rather than focusing on those other important
aspects, texting becomes detrimental. Students' enjoyment of
reading, their schoolwork, and their relationships with others
are all negatively affected by text messaging.

*The student
identifies an issue,
or problem, and
states her thesis
as an evaluative
claim that attempts
to correct a
misconception.*

Due to the mass appeal of text messaging, students pass
their free time chatting through their cell phones rather than
enjoying a great book. Texting is so widespread because 25
percent of students under age eight, 89 percent of students ages
eleven to thirteen, and over 95 percent of students over age
fifteen have a cell phone ("Mobile Phones"). On average, 75.6
million text messages are sent in a day, with 54 percent
of the population texting more than five times per day
("Mobile Phones"). In contrast to the time they spend texting,
fifteen- to twenty-four-year-olds read a mere seven minutes per
day for fun and only 1.25 hours a week (NEA 10), which is less
than half the time that seventh-grade students spend texting:
2.82 hours a week (Bryant et al.). While more than half of the
population texts every day, almost as many (43 percent) have
not read a single book in the past year (NEA 7). It seems there
is a direct correlation between reading and texting because,
as text messaging increases in popularity, reading decreases.
The National Endowment for the Arts surveyed eighteen- to
twenty-four-year-olds and discovered that the enjoyment of
reading in this age group is declining the fastest. Inversely, it
is the group that sends the most text messages: 142 billion a
year (NEA 10). From 1992 to 2002, 2.1 million potential readers,
aged eighteen to twenty-four years old, were lost (NEA 27).
As proved by the direct correlation, reading does not have

*She summarizes
research, placing
the conversation
in a larger context.
Her citations
also indicate that
the problem she
identifies is relevant
and timely.*

*She uses evidence
to support her
thesis — that
we take for
granted a mode of
communication that
actually threatens
the development of
literacy.*

186 CHAPTER 11 | FROM FORMULATING TO DEVELOPING A THESIS

Stafford 2

She refines her thesis, first stating what people assume is true and then offering a corrective in the second part of her thesis.

the same appeal because of texting. Students prefer to spend time in the technological world rather than sitting with a book.

However, reading well is essential to being successful academically. Although some argue that text messages force students to think quickly and allow them to formulate brief responses to questions, their habit is actually stifling creativity. When a group of twenty students was given a chance to write responses to open-ended questions, the students who owned cell phones with text messaging wrote much less. They also had more grammatical errors, such as leaving apostrophes out of contractions and substituting the letter "r" for the word "are"

She also makes a secondary claim related to her thesis.

(Ward). Because of text messages, students perceive writing as a fun way to communicate with friends and not as a way to strongly voice an opinion. Students no longer think of writing as academic, but rather they consider it social. For instance, in Scotland, a thirteen-year-old student wrote this in a school essay about her summer vacation: "My smmr hols wr CWOT. B4 we used 2 go to NY 2C my bro, & 3 kids FTF ILNY, its gr8 . . ." (Ward). She used writing that would appear in a text message for

And she elaborates on this claim to point out one of the detrimental effects of texting.

a friend rather than in a report for school. Furthermore, students who text become so accustomed to reading this type of shorthand lingo that they often overlook it in their own writing (O'Connor). This means that teachers have to spend even longer correcting these bad habits. Regardless, Lily Huang, a writer for *Newsweek*, believes that text messages increase literacy because a student

The student presents a possible counterargument from a published writer and then restates her thesis in an effort to correct a misconception.

must first know how to spell a word to abbreviate it in texting. However, texting affects not only the way that students write, but also the way in which they think about language. As a critic of Huang's article writes, "Habitual use of shorthand isn't just about choppy English, but choppy thinking" (Muffie). Writers who text will have trouble thinking creatively, and will especially have trouble composing intricate works like poetry because of the abridged way of thinking to which they are accustomed.

Outside of school, students' interactions with one another are similarly altered. Three in five teens would argue with a friend and one in three would break up with someone through a text message ("Technology Has Tremendous Impact"). Text messaging is now the most popular way for students to arrange to meet with friends, have a quick conversation, contact

Stafford 3

She restates an evaluative claim that runs through the essay like the skewer we discussed earlier.

a friend when bored, or invite friends to a party ("Technology Has Tremendous Impact"). Eight out of ten teens would rather text than call ("Mobile Phones"). Although it is true that text messaging has made conversations much simpler and faster, it has not improved communication. Texting may make it more convenient to stay in contact with friends, but it does not ensure that the contact is as beneficial as talking in person.

Text messages do not incorporate all of the body language and vocal inflections that a face-to-face conversation does. These nonverbal cues are essential to fully comprehending what is being communicated. Only 7 percent of a message is verbal. When the message is not communicated face-to-face, 93 percent of that message is lost ("Importance of Nonverbal"), and this nonverbal message is crucial to maintaining close relationships. According to Don McKay, a contributor to healthinfosource.com, the most important aspect of lasting friendships is effective communication. Friends must be able to convey emotions and empathize with others (McKay). However, friends who communicate solely through text messages will miss out on any truly personal interaction because they can never see the other person's posture, body language, or gestures.

She provides current research to support her thesis.

She concludes by restating her premise about the value of reading and her evaluation of texting as a form of communication that erodes what she considers the very definition of literacy.

All of the negative effects of text messaging additionally deteriorate literacy. The enjoyment of reading leads to avid readers who eagerly absorb written words. A devotion to schoolwork encourages students to read so that they may be informed about important topics. Through book clubs and conversations about great literature, even relationships can foster a love for reading. However, text messaging is detracting from all three. In today's society, literacy is important. Schools focus on teaching English at an early age because of the active role that it forces students to take (Le Guin). While students can passively text message their friends, they need to focus on reading to enjoy it. In order to really immerse themselves in the story, they need to use a higher level of thinking than that of texting. This learning is what causes avid readers to become so successful. Those who read for fun when they are young score better on standardized tests, are admitted to more selective universities, and are able to secure the most competitive jobs (NEA 69). The decline in literacy caused by text messaging

She also concludes with a claim in which she proposes that students need to elevate the way they read and write.

5

Stafford 4

could inevitably cost a student a selective job. If students spent less time texting and more time reading, it could give them an advantage over their peers. Imagine a scenario between classes without any students' eyes to the ground. Imagine that Notre Dame students are not texting acquaintances hours away. Perhaps instead they are all carrying a pen and notebook and writing a letter to their friends. Maybe they are conversing with those around them. Instead of spending time every week text messaging, they are reading. When those other students text "lol," it no longer is an abbreviation for "laugh out loud," but for "loss of literacy."

Works Cited

Bryant, J. Alison, et al. "IMing, Text Messaging, and Adolescent Social Networks." *Journal of Computer-Mediated Communication*, vol. 11, no. 2, Jan. 2006, pp. 577–92.

Huang, Lily. "Technology: Textese May be the Death of English." *Newsweek*, 1 Aug. 2008, www.newsweek.com/ technology-textese-may-be-death-english-87727.

"The Importance of Nonverbal Communication." *EruptingMind Self Improvement Tips*, 2008, www.eruptingmind.com/ the-importance-of-nonverbal-communication/.

Le Guin, Ursula K. "Staying Awake: Notes on the Alleged Decline of Reading." *Harper's Magazine*, Feb. 2008, harpers.org/ archive/2008/02/staying-awake/.

McKay, Don. "Communication and Friendship." *EzineArticles*, 22 Feb. 2006, ezinearticles.com/?Communication-And -Friendship&id=150491.

"Mobile Phones, Texting, and Literacy." *National Literacy Trust*, 2008, www.literacytrust.org.uk/news/mobile_phones _texting_and_literacy.

Muffie. Comment on "Technology: Textese May be the Death of English," by Lily Huang. *Newsweek*, 18 Aug. 2008, www.newsweek.com/technology-textese-may-be-death -english-87727.

Stafford 5

O'Connor, Amanda. "Instant Messaging: Friend or Foe of
Student Writing?" *New Horizons for Learning*, Johns Hopkins
School of Education, Mar. 2005, education.jhu.edu/PD/
newhorizons/strategies/topics/literacy/articles/
instant-messaging/.

"Technology Has Tremendous Impact on How Teens
Communicate." *Cellular-news*, 19 Feb. 2007,
www.cellular-news.com/story/22146.php.

To Read or Not To Read: A Question of National Consequence.
National Endowment for the Arts, Nov. 2007, www.arts.gov/
publications/read-or-not-read-question-national
-consequence-0.

Ward, Lucy. "Texting 'Is No Bar to Literacy.'" *The Guardian*,
23 Dec. 2004, www.theguardian.com/technology/2004/
dec/23/schools.mobilephones.

12

From Synthesis to Researched Argument

A **synthesis** is a discussion that forges connections between the arguments of two or more authors. Like a summary (discussed in Chapter 8), a synthesis requires you to understand the key claims of each author's argument, including his or her use of supporting examples and evidence. Also like a summary, a synthesis requires you to present a central idea, a *gist*, to your readers. But in contrast to a summary, which explains the context of a source, a synthesis creates a context for your own argument. That is, when you write a synthesis comparing two or more sources, you demonstrate that you are aware of the larger conversation about the issue and begin to claim your own place in that conversation.

Comparing different points of view prompts you to ask why they differ. It also makes you more aware of *counterarguments*—passages where claims conflict ("writer X says this, but writer Y asserts just the opposite") or at least differ ("writer X interprets this information this way, while writer Y sees it differently"). And it starts you formulating your own counterarguments: "Neither X nor Y has taken this into account. What if they had?"

Keep in mind that the purpose of a synthesis is not merely to list the similarities and differences you find in different sources or to assert your agreement with one source as opposed to others. Instead, it sets up your argument. Once you discover connections among texts, you have to decide what those connections mean to you and your readers. What bearing do they have on your own thinking? How can you make use of them in your argument?

190

WRITING A SYNTHESIS

To compose an effective synthesis, you must (1) make connections among ideas in different texts, (2) decide what those connections mean, and (3) formulate the gist of what you've read, much like you did when you wrote a summary. The difference is that in a synthesis, your gist should be a succinct statement that brings into focus not the central idea of one text but the relationship among different ideas in multiple texts.

To help you grasp strategies of writing a synthesis, read the following essays from activist Paul Rogat Loeb, who writes about building community through grassroots activism; educators Anne Colby and Thomas Ehrlich, whose work with the Carnegie Foundation for Teaching and Learning focuses on the reasons why young people, especially undergraduates, need to be more civically engaged in their communities; and Laurie Ouellette, a professor of communication studies who writes about media and the recent trend toward the media's efforts to do good works in local communities at a time when the federal government in the United States has cut social programs and continues to rely on private entities to support families in need. We have annotated these readings not only to comment on the ideas that these authors have put forth, but also to model some of the ways that you might annotate texts as a useful first step in writing a synthesis.

PAUL ROGAT LOEB

Making Our Lives Count
(from *Soul of a Citizen*)

Paul Rogat Loeb is an American social and political activist. A graduate of Stanford University, he has published widely in both newspapers and journals. *Hope in Hard Times* is one of several books that he has written and depicts ordinary Americans involved in grassroots peace activism, while *Soul of a Citizen* seeks to inspire civic engagement activism. His book *The Impossible Will Take a Little While*, an anthology of the achievements of activists in history who faced enormous obstacles, was named the #4 political book of 2004 by the History Channel and the American Book Association and won the Nautilus Book Award for the best social change book that year.

192 CHAPTER 12 | FROM SYNTHESIS TO RESEARCHED ARGUMENT

> Souls are like athletes that need opponents worthy of them if they are to be tried and extended and pushed to the full use of their powers.
>
> —THOMAS MERTON

***

Cites research to emphasize the value of human interaction.

"Heart," "spark," "spirit"—whatever word we use for the mysterious force that animates us, its full potential cannot be realized in isolation. Indeed, according to developmental psychologists, individual growth is possible only through interaction with the human and natural world, and through experiences that challenge us. "Souls are like athletes," wrote the Trappist monk Thomas Merton, "that need opponents worthy of them if they are to be tried and extended and pushed to the full use of their powers."

Acknowledges that many of us are aware of the value of voicing our own needs and taking care of ourselves, and sets up the argument about community building.

Many of us may already know the value of stretching our souls in personal life. We know the virtue of learning to voice our needs, fight for our choices, and recover from psychological intimidation. This process may require acknowledging painful truths, withstanding conflict, standing firm on what seems like shaky ground. We may need to question familiar habits, overcome self-doubt, and begin to separate who we really are from the roles we've been taught. Jungian analysts like James Hillman would say that by taking these steps we reconnect with what the Greeks called the *daimon,* the "acorn" of character at the core of our being. Psychiatrist M. Scott Peck described spiritual healing as "an ongoing process of becoming increasingly conscious."

Expresses concern that we may be less likely to think about our well-being as connected to others in the public sphere. Also identifies with those who may be reluctant to be assertive in the public sphere because they fear their voices won't be heard.

We are slower to attempt such transformations in the public sphere. Self-assertion there requires us not only to modify our outlook and behavior but also to confront a bewildering and often disorienting maze of institutions and individuals, powers and principalities. So we stay silent in the face of common choices that we know are unwise or morally troubling. We keep our opinions to ourselves, because we doubt our voices will be heard, mistrust our right to speak, or fear the consequences if we do speak out. We feel we lack essential political skills. Like ... Rosa Parks before her first NAACP meeting, we simply do not know we have it in us.

Yet coming out of one's cocoon in the public sphere is just as necessary to self-realization as it is in the private. I once told a young Puerto Rican activist about the notion, common among many of his fellow students, that they'd lose their identity by getting involved—find themselves "swallowed up" by the movements they joined. He laughed and said the reverse was true. "You learn things you never knew about yourself. You get pushed to your limits. You meet people who make you think and push you further. You don't lose your identity. You begin to find out who you really are. I feel sad for people who will never have this experience."

Elaborates on his point that human connection is necessary. Uses an anecdote to show how getting involved with others helps us better understand who we are as individuals.

You begin to find out who you really are. The implication is clear enough: We become human only in the company of other human beings. And this involves both opening our hearts and giving voice to our deepest convictions. The biblical vision of *shalom* describes this process with its concept of "right relationships" with our fellow humans, and with all of God's creation. The turning point for the Buddha, writes James Hillman, came only "when he left his protected palace gardens to enter the street. There the sick, the dead, the poor, and the old drew his soul down into the question of how to live life in the world." As Hillman stresses, the Buddha became who he was precisely by leaving the cloistered life. A doctor I know works in a low-income clinic because, she says, "seeing the struggles of others helps me be true to myself. It helps me find out how people in very different circumstances live out their humanity." Community involvement, in other words, is the mirror that best reflects our individual choices, our strengths and weaknesses, our accomplishments and failures. It allows our lives to count for something.

Reiterates his point that interacting with others teaches us about who we are and what we value. Cites the work of a scholar who studies Buddhism and a doctor who believes her work in low-income communities has helped her be a better version of herself.

Community involvement helps us see that we matter.

The Cost of Silence

Offers an illustration to support the value of activism but also shows that speaking out for what we value can have its costs.

Twenty years after Harvard Law School hired him as its first fulltime African American professor, Derrick Bell took an unpaid protest leave, refusing to teach until the school hired a minority woman to its faculty. It was not a decision made in haste. Bell had long campaigned for this. But each time a new position opened, the Law School somehow could find not a single minority female candidate in the world who was worthy enough to hire. The school's resistance continued despite Bell's stand. After three years, the school forced him to resign. His conscience had cost him a tenured job at the most prestigious law school in America.

What might seem like failure can actually be a factor that bolsters our commitment to make a difference.

Yet Bell didn't feel defeated. Quite the opposite. His public stance had preserved his core identity and integrity. "It is the determination to protect our sense of who we are," he writes, "that leads us to risk criticism, alienation, and serious loss while most others, similarly harmed, remain silent."

Helps readers understand that remaining silent about issues that matter can be more costly than failed action.

What Bell means is that silence is more costly than speaking out, because it requires the ultimate sacrifice—the erosion of our spirit. The toll we pay for stifling our emotions in personal life is fairly obvious. Swallowed words act like caustic acids, eating at our gut. If the condition persists and the sentiments are sufficiently intense, we grow numb, detached, dead to the world around us. When, however, we take steps to redress our private losses and sorrows, we often feel a renewed sense of strength and joy, of reconnecting with life.

One cost to remaining silent is that we are no longer true to ourselves and we lose our ability to be whole human beings.

A similar process occurs when we want to address public issues but stay silent. It takes energy to mute our voices while the environment is ravaged, greed runs rampant, and families sleep in the streets. It takes energy to distort our words and actions because we fear the consequences of speaking out. It takes energy, in other words, to sustain what the psychiatrist Robert Jay Lifton calls "the broken connection," splitting our lives from our values. Like autistic children, we can blank out the voices of our fellow human beings. But if we do, we risk the decay of our humanity. When we shrink from the world, our souls shrink, too.

Cites additional research to explain how serving our communities with others can have an effect on us physically, not just psychologically, and contribute to our health and well-being.

Social involvement reverses this process, releas- 10 ing our choked-off energy, overcoming the psychic paralysis that so many of us feel, reintegrating mind and heart, body and soul, so that we can speak in one voice—our own—and mean what we say. There's even a physical corollary to this integration. In *The Healing Power of Doing Good*, Allan Luks describes various studies that confirm what he calls the "helper's high." People who volunteer in their communities experience significantly greater physical pleasure and well-being in the process of their work, a general sense of increased energy, and in some cases an easing of chronic pain. A Harvard School of Public Health study found that African Americans who challenged repeated discrimination had lower blood pressure than those who did not. So taking stands for what we believe may help us save more than our souls.

Cites further evidence to explain the importance of acting on our convictions.

Sociologist Parker Palmer describes the result- 11 ing unleashing of truth, vision, and strength in the lives of people like Rosa Parks, Vaclav Havel, Nelson Mandela, and Dorothy Day, who've acted on their deepest beliefs. "These people," he wrote, "have understood that no punishment could be worse than the one we inflict on ourselves by living a divided life." And nothing could be more powerful than the decision to heal that rift, "to stop acting differently on the outside from what they knew to be true inside."

Learned Helplessness

Laments the extent to which American culture seems to work against the idea of activism, community work, and human agency—the ability to envision change and the capacity to act on our convictions in meaningful ways.

America's predominant culture insists that little we 12 do can matter. It teaches us not to get involved in shaping the world we'll pass on to our children. It encourages us to leave such important decisions to others—whether they be corporate and government leaders, or social activists whose lifestyles seem impossibly selfless or foreign. Sadly, and ironically, in

196   CHAPTER 12 | FROM SYNTHESIS TO RESEARCHED ARGUMENT

a country born of a democratic political revolution, to be American in recent years is too often to be apolitical. For many, civic withdrawal has become the norm. The 2008 presidential campaign challenged this trend by inspiring vast numbers of previously disengaged citizens to volunteer in ways that shifted not only the presidential race, but also close races for the Senate, the House, and state governorships. But even then over a third of potentially eligible Americans ended up staying home. And despite all the passionate volunteers, far more citizens did little beyond casting their vote. Absent a highly contested election, it's easier still to sit on the sidelines and simply hope our leaders will take care of things.

Argues that we need to adopt a view of democratic engagement that our Founding Fathers offered.

Overcoming our instinctive civic withdrawal requires courage. It requires learning the skills and developing the confidence to participate.... It also requires creating a renewed definition of ourselves as citizens—something closer to the nation of active stakeholders that leaders like Thomas Jefferson had in mind.

13

The importance of citizens' direct participation in a democracy was expressed thousands of years ago, by the ancient Greeks. In fact, they used the word "idiot" for people incapable of involving themselves in civic life. Now, the very word "political" has become so debased in our culture that we use it to describe either trivial office power plays or leaders who serve largely personal ambitions. We've lost sight of its original roots in the Greek notion of the *polis*: the democratic sphere in which citizens, acting in concert, determine the character and direction of their society. "All persons alike," wrote Aristotle, should share "in the government to the utmost."

14

Uses a play to illustrate the extent to which it is not enough to focus on problems without taking action.

Reclaiming this political voice requires more than just identifying problems, which itself can feed our sense of overload. I think of an Arthur Miller play, *Broken Glass*, whose heroine obsesses while Hitler steadily consolidates his power. From her safe home in Brooklyn, she reads newspaper articles about *Kristallnacht:* synagogues smashed and looted; old

15

men forced to scrub streets with toothbrushes while storm troopers laugh at them; and finally, children shipped off to the camps in cattle cars. Her concern contrasts with the approach of her family and friends, who insist, despite the mounting evidence, that such horrors are exaggerated. Yet she does nothing to address the situation publicly, except to grow more anxious. Eventually she becomes psychosomatically paralyzed.

The approach Miller's protagonist takes toward the horrors of Nazism echoes that of far too many people who spend hours following every twist and turn of the twenty-four-hour news cycle, yet never take action that might address them. It also resembles the condition of learned helplessness. People who suffer from severe depression, psychologist Martin Seligman found, do so less as a result of particular unpleasant experiences than because of their "explanatory style"—the story they tell themselves about how the world works. Depressed people have become convinced that the causes of their difficulties are permanent and pervasive, inextricably linked to their personal failings. There's nothing to be done because nothing can be done. This master narrative of their lives excuses inaction; it provides a rationale for remaining helpless. In contrast, individuals who function with high effectiveness tend to believe that the problems they face result from factors that are specific, temporary, and therefore changeable. The story they live by empowers them.

The story we tell ourselves about the world can either lead us to a feeling of helplessness or a sense of empowerment — that there are things we can do to create change.

This is not to say that change is easy, nor that everyone is in an equal position to bring it about. Some individuals and groups in America possess far more material and organizational resources than others. This reflects our deep social and economic inequities. But as *Tikkun* magazine founder Rabbi Michael Lerner has observed, we often fail to use the resources we do have, which may be of a different kind. "Most of us," Lerner says, "have been subjected to a set of experiences in our childhood and adult lives that makes us feel that we do not deserve to have power." Consequently, we can't imagine changing the direction of our society. We decide that things are worse than they actually are—a condition Lerner refers to as "surplus powerlessness."...

The illusion of powerlessness can just as easily afflict the fortunate among us. I know many people who are confident and successful in their work and have loving personal relationships, yet can hardly conceive of trying to work toward a more humane society. Materially comfortable and professionally accomplished, they could make important social contributions. Instead they restrict their search for meaning and integrity to their private lives. Their sense of shared fate extends only to their immediate families and friends. Despite their many advantages, they, too, have been taught an "explanatory style" that precludes participation in public life, except to promote the most narrow self-interest.

Points out that some of the most well-off people are driven by self-interest when they might use their wealth to make important "social contributions."

Whatever our situations, we all face a choice. We can ignore the problems that lie just beyond our front doors; we can allow decisions to be made in our names that lead to a meaner and more desperate world. We can yell at the TV newscasters and complain about how bad things are, using our bitterness as a hedge against involvement. Or we can work, as well as we can, to shape a more generous common future.

Leaves us with a clear decision about whether or not we allow others to make choices for us or to take on the responsibility of working for the common good.

ANNE COLBY AND THOMAS EHRLICH, WITH ELIZABETH BEAUMONT AND JASON STEPHENS
Undergraduate Education and the Development of Moral and Civic Responsibility

At the time that the two primary authors published this essay, they worked at the Carnegie Foundation for the Advancement of Teaching, a U.S.-based education policy and research center founded by Andrew Carnegie in 1905. The foundation embraces a commitment to developing networks of ideas, individuals, and institutions to advance teaching and learning. Anne Colby holds a PhD in psychology from Columbia and currently serves as a consulting professor at Stanford University. Prior to that, she was director of the Henry Murray Research Center at Harvard University. With Thomas Ehrlich, she published *Educating for Democracy: Preparing Undergraduates for Responsible Political Engagement* and won the 2013 Frederic W. Ness Book Award for their book *Rethinking Undergraduate Business Education: Liberal Learning for the Profession*. Thomas Ehrlich is a consulting professor at the Stanford Graduate School of Education. He is a graduate of Harvard College and Harvard Law School and holds five honorary degrees. Professor Ehrlich has previously served as president of Indiana University, provost of the University of Pennsylvania, and dean of Stanford Law School. His most recent book (2013) is *Civic Work, Civic Lessons: Two Generations Reflect on Public Service*.

■ ■ ■

Shares a concern that Loeb expresses about trends toward increased individualism and lack of civic engagement. Especially interested in reaching out to undergraduates, whereas Loeb addresses a more general audience.

We are among those increasingly concerned about two related trends in contemporary American culture—excessive individualism and moral relativism on the one hand and popular disdain for civic engagement, particularly political involvement, on the other. In our view, undergraduate years are an important time for developing in students moral and civic responsibility that can help reverse these trends. This essay describes our work-in-progress, under the auspices of the Carnegie Foundation for the Advancement of Teaching, to analyze the American undergraduate scene in terms of efforts to promote students' moral and civic responsibility and to encourage our colleges and universities to strengthen those efforts.

Stresses the responsibility that universities and colleges have to encourage students to be involved.

As concerned with morality as with civic engagement, which is a departure from Loeb. Maintains that moral and civic responsibility are inextricably linked.

Some people who have written about these issues have focused exclusively on civic responsibility, avoiding the more controversial area of morality (e.g., Barber, 1998). We include moral as well as civic responsibility in the scope of our project, because we believe the two are inseparable. Our democratic principles, including tolerance and respect for others, procedural impartiality, and concern for both the rights of the individual and the welfare of the group, are all grounded in moral principles. Likewise, the problems that the civically engaged citizen must confront always include strong moral themes—for example, fair access to resources such as housing, the moral obligation to consider future generations in making environmental policy, and the conflicting claims of multiple stakeholders in community decision-making. None of these issues can be adequately resolved

Elaborates on how moral principles are tied to democratic principles. Contends that decision making relies on having a "strong moral compass."

200 CHAPTER 12 | FROM SYNTHESIS TO RESEARCHED ARGUMENT

Educators must commit themselves to teaching civic responsibility and morality.

without a consideration of moral questions. A person can become civically and politically active without good judgment and a strong moral compass, but it is hardly wise to promote that kind of involvement. Because civic responsibility is inescapably threaded with moral values, we believe that higher education must aspire to foster both moral and civic maturity and must confront educationally the many links between them.

Defines moral engagement in broad terms to promote thoughtful reflection and call upon institutions of higher education to foster moral engagement.

What do we mean by "moral" and by "civic"? We consider "moral," in its broadest sense, to include matters of values both personal and public. As we use the term, "morality" is not confined to a specific sphere of life or action, nor is it necessarily tied to religion. In advocating moral engagement, we are not promoting any particular moral or meta-ethical viewpoint. Rather, we are interested in fostering more thoughtful moral reflection generally and the adoption of viewpoints and commitments that emerge from reasoned consideration. We believe that higher education should encourage and facilitate the development of students' capacities to examine complex situations in which competing values are often at stake, to employ both substantive knowledge and moral reasoning to evaluate the problems and values involved, to develop their own judgments about those issues, and then to act on their judgments.

3

Defines civic engagement as a necessary means for sustaining a democracy that encompasses both thoughtful reflection and subsequent action.

We consider "civic" to range over all social spheres beyond the family, from neighborhoods and local communities to state, national, and cross-national arenas. Political engagement is a particular subset of civic engagement that is required for sustaining American democracy. We are not promoting a single type of civic or political engagement, but instead urging that the effective operation of social systems and the successful achievement of collective goals demand the time, attention, understanding, and action of all citizens. Institutions of higher education have both the opportunity and obligation to cultivate in their graduates an appreciation for the responsibilities and rewards of civic engagement, as well as to

4

foster the capacities necessary for thoughtful participation in public discourse and effective participation in social enterprises.

In general terms, we believe that a morally and civically responsible individual recognizes himself or herself as a member of a larger social fabric and therefore considers social problems to be at least partly his or her own; such an individual is willing to see the moral and civic dimensions of issues, to make and justify informed moral and civic judgments, and to take action when appropriate.

We believe that moral and civic development is enhanced by mutually interdependent sets of knowledge, virtues, and skills. Because they are interdependent, no simple listing of attributes is adequate. Such a listing may imply that the elements involved have precise definitions and parameters that might be gained through a single course or even from reading a few books. We have come to understand through studying various colleges and universities that this is not the case. Instead, enriching the moral and civic responsibility of all members of the campus community is best achieved through the cumulative, interactive effect of numerous curricular and extracurricular programs, within an environment of sustained institutional commitment to these overarching goals....

Included in the core knowledge we consider integral to moral and civic learning is knowledge of basic ethical concepts and principles, such as justice and equity, and how they have been interpreted by various seminal thinkers. Also included is a comprehension of the diversity of American society and global cultures, and an understanding of both the institutions and processes of American and international civic, political, and economic affairs. Finally, deep substantive knowledge of the particular issues in which one is engaged is critical.

This core of knowledge cannot be separated from the virtues and skills that a morally and civically responsible individual should strive to attain. The virtues and skills we have in mind are not distinct to moral and civic learning but are necessary for active

The teaching of civic and moral engagement should occur in different fields of study and programs supported by a national organization such as the Carnegie Foundation for the Advancement of Teaching.

Avoids defining values that can inform judgment, but offers a description of core knowledge and concepts that educators should impart to their students.

Core knowledge of key issues and an understanding of civic, political, and economic concerns should go hand in hand with moral and civic learning.

202 CHAPTER 12 | FROM SYNTHESIS TO RESEARCHED ARGUMENT

engagement in many personal and professional realms. Among the core virtues is the willingness to engage in critical self-examination and to form reasoned commitments, balanced by open-mindedness and a willingness to listen to and take seriously the ideas of others. Moral and civic responsibility also requires honesty in dealings with others, and in holding oneself accountable for one's action and inactions.

Elaborates upon the idea of community building that Loeb introduces, particularly empathy, trust, and compassion.

Without a basis of trust, and habits of cooperation, no community can operate effectively. Empathy and compassion are also needed, not only for relating to those in one's immediate social sphere, but for relating to those in the larger society as well. Willingness to form moral and civic commitments and to act on those is a core virtue that puts the others into practice.

Finally, the core skills of moral and civic responsibility are essential for applying core knowledge and virtues, transforming informed judgments into action. They include the abilities to recognize the moral and civic dimensions of issues and to take a stand on those issues. But they also include skills that apply to much broader arenas of thought and behavior, such as abilities to communicate clearly orally and in writing, to collect, organize, and analyze information, to think critically and to justify positions with reasoned arguments, to see issues from the perspectives of others and to collaborate with others. They also include the ability and willingness to lead, to build a consensus, and to move a group forward under conditions of mutual respect.

Maintains that to act requires applying core knowledge and values, in contrast to Loeb, who uses evidence from sociology, health, and psychology to inspire people to become civically and politically engaged.

9

LAURIE OUELLETTE

Citizen Brand: ABC and the Do Good Turn in US Television

Laurie Ouellette is a professor of communication studies at the University of Minnesota. The author of *Lifestyle TV* and coauthor of *Better Living through Reality TV: Television and Post-Welfare Citizenship*, she has published extensively about public broadcasting, TV history, fashion and style, self-help culture, and social media.

> The greatest moments in life are not concerned with selfish achievement, but rather with the things we do for other people.
>
> —Walt Disney

***

Better Communities and Corporate Citizens

Introduces the idea of corporate sponsorship of community involvement and raises the question of what has motivated this kind of initiative to involve viewers, actors, and the like.

In 2002, ABC launched its long-running Better Community public outreach campaign, with a mission of advancing the television network's standing as a corporate citizen through "community outreach efforts that serve the public interest, inform and inspire."... Encompassing announcements urging TV viewers to perform community service, as well as an online guide to volunteering and a slate of popular entertainment programs showcasing corporate and personal humanitarianism, the campaign positioned ABC as a socially responsible corporate citizen. More than this, it constituted ABC as a gateway to a Better Community comprising network stars, nonprofit partners, commercial sponsors, and socially conscious TV viewers who—much more than other television consumers—contribute resources (time and money) to the well-being of the communities in which they live. Why would ABC pursue what it claimed to be the "comprehensive and recognizable public service initiative" on US television in the wake of deregulatory policies? To make sense of the Better Community initiative—and the television industry's investment in civic empowerment more broadly—it is useful to trace the burgeoning and deeply intertwined currency of communitarian discourse and corporate social responsibility.

Uses the term "civic empowerment," which is different from Loeb, as well as Colby and her colleagues. Also introduces the word "communitarian" to the conversation.

Offers some historical perspective and describes some of the economic reforms in government that have placed more responsibility on private citizens, among others, to support children and families living in poverty.

The Better Community campaign appeared in the midst of the reinvention of government in the US, an assemblage of reforms encompassing public sector downsizing, the encouragement of public–private partnerships, the outsourcing of many government services to commercial firms, and the dismantling of welfare programs.... ABC translated a bipartisan call for private initiative and personal responsibility as empowering alternatives to big government into

204 CHAPTER 12 | FROM SYNTHESIS TO RESEARCHED ARGUMENT

TV stations like ABC interpreted the call for more private and personal responsibility as a way to promote volunteerism and their own interests. Community activism would replace social welfare programs, while the government fostered a free, unregulated economic market.

fifteen-second public service announcements that doubled as station promotions, and advertising stuffed entertainment revolving around corporate giving and volunteerism. The campaign embraced the entrepreneurial zeal guiding political reform, but it also inserted the ABC television network and its viewers into communitarian solutions to the underside of unfettered capitalism. Like other examples of do good television, the Better Community campaign exemplifies an enterprising turn in governing and at the same time seeks to help overcome the consequences of a pure market logic in the civic realm.

Corporate social responsibility seems separate from political interests while still supporting democracy, but corporate involvement has its roots in efforts by both former presidents Bush and Clinton to find alternatives to welfare programs.

Community is an especially popular corporate civic objective due to its positive currency and safe distance from unruly political activism or controversy. The turn to community, which is also a dominant theme in do good television, is also closely intertwined with communitarian political discourses and strategies of governing. Communitarianism is an applied political philosophy that endorses market capitalism and limited public powers but calls for additional changes to ensure the civic functionality of democratic societies. It advocates the nourishing of voluntary associations as a buffer between the downsized welfare state and the competitive self-interest found in the commercial marketplace.... Both the Clinton and Bush administrations adopted communitarian models of "governing through community," from the designation of community empowerment zones as an alternative to public housing programs (Clinton) to the creation of

Observes that an ethic of communitarianism derives from policy, in contrast to the moral argument that Colby and her colleagues describe or the humanitarian principles that Loeb explains. Communitarianism has become necessary in the absence of government-supported programs.

the Office of Faith-Based and Community Initiatives to "nourish dispersed religious and civil alternatives to public welfare programs" and a USA Freedom Corps Volunteer Network to mobilize citizens into "armies of compassion" (Bush). Bush also entrusted the new President's Council on National and Community Service, composed of leaders from business, entertainment, sports, the nonprofit sector, education, and media, to help the White House cultivate a stronger ethic of service and responsibility in the US. While there were crucial differences between Clinton and Bush, the point to be made here is that community has become an objective of governing across political regimes. This matters for our purposes for two reasons: First, good communities (like good citizens) are not born but made—constituted through policies, political discourses, and cultural technologies such as television. Second, as Nikolas Rose persuasively contends, community has become "another word for citizenship" that stresses civic duties rather than collective entitlements. Rose sees the uptake of communitarianism as a substitute for a diminishing social contract—an intervention that softens the "harshest dimensions of neo-capitalist restructuring" by encouraging citizens to serve associations (neighborhoods, localities, social networks, families) that are "decidedly private and which more or less absolve the state of responsibility for society." ...

In the US, communitarianism is closely associated with prominent scholar and political consultant Amitai Etzioni.... In his many books, speeches, and ongoing work with the Institute for Communitarian Studies at George Washington University, Etzioni promotes an understanding of community as a counterbalance to a model of society created in the image of the "marketplace, in which self-serving individuals compete with one another." ... Communities, he contends, also offset the need for public oversight by reinforcing a voluntary moral order rooted in "traditional values" of respectability, responsibility, and independence. Conceived as dispersed, self-managed ethical zones, community poses an alternative not only to the welfare state but also to the model of democracy associated with broadcast regulation and earlier interpretations of the public interest in television. As Rose points out, community as conceived by Etzioni and other influential thinkers offers a way to "regenerate society" that comes not from "law, information, reason, or deliberative democracy" but from moral "dialogue and action" within voluntary associations....

4

Traces the term "communitarianism" to one scholar who developed a model of communitarian values that seems to mirror those of Colby and her colleagues, given their similar emphasis on "moral dialogue and action."

206 CHAPTER 12 | FROM SYNTHESIS TO RESEARCHED ARGUMENT

Cites Putnam's study reported in Bowling Alone and reiterates concerns of others about the decline of volunteerism and civic engagement. This decline seems connected, according to another scholar, Rose, to a number of social problems.

While Etzioni naturalizes the space of community, he concedes that citizens *must be trained* to "participate in communitarian society." Even those who have "acquired virtue" will require ongoing guidance, "for if left to their own devices... [they] gradually lose much of their commitment to values."... What Rose calls technologies of community have proliferated since the 1990s, offering tutelage and instruction. This is partly a response to widely circulating reports of declining volunteerism, everyday philanthropy, and civic engagement in the US. Robert Putnam's influential study *Bowling Alone* lamented the collapse of voluntary associations, indicating that few contemporary Americans demonstrate the civic propensities that Alexis de Tocqueville credited with the "capacity to make democracy work."... By the mid-1990s, barely one American in three reported any charitable giving in the previous month, and fewer than two in five claimed even "occasional religious giving," according to Putnam's study.... These trends paralleled an equally sharp reduction in participation in community institutions, from lodges to parent-teacher associations.... As Rose points out, the "decline of community" ascribed to these trends was also held responsible for a slew of civic problems, from "drugs, crime and alienation, to family breakdown and the loss of good neighborliness."... For Putnam (who penned Bush's 2001 inaugural speech), any attempt to reinvent government also needed to "revitalize" community and its subjects.

While communitarianism gained currency, corporate social responsibility was also actively encouraged as a dimension of governmental reform. Both Clinton and Bush called on the corporate sector to partner in social programs and fill gaps left by the divested welfare state. As Andrew Barry argues, the market's willingness to take on responsibility for ethical problems is not surprising. In an era when "direct state control has declined," he explains, corporations are increasingly expected to "perform the job of government at

Introduces the term "cause marketing," which combines the ideas of corporate social responsibility and profit. This concept highlights the role that businesses have taken on in the context of economic reform and the responsibility of businesses to make money. It seems that corporate social responsibility is a key to financial success.

a distance."... Yet, the rise of cause marketing, corporate philanthropy, and other manifestations of what Barry calls ethical capitalism are only viable to the extent that they are also profitable. The age of paternalistic philanthropy, exemplified by Andrew Carnegie's view of wealth as a "sacred trust, which its possessor was bound to administer for the good of the community," passed some time ago.... In 1970, Milton Friedman, a leading figure of the Chicago school of neoliberalism, unapologetically declared in the *New York Times*, "The social responsibility of business is to increase profits."... Nonetheless, corporations have increasingly embraced objectives (fundraising for cures, promoting recycling, citizenship training) that blur boundaries between public and private, governing and profiteering. According to business historian David Vogel, this development is not only the outcome of public sector downsizing and government at a distance. As the entrepreneurial spirit was reforming the welfare state, many corporations were discovering a lucrative "market for virtue." Today, says Vogel, corporate social responsibility is approached not as an unprofitable duty but as the key to successful profit maximization....

Cites one scholar who reiterates a concern the author shares: corporate social responsibility has become a means for creating wealth rather than a virtuous act of being involved in "ethical issues" and "civic affairs."

In his genealogy of corporate social responsibility, Vogel argues that contemporary advocates of ethical capitalism have basically accepted "Friedman's position that the primary responsibility of companies is to create wealth for their shareholders"—with an important twist: in order for companies to maximize profit, he explains, the prevailing assumption is that "they must now act virtuously." In other words, social responsibility is enacted less as a paternalistic duty than as a competitive business strategy. "Never before has the claim that corporate virtue can and should be profitable enjoyed so much currency or influence," Vogel writes.... The new tendency to approach social responsibility as an instrument of profitability is the outcome of the neoliberal reforms, including deregulation and expanded entrepreneurialism, that Friedman and his colleagues promoted, and that spawned a

208 CHAPTER 12 | FROM SYNTHESIS TO RESEARCHED ARGUMENT

Points out that the trend toward "citizen branding" represents this shift in emphasis away from civic engagement for its own sake toward profitability. Doing so has entailed masking the profit motive to project an image of a company committed to doing good work in the community.

perceived need for greater corporate involvement in ethical issues and civic affairs....

The concept of the citizen brand, which has revolutionized marketing in recent years, takes this a step further by placing corporations and consumer culture at the center of governing and citizenship. In his book *Citizen Brand: 10 Commandments Transforming Brand Culture in a Consumer Democracy* (2002), Mark Gobé argues that corporations that wish to increase profits will have to distance themselves from the greed and exploitation associated with deregulated global capitalism. One way of doing so, he suggests, is to integrate do good activities into business plans and branding strategies so that an image of trust and ethics can be built on a "real dedication to being part of human solutions around the world." ... In his manual *Citizen Brands: Putting Society at the Heart of Your Business* (2003), Michael Willmott agrees that citizenship must "be a part of branding" and explains how the public interest can be harnessed as a form of market intelligence.... As one example, he suggests that public support for community (bolstered by the policies and discourses discussed earlier) can be appropriated as an objective of corporate citizenship and channeled into "economic success." ...

The Better Community campaign exemplifies the ethical turn in capitalism, presented not as an obligation (which might imply public oversight) but as ABC's *choice* to advance an empowering civic agenda. ABC is positioned at the center of communitarian strategies for activating citizens and buffering the consequences of privatization and welfare reform. Public outreach entails channeling the demands being placed on individuals and communities into the ethical value of the ABC network. It is not coincidental that the Better Community project is overseen entirely by ABC Corporate Initiatives, for its approach to doing good is much more compatible with new directions in marketing and branding than were earlier (unrealized) public service ideals emphasizing rational debate and an informed citizenry.

Citizen Disney and the Rebranding of ABC

Disney, overseeing the rebranding of ABC, represents the trend the author has described — taking on the role of responsible corporate citizen and promoting the role of the good citizen.

The Disney Corporation, the parent corporation of ABC, is a prime example of the multilayered use of community as a technology of governing, a strategic business practice, and a branding strategy. The Disney Corporation, the largest media conglomerate in the world, characterizes itself as a good neighbor visibly committed to social responsibility (exemplified by employee volunteer programs and corporate giving) and humanitarian causes—particularly community and the environment. Disney has diffused these commitments across its corporate holdings, including film studios, theme parks, television networks, and cable channels.... The Disney-owned ESPN channel incorporates volunteerism and community service into its operations, enticing employees and "sports enthusiasts" at home to make a difference by volunteering on behalf of nonprofit organizations. The (now defunct) SOAPNet partnered with volunteer events in Hollywood and sponsored community outreach programs in public schools, using soap opera clips to promote family, responsibility, and communication skills. The Disney-ABC Television Group, which oversees the Disney Channel and ABC, is also dedicated to "serving and inspiring individuals and communities through a variety of public service initiatives and outreach programs." Disney-ABC claims that it "proudly supports non-profit organizations in their endeavors to make the world a better place," while its television channels—with their capacity to reach millions of people—provide "ideal platforms to inspire viewers to drive positive change in their communities." ...

Attributes Disney's investment in humanitarian endeavors to changes in federal policies. While writers such as Putnam and Etzioni might lament the fragmentation of community, media is also now responsible for increased civic engagement and community building.

Disney's investment in community and volunteerism is related to the reinvention of government. Disney was a corporate partner in the Bush White House's efforts to encourage volunteerism as a solution to postwelfare needs and problems. Disney also sponsored the National Conference on Volunteering and Service organized by the Corporation for National Community Service, the Points of Light

Foundation, and the USA Freedom Corps. At the 2005 meeting, leaders from government and the corporate sector met to devise strategies for developing volunteer service (a term used to describe everything from corporate giving to bake sales) to meet America's "pressing social needs." The responsibilities bestowed upon corporations and individual citizens were evident by the keynote speeches: US Department of Health and Human Services secretary Mike Leavitt lectured on the importance of "economic goodness" and the closing remarks were delivered by Mark Victor Hansen, best-selling author of the Christian self-help book *Chicken Soup for the Soul....* It is telling, but not surprising, that culture industries and popular media figured heavily in the brainstorming session. Although communitarians (including Etzioni and Putnam) condemn mass media as a factor in the decline of community, television and the web are also recognized as useful instruments for retraining citizens and rebuilding voluntary associations independently of big government. ABC's Better Community campaign is one such technology, operating at a distance from the state to constitute responsibility for post-welfare society as a corporate and community affair.

Despite the benefits of citizen branding, the author again reminds us that we cannot ignore the profit motive of companies that have fulfilled a role once played by the federal government in what is now a postwelfare state. To what extent are these roles in conflict with one another?

ABC has inserted itself into the communitarian space between the uncaring market and so-called welfare dependency. The question remains: If corporate social responsibility is now practiced as a profit-making endeavor, as Vogel suggests, how does the Better Community campaign fuel ABC's and Disney's coffers? To understand how valuable commitments to ethical business and community building have become for the cultural industries, it is worth juxtaposing the current approach to public service with the "all-business" mentality unleashed by broadcast deregulation. While Disney has always billed itself as an all-American company committed to traditional values, the media mergers and takeovers of the 1980s led all conglomerates to an intensified focus on the bottom line. Within an increasingly competitive industrial climate, former Disney CEO Michael Eisner confessed in a 1981 memo, "We have no obligation to make history; we have no obligation to make art; we have no obligation to make a statement; to make money is our only objective." ... Sounding a lot like Milton Friedman a decade earlier, Eisner acknowledged that the company's primary, indeed sole, purpose was to maximize profits for shareholders. As late as 1997, the ABC television network (recently purchased by Disney) owned up to a similar sentiment with its TV is Good branding campaign. Mocking any notion that television should serve a purpose higher than producing wealth, the spots proudly positioned ABC as a venue for the hedonistic consumption of trivial entertainment. Pitting TV viewers seeking pleasure and escape against the concerns of do good reformers, the advertisements offered tongue-in-cheek advice such as "Life is short. Watch TV" and "Don't worry, you've got billions of brain cells."

ABC's attempt to brand the right to consume television with no redeeming attributes was short-lived. In 2002, the network switched gears dramatically with what it called the most visible public service campaign on television. Branded as ABC—A Better Community, the campaign generated more than 100 public service announcements to date, in which ABC stars urge TV viewers to "make a difference" in their communities. Early in the campaign, the talent read quotations by famous historical figures in order to situate ABC within a recognizable genealogy of ethical activity and public service. Interspersed with pitches for automobiles, mouthwash, and diet soda were reminders that: *"You make a living by what you get, but you make a life by what you give"* (Winston Churchill); *"Everyone has the power for greatness ... because greatness is determined by service"* (Dr. Martin Luther King Jr.); *"No man can sincerely help another without helping himself"* (Ralph Waldo Emerson); *"The best way to find yourself ... is to lose yourself in the service of others"* (Mahatma Gandhi); and *"The greatest moments in life are not concerned with selfish*

Describes how ABC and Disney rebranded themselves with public service announcements and connecting their work in media with public service.

13

achievement, but rather with the things we do for other people" (Walt Disney).

Visually framed by the ABC Better Community logo, accompanied by inspirational music and ending with a call to action (including a visit to the ABC website), the spots linked ABC to an iconic pantheon of civic leadership. Within the logic of the campaign, the political differences between entrepreneurs like Disney and activists like King were insignificant; what mattered was their shared commitment to doing good—a moral disposition to which the ABC audience should aspire. Once ABC had established its ethical credibility, the inspirational passages were dropped and well-known ABC stars such as George Lopez (*The George Lopez Show*), Nicollette Sheridan (*Desperate Housewives*), and Evangeline Lilly (*Lost*) urged TV viewers to take specific actions, like becoming a mentor or cleaning up a neighborhood park. The stars took over as civic tutors in the new promotions, guiding the conduct of individuals while also constituting ABC as a Better Community on the basis of values presumably shared by executives, talent, and audiences. While the initial spots had selectively linked civic progress to the legacy of political figures like King, the announcements that followed disassociated good citizenship from any reminder of grassroots activism or critique. What was radical about the campaign, however, was its aggressive attempt to move TV viewers away from their sets, into civic life. Breaking commercial television's associations with leisure, domesticity, and passive consumption, it recast the ABC audience as an active community of unselfish, civically responsible people. The imagined viewer was addressed as an ethical subject who, with gentle reminders and practical advice, could make a difference in the world outside commercial television. In this way the public service campaign provides what Etzioni calls the training required to "restrain impulses," "delay gratification," and balance "pleasure and living up to one's moral commitments."...

14

Takes a critical stance toward ABC's rebranding that associated their calls for public service with Martin Luther King's leadership during the civil rights movement. Ignoring differences enabled ABC to project an image that is problematic but clearly served ABC's goals.

Acknowledges the extent to which this strategy was able to position ABC as an ethical corporation and viewers as responsible citizens.

In 2006, ABC re-launched the Better Community *15* initiative with much fanfare. The renewed commitment to community service provided the occasion for a new round of publicity kicked off by a special announcement from actress Geena Davis. Davis, who portrayed the first female president of the US on ABC's (now-canceled) drama *Commander-in-Chief*, addressed the audience during a special network showing of *The Ten Commandments*. Drawing civic credibility from her television character and a moral compass from the biblical film, she reiterated the ABC network's unique contributions to community service and volunteerism. Davis also reminded viewers of their crucial role in realizing the network's mission by making a difference in the communities in which they live. Here as before, the Better Community was doubly constituted as an imagined community whose membership involved consuming ABC, and as the outcome of suggested civic actions. Carried out across multiple sites, these actions supported the communitarian turn in government while also providing coveted ethical value to the ABC brand.

Illustrates the way media corporations can use celebrities to add credibility to their message, even when the reference is a fictional character on TV.

The profitability of corporate social responsibil- *16* ity and community is realized in the generation of brand identity and value. The stakes are high for a mass television network in the age of cultural fragmentation and niche marketing. As one handbook on the television business explains, "In a world with dozens and eventually hundreds of television channels, those with the most clearly differentiated brands would be the ones most likely to succeed."... ABC combines the concept of the citizen brand with the brand community to differentiate the network's compassion and civic relevance. "Brand community" is a relatively new term used by market researchers to describe a "specialized, non-geographically bound community, based on a structured set of social relationships among admirers of a brand."... Like other communities, brand communities are believed to possess "a shared consciousness, rituals and traditions, and a sense of moral responsibility."... The Better

Adds one more term, "brand community," to describe corporations' efforts to distinguish their product from others in an increasingly competitive market and foster the development of a community that shares their values — in this case, the shared sense of ethical responsibility.

> Community campaign envisions the mass audience as a brand community composed of ABC viewers, each of whom exercises ethical dispositions and capacities within existing institutions (schools, hospitals, charities) and spaces (neighborhoods, parks, municipalities). Although this ethical activity takes place outside television culture, it can only be realized through the ABC brand, which activates and rewards action with affirmation and belonging. ABC operates as what Celia Lury calls a branded interface—not only to the consumption of television but to the duties and practices of contemporary citizenship.... TV is no longer good in the self-interested sense evoked by the earlier ABC campaign. ABC is the gateway for civic obligations in the double service of the "community" and the Better Community brand.

■ Make Connections among Different Texts

The texts by Loeb, Colby and her colleagues, and Ouellette all deal with some aspect of civic engagement, activism, and community building. The authors write about efforts to motivate people to work with one another to foster the health of communities based on moral or humanistic principles or to take up the call to compensate for changing economic policies. The texts are very much in conversation with one another, as the authors focus on relevant experiences and research to convey what they see as the value of civic and political engagement. However, each author offers a slightly different perspective that forces readers to ask if morality has a place in the ways we conceptualize civic engagement, the role that colleges and universities should play in promoting civic engagement in the undergraduate curriculum, or the extent to which corporations' commitment to community building is in conflict with their profit motives.

- Loeb urges readers to value the human connection that results from working together for the common good of a community and uses research to convey the psychological and physiological benefits of doing so. He also brings into focus the consequences of silence and the disconnect that can occur when we see injustice and fail to act.

- Colby and her colleagues share Loeb's perceptions about the value of community engagement but argue that teaching moral principles and core knowledge can have the positive effect of serving as a compass or guide for action. Though the authors are reluctant to identify specific values that they believe students should learn, they are particularly interested in the education of undergraduates and see the importance of helping students develop the ability to make informed judgments.

- Ouellette takes a different approach when she uses ABC as a case example to document the ways corporations have taken on the responsibility of serving families in need with changes in economic policy. In telling this story, she affirms the value of building community and shows that media can foster community; however, she also seems to question the profit-making motive that underlies the branding of corporations as civically engaged.

■ Decide What Those Connections Mean

Having annotated the selections, we filled out the worksheet in Figure 12.1, making notes in the grid to help us see the three texts in relation to one another. Our worksheet included columns for

- author and source information,
- the gist of each author's argument,
- supporting examples and illustrations,
- counterarguments, and
- our own thoughts.

A worksheet like this one can help you concentrate on similarities and differences in the texts to determine what the connections among texts mean. Of course, you can design your own worksheet as well, tailoring it to your needs and preferences. If you want to take very detailed notes about your authors and sources, for example, you may want to have separate columns for each.

Once you start making connections, including points of agreement and disagreement, you can start identifying counterarguments in the reading—that perhaps educators should not be inclined to teach morality in their classes and that the human connection that Loeb describes will serve as a sufficient motive for acting on behalf of the common good in a given community. Perhaps we need to look more critically at a corporation's interest in communities where their executives do not live, work, go to school, and shop. Identifying questions and even counterarguments can give you a sense of what is at issue for each author and what is at stake. And how can we test the claims that experts make about how policies have affected the health and well-being of communities where many children and families may be feeling the consequences of policies designed to shift the responsibility from the federal government to private corporations and private agencies? What causes the fragmentation that concerns some of the authors cited in these essays? What are the best ways to build community? For that matter, how effective have media corporations been in fostering the health of communities and a shared sense of responsibility?

216 CHAPTER 12 | FROM SYNTHESIS TO RESEARCHED ARGUMENT

▪ Formulate the Gist of What You've Read

Remember that your gist should bring into focus the relationship among different ideas in multiple texts. Looking at the information juxtaposed on the worksheet (Figure 12.1), you can begin to construct the gist of your synthesis:

- Paul Loeb cites studies and uses his own experiences to motivate readers to be more civically engaged in their communities, to resist focusing on their own interests, and to enter into relationships with others to fulfill what it means to be human. He addresses those readers who may be discouraged by others who would silence or ignore their voices and commit themselves to speaking out about the issues that concern them. He points out the consequences of remaining silent and explains that we should not be discouraged by our "failed" attempts to create change.

- Anne Colby and her colleagues share a common concern that Loeb expresses about trends toward increased individualism and lack of civic engagement. The authors are especially interested in reaching out to undergraduates and speak to the need to equip young people with the kinds of tools that would enable them to translate what they are learning into actions they can take as civic-minded, politically engaged citizens. One of those tools is judgment, and the best way to teach judgment is by imparting values and core knowledge that can serve as a moral compass and guide action.

- Ouellette broadens the discussion of civic engagement and political action by looking at the branding of corporations as socially responsible "citizens." Her analysis explains the extent to which presidents Clinton and then Bush reached out to businesses to provide initiatives to support children and families in need given changes in federal economic policies.

How do you formulate this information into a gist? You can use a transition word such as *although* or *however* to connect ideas that different authors bring together while conveying their differences. Thus, a gist of these essays might read:

GIST OF A SYNTHESIS

As a response to increased fragmentation of American society, Paul Loeb and Anne Colby and her colleagues underscore the reasons individuals need to be more involved in both civic and political engagement. They help highlight the ways human interaction makes us more fully human and the extent to which community engagement fulfills the Founding Fathers' vision of democracy. However, Laurie Ouellette broadens readers' understanding of why it is necessary to be more involved. She focuses on changes in economic policy in the United States that have shifted funding for families and children with the greatest needs to private entities and corporations.

Author and Source	Gist of Argument	Examples/Illustrations	Counterarguments/Challenging Assumptions	What I Think
Paul Rogat Loeb "Making Our Lives Count" from *Soul of a Citizen*	Argues that connecting to others through civic participation and working for the common good is what makes us more fully human.	Uses research from psychology, public health, and sociology, as well as personal stories to explain the value of community involvement. He also describes a number of negative effects of failing to be engaged and living with the disconnect between our convictions and our decision not to act on those convictions.	If there is a counterargument, it is implied when Loeb anticipates readers who have been silenced and feel their points of view do not matter. These readers are skeptical of the benefits of engagement.	The examples serve as compelling reasons to be involved, but I also understand why others feel that their voices might not be heard or taken seriously. This is often the case, but remaining silent can also be difficult. I also appreciate his point about failure. What might seem like failure can actually be a factor that bolsters our commitment to make a difference.
Anne Colby and Thomas Ehrlich with Elizabeth Beaumont and Jason Stephens "Undergraduate Education and the Development of Moral and Civic Responsibility"	Shares the concern Loeb raises—that there is a growing trend away from being civically and politically engaged. The authors add that moral principles are inextricably tied to democratic principles of rights, respect, tolerance, and community.	Limits the argument to the authors' own conceptions of civic and moral engagement, as well as the kind of core knowledge that is necessary to translate judgments into actions that people can take in a participant democracy.	Recognizes the extent to which the focus on moral engagement sets the authors' ideas apart from others like Loeb who try to motivate people to be civically engaged. It is implicit that others may feel uncomfortable with an argument that includes moral engagement, and the authors are careful to explain that they do not have a specific set of values in mind. Still, the counterargument may very well be that educators should not blur the line between the subject they teach and values.	I agree that universities should take more responsibility for the communities they are a part of. Classes in political science might address both theories of government and action—not just voting but community involvement. I am not sure I agree that professors should teach values.

AUTHOR AND SOURCE	GIST OF ARGUMENT	EXAMPLES/ILLUSTRATIONS	COUNTERARGUMENTS/CHALLENGING ASSUMPTIONS	WHAT I THINK
Laurie Ouellette "Citizen Brand: ABC and the Do Good Turn in US Television"	Examines the reasons corporate social responsibility has emerged in recent years, emphasizing shifts in government policies that placed greater responsibility on the private sector for supporting children and families living in poverty. Argues that initiatives like "The Better Community" campaign are not altogether altruistic and serve corporate interests in creating wealth for their stakeholders.	Uses case examples of ABC's Better Community public outreach campaign and ABC's parent company to illustrate roles that corporations have taken on. On the one hand, they have taken on the mantle of social responsibility, and on the other hand, they use social responsibility as a marketing tool to create profits.	Acknowledges the value of ABC's strategy of positioning itself as a socially conscious corporation. However, looks critically at efforts that associate the leadership of figures such as Martin Luther King and the grassroots movement of the Civil Rights struggle with civic-minded projects that ABC has promoted. Also questions whose interests are served when corporations promote civic engagement as a profit-making venture.	I hadn't really thought about the economic factors that have prompted corporations to be more invested in community development. I am a little skeptical of the role that corporations can or should play in communities and worry that their motives blur, serving a community as a good in itself and doing so to make money.

FIGURE 12.1   Worksheet for Writing a Synthesis

WRITING A SYNTHESIS **219**

Having drafted the gist, we returned to our notes on the worksheet to complete the synthesis, presenting examples and using transitions to signal the relationships among the texts and their ideas. Here is our brief synthesis of the three texts:

The gist of our synthesis.

As a response to increased fragmentation of society, Paul Loeb and Anne Colby and her colleagues underscore the reasons why individuals need to be more involved in both political and civic engagement. They help highlight the ways human interaction makes us more fully human and the extent to which community engagement fulfills the Founding Fathers' vision of democracy. Loeb's research in psychology, public health, and sociology also demonstrates the ways that community engagement contributes to our own sense of well-being. Colby and her colleagues share Loeb's outlook, but they add that moral principles are inextricably tied to democratic principles of rights, respect, tolerance, and community. They also argue that individuals need tools to make decisions, especially a core knowledge of key issues and a moral compass to serve as a guide to action that is aimed at the common good. Still, they recognize the extent to which their focus on moral engagement sets their ideas apart from others like Loeb who try to motivate people to be civically engaged. It is implicit that others may feel uncomfortable with an argument that includes moral engagement, and the authors are careful to explain that they do not have a specific set of values in mind.

1

Transition: There is an alternative reason individuals should be civically and politically engaged.

However, Laurie Ouellette broadens readers' understanding of why it is necessary to be more involved. This is especially true when she focuses her analysis on changes in economic policy in the United States that have shifted funding for families and children with the greatest needs to private entities and corporations. In pointing to this shift in policy, she shows how corporations such as Disney have rebranded themselves as socially responsible, marketing themselves in a way that appeals to viewers who share a view of themselves as altruistic. Thus, Ouellette helps show that there are reasons beyond the humanizing principles that Loeb advances and the kinds of values that Colby and her colleagues believe are inextricably tied to teaching and learning in institutions of higher education. That is, communities may appear to be more fragmented than ever before, but the urgency created by government social welfare programs serves as a pragmatic call to service that we cannot ignore.

2

Evidence demonstrates that the urgency of a changing economy is a strong factor in motivating individuals to get involved, especially when sponsored by corporations that have been given the responsibility to fulfill what was an obligation of the federal government.

220   CHAPTER 12 | FROM SYNTHESIS TO RESEARCHED ARGUMENT

One formulation of an argument that emerges from the three texts. The transition "yet" and the questions posed set up the direction of what is to follow.

While some may argue that corporations act out of self-interest in branding themselves as socially responsible, evidence indicates that the media may be more successful at motivating individuals to be involved than other means. Yet in considering the reasons why it is important to be an engaged citizen, whether as individuals or as a corporation, Ouellette, among others, forces us to ask whose interests are served when any of us becomes invested in communities where we do not live, work, shop, or go to school. Despite the benefits of citizen branding, Ouellette reminds us that we cannot ignore the profit motive of companies that have fulfilled a role once played by the federal government in what is now a postwelfare state. To what extent, if at all, are these roles in conflict with one another? For that matter, what values should guide investments and personal responsibility in reaching out to communities with the greatest needs?

3

Writing a synthesis, like writing a summary, is principally a strategy for framing your own argument. It's one thing to synthesize what you read and convey to your readers how various points in a conversation intersect and diverge. It's quite another to write yourself into the conversation. This entails thinking critically about what you are reading, raising questions, conducting further research, and taking a stance based on your own understanding of what you have read, what you believe and value, and the available evidence.

Steps to Writing a Synthesis

1 **Make connections between and among different texts.** Annotate the texts you are working with, with an eye to comparing them. As you would for a summary, note major points in the texts, choose relevant examples, and formulate the gist of each text.

2 **Decide what those connections mean.** Fill out a worksheet to compare your notes on the different texts, track counterarguments, and record your thoughts. Decide what the similarities and differences mean to you and what they might mean to your readers.

3 **Formulate the gist of what you've read.** Identify an overarching idea that brings together the ideas you've noted, and write a synthesis that forges connections and makes use of the examples you've noted. Use transitions to signal the direction of your synthesis.

WRITING A SYNTHESIS **221**

A Practice Sequence: Writing a Synthesis

1 To practice the strategies for synthesizing that we describe in this chapter, read the following three essays, which focus on the role that online media play in conveying information to diverse groups of readers or viewers. As you discuss the strategies the authors use to develop their arguments, consider these questions:

- How would you explain the popularity of blogs, Twitter, and YouTube?
- What themes have the writers focused on as they have sought to enter the conversation surrounding the use of electronic media?
- To what extent do you think the criticisms of media presented by the authors are legitimate?
- Do blogs, Twitter, and YouTube pose a threat to traditional journalism?
- Do you think that blogs, Twitter, and YouTube add anything to print journalism? If so, what?

2 To stimulate a conversation, or a debate, we suggest that you break up into four different groups:

Group 1: Print journalism

Group 2: Blogs

Group 3: Twitter

Group 4: YouTube

Students in each group should prepare an argument indicating the strengths and limitations of the particular mode of communication that they represent. In preparing the argument, be sure to acknowledge what other modes of communication might add to the ways we learn about news and opinions. One student from each group will present this argument to the other groups.

3 Based on the discussion you have had in exercise 1 and/or exercise 2, write a synthesis of the three essays using the steps we have outlined in this chapter.

- Summarize each essay.
- Explain the ways in which the authors' arguments are similar or different, using examples and illustrations to demonstrate the similarities and differences.
- Formulate an overall gist that synthesizes the points each author makes.

222 CHAPTER 12 | FROM SYNTHESIS TO RESEARCHED ARGUMENT

DAN KENNEDY

Political Blogs: Teaching Us Lessons about Community

Dan Kennedy, an assistant professor of journalism at Northeastern University, writes on media issues for *The Guardian* and for *CommonWealth* magazine. His blog, Media Nation, is online at dankennedy.net.

■ ■ ■

The rise of blogging as both a supplement and a challenge to traditional journalism has coincided with an explosion of opinion mongering. Blogs—and the role they play in how Americans consume and respond to information—are increasingly visible during our political season, when our ideological divide is most apparent. From nakedly partisan sites such as Daily Kos on the left and Little Green Footballs on the right, to more nuanced but nevertheless ideological enterprises such as Talking Points Memo, it sometimes seems there is no room in blogworld for straight, neutral journalism.

1

The usual reasons given for this are that reporting is difficult and expensive and that few bloggers know how to research a story, develop and interview sources, and assemble the pieces into a coherent, factual narrative. Far easier, so this line of thinking goes, for bloggers to sit in their pajamas and blast their semi-informed opinions out to the world.

2

There is some truth to this, although embracing this view wholeheartedly requires us to overlook the many journalists who are now writing blogs, as well as the many bloggers who are producing journalism to a greater or lesser degree. But we make a mistake when we look at the opinion-oriented nature of blogs and ask whether bloggers are capable of being "objective," to use a hoary and now all but meaningless word. The better question to ask is why opinion-oriented blogs are so popular—and what lessons the traditional media can learn from them without giving up their journalistic souls.

3

Perhaps what's happening is that the best and more popular blogs provide a sense of community that used to be the lifeblood of traditional news organizations and, especially, of newspapers. Recently I reread part of Jay Rosen's book, *What Are Journalists For?*, his 1999 postmortem on the public journalism movement. What struck me was Rosen's description of public journalism's origins, which were grounded in an attempt to recreate a sense of community so that people might discover a reason to read newspapers. "Eventually I came to the conclusion ... that journalism's purpose was to see the public into fuller existence," Rosen writes. "Informing people followed that."

4

Rosen's thesis—that journalism could only be revived by reawakening the civic impulse—is paralleled by Robert Putnam's 2000 book, *Bowling Alone*, in which he found that people who sign petitions, attend public meetings, and participate in religious and social organizations are more likely to be newspaper readers than those who do not. "Newspaper readers are older, more educated, and more rooted in their communities than is the average American," Putnam writes.

Unfortunately for the newspaper business, the traditional idea of community, based mainly on geography, remains as moribund today as it was when Rosen and Putnam were analyzing its pathologies. But if old-fashioned communities are on the decline, the human impulse to form communities is not. And the Internet, as it turns out, is an ideal medium for fostering a new type of community in which people have never met, and may not even know each other's real names, but share certain views and opinions about the way the world works. It's interesting that Rosen has become a leading exponent of journalism tied to these communities, both through his PressThink blog and through NewAssignment.net, which fosters collaborations between professional and citizen journalists.

Attitude First, Facts Second

This trend toward online community-building has given us a mediascape in which many people—especially those most interested in politics and public affairs—want the news delivered to them in the context of their attitudes and beliefs. That doesn't mean they want to be fed a diet of self-reinforcing agit-prop (although some do). It does mean they see their news consumption as something that takes place within their community, to be fit into a preexisting framework of ideas that may be challenged but that must be acknowledged.

Earlier this year John Lloyd, a contributing editor for the *Financial Times*, talked about the decline of just-the-facts journalism on *Open Source*, a Web-based radio program hosted by the veteran journalist Christopher Lydon. It has become increasingly difficult, Lloyd said, to report facts that are not tied to an ideological point of view. The emerging paradigm, he explained, may be "that you can only get facts through by attaching them to a very strong left-wing, right-wing, Christian, atheist position. Only then, only if you establish your bona fides within this particular community, will they be open to facts."

No less a blogging enthusiast than Markos Moulitsas, founder of Daily Kos, has observed that political blogs are a nonentity in Britain, where the newspapers themselves cater to a wide range of different opinions. "You look at the media in Britain, it's vibrant and it's exciting and it's fun, because they're all ideologically tinged," Moulitsas said at an appearance in Boston last fall. "And that's a good thing, because people buy them and understand that their viewpoints are going to be represented."

The notion that journalism must be tied to an ideological community may seem disheartening to traditionalists. In practice, though, journalism based on communities of shared interests and beliefs can be every bit as valuable as the old model of objectivity, if approached with rigor and respect for the truth. *10*

Last year, for instance, Talking Points Memo (TPM) and its related blogs helped break the story of how the U.S. Department of Justice had fired eight U.S. attorneys for what appeared to be politically motivated reasons, a scandal that led to the resignation of Attorney General Alberto Gonzales. TPM's reporting was based in part on information dug up and passed along by its liberal readership. The founder and editor, Joshua Micah Marshall, received a George Polk Award, but it belonged as much to the community he had assembled as it did to him personally. *11*

Of course, we still need neutral, non-opinionated journalism to help us make sense of the world around us. TPM's coverage of the U.S. attorneys scandal was outstanding, but it was also dismissive of arguments that it was much ado about nothing, or that previous administrations had done the same or worse. Liberals or conservatives who get all of their news from ideologically friendly sources don't have much incentive to change their minds. *12*

Connecting to Communities of Shared Interests

Even news outlets that excel at traditional, "objective" journalism do so within the context of a community. Some might not find liberal bias in the news pages of the *New York Times*, as the paper's conservative critics would contend, but there's little doubt that the *Times* serves a community of well-educated, affluent, culturally liberal readers whose preferences and tastes must be taken into account. Not to be a journalistic relativist, but all news needs to be evaluated within the context in which it was produced, even an old-fashioned, inverted-pyramid-style dispatch from the wires. Who was interviewed? Who wasn't? Why? These are questions that must be asked regardless of the source. *13*

We might now be coming full circle as placeblogs—chatty, conversational blogs that serve a particular geographic community—become more prevalent. Lisa Williams, founder of H20town, a blog that serves her community of Watertown, Massachusetts, believes that such forums could help foster the sense of community that is a necessary *14* precondition to newspaper readership. Williams also runs a project called Placeblogger.com, which tracks local blogs around the world.

"The news creates a shared pool of stories that gives us a way to talk to people who aren't family or close friends or people who we will never meet—in short, our fellow citizens," Williams says by e-mail. "The truth is, people still want those neighbor-to-neighbor contacts, but the traditional ways of doing it don't fit into the lives that people are actually living today. Your core audience is tired, sitting on the couch with their laptop, and watching *Lost* with one eye. Give them someone to sit with."

Critics of blogs have been looking at the wrong thing. While traditionalists disparage bloggers for their indulgence of opinion and hyperbole, they overlook the sense of community and conversation that blogs have fostered around the news. What bloggers do well, and what news organizations do poorly or not at all, is give their readers someone to sit with. News consumers—the public, citizens, us—still want the truth. But we also want to share it and talk about it with our like-minded neighbors and friends. The challenge for journalism is not that we'll lose our objectivity; it's that we won't find a way to rebuild a sense of community.

JOHN DICKERSON

Don't Fear Twitter

John Dickerson is a political columnist for *Slate* magazine and chief Washington correspondent for CBS News. Before joining *Slate*, Dickerson covered politics for *Time* magazine, including four years as the magazine's White House correspondent. Dickerson has also written for the *New York Times* and *Washington Post* and is a regular panelist on *Washington Week in Review*. This essay first appeared in the Summer 2008 issue of *Nieman Reports*.

■　■　■

If I were cleverer, this piece on Twitter and journalism would fit in Twitter's 140-character limitation. The beauty of Twitter when properly used—by both the reader and the writer—is that everyone knows what it is. No reader expects more from Twitter than it offers, and no one writing tries to shove more than necessary into a Twitter entry, which is sometimes called a Tweet, but not by me, thank you.

Not many people know what Twitter is, though, so I'm going to go on for a few hundred words. Twitter is a Web site that allows you to share your thoughts instantly and on any topic with other people in the Twitter network as long as you do so in tight little entries of 140 characters

226   CHAPTER 12 | FROM SYNTHESIS TO RESEARCHED ARGUMENT

or less. If you're wondering how much you can write with that space limitation, this sentence that you're reading right now hits that mark perfectly.

For some, journalism is already getting smaller. Newspapers are shrinking. Serious news is being pushed aside in favor of entertainment and fluff stories. To many journalists and guardians of the trade, the idea that any journalist would willingly embrace a smaller space is horrifying and dumb. One journalism professor drew himself up to his full height and denounced Twitter journalism—or microjournalism, as someone unfortunately called it—as the ultimate absurd reduction of journalism. (I think he may have dislodged his monocle, he was waving his quill pen so violently.) Venerable CBS newsman Roger Mudd had a far lighter touch when he joked to me that he could barely say the word "texting" when he and I were talking about the idea of delivering a couple of sentences and calling it journalism.

We can all agree that journalism shouldn't get any smaller, but Twitter doesn't threaten the traditions of our craft. It adds, rather than subtracts, from what we do.

As I spend nearly all of my time on the road these days reporting on the presidential campaigns, Twitter is the perfect place for all of those asides I've scribbled in the hundreds of notebooks I have in my garage from the campaigns and stories I've covered over the years. Inside each of those notebooks are little pieces of color I've picked up along the way. Sometimes these snippets are too off-topic or too inconsequential to work into a story. Sometimes they are the little notions or sideways thoughts that become the lead of a piece or the kicker. All of them now have found a home on Twitter.

As journalists we take people places they can't go. Twitter offers a little snapshot way to do this. It's informal and approachable and great for conveying a little moment from an event. Here's an entry from a McCain rally during the Republican primaries: "Weare, NH: Audience man to McCain: 'I heard that Hershey is moving plants to Mexico and I'll be damned if I'm going to eat Mexican chocolate.'" In Scranton covering Barack Obama I sent this: "Obama: 'What's John McCain's problem?' Audience member: 'He's too old.' Obama: 'No, no that's not the problem. There are a lot of wise people....'" With so many Democrats making an issue of McCain's age, here was the candidate in the moment seeming to suggest that critique was unfair.

Occasionally, just occasionally, reporters can convey a piece of news that fits into 140 characters without context. If Twitter had been around when the planes hit the World Trade Center, it would have been a perfect way for anyone who witnessed it to convey at that moment what they'd seen or heard. With Twitter, we can also pull back the curtain on our lives a little and show readers what it's like to cover a campaign. ("Wanna be a reporter? On long bus rides learn to sleep in your own hand.")

The risk for journalism, of course, is that people spend all day Twittering and reading other people's Twitter entries and don't engage with the news in any other way. This seems a pretty small worry. If written the right way, Twitter entries build a community of readers who find their way to longer articles because they are lured by these moment-by-moment observations. As a reader, I've found that I'm exposed to a wider variety of news because I read articles suggested to me by the wide variety of people I follow on Twitter. I'm also exposed to some keen political observers and sharp writers who have never practiced journalism. 8

Twitter is not the next great thing in journalism. No one should try to make Twitter do more than it can and no reader should expect too much from a 140-character entry. As for the critics, their worries about Twitter and journalism seem like the kind of obtuse behavior that would make a perfect observational Twitter entry: "A man at the front of the restaurant is screaming at a waiter and gesticulating wildly. The snacks on the bar aren't a four-course meal!" 9

STEVE GROVE

YouTube: The Flattening of Politics

Steve Grove is director of Google News Lab, and formerly directed all news, political programming, and citizen journalism for YouTube. He has been quoted as saying that he regards himself less as an editor than as a curator of the Web site's "chaotic sea of content." A native of Northfield, Minnesota, he worked as a journalist at the *Boston Globe* and ABC News before moving to YouTube.

For a little over a year, I've served as YouTube's news and political director — perhaps a perplexing title in the eyes of many journalists. Such wonderment might be expected since YouTube gained its early notoriety as a place with videos of dogs on skateboards or kids falling off of trampolines. But these days, in the ten hours of video uploaded to YouTube every minute of every day (yes — every minute of every day), an increasing amount of the content is news and political video. And with YouTube's global reach and ease of use, it's changing the way that politics — and its coverage — is happening. 1

Each of the sixteen one-time presidential candidates had YouTube channels; seven announced their candidacies on YouTube. Their staffs 2 uploaded thousands of videos that were viewed tens of millions of times. By early March of this year, the Obama campaign was uploading two to three videos to YouTube every day. And thousands of advocacy groups and nonprofit organizations use YouTube to get their election messages into the conversation. For us, the most exciting aspect is that ordinary people continue to use YouTube to distribute their own political content; these range from "gotcha" videos they've taken at campaign rallies to questions for the candidates, from homemade political commercials to video mash-ups of mainstream media coverage.

What this means is that average citizens are able to fuel a new meritocracy for political coverage, one unburdened by the gatekeeping "middleman." Another way of putting it is that YouTube is now the world's largest town hall for political discussion, where voters connect with candidates—and the news media—in ways that were never before possible.

In this new media environment, politics is no longer bound by traditional barriers of time and space. It doesn't matter what time it is, or where someone is located—as long as they have the means to connect through the Web, they can engage in the discussion. This was highlighted in a pair of presidential debates we produced with CNN during this election cycle during which voters asked questions of the candidates via YouTube videos they'd submitted online. In many ways, those events simply brought to the attention of a wider audience the sort of exchanges that take place on YouTube all the time....

News Organizations and YouTube

Just because candidates and voters find all sorts of ways to connect directly on YouTube does not mean there isn't room for the mainstream media, too. In fact, many news organizations have launched YouTube channels, including the Associated Press, the *New York Times*, the BBC, CBS, and the *Wall Street Journal*.

Why would a mainstream media company upload their news content to YouTube?

Simply put, it's where eyeballs are going. Research from the Pew Internet & American Life project found that 37 percent of adult Internet users have watched online video news, and well over half of online adults have used the Internet to watch video of any kind. Each day on YouTube hundreds of millions of videos are viewed at the same time that television viewership is decreasing in many markets. If a mainstream news organization wants its political reporting seen, YouTube offers visibility without a cost. The ones that have been doing this for a while rely on a strategy of building audiences on YouTube and then trying to drive viewers back to their Web sites for a deeper dive into the content. And these organizations can earn revenue as well by running ads against their video content on YouTube.

In many ways, YouTube's news ecosystem has the potential to offer much more to a traditional media outlet. Here are some examples:

1. **Interactivity:** YouTube provides an automatic focus group for news content. How? YouTube wasn't built as merely a "series of tubes" to distribute online video. It is also an interactive platform. Users comment on, reply to, rank, and share videos with one another and form communities around content that they like. If news organizations want to see how a particular piece of content will resonate with audiences, they have an automatic focus group waiting on YouTube. And that focus group isn't just young people: 20 percent of YouTube users are over age 55—which is the same percentage that is under 18. This means the YouTube audience roughly mirrors the national population.

2. **Partner with audiences:** YouTube provides news media organizations new ways to engage with audiences and involve them in the programming. Modeled on the presidential debates we cohosted last year, YouTube has created similar partnerships, such as one with the BBC around the mayoral election in London and with a large public broadcaster in Spain for their recent presidential election. Also on the campaign trail, we worked along with Hearst affiliate WMUR-TV in New Hampshire to solicit videos from voters during that primary. Hundreds of videos flooded in from across the state. The best were broadcast on that TV station, which highlighted this symbiotic relationship: On the Web, online video bubbles the more interesting content to the top and then TV amplifies it on a new scale. We did similar arrangements with news organizations in Iowa, Pennsylvania, and on Super Tuesday, as news organizations leveraged the power of voter-generated content. What the news organizations discover is that they gain audience share by offering a level of audience engagement—with opportunities for active as well as passive experiences.

For news media organizations, audience engagement is much easier to achieve by using platforms like YouTube than it is to do on their own. And we just made it easier: Our open API (application programming interface), nicknamed "YouTube Everywhere"—just launched a few months ago—allows other companies to integrate our upload functionality into their online platforms. It's like having a mini YouTube on your Web site and, once it's there, news organizations

230 CHAPTER 12 | FROM SYNTHESIS TO RESEARCHED ARGUMENT

can encourage—and publish—video responses and comments on the reporting they do.

Finally, reporters use YouTube as source material for their stories. *10* With hundreds of thousands of video cameras in use today, there is a much greater chance than ever before that events will be captured—by someone—as they unfold. No need for driving the satellite truck to the scene if someone is already there and sending in video of the event via their cell phone. It's at such intersections of new and old media that YouTube demonstrates its value. It could be argued, in fact, that the YouTube platform is the new frontier in newsgathering. On the election trail, virtually every appearance by every candidate is captured on video—by someone—and that means the issues being talked about are covered more robustly by more people who can steer the public discussion in new ways. The phenomenon is, of course, global, as we witnessed last fall in Burma (Myanmar) after the government shut down news media outlets during waves of civic protests. In time, YouTube was the only way to track the violence being exercised by the government on monks who'd taken to the streets. Videos of this were seen worldwide on YouTube, creating global awareness of this situation—even in the absence of journalists on the scene.

Citizen journalism on YouTube—and other Internet sources—is *11* often criticized because it is produced by amateurs and therefore lacks a degree of trustworthiness. Critics add that because platforms like YouTube are fragmenting today's media environment, traditional newsrooms are being depleted of journalists, and thus the denominator for quality news coverage is getting lower and lower. I share this concern about what is happening in the news media today, but I think there are a couple of things worth remembering when it comes to news content on YouTube.

Trusting What We See

When it comes to determining the trustworthiness of news content on *12* YouTube, it's important to have some context. People tend to know what they're getting on YouTube, since content is clearly labeled by username as to where it originated. A viewer knows if the video they're watching is coming from "jellybean109" or "thenewyorktimes." Users also know that YouTube is an open platform and that no one verifies the truth of content better than the consumer. The wisdom of the crowd on YouTube is far more likely to pick apart a shoddy piece of "journalism" than it is to elevate something that is simply untrue. In fact, because video is ubiquitous and so much more revealing and compelling than text, YouTube can provide a critical fact-checking platform in today's media environment. And in some ways, it offers a backstop for accuracy since a journalist can't afford to get the story wrong; if they do, it's likely that someone else who was there got it right — and posted it to YouTube.

Scrutiny cuts both ways. Journalists are needed today for the work they do as much as they ever have been. While the wisdom of crowds might provide a new form of fact checking, and the ubiquity of technology might provide a more robust view of the news, citizens desperately need the Fourth Estate to provide depth, context, and analysis that only comes with experience and the sharpening of the craft. Without the work of journalists, the citizens — the electorate — lose a critical voice in the process of civic decision making.

This is the media ecosystem in which we live in this election cycle. Candidates and voters speak directly to one another, unfiltered. News organizations use the Internet to connect with and leverage audiences in new ways. Activists, issue groups, campaigns, and voters all advocate for, learn about, and discuss issues on the same level platform. YouTube has become a major force in this new media environment by offering new opportunities and new challenges. For those who have embraced them — and their numbers grow rapidly every day — the opportunity to influence the discussion is great. For those who haven't, they ignore the opportunity at their own peril.

AVOIDING PLAGIARISM

Whether you paraphrase, summarize, or synthesize, it is essential that you acknowledge your sources. Academic writing requires you to use and document sources appropriately, making clear to readers the boundaries between your words and ideas and those of other writers. Setting boundaries can be a challenge because so much of academic writing involves interweaving the ideas of others into your own argument. Still, you must acknowledge your sources. It's only fair. Imagine how you would feel if you were reading a text and discovered that the writer had incorporated a passage from one of your papers, something you had slaved over, without giving you credit. You would see yourself as a victim of plagiarism, and you would be justified in feeling very angry indeed.

In fact, **plagiarism** — the unacknowledged use of another's work, passed off as one's own — is a serious breach of academic integrity, and colleges and universities deal with it severely. If you are caught plagiarizing in your work for a class, you can expect to fail that class and you may even be expelled from your college or university. Furthermore, although a failing grade on a paper or in a course, honestly come by, is unlikely to deter an employer from hiring you, the stigma of plagiarism can come back to haunt you when you apply for a job. Any violation of the principles set forth in Table 12.1 could have serious consequences for your academic and professional career.

232 CHAPTER 12 | FROM SYNTHESIS TO RESEARCHED ARGUMENT

TABLE 12.1 Principles Governing Plagiarism

1. All written work submitted for any purpose is accepted as your own work. This means it must not have been written, even in part, by another person.

2. The wording of any written work you submit is assumed to be your own. This means you must not submit work that has been copied, wholly or partially, from a book, an article, an essay, a newspaper, another student's paper or notebook, or any other source. Another writer's phrases, sentences, or paragraphs can be included only if they are presented as quotations and the source acknowledged.

3. The ideas expressed in a paper or report are assumed to originate with you, the writer. Written work that paraphrases a source without acknowledgment must not be submitted for credit. Ideas from the work of others can be incorporated in your work as starting points, governing issues, illustrations, and the like, but in every instance the source must be cited.

4. Remember that any online materials you use to gather information for a paper are also governed by the rules for avoiding plagiarism. You need to cite electronic sources as well as printed and other sources.

5. You may correct and revise your writing with the aid of reference books. You also may discuss your writing with your peers in a writing group or with peer tutors at your campus writing center. However, you may not submit writing that has been revised substantially by another person.

Even if you know what plagiarism is and wouldn't intentionally plagiarize, watch out for unintentional plagiarism. Again, paraphrasing can be especially tricky: Attempting to restate a passage without using the original words and sentence structure is, to a certain extent, an invitation to plagiarism. If you remember that your paper is *your* argument, and understand that any paraphrasing, summarizing, or synthesizing should reflect *your* voice and style, you will be less likely to have problems with plagiarism. Your paper should sound like you. And, again, the surest way to protect yourself is to cite your sources and carefully check your work.

Steps to Avoiding Plagiarism

1 **Always cite the source.** Signal that you are paraphrasing, summarizing, or synthesizing by identifying your source at the outset — "According to Laurie Ouellette," "Paul Loeb argues," "Anne Colby and her colleagues ... point out." And if possible, indicate the end of the paraphrase, summary, or synthesis with relevant page references to the source. If you cite a source several times in your paper, don't assume that your first citation has you covered; acknowledge the source as often as you use it.

2 **Provide a full citation in your bibliography.** It's not enough to cite a source in your paper; you must also provide a full citation for every source you use in the list of sources at the end of your paper.

INTEGRATING QUOTATIONS INTO YOUR WRITING

When you integrate quotations into your writing, bear in mind a piece of advice we've given you about writing the rest of your paper: Take your readers by the hand and lead them step by step. When you quote other authors to develop your argument—using their words to support your thinking or to address a counterargument—discuss and analyze the words you quote, showing readers how the specific language of each quotation contributes to the larger point you are making in your essay. When you integrate quotations, then, there are three basic things you want to do: (1) Take an active stance, (2) explain the quotations, and (3) attach short quotations to your own sentences.

■ Take an Active Stance

Critical reading requires that you adopt an active stance toward what you read—that you raise questions in response to a text. You should be no less active when you are using other authors' texts to develop your own argument.

Taking an active stance when you are quoting means knowing when to quote. Don't quote when a paraphrase or summary will convey the information from a source more effectively. More important, you have to make fair and wise decisions about what and how much you should quote to make your argument.

- You want to show that you understand the writer's argument, and you want to make evenhanded use of it in your own argument. It's not fair (or wise) to quote selectively—choosing only passages that support your argument—when you know you are distorting the argument of the writer you are quoting.

- Remember that your ideas and argument—your thesis—are what is most important to the readers and what justifies a quotation's being included at all. It's not wise (or fair to yourself) to flesh out your paper with an overwhelming number of quotations that could make readers think that you do not know your topic well or do not have your own ideas. Don't allow quotations to take over your paragraphs.

Above all, taking an active stance when you quote means taking control of your writing. You want to establish your own argument and guide your readers through it, allowing sources to contribute to but not dictate its direction. You are responsible for plotting and pacing your essay. Always keep in mind that your thesis is the skewer that runs through every paragraph, holding all of the ideas together. When you use quotations, then, you must organize them to enrich, substantiate, illustrate, and help support your central claim or thesis.

234   CHAPTER 12 | FROM SYNTHESIS TO RESEARCHED ARGUMENT

■ Explain the Quotations

When you quote an author to support or advance your argument, make sure that readers know exactly what they should learn from the quotation.

Read the excerpt below from one student's early draft of an argument that focuses on the value of service learning in high schools. The student reviews several relevant studies—but then simply drops in a quotation, expecting readers to know what they should pay attention to in it.

> Other research emphasizes community service as an integral and integrated part of moral identity. In this understanding, community service activities are not isolated events but are woven into the context of students' everyday lives (Yates, 1995); the personal, the moral, and the civic become "inseparable" (Colby, Ehrlich, Beaumont, & Stephens, 2003, p. 15). In their study of minority high schoolers at an urban Catholic school who volunteered at a soup kitchen for the homeless as part of a class assignment, Youniss and Yates (1999) found that the students underwent significant identity changes, coming to perceive themselves as lifelong activists. The researchers' findings are worth quoting at length here because they depict the dramatic nature of the students' changed viewpoints. Youniss and Yates wrote,
>
> > Many students abandoned an initially negative view of homeless people and a disinterest in homelessness by gaining appreciation of the humanity of homeless people and by showing concern for homelessness in relation to poverty, job training, low-cost housing, prison reform, drug and alcohol rehabilitation, care for the mentally ill, quality urban education, and welfare policy. Several students also altered perceptions of themselves from politically impotent teenagers to involved citizens who now and in the future could use their talent and power to correct social problems. They projected articulated pictures of themselves as adult citizens who could affect housing policies, education for minorities, and government programs within a clear framework of social justice. (p. 362)

The student's introduction to the quoted passage provided a rationale for quoting Youniss and Yates at length, but it did not help her readers see how the research related to her argument. The student needed to frame the quotation for her readers. Instead of introducing the quotation by saying "Youniss and Yates wrote," she should have made clear that the study supports the argument that community service can create change. A more appropriate frame for the quotation might have been a summary like this one:

Frames the quoted material, explaining it in the context of the student's argument.

One particular study underscores my argument that service can motivate change, particularly when that change begins within the students who are involved in service. Youniss and Yates (1999) wrote that over the course of their research, the students developed both an "appreciation of the humanity of homeless people" and a sense that they would someday be able to "use their talent and power to correct social problems" (p. 362).

In the following example, notice that the student writer uses Derrick Bell's text to say something about how the effects of desegregation have been muted by political manipulation.* The writer shapes what he wants readers to focus on, leaving nothing to chance.

> The effectiveness with which the meaning of *Brown v. Board of Education* has been manipulated, Derrick Bell argued, is also evidenced by the way in which such thinking has actually been embraced by minority groups. Bell claimed that a black school board member's asking "But of what value is it to teach black children to read in all-black schools?" indicates this unthinking acceptance that whiteness is an essential ingredient to effective schooling for blacks. Bell continued:
>
>> The assumption that even the attaining of academic skills is worthless unless those skills are acquired in the presence of white students illustrates dramatically how a legal precedent, namely the Supreme Court's decision in Brown v. Board of Education, has been so constricted even by advocates that its goal — equal educational opportunity — is rendered inaccessible, even unwanted, unless it can be obtained through racial balancing of the school population. (p. 255)
>
> Bell's argument is extremely compelling, particularly when one considers the extent to which "racial balancing" has come to be defined in terms of large white majority populations and small nonwhite minority populations.

Notice that the student's last sentence helps readers understand what the quoted material suggests and why it's important by embedding and extending Bell's notion of racial balancing into his explanation.

In sum, you should always explain the information that you quote so that your readers can see how the quotation relates to your own argument. ("Take your readers by the hand ...") As you read other people's writing, keep an eye open to the ways writers introduce and explain the sources they use to build their arguments.

■ Attach Short Quotations to Your Sentences

The quotations we discussed above are **block quotations,** lengthy quotations of more than five lines that are set off from the text of a paper with indention. Make shorter quotations part of your own sentences so that your readers can easily follow along and understand how the quotations connect to your argument. How do you make a quotation part of your own sentences? There are two main methods:

*This quotation is from Derrick Bell's *Silent Covenants: Brown v. Board of Education and the Unfulfilled Hopes for Racial Reform* (New York: Oxford UP, 2005).

236 CHAPTER 12 | FROM SYNTHESIS TO RESEARCHED ARGUMENT

- Integrate quotations within the grammar of your writing.
- Attach quotations with punctuation.

If possible, use both to make your integration of quotations more interesting and varied.

Integrate quotations within the grammar of a sentence. When you integrate a quotation into a sentence, the quotation must make grammatical sense and read as if it is part of the sentence:

> Fine, Weiss, and Powell (1998) expanded upon what others call "equal status contact theory" by using a "framework that draws on three traditionally independent literatures — those on community, difference, and democracy" (p. 37).

If you add words to the quotation, use square brackets around them to let readers know that the words are not original to the quotation:

> Smith and Wellner (2002) asserted that they "are not alone [in believing] that the facts have been incorrectly interpreted by Mancini" (p. 24).

If you omit any words in the middle of a quotation, use an **ellipsis**, three periods with spaces between them, to indicate the omission:

> Riquelme argues that "Eliot tries ... to provide a definition by negations, which he also turns into positive terms that are meant to correct misconceptions" (p. 156).

If you omit a sentence or more, make sure to put a period before the ellipsis points:

> Eagleton writes, "What Eliot was in fact assaulting was the whole ideology of middle-class liberalism.... Eliot's own solution is an extreme right-wing authoritarianism: men and women must sacrifice their petty 'personalities' and opinions to an impersonal order" (p. 39).

Whatever you add (using square brackets) or omit (using ellipses), the sentence must read grammatically. And, of course, your additions and omissions must not distort the author's meaning.

> Leah is also that little girl who "stares at her old street and look[s] at the abandoned houses and cracked up sidewalks."

Attach quotations with punctuation. You also can attach a quotation to a sentence by using punctuation. For example, this passage attaches the run-in quotation with a colon:

> For these researchers, there needs to be recognition of differences in a way that will include and accept all students. Specifically, they raised this key question: "Within multiracial settings, when are young people invited to discuss, voice, critique, and re-view the very notions of race that feel so fixed, so hierarchical, so damaging, and so accepted in the broader culture?" (p. 132).

In conclusion, if you don't connect quotations to your argument, your readers may not understand why you've included them. You need to explain a significant point that each quotation reveals as you introduce or end it. This strategy helps readers know what to pay attention to in a quotation, particularly if the quotation is lengthy.

Steps to Integrating Quotations into Your Writing

1 **Take an active stance.** Your sources should contribute to your argument, not dictate its direction.

2 **Explain the quotations.** Explain what you quote so your readers understand how each quotation relates to your argument.

3 **Attach short quotations to your sentences.** Integrate short quotations within the grammar of your own sentences, or attach them with appropriate punctuation.

A Practice Sequence: Integrating Quotations

1 Using several of the sources you are working with in developing your paper, try integrating quotations into your essay. Be sure you are controlling your sources. Carefully read the paragraphs where you've used quotations. Will your readers clearly understand why the quotations are there—the points the quotations support? Do the sentences with quotations read smoothly? Are they grammatically correct?

2 Working in a small group, agree on a substantial paragraph or passage (from this book or some other source) to write about. Each member should read the passage and take a position on the ideas, and then draft a page that quotes the passage using both strategies for integrating these quotations. Compare what you've written, examining similarities and differences in the use of quotations.

AN ANNOTATED STUDENT RESEARCHED ARGUMENT: SYNTHESIZING SOURCES

The student who wrote the essay "A Greener Approach to Groceries: Community-Based Agriculture in LaSalle Square" did so in a first-year writing class that gave students the opportunity to volunteer in the local community. For this assignment, students were asked to explore debates

238 CHAPTER 12 | FROM SYNTHESIS TO RESEARCHED ARGUMENT

about community and citizenship in contemporary America and to focus their research and writing on a social justice–related issue of their choice. The context of the course guided their inquiry as all the students in the course explored community service as a way to engage meaningfully and to develop relationships in the community.

We have annotated her essay to show the ways that she summarized and paraphrased research to show the urgency of the problem of food insecurity that exists around the world and to offer possible solutions. Notice how she synthesizes her sources, taking an active stance in using what she has read to advance her own argument.

Paul 1

Nancy Paul
Professor McLaughlin
English 2102
May 11, 20—

A Greener Approach to Groceries:
Community-Based Agriculture in LaSalle Square

In our post–9/11 society, there is incessant concern for the *1* security of our future. Billions of dollars are spent tightening borders, installing nuclear detectors, and adjudicating safety measures so that the citizens of the United States can grow and prosper without fear. Unfortunately, for some urban poor, the threat from terrorism is minuscule compared to the cruelty of their immediate environment. Far from the sands of the Afghan plains and encapsulated in the midst of inner-city deterioration, many find themselves in gray-lot

The student's thesis
deserts devoid of vegetation and reliable food sources. Abandoned by corporate supermarkets, millions of Americans are maimed by a "food insecurity" — the nutritional poverty that cripples them developmentally, physically, and psychologically.

The midwestern city that surrounds our university has a *2* food-desert sitting just west of the famously lush campus. Known as LaSalle Square, it was once home to the lucrative Bendix plant and has featured both a Target and a Kroger supermarket in recent years.

She calls attention to both the immediacy and urgency of the problem
But previous economic development decisions have driven both stores to the outskirts of town, and without a local supplier, the only food available in the neighborhood is prepackaged and sold at the few small convenience stores. This available food is virtually devoid

AN ANNOTATED STUDENT RESEARCHED ARGUMENT: SYNTHESIZING SOURCES **239**

Paul 2

of nutrition and inhibits the ability of the poor to prosper and thrive. Thus, an aging strip mall, industrial site, and approximately three acres of an empty grass lot between the buildings anchor — and unfortunately define — the neighborhood.

She proposes a possible solution.

While there are multiple ways of providing food to the destitute, I am proposing a co-op of community gardens built on the grassy space in LaSalle Square and on smaller sites within the neighborhood, supplemented by extra crops from Michiana farmers, which would supply fresh fruit and vegetables to be sold or distributed to the poor. Together the co-op could meet the nutritional needs of the people, provide plenty of nutritious food, not cost South Bend any additional money, and contribute to neighborhood revitalization, yielding concrete increases in property values. Far from being a pipe dream, LaSalle Square already hosted an Urban Garden Market this fall, so a co-op would simply build upon the already recognized need and desire for healthy food in the area. Similar coalitions around the world are harnessing the power of community to remedy food insecurity without the aid of corporate enterprise, and South Bend is perfectly situated to reproduce and possibly exceed their successes.

She places her solution in a larger context to indicate its viability.

Many, myself previously included, believe that the large-volume, cheap industrialization of food and the welfare system have obliterated hunger in the United States. Supermarkets like Wal-Mart and Kroger seem ubiquitous in our communities, and it is difficult to imagine anyone being beyond their influence. However, profit-driven corporate business plans do not mix well with low-income, high-crime populations, and the gap between the two is growing wider. This polarization, combined with the vitamin deficiency of our high-fructose corn syrup society, has created food deserts in already struggling communities where malnutrition is the enemy *inconnu* of the urban poor.

More context

LaSalle Square's food insecurity is typical of many urban areas. The grocery stores that used to serve the neighborhood have relocated to more attractive real estate on the outskirts of the city, and only local convenience stores, stocking basic necessary items and tobacco products, remain profitable. Linda Wolfson, a member of the steering committee for the LaSalle Square Redevelopment Plan, notes that if the community was fiscally healthy, it would be reasonable

Paul 3

to expect the inhabitants to simply drive the six miles to the strip mall district, but unfortunately many are marginally employed and do not have access to cars. For them, it is economically irresponsible to spend the extra money to get to the supermarket, and so they feed their families on the cheap soda, chips, and processed food

Synthesizing helps illustrate the extent of the problem and bolster her view that the poor suffer the most from the problem she identifies (Garnett; Smith; Brown and Carter).

that are readily available at the convenience store. Especially since high-calorie, low-nutrient, packaged food tends to be denser, urban mothers find that it helps their children feel full (Garnett). Sadly, a health investigation released in 2006 concluded that by the age of three, more than one-third of urban children are obese, due in large part to the consumption of low-quality food obtained from corner stores (Smith). A recent analysis of urban stores in Detroit found that only 19 percent offer the healthy food array suggested by the FDA food pyramid (Brown and Carter 5). The food that is offered contains 25 percent less nutrient density, and consequently, underprivileged socioeconomic populations consume significantly lower levels of the micronutrients that form the foundation for proper protein and brain

Here she paraphrases findings.

development. In a recent study of poor households, it was found that two-thirds of children were nutritionally poor and that more than 25 percent of women were deficient in iron, vitamin A, vitamin C, vitamin B6, thiamin, and riboflavin (Garnett). Of course, some may challenge the relevance of these vitamins and nutrients since they are not something the average person consciously incorporates into his or her diet on a daily basis. Yet modern research, examining the severely homogenous diets of the poor, has found severe developmental consequences associated with the lack of nutritional substance. For those afflicted, these deficiencies are not simply inconvenient, but actually exacerbate their plight and hinder their progress toward a sustainable lifestyle.

The human body is a complex system that cannot be sustained merely on the simple sugars and processed carbohydrates that comprise most cheap and filling foodstuffs, and research shows a relationship between nutritional deficiencies and a host of cognitive and developmental impairments that are prevalent in the undernourished families from urban America. Standardized tests of impoverished siblings, one of whom received nutritional supplements and the other who did not, showed cognitive gains in the well-

AN ANNOTATED STUDENT RESEARCHED ARGUMENT: SYNTHESIZING SOURCES **241**

Paul 4

Again she both summarizes and cites a relevant study to advance her argument.

nourished child as well as increased motor skills and greater interest in social interactions when compared to the other child. In the highly formative toddler years, undernutrition can inhibit the myelination of nerve fibers, which is responsible for neurotransmitting and proper brain function. Collaborators Emily Tanner from the University of Oxford and Matia Finn-Stevenson from Yale University published a comprehensive analysis of the link between nutrition and brain development in 2002. Their analysis, which they linked to social policy, indicated that a shortage of legumes and leafy green vegetables, which are nearly impossible to find in corner stores, is the leading cause of the iron-deficiency anemia afflicting 25 percent of urban children. This extreme form of anemia is characterized by impaired neurotransmission, weaker memory, and reduced attention span (Tanner and Finn-Stevenson 186). For those who do not have access to the vitamins, minerals, and micronutrients found in fruits and vegetables, these maladies are not distant risks, but constant, inescapable threats.

In light of these severe consequences of undernutrition, the term "food insecurity" encapsulates the condition wherein the economically disadvantaged are vulnerable simply because their bodies are unable to receive adequate fuel for optimal functioning. Just as one cannot expect a dry, parched plant to bloom and pollinate a garden, by constraining the development of individuals, food insecurity also constrains the development of the neighborhoods in which the individuals contribute. For the health of a city and its communities, all roadblocks to progress must be removed, and food insecurity must be cut out at its roots so that individuals have the resources for advancement. 7

As socially conscious citizens and local governments have recognized the prevalence and danger of food insecurity in inner cities, there have been attempts at a remedy. Obviously, the easiest solution is simply to introduce a grocery store that would provide a variety of quality, healthful foods. However, for big-box supermarkets driven by the bottom line, urban areas are less than desirable business locales from a standpoint of both profitability and maintenance. It is simply irrational for a supermarket to invest in an urban area with less revenue potential, size constraints, an 8

Paul 5

unattractive locale, and an increased threat of theft and defacement when it is so easy to turn a profit in spacious and peaceful suburbia (Eisenhauer 131). Supermarkets must have significant incentive, beyond humanitarian ends, if they are to take the financial risk of entering a poor, urban marketplace.

She takes an active stance in citing initiatives that could be applied more effectively to alleviate the problem of food insecurity.

Certain cities are using the power of Tax Increment Financing (TIF) districts to encourage supermarkets to invest in urban centers. Under these redevelopment laws, tax revenues from retail development or other commercial enterprises are devoted, for a specified number of years, to infrastructural improvement of the district ("TIF Reform"). This approach has been effective in enticing new businesses; in fact, the exterior growth around South Bend is the result of a TIF district established in the late 1980s. LaSalle Square is currently part of a TIF district, but there is discussion as to how the TIF monies should best be applied (Wolfson). It may be possible to use the power of the TIF to encourage another large retailer such as Kroger to establish a presence in the square, but a smaller enterprise may be a better option. Experts indicate that for the destitute and

She paraphrases a researcher's findings.

food-insecure, reliance on a corporate entity is not optimal. Elizabeth Eisenhauer, a researcher from the State University of New York, investigated the interplay between supermarkets and the urban poor; she concluded that large big-box stores lack a commitment to the communities they serve and can be relied on only when it is clear they will make a profit, which may or may not happen when TIF benefits expire (131). Even when a portion of proceeds is used in the community, the majority of the cash flow from a supermarket is going to a corporate headquarters elsewhere, not directly supporting the surrounding neighborhood. Likewise, while some employees may be local, the highest-salary management positions are generally given to outsiders, making the stores and their employees set apart, rather than integrated into the neighborhood (Eisenhauer 130). Certainly a supermarket in an urban area will greatly contribute to the reduction of food insecurity, but it is not the only available option, and the city of South Bend is ripe for alternative solutions. The city is primed for a cooperative effort that could shift the paradigm for urban renewal from a quick, corporate solution, to a long-term enterprise built on community contributions and under local control.

AN ANNOTATED STUDENT RESEARCHED ARGUMENT: SYNTHESIZING SOURCES   **243**

Paul 6

She cites a number of examples as evidence to demonstrate the viability of the solution she offers.

Around the globe, many destitute urban areas have found the means to reverse nutritional poverty through a literal and figurative grassroots effort. In an effort to avoid packaged, convenience store food, neighbors in the Bronx, San Francisco, Los Angeles, London, and most successfully in Philadelphia, have been planting their own crops right in the heart of the city (Brown and Carter 3-4). Truly farming the food desert, coalitions that link community gardens, local farmers, and urban markets are providing healthy, sustainable food sources without a supermarket. Interestingly, in the process, such coalitions are generating jobs, increasing property value, and, in some cases, actually reversing the effects of poverty. The city of South Bend, uniquely situated in the breadbasket of the United States, is in the perfect position to launch a "greening" effort, modeled after the successes in other parts of the world, which would both solve the problem of food insecurity of LaSalle Square and invigorate the local economy.

10

While modern Americans have the tendency to think that food production should be, and always has been, industrialized, countries around the world, especially economically disadvantaged nations, are

11

The use of multiple sources would make her case even stronger than using just one source of information, in this case Brown and Carter.

exemplifying the possibilities of local gardening efforts. Far removed from industrial farms, Cubans grow half their vegetables within the city; vacant land in Russian cities produces 80 percent of the nation's vegetables, and specifically in Moscow, 65 percent of families contribute to food production. Singapore has 10,000 urban farmers, and nearly half of the residents of Vancouver grow food in their gardens (Brown and Carter 10). These habits are not simply a novelty; rather, populations that garden tend to be healthier, eating six out of the fourteen vegetable categories more regularly than nongardeners and also consuming fewer sweet and sugary foods per capita (Brown and Carter 13). These data, compiled by the North American Urban Agriculture Committee, were synthesized from the *Journal of Public Health Policy* and the *Journal of Nutrition Education* and show the interrelatedness of nutritional access and availability to healthy personal choices. While these trends toward healthful lifestyles and gardening have been gaining ground slowly in the United States, when food insecurity and poverty take their toll, cities are finding that urban agriculture is an increasingly attractive and profitable alternative.

Paul 7

American communities have shown that creativity and collaboration can be quite effective at reversing food insecurity. The Garden Project of the Greater Lansing Food Bank has successfully combined gardening and Midwest access to local farms to bring food security to urban residents and senior citizens. Their eighteen community gardens and volunteers provide fresh fruits and vegetables year-round to low-income families, food pantries, the elderly, and social service organizations. Completely bypassing the commercial market, the Garden Project has trained 500 families to grow their own food in backyard plots so that they can always have healthy food in the midst of the city (Brown and Carter 1). The gardens are supplemented by a process known as "gleaning," in which volunteers harvest extra crops from local farmers that would otherwise go to waste, and deliver it to residents of subsidized housing ("Gleaning"). In 2008 alone, the Garden Project actively involved 2,500 individual gardeners and was able to provide over 250,000 pounds of produce from gleaning alone, plus the yields of the community plots that were used directly by the gardeners ("GLFB Facts"). This Lansing coalition serves over 5,000 individuals per month, yet only 4,400 reside under the poverty line in the LaSalle Square area (*City-Data.com*). If half of the inhabitants of LaSalle Square became engaged in the gardening effort, a similar collaboration could meet the needs of the region, and greater participation could yield an excess.

> *She synthesizes different sources to make her point.*

Similar efforts have demonstrated not only that inner-city food production is achievable but also that it can be cost-effective and self-sufficient, unlike a food bank. Frustrated by the inner-city downturn she describes as "an overgrown dog toilet," industrious London entrepreneur Julie Brown created a community gardening company aimed at providing unmechanized, local, sustainable food. The company, Growing Communities, uses organic box gardens and small farms to supply more than 400 homes with weekly deliveries of organic fruits and vegetables. After a ten-year investment in local farmers and mini-gardens within the city, Growing Communities is now financially independent and generates over $400,000 per year (Willis 53). Compelled by both capitalism and social concern, Brown's efforts have shown that community-supported agriculture not

> *In this paragraph, she summarizes research to address the possible counter-argument.*

AN ANNOTATED STUDENT RESEARCHED ARGUMENT: SYNTHESIZING SOURCES   **245**

Paul 8

only is possible but can be profitable as well! Our own community agriculture program should not be an entrepreneurial endeavor, but Brown's work in London indicates that it need not be a financial burden to the city either. Rather, the co-op would be financially self-sufficient, with the potential to generate revenues and fiscal growth in the city.

There are environmental factors that make South Bend an even better place to launch a profitable community agriculture program than London. Chiefly, South Bend has many more farms in the immediate vicinity than Ms. Brown could ever have dreamed of in the U.K. While Brown was limited to twenty-five local farms within 100 miles of the city, South Bend has over fifty farms within 25 miles of LaSalle Square (*Local Harvest*). Offering a broader production base creates more potential for profits by decreasing transportation time and increasing product, thereby making it easier for a coalition to become financially self-sufficient in a shorter time frame than Ms. Brown's ten-year plan.

14

She again cites research to address the counter-argument.

Urban Philadelphia has led the way in demonstrating the profitability of community solutions to food insecurity through an offshoot of the Pennsylvania Horticultural Society (PHS) known as Philadelphia Greens. Since the 1970s, this coalition has reclaimed parks, planted trees, and created community gardens, both to revitalize the neighborhood and to serve the nutritionally and economically poor. Through a process that plants trees, builds wooden fences, and gardens the more than 1,000 vacant lots of Philadelphia, PHS combines housing projects and reclaimed space to "green" and reinvigorate the neighborhood ("The Effects"). Since LaSalle Square is essentially a large empty grassy area at the moment, a community agricultural co-op should turn this vacant lot and others in the neighborhood into community gardens, which would work in tandem with the gleaning from local farms. Similar to the Philadelphia project, these gardens would simultaneously yield produce and improve the appearance of the neighborhood.

15

One PHS project, in the New Kensington neighborhood of north Philadelphia, was the subject of a recent socioeconomic study conducted by the University of Pennsylvania's renowned Wharton School of Business. In the New Kensington area, PHS recently planted

16

Paul 9

480 new trees, cleaned 145 side yards, developed 217 vacant lots, and established 15 new community gardens. The effort was a model of the collaborative strategy between PHS and the local community development corporation, making it the ideal subject of the Wharton

She summarizes a study and then paraphrases. study. The findings, published in 2004, showed significant increases in property values around the PHS greening projects and were the first step in quantifying the fiscal returns of neighborhood greening beyond the qualitative benefits of remedying food insecurity. After analyzing the sales records of thousands of New Kensington homes between 1980 and 2003, the study reported that PHS greening had led to a $4 million gain in property value from tree plantings alone and a $12 million gain from vacant lot improvements. Simply greening a vacant lot increased nearby property values by as much as 30 percent ("Seeing Green"). While a supermarket might modestly improve property values for those immediately near the store, community greening involves multiple plots across an area, benefiting many more people and properties. The Wharton study showed that community greening would provide increases in the value of any property near a green space, up to multiple millions of dollars. The New Kensington neighborhood covers 1.4 square miles, which is approximately the size of LaSalle Square, so while the overall property values are lower simply because South Bend is a smaller city, the gains might be proportional (*City-Data.com*). It is reasonable to believe that cleaning up LaSalle Square and planting gardens would quantitatively benefit the fiscal situation of the city and increase assets of the homeowners while subsequently improving the quality of life over many acres.

Certainly there are challenges to the sort of dynamical, community-based solution that I am proposing. Such an agricultural co-op hinges on the participation of the people it serves and cannot be successful without the dedicated support of the neighborhood. It could be noted that lower-income economic groups are less socially involved than their higher-income counterparts, and some might believe that they are unlikely to contribute to, or care about, a greening effort. Yet I believe that there is a distinction between political involvement and neighborhood interaction. Middle-class Americans are conscious of gas prices and the fluctuations of the

Paul 10

stock market that affect their job security and ability to provide for their families; yet the unemployed poor without cars must rely on their neighborhoods to eke out a living. Their sustenance comes not from a salary, but from odd jobs, welfare, and the munificence of fate. The battle to put food on the table is more familiar to the poor than foreign conflict and is one that they fight every day. Therefore, while the poor are less inclined to vote or worry about governmental affairs because of the difficulties associated simply with daily living, they are acutely aware of their immediate surroundings and how those surroundings challenge or contribute to their success. This position makes them uniquely inclined to invest in the betterment of their surroundings since it can have a dramatic effect on their personal lives. The real success of the sustainable food movement may come from harnessing the power of urban communities that can derive great, immediate, and lasting benefit from neighborhood revitalization.

In this paragraph, she takes an active stance in using research to alleviate fears that the local community would have to start from scratch with limited expertise.

It has been argued that urban growers, especially from lower socioeconomic classes, do not have the expertise or knowledge base to generate successful yields that will ensure food security. Fortunately, agriculture is Indiana's fourth-largest industry, and the state boasts over 63,000 farms ("A Look"). In addition to the many inhabitants of LaSalle Square who have a background in agriculture, there is a wealth of knowledge about proper planting methods available from the farmers around the local area. Many of these farmers have already shown a willingness to help by selling or donating their produce to the local Urban Market. Additionally, national urban agriculture nonprofit groups, such as Master Gardening and Cooperative Extension, offer free public education to cities beginning community agriculture programs, and some will even perform on-site training (Brown and Carter 16). By harnessing the assets of local, gratuitous knowledge and supplementing that knowledge with national support groups, South Bend has multiple resources available to train and encourage its burgeoning urban farmers.

18

The economic and nutritional gains of the people would only be heightened by the personal well-being that is born of interpersonal collaboration that crosses racial and social

19

Paul 11

boundaries. Such an effort is ambitious; it will indeed require the time and talents of many people who care about the health of their community. But the local community is rich with the necessary seeds for such a project, which may, in time, blossom and grow to feed its people.

Paul 12

Works Cited

Brown, Katherine H., and Anne Carter. *Urban Agriculture and Community Food Security in the United States: Farming from the City Center to the Urban Fringe*. Community Food Security Coalition, Oct. 2003.

City-Data.com. Advameg, 16 Apr. 2008, www.city-data.com/city/South-Bend-Indiana.html.

"The Effects of Neighborhood Greening." *Pennsylvania Horticultural Society*, Jan. 2001, phsonline.org/programs/effects-of-neighborhood-greening.

Eisenhauer, Elizabeth. "In Poor Health: Supermarket Redlining and Urban Nutrition." *GeoJournal*, vol. 53, no. 2, Feb. 2001, pp. 125–33.

Garnett, Tara. "Farming the City." *The Ecologist*, vol. 26, no. 6, Nov./Dec. 1996, p. 299.

"Gleaning." *Greater Lansing Food Bank*, greaterlansingfoodbank.org/programs/programs-home/the-garden-project/gleaning/. Accessed 15 Apr. 20—.

"GLFB Facts." *Greater Lansing Food Bank*, greaterlansingfoodbank.org/our-impact/fact-sheet/. Accessed 15 Apr. 20—.

LocalHarvest. Local Harvest, 2008, www.localharvest.org/south-bend-in.

"A Look at Indiana Agriculture." *National Agriculture in the Classroom*, www.agclassroom.org/kids/ag_facts.htm. Accessed 18 Apr. 20—.

AN ANNOTATED STUDENT RESEARCHED ARGUMENT: SYNTHESIZING SOURCES **249**

Paul 13

"Seeing Green: Study Finds Greening Is a Good Investment."
Pennsylvania Horticultural Society, 2005, phsonline.org/
programs/seeing-green.

Smith, Stephen. "Obesity Battle Starts Young for Urban Poor." *The
Boston Globe*, 29 Dec. 2006, archive.boston.com/news/nation/
articles/2006/12/29/obesity_battle_starts_young_for_urban
_poor/.

Tanner, Emily M., and Matia Finn-Stevenson. "Nutrition and Brain
Development: Social Policy Implications." *American Journal of
Orthopsychiatry*, vol. 72, no. 2, Apr. 2002, pp. 182–93.

"TIF Reform." *New Rules Project*, Institute for Local Self-Reliance,
2008, ilsr.org/rule/tif-reform/.

Willis, Ben. "Julie Brown of Growing Communities." *The Ecologist*,
vol. 38, no. 5, June 2008, pp. 58–61.

Wolfson, Linda. Personal interview, 20 Apr. 20—.

A Practice Sequence: Thinking about Copyright

1 Now that you have read about steps to avoiding plagiarism
(pp. 231–232) and Nancy Paul's essay on community gardens
(p. 238) we would like you to examine the idea of copyright. That
is, who owns the rights to images that the organizers of a community garden use to market their idea? What if you wanted to use
that image in a paper? Or what if you wanted to use a published
ad in your own paper? Under what circumstances would you be
able to use that ad for your own purposes?

2 After conducting your own inquiry into copyright, what would
you conclude about the need to document the use of images,
ideas, and text? Are the guidelines clear or are there some ambig-
uous areas for what to cite and how? What advice would you give
your peers?

13

From Ethos to Logos
Appealing to Your Readers

Your understanding of your readers influences how you see a particular situation, define an issue, explain the ongoing conversation surrounding that issue, and formulate a question. You may need to read widely to understand how different writers have dealt with the issue you address. And you will need to anticipate how others might respond to your argument—whether they will be sympathetic or antagonistic—and to compose your essay so that readers will "listen" whether or not they agree with you.

To achieve these goals, you will no doubt use reason in the form of evidence to sway readers. But you can also use other means of persuasion. That is, you can use your own character, by presenting yourself as someone who is knowledgeable, fair, and just, and you can appeal to your readers' emotions. Although you may believe that reason alone should provide the means for changing people's minds, people's emotions also color the way they see the world.

Your audience is more than your immediate reader—your instructor or a peer. Your audience encompasses those you cite in writing about an issue and those you anticipate responding to your argument. This is true no matter what you write about, whether it be an interpretation of the novels of a particular author, an analysis of the cultural work of horror films, the ethics of treating boys and girls differently in schools, or the moral issues surrounding homelessness in America.

In this chapter we discuss different ways of engaging your readers, centering on three kinds of appeals: **ethos**, appeals from character; **pathos**, appeals to emotion; and **logos**, appeals to reason. *Ethos, pathos,* and *logos* are terms derived from ancient Greek writers, but they are still of great value today when considering how to persuade your audience. Readers

250

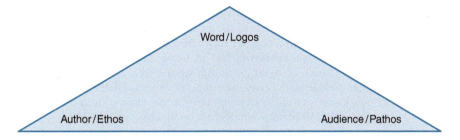

FIGURE 13.1 The Rhetorical Triangle

will judge your writing on whether or not you present an argument that is fair and just, one that creates a sense of goodwill. All three appeals rely on these qualities.

Figure 13.1, the **rhetorical triangle**, visually represents the interrelationship among ethos, pathos, and logos. Who we think our readers are (pathos: which of their emotions do we appeal to?) influences decisions about the ways we should represent ourselves to them (ethos: how can we come across as fair, credible, and just?). In turn, we use certain patterns of argument (logos: how do we arrange our words to make our case?) that reflect our interpretation of the situation to which we respond and that we believe will persuade readers to accept our point of view. Effective communication touches on each of the three points of the triangle. Your task as a writer is to determine the proper balance of these different appeals in your argument, based on your thesis, the circumstances, and your audience.

CONNECTING WITH READERS: A SAMPLE ARGUMENT

To see how an author connects with his audience, read the following excerpt from James W. Loewen's book *Lies My Teacher Told Me: Everything Your American History Textbook Got Wrong*. As you read the excerpt, note Loewen's main points and select key examples that illustrate his argument. As a class, test the claims he makes: To what extent do you believe that what Loewen argues is true? This may entail recalling your own experiences in high school history classes or locating one or more of the books that Loewen mentions.

JAMES W. LOEWEN

The Land of Opportunity

In addition to *Lies My Teacher Told Me* (1995, 2007), James Loewen, who holds a PhD in sociology, has written several other books, including *Lies across America: What Our Historic Sites Get Wrong* (1999) and *Sundown Towns: A Hidden Dimension of American Racism* (2005). As the titles of

252 CHAPTER 13 | FROM ETHOS TO LOGOS: APPEALING TO YOUR READERS

these books suggest, Loewen is a writer who questions the assumptions about history that many people take for granted. This is especially true of the following excerpt, from a chapter in which Loewen challenges a common American belief—that everyone has an equal chance in what he calls the "land of opportunity"—by arguing that we live in a class system that privileges some people and raises barriers for others. History textbook writers, he points out, are guilty of complicity in this class system because they leave a great deal of history out of their textbooks.

■ ■ ■

High school students have eyes, ears, and television sets (all too many have their own TV sets), so they know a lot about relative privilege in America. They measure their family's social position against that of other families, and their community's position against other communities. Middle-class students, especially, know little about how the American class structure works, however, and nothing at all about how it has changed over time. These students do not leave high school merely ignorant of the workings of the class structure; they come out as terrible sociologists. "Why are people poor?" I have asked first-year college students. Or, if their own class position is one of relative privilege, "Why is your family well-off?" The answers I've received, to characterize them charitably, are half-formed and naïve. The students blame the poor for not being successful. They have no understanding of the ways that opportunity is not equal in America and no notion that social structure pushes people around, influencing the ideas they hold and the lives they fashion.

High school history textbooks can take some of the credit for this state of affairs. Some textbooks do cover certain high points of labor history, such as the 1894 Pullman strike near Chicago that President Cleveland broke with federal troops, or the 1911 Triangle Shirtwaist fire that killed 146 women in New York City, but the most recent event mentioned in most books is the Taft-Hartley Act of sixty years ago. No book mentions any of the major strikes that labor lost in the late twentieth century, such as the 1985 Hormel meatpackers' strike in Austin, Minnesota, or the 1991 Caterpillar strike in Decatur, Illinois—defeats that signify labor's diminished power today. Nor do most textbooks describe any continuing issues facing labor, such as the growth of multinational corporations and their exporting of jobs overseas. With such omissions, textbook authors can construe labor history as something that happened long ago, like slavery, and that, like slavery, was corrected long ago. It logically follows that unions now appear anachronistic. The idea that they might be necessary for workers to have a voice in the workplace goes unstated.

These books' poor treatment of labor history is magnificent compared to their treatment of social class. *Nothing* that textbooks discuss—not even strikes—is ever anchored in any analysis of social class.[1] This amounts to delivering the footnotes instead of the lecture! Half of the eighteen high school American history textbooks I examined contain no index listing at all for *social class, social stratification, class structure, income distribution, inequality*, or any conceivably related topic. Not one book lists *upper class* or *lower class*. Three list *middle class*, but only to assure students that America is a middle-class country. "Except for slaves, most of the colonists were members of the 'middling ranks,'" says *Land of Promise*, and nails home the point that we are a middle-class country by asking students to "describe three 'middle-class' values that united free Americans of all classes." Several of the textbooks note the explosion of middle-class suburbs after World War II. Talking about the middle class is hardly equivalent to discussing social stratification, however. On the contrary, as Gregory Mantsios has pointed out, "such references appear to be acceptable precisely because they mute class differences."[2]

Stressing how middle-class we all are is increasingly problematic today, because the proportion of households earning between 75 percent and 125 percent of the median income has fallen steadily since 1967. The Reagan-Bush administrations accelerated this shrinkage of the middle class, and most families who left its ranks fell rather than rose.[3] As late as 1970, family incomes in the United States were only slightly less equal than in Canada. By 2000, inequality here was much greater than Canada's; the United States was becoming more like Mexico, a very stratified society.[4] The Bush II administration, with its tax cuts aimed openly at the wealthy, continued to increase the gap between the haves and have-nots. This is the kind of historical trend one would think history books would take as appropriate subject matter, but only five of the eighteen books in my sample provide any analysis of social stratification in the United States. Even these fragmentary analyses are set mostly in colonial America. Boorstin and Kelley, unusual in actually including *social class* in its index, lists only *social classes in 1790* and *social classes in early America*. These turn out to be two references to the same paragraph, which tells us that England "was a land of rigid social classes," while here in America "social classes were much more fluid." "One great difference between colonial and European society was that the colonists had more social mobility," echoes *The American Tradition*. Never mind that the most violent class conflicts in American history—Bacon's Rebellion and Shays's Rebellion—took place in and just after colonial times. Textbooks still say that colonial society was relatively classless and marked by upward mobility.

And things have only gotten rosier since. "By 1815," *The Challenge of Freedom* assures us, two classes had withered away and "America was a country of middle class people and of middle class goals." This book returns repeatedly, every fifty years or so, to the theme of how open opportunity is in America. The stress on upward mobility is striking. There is almost nothing in any of these textbooks about class inequalities or barriers of any kind to social mobility. "What conditions made it possible for poor white immigrants to become richer in the colonies?" *Land of Promise* asks. "What conditions made/make it difficult?" goes unasked. Boorstin and Kelley close their sole discussion of social class (in 1790, described above) with the happy sentence, "As the careers of American Presidents would soon show, here a person might rise by hard work, intelligence, skill, and perhaps a little luck, from the lowest positions to the highest."

If only that were so! Social class is probably the single most important variable in society. From womb to tomb, it correlates with almost all other social characteristics of people that we can measure. Affluent expectant mothers are more likely to get prenatal care, receive current medical advice, and enjoy general health, fitness, and nutrition. Many poor and working-class mothers-to-be first contact the medical profession in the last month, sometimes the last hours, of their pregnancies. Rich babies come out healthier and weighing more than poor babies. The infants go home to very different situations. Poor babies are more likely to have high levels of poisonous lead in their environments and their bodies. Rich babies get more time and verbal interaction with their parents and higher quality day care when not with their parents. When they enter kindergarten, and through the twelve years that follow, rich children benefit from suburban schools that spend two to three times as much money per student as schools in inner cities or impoverished rural areas. Poor children are taught in classes that are often 50 percent larger than the classes of affluent children. Differences such as these help account for the higher school-dropout rate among poor children.

Even when poor children are fortunate enough to attend the same school as rich children, they encounter teachers who expect only children of affluent families to know the right answers. Social science research shows that teachers are often surprised and even distressed when poor children excel. Teachers and counselors believe they can predict who is "college material." Since many working-class children give off the wrong signals, even in first grade, they end up in the "general education" track in high school. "If you are the child of low-income parents, the chances are good that you will receive limited and often careless attention from adults in your high school," in the words of Theodore Sizer's bestselling study of American high schools, *Horace's Compromise*. "If you are the child of upper-middle-income parents, the chances are good that you will receive substantial and careful attention."[5] Researcher Reba Page has provided vivid accounts of how high school American history courses use rote learning to turn off lower-class students.[6] Thus schools have put into practice Woodrow Wilson's recommendation: "We want one class of persons to have a liberal education, and we want another class of persons, a very much larger class of necessity in every society, to forgo the privilege of a liberal education and fit themselves to perform specific difficult manual tasks."[7]

As if this unequal home and school life were not enough, rich teenagers then enroll in the Princeton Review or other coaching sessions for the Scholastic Aptitude Test. Even without coaching, affluent children are advantaged because their background is similar to that of the test makers, so they are comfortable with the vocabulary and subtle subcultural assumptions of the test. To no one's surprise, social class correlates strongly with SAT scores.

All these are among the reasons that social class predicts the rate of college attendance and the type of college chosen more effectively than does any other factor, including intellectual ability, however measured. After college, most affluent children get white-collar jobs, most working-class children get blue-collar jobs, and the class differences continue. As adults, rich people are more likely to have hired an attorney and to be a member of formal organizations that increase their civic power. Poor people are more likely to watch TV. Because affluent families can save some money while poor families must spend what they make, wealth differences are ten times larger than income differences. Therefore most poor and working-class families cannot accumulate the down payment required to buy a house, which in turn shuts them out from our most important tax shelter, the write-off of home mortgage interest. Working-class parents cannot afford to live in elite subdivisions or hire high-quality day care, so the process of educational inequality replicates itself in the next generation. Finally, affluent Americans also have longer life expectancies than lower- and working-class people, the largest single cause of which is better access to health care. Echoing the results of Helen Keller's study of blindness, research has determined that poor health is not distributed randomly about the social structure but is concentrated in the lower class. Social Security then become a huge transfer system, using monies contributed by all Americans to pay benefits disproportionately to longer-lived affluent Americans.

Ultimately social class determines how people think about social class. When asked if poverty in America is the fault of the poor or the fault of the system, 57 percent of business leaders blamed the poor; just 9 percent blamed the system. Labor leaders showed sharply reversed choices: only 15 percent said the poor were at fault while 56 percent blamed the system. (Some people replied "don't know" or chose a middle position.) The largest single difference between our two main political parties lies in how their members think about social class: 55 percent of Republicans blamed the poor for their poverty, while only 13 percent blamed the system for it; 68 percent of Democrats, on the other hand, blamed the system, while only 5 percent blamed the poor.[8]

Few of these statements are news, I know, which is why I have not bothered to document most of them, but the majority of high school students do not know or understand these ideas. Moreover, the processes have changed over time, for the class structure in America today is not the same as it was in 1890, let alone in colonial America. Yet in the most recent *American Pageant*, for example, social class goes unmentioned in the twentieth century. Many teachers compound the problem by avoiding talking about social class in the twenty-first. A study of history and social studies teachers "revealed that they had a much broader knowledge of the economy, both academically and experientially, than they admitted in class." Teachers "expressed fear that students might find out about the injustices and inadequacies of their economic and political institutions."[9] By never blaming the system, American history courses thus present Republican history.

Notes

1. Jean Anyon, "Ideology and United States History Textbooks," *Harvard Educational Review* 49, no. 3 (8/1979): 373.

2. Gregory Mantsios, "Class in America: Myths and Realities," in Paula S. Rothernberg, ed., *Racism and Sexism: An Integrated Study* (New York: St. Martin's, 1988), 56.

3. Ibid., 60; Kevin Phillips, *The Politics of Rich and Poor* (New York: Random House, 1990); Robert Heilbroner, "Lifting the Silent Depression," *New York Review of Books*, 10/24/1991, 6; and Sylvia Nasar, "The Rich Get Richer," *New York Times*, 8/16/1992. Stephen J. Rose, *Social Stratification in the United States* (New York: New Press, 2007), is a posterbook that shows graphically the shrinkage of the middle class between 1979 and 2004.

4. "Income Disparity Since World War II—The Gini Index," in "Gini co-efficient," en.wikipedia.org/wiki/Gini_coefficient, 9/2006.

5. Sizer quoted in Walter Karp, "Why Johnny Can't Think," *Harper's*, 6/1985, 73.

6. Reba Page, "The Lower-Track Students' View of Curriculum," (Washington, D.C.: American Education Research Association, 1987).

7. Woodrow Wilson quoted in Lewis H. Lapham, "Notebook," *Harper's*, 7/1991, 10.

8. Survey data from about 1979 reported in Sidney Verba and Gary Orren, *Equality in America* (Cambridge: Harvard University Press, 1985), 72–75.

9. Linda McNeil, "Defensive Teaching and Classroom Control," in Michael W. Apple and Lois Weis, eds., *Ideology and Practice in Schooling* (Philadelphia: Temple University Press, 1983), 116.

Reading as a Writer

1. List what you think are Loewen's main points. What appeals does he seem to draw on most when he makes those points: appeals based on his own character (ethos), on the emotions of his reader (pathos), or on the reasonableness of his evidence (logos)? Are the appeals obvious or difficult to tease out? Does he combine them? Discuss your answers with your classmates.

2. Identify what you think is the main claim of Loewen's argument, and choose key examples to support your answer. Compare your chosen claim and examples to those chosen by your classmates. Do they differ significantly? Can you agree on Loewen's gist and his key examples?

3. As a class, test the claims Loewen makes by thinking about your own experiences in high school history classes. Do you remember finding out that something you were taught from an American history textbook was not true? Did you discover on your own what you considered to be misrepresentations in or important omissions from your textbook? If so, did these misrepresentations or omissions tend to support or contradict the claims about history textbooks that Loewen makes?

APPEALING TO ETHOS

Although we like to believe that our decisions and beliefs are based on reason and logic, in fact they are often based on what amounts to character judgments. That is, if a person you trust makes a reasonable argument for one choice, and a person you distrust makes a reasonable argument for another choice, you are more likely to be swayed by the argument of the person you trust. Similarly, the audience for your argument will be more disposed to agree with you if its members believe you are a fair, just person who is knowledgeable and has good judgment. Even the most well-developed argument will fall short if you do not leave this kind of impression on your readers. Thus, it is not surprising that ethos may be the most important component of your argument.

258   CHAPTER 13 | FROM ETHOS TO LOGOS: APPEALING TO YOUR READERS

There are three strategies for evoking a sense of ethos:

1. Establish that you have good judgment.
2. Convey to readers that you are knowledgeable.
3. Show that you understand the complexity of the issue.

These strategies are interrelated: A writer who demonstrates good judgment is more often than not someone who is both knowledgeable about an issue and who acknowledges the complexity of it by weighing the strengths *and* weaknesses of different arguments. However, keep in mind that these characteristics do not exist apart from what readers think and believe.

■ Establish That You Have Good Judgment

Most readers of academic writing expect writers to demonstrate good judgment by identifying a problem that readers agree is worth addressing. In turn, good judgment gives writers credibility.

Loewen crafts his introduction to capture the attention of educators as well as concerned citizens when he claims that students leave high school unaware of class structure and as a consequence "have no understanding of the ways that opportunity is not equal in America and no notion that social structure pushes people around, influencing the ideas they hold and the lives they fashion" (para. 1). Loewen does not blame students, or even instructors, for this lack of awareness. Instead, he writes, "textbooks can take some of the credit for this state of affairs" (para. 2) because, among other shortcomings, they leave out important events in "labor history" and relegate issues facing labor to the past.

Whether an educator—or a general reader for that matter—will ultimately agree with Loewen's case is, at this point, up for grabs, but certainly the possibility that high schools in general, and history textbooks in particular, are failing students by leaving them vulnerable to class-based manipulation would be recognized as a problem by readers who believe America should be a society that offers equal opportunity for all. At this point, Loewen's readers are likely to agree that the problem of omission he identifies may be significant if its consequences are as serious as he believes them to be.

Writers also establish good judgment by conveying to readers that they are fair-minded and just and have the best interests of readers in mind. Loewen is particularly concerned that students understand the persistence of poverty and inequality in the United States and the historical circumstances of the poor, which they cannot do unless textbook writers take a more inclusive approach to addressing labor history, especially "the growth of multinational corporations and their exporting of jobs overseas" (para. 2). It's not fair to deny this important information to students, and it's not fair to the poor to leave them out of official histories of the United

States. Loewen further demonstrates that he is fair and just when he calls attention in paragraph 6 to the inequality between rich and poor children in schools, a problem that persists despite our forebears' belief that class would not determine the fate of citizens of the United States.

■ Convey to Readers That You Are Knowledgeable

Being thoughtful about a subject goes hand in hand with being knowledgeable about the subject. Loewen demonstrates his knowledge of class issues and their absence from textbooks in a number of ways (not the least of which is his awareness that a problem exists—many people, including educators, may not be aware of this problem).

In paragraph 3, Loewen makes a bold claim: "*Nothing* that textbooks discuss—not even strikes—is ever anchored in any analysis of social class." As readers, we cannot help wondering: How does the author know this? How will he support this claim? Loewen anticipates these questions by demonstrating that he has studied the subject through a systematic examination of American history textbooks. He observes that half of the eighteen textbooks he examined "contain no index listing at all for *social class, social stratification, class structure, income distribution, inequality*, or any conceivably related topic" and that "not one book lists *upper class* or *lower class*." Loewen also demonstrates his grasp of class issues in American history, from the "violent class conflicts" that "took place in and just after colonial times" (para. 4), which contradict textbook writers' assertions that class conflicts did not exist during this period, to the more recent conflicts in the 1980s and early 1990s (paras. 2 and 4).

Moreover, Loewen backs up his own study of textbooks with references to a number of studies from the social sciences to illustrate that "social class is probably the single most important variable in society" (para. 6). Witness the statistics and findings he cites in paragraphs 6 through 10. The breadth of Loewen's historical knowledge and the range of his reading should convince readers that he is knowledgeable, and his trenchant analysis contributes to the authority he brings to the issue and to his credibility.

■ Show That You Understand the Complexity of a Given Issue

Recognizing the complexity of an issue helps readers see the extent to which authors know that any issue can be understood in a number of different ways. Loewen acknowledges that most of the history he recounts is not "news" (para. 11) to his educated readers, who by implication "know" and "understand" his references to historical events and trends. What may be news to his readers, he explains, is the extent to which class structure in the United States has changed over time. With the steady erosion of middle-class households since 1967, "class inequalities" and "barriers . . . to social mobility" (para. 5) are limiting more and more Americans' access to even the most fundamental of opportunities in a democratic society—health care and education.

Still, even though Loewen has introduced new thinking about the nature of class in the United States and has demonstrated a provocative play of mind by examining an overlooked body of data (high school history textbooks) that may influence the way class is perceived in America, there are still levels of complexity he hasn't addressed explicitly. Most important, perhaps, is the question of why history textbooks continue to ignore issues of class when there is so much research that indicates its importance in shaping the events history textbooks purport to explain.

Steps to Appealing to Ethos

1 **Establish that you have good judgment.** Identify an issue your readers will agree is worth addressing, and demonstrate that you are fair-minded and have the best interests of your readers in mind when you address it.

2 **Convey to readers that you are knowledgeable.** Support your claims with credible evidence that shows you have read widely on, thought about, and understand the issue.

3 **Show that you understand the complexity of the issue.** Demonstrate that you understand the variety of viewpoints your readers may bring—or may not be able to bring—to the issue.

APPEALING TO PATHOS

An appeal to pathos recognizes that people are moved to action by their emotions as well as by reasonable arguments. In fact, pathos is a vital part of argument that can predispose readers one way or another. Do you want to arouse readers' sympathy? Anger? Passion? You can do that by knowing what readers value.

Appeals to pathos are typically indirect. You can appeal to pathos by using examples or illustrations that you believe will arouse the appropriate emotions and by presenting them using an appropriate tone.

To acknowledge that writers play on readers' emotions is not to endorse manipulative writing. Rather, it is to acknowledge that effective writers use all available means of persuasion to move readers to agree with them. After all, if your thoughtful reading and careful research have led you to believe that you must weigh in with a useful insight on an important issue, it stands to reason that you would want your argument to convince your readers to believe as strongly in what you assert as you do.

For example, if you genuinely believe that the conditions some families are living in are abysmal and unfair, you want your readers to believe it too. And an effective way to persuade them to believe as you do, in addition to convincing them of the reasonableness of your argument and of your own good character and judgment, is to establish a kind of emotional common ground in your writing—the common ground of pathos.

■ Show That You Know What Your Readers Value

Let's consider some of the ways James Loewen signals that he knows what his readers value.

In the first place, Loewen assumes that readers feel the same way he does: Educated people should know that the United States has a class structure despite the democratic principles that the nation was founded on. He also expects readers to identify with his unwillingness to accept the injustice that results from that class structure. He believes that women living in poverty should have access to appropriate health care, that children living in poverty should have a chance to attend college, and that certain classes of people should not be written off to, as Woodrow Wilson recommended, "perform specific difficult manual tasks" (para. 7).

Time and again, Loewen cites examples that reveal that the poor are discriminated against by the class structure in the United States not for lack of ability, lack of desire, lack of ambition, or lack of morality, but for no better reason than lack of money—and that such discrimination has been going on for a long time. He expects that his readers also will find such discrimination an unacceptable affront to their values of fair play and democracy and that they will experience the same sense of outrage that he does.

■ Use Illustrations and Examples That Appeal to Readers' Emotions

You can appeal to readers' emotions indirectly through the illustrations and examples you use to support your argument.

For instance, in paragraph 2, Loewen contends that textbook writers share responsibility for high school students' not knowing about the continued relevance of class issues in American life. Loewen's readers—parents, educators, historians—may very well be angered by the omissions he points out. Certainly he would expect them to be angry when they read about the effects of economic class on the health care expectant mothers and then their children receive (para. 6) and on their children's access to quality education (paras. 6–8). In citing the fact that social class "correlates strongly with SAT scores" (para. 8) and so "predicts the rate of college attendance and the type of college chosen" (para. 9), Loewen forces

262   CHAPTER 13 | FROM ETHOS TO LOGOS: APPEALING TO YOUR READERS

his readers to acknowledge that the educational playing field is far from level.

Finally, he calls attention to the fact that accumulated wealth accounts for deep class divisions in our society—that the inability to save prevents the poor from hiring legal counsel, purchasing a home, or taking advantage of tax shelters. The result, Loewen observes, is that "educational inequality replicates itself in the next generation" (para. 9).

Together, these examples strengthen both Loewen's argument and what he hopes will be readers' outrage that history textbooks do not address class issues. Without that information, Americans cannot fully understand or act to change the existing class structure.

■ Consider How Your Tone May Affect Your Audience

The **tone** of your writing is your use of language that communicates your attitude toward yourself, your material, and your readers. Of course, your tone is important in everything you write, but it is particularly crucial when you are appealing to pathos.

When you are appealing to your readers' emotions, it is tempting to use loaded, exaggerated, and even intemperate language to convey how you feel (and hope your readers will feel) about an issue. Consider these sentences: "The Republican Party has devised the most ignominious means of filling the pockets of corporations." "These wretched children suffer heartrending agonies that can barely be imagined, much less described." "The ethereal beauty of the Brandenburg concertos thrill one to the deepest core of one's being." All of these sentences express strong and probably sincere beliefs and emotions, but some readers might find them overwrought and coercive and question the writer's reasonableness.

Similarly, some writers rely on irony or sarcasm to set the tone of their work. **Irony** is the use of language to say one thing while meaning quite another. **Sarcasm** is the use of heavy-handed irony to ridicule or attack someone or something. Although irony and sarcasm can make for vivid and entertaining writing, they also can backfire and end up alienating readers. The sentence "Liberals will be pleased to hear that the new budget will be making liberal use of their hard-earned dollars" may entertain some readers with its irony and wordplay, but others may assume that the writer's attitude toward liberals is likely to result in an unfairly slanted argument. And the sentence "In my opinion, there's no reason why Christians and Muslims shouldn't rejoice together over the common ground of their both being deluded about the existence of a God" may please some readers, but it risks alienating those who are uncomfortable with breezy comments about religious beliefs. Again, think of your readers and what they value, and weigh the benefits of a clever sentence against its potential to detract from your argument or offend your audience.

APPEALING TO PATHOS   **263**

You often find colorful wording and irony in op-ed and opinion pieces, where a writer may not have the space to build a compelling argument using evidence and has to resort to shortcuts to readers' emotions. However, in academic writing, where the careful accumulation and presentation of evidence and telling examples are highly valued, the frequent use of loaded language, exaggeration, and sarcasm is looked on with distrust.

Consider Loewen's excerpt. Although his outrage comes through clearly, he never resorts to hectoring. For example, in paragraph 1, he writes that students are "ignorant of the workings of the class structure" and that their opinions are "half-formed and naïve." But he does not imply that students are ignoramuses or that their opinions are foolish. What they lack, he contends, is understanding. They need to be taught something about class structure that they are not now being taught. And paragraph 1 is about as close to name-calling as Loewen comes. Even textbook writers, who are the target of his anger, are not vilified.

Loewen does occasionally make use of irony, for example in paragraph 4, where he points out inconsistencies and omissions in textbooks: "Never mind that the most violent class conflicts in American history— Bacon's Rebellion and Shays's Rebellion—took place in and just after colonial times. Textbooks still say that colonial society was relatively classless and marked by upward mobility. And things have only gotten rosier since." But he doesn't resort to ridicule. Instead, he relies on examples and illustrations to connect with his readers' sense of values and appeal to their emotions.

Steps to Appealing to Pathos

1 **Show that you know what your readers value.** Start from your own values and imagine what assumptions and principles would appeal to your readers. What common ground can you imagine between your values and theirs? How will it need to be adjusted for different kinds of readers?

2 **Use illustrations and examples that appeal to readers' emotions.** Again, start from your own emotional position. What examples and illustrations resonate most with you? How can you present them to have the most emotional impact on your readers? How would you adjust them for different kinds of readers?

3 **Consider how your tone may affect your audience.** Be wary of using loaded, exaggerated, and intemperate language that may put off your readers; and be careful in your use of irony and sarcasm.

264 CHAPTER 13 | FROM ETHOS TO LOGOS: APPEALING TO YOUR READERS

A Practice Sequence: Appealing to Ethos and Pathos

Discuss the language and strategies the writers use in the following passages to connect with their audience, in particular their appeals to both ethos and pathos. After reading each excerpt, discuss who you think the implied audience is and whether you think the strategies the writers use to connect with their readers are effective or not.

1   Almost a half century after the U.S. Supreme Court concluded that Southern school segregation was unconstitutional and "inherently unequal," new statistics from the 1998–99 school year show that segregation continued to intensify throughout the 1990s, a period in which there were three major Supreme Court decisions authorizing a return to segregated neighborhood schools and limiting the reach and duration of desegregation orders. For African American students, this trend is particularly apparent in the South, where most blacks live and where the 2000 Census shows a continuing return from the North. From 1988 to 1998, most of the progress of the previous two decades in increasing integration in the region was lost. The South is still much more integrated than it was before the civil rights revolution, but it is moving backward at an accelerating rate.

> —GARY ORFIELD, "Schools More Separate:
> Consequences of a Decade of Resegregation"

2   When the judgment day comes for every high school student—that day when a final transcript is issued and sent to the finest institutions, with every sin of class selection written as with a burning chisel on stone—on that day a great cry will go up throughout the land, and there will be weeping, wailing, gnashing of teeth, and considerable grumbling against guidance counselors, and the cry of a certain senior might be, "WHY did no one tell me that Introduction to Social Poker wasn't a solid academic class?" At another, perhaps less wealthy school, a frustrated and under-nurtured sculptress will wonder, "Why can't I read, and why don't I care?" The reason for both of these oversights, as they may eventually discover, is that the idea of the elective course has been seriously mauled, mistreated, and abused under the current middle-class high school system. A significant amount of the blame for producing students who are stunted, both cognitively and morally, can be traced back to this pervasive fact. Elective courses, as shoddily planned and poorly funded as they may be, constitute the only formation that many students get in their own special types of intelligences. Following the model of Howard Gardner, these may

be spatial, musical, or something else. A lack of stimulation to a student's own intelligence directly causes a lack of identification with the intelligence of others. Instead of becoming moderately interested in a subject by noticing the pleasure other people receive from it, the student will be bitter, jealous, and without empathy. These are the common ingredients in many types of tragedy, violent or benign. Schools must take responsibility for speaking in some way to each of the general types of intelligences. Failure to do so will result in students who lack skills, and also the inspiration to comfort, admire, emulate, and aid their fellow humans.

"All tasks that really call upon the power of attention are interesting for the same reason and to an almost equal degree," wrote Simone Weil in her *Reflections on Love and Faith*, her editor having defined attention as "a suspension of one's own self as a center of the world and making oneself available to the reality of another being." In Parker Palmer's *The Courage to Teach*, modern scientific theorist David Bohm describes "a holistic underlying implicate order whose information unfolds into the explicate order of particular fields." Rilke's euphemism for this "holistic . . . implicate order," which Palmer borrows, is "the grace of great things." Weil's term would be "God." However, both agree that eventual perception of this singular grace, or God, is accessible through education of a specific sort, and for both it is doubtless the most necessary experience of a lifetime. Realizing that this contention is raining down from different theorists, and keeping in mind that the most necessary experience of a lifetime should not be wholly irrelevant to the school system, educators should therefore reach the conclusion that this is a matter worth looking into. I assert that the most fruitful and practical results of their attention will be a wider range of electives coupled with a new acknowledgment and handling of them, one that treats each one seriously.

—ERIN MEYERS,
"The Educational Smorgasbord as Saving Grace"

APPEALING TO LOGOS: USING REASON AND EVIDENCE TO FIT THE SITUATION

To make an argument persuasive, you need to be in dialogue with your readers, using your own character (ethos) to demonstrate that you are a reasonable, credible, and fair person and to appeal to your readers'

266   CHAPTER 13 | FROM ETHOS TO LOGOS: APPEALING TO YOUR READERS

emotions (pathos), particularly their sense of right and wrong. Both types of appeal go hand in hand with appeals to logos, using converging pieces of evidence—statistics, facts, observations—to advance your claim. Remember that the type of evidence you use is determined by the issue, problem, situation, and readers' expectations. As an author, you should try to anticipate and address readers' beliefs and values. Ethos and pathos are concerned with the content of your argument; logos addresses both form and content.

An argument begins with one or more premises and ends with a conclusion. A **premise** is an assumption that you expect your readers to agree with, a statement that is either true or false—for example, "Alaska is cold in the winter"—that is offered in support of a claim. That claim is the **conclusion** you want your readers to draw from your premises. The conclusion is also a sentence that is either true or false.

For instance, Loewen's major premise is that class is a key factor in Americans' access to health care, education, and wealth. Loewen also offers a second, more specific premise: that textbook writers provide little discussion of the ways class matters. Loewen crafts his argument to help readers draw the following conclusion: "We live in a class system that runs counter to the democratic principles that underlie the founding of the United States, and history textbooks must tell this story. Without this knowledge, citizens will be uninformed."

Whether readers accept this as true depends on how Loewen moves from his initial premises to reach his conclusion—that is, whether we draw the same kinds of inferences, or reasoned judgments, that he does. He must do so in a way that meets readers' expectations of what constitutes relevant and persuasive evidence and guides them one step at a time toward his conclusion.

There are two main forms of argument: deductive and inductive. A **deductive argument** is an argument in which the premises support (or appear to support) the conclusion. If you join two premises to produce a conclusion that is taken to be true, you are stating a **syllogism.** This is the classic example of deductive reasoning through a syllogism:

1. All men are mortal. (First premise)
2. Socrates is a man. (Second premise)
3. Therefore, Socrates is mortal. (Conclusion)

In a deductive argument, it is impossible for both premises to be true and the conclusion to be false. That is, the truth of the premises means that the conclusion must also be true.

By contrast, an **inductive argument** relies on evidence and observation to reach a conclusion. Although readers may accept a writer's premises as true, it is possible for them to reject the writer's conclusion.

Let's consider this for a moment in the context of Loewen's argument. Loewen introduces the premise that class matters, then offers the more specific premise that textbook writers leave class issues out of their narratives of American history, and finally draws the conclusion that citizens need to be informed of this body of knowledge in order to create change:

1. Although class is a key factor in Americans' access to health care, education, and wealth, students know very little about the social structure in the United States.
2. In their textbooks, textbook writers do not address the issue of class, an issue that people need to know about.
3. Therefore, if people had this knowledge, they would understand that poverty cannot be blamed on the poor.

Notice that Loewen's premises are not necessarily true. For example, readers could challenge the premise that "textbook writers do not address issues of class." After all, Loewen examined just eighteen textbooks. What if he had examined a different set of textbooks? Would he have drawn the same conclusion? And even if Loewen's evidence convinces us that the two premises are true, we do not have to accept that the conclusion is true.

The conclusion in an inductive argument is never definitive. That is the nature of any argument that deals with human emotions and actions. Moreover, we have seen throughout history that people tend to disagree much more on the terms of an argument than on its form. Do we agree that Israel's leaders practice apartheid? (What do we mean by *apartheid* in this case?) Do we agree with the need to grant women reproductive rights? (When does life begin?) Do we agree that all people should be treated equally? (Would equality mean equal access to resources or to outcomes?)

Deductive arguments are conclusive. In a deductive argument, the premises are universal truths—laws of nature, if you will—and the conclusion must follow from those premises. That is, a^2 plus b^2 always equals c^2, and humans are always mortal.

By contrast, an inductive argument is never conclusive. The premises may or may not be true; and even if they are true, the conclusion may be false. We might accept that class matters and that high school history textbooks don't address the issue of class structure in the United States; but we still would not know that students who have studied social stratification in America will necessarily understand the nature of poverty. It may be that social class is only one reason for poverty; or it may be that textbooks are only one source of information about social stratification in the United States, that textbook omissions are simply not as serious as Loewen claims. That the premises of an argument are true establishes only that the conclusion is probably true and, perhaps, true only for some readers.

268 CHAPTER 13 | FROM ETHOS TO LOGOS: APPEALING TO YOUR READERS

Inductive argument is the basis of academic writing; it is also the basis of any appeal to logos. The process of constructing an inductive argument involves three steps:

1. State the premises of your argument.
2. Use credible evidence to show readers that your argument has merit.
3. Demonstrate that the conclusion follows from the premises.

In following these three steps, you will want to determine the truth of your premises, help readers understand whether or not the inferences you draw are justified, and use word signals to help readers fully grasp the connections between your premises and your conclusion.

■ State the Premises of Your Argument

Stating a premise establishes what you have found to be true and what you want to persuade readers to accept as truth as well. Let's return to Loewen, who asserts his premise at the very outset of the excerpt: "Middle-class students . . . know little about how the American class structure works . . . and nothing at all about how it has changed over time." Loewen elaborates on this initial premise a few sentences later, arguing that students "have no understanding of the ways that opportunity is not equal in America and no notion that the social structure pushes people around, influencing the ideas they hold and the lives they fashion."

Implicit here is the point that class matters. Loewen makes this point explicit several paragraphs later, where he states that "social class is probably the single most important variable in society" (para. 6). He states his second, more specific premise in paragraph 2: "High school history textbooks can take some of the credit for this state of affairs." The burden of demonstrating that these premises are true is on Loewen. If readers find that either of the premises is not true, it will be difficult, if not impossible, for them to accept his conclusion that with more knowledge, people will understand that poverty is not the fault of the poor (para. 10).

■ Use Credible Evidence

The validity of your argument depends on whether the inferences you draw are justified, and whether you can expect a reasonable person to draw the same conclusion from those premises. Loewen has to demonstrate throughout (1) that students do not have much, if any, knowledge about the class structure that exists in the United States and (2) that textbook writers are in large part to blame for this lack of knowledge. He also must help readers understand how this lack of knowledge contributes to (3) his conclusion that greater knowledge would lead Americans to understand that poor

APPEALING TO LOGOS: USING REASON AND EVIDENCE TO FIT THE SITUATION **269**

people are not responsible for poverty. He can help readers with the order in which he states his premises and by choosing the type and amount of evidence that will enable readers to draw the inferences that he does.

Interestingly, Loewen seems to assume that one group of readers—educators—will accept his first premise as true. He does not elaborate on what students know or do not know. Instead, he moves right to his second premise, which involves first acknowledging what high school history textbooks typically cover, then identifying what he believes are the important events that textbook writers exclude, and ultimately asserting that textbook discussions of events in labor history are never "anchored in any analysis of social class" (para. 3). He supports this point with his own study of eighteen textbooks (paras. 3–5) before returning to his premise that "social class is probably the single most important variable in society" (para. 6). What follows is a series of observations about the rich and references to researchers' findings on inequality (paras. 7–9). Finally, he asserts that "social class determines how people think about social class" (para. 10), implying that fuller knowledge would lead business leaders and conservative voters to think differently about the source of poverty. The question to explore is whether or not Loewen supports this conclusion.

■ Demonstrate That the Conclusion Follows from the Premises

Authors signal their conclusion with words like *consequently*, *finally*, *in sum*, *in the end*, *subsequently*, *therefore*, *thus*, *ultimately*, and *as a result*. Here is how this looks in the structure of Loewen's argument:

1. Although class is a key factor in Americans' access to health care, education, and wealth, students know very little about the social structure in the United States.

2. In their textbooks, textbook writers do not address the issue of class, an issue that people need to know about.

3. Ultimately, if people had this knowledge, they would understand that poverty cannot be blamed on the poor.

We've reprinted much of paragraph 9 of Loewen's excerpt below. Notice how Loewen pulls together what he has been discussing. He again underscores the importance of class and achievement ("All these are among the reasons"). And he points out that access to certain types of colleges puts people in a position to accumulate and sustain wealth. Of course, this is not true of the poor "because affluent families can save some money while poor families must spend what they make." This causal relationship ("Because") heightens readers' awareness of the class structure that exists in the United States.

> All these are among the reasons that social class predicts the rate of college attendance and the type of college chosen more effectively than does any other factor, including intellectual ability, however measured. After college,

most affluent children get white-collar jobs, most working-class children get blue-collar jobs, and the class differences continue. As adults, rich people are more likely to have hired an attorney and to be a member of formal organizations that increase their civic power. Poor people are more likely to watch TV. <u>Because</u> affluent families can save some money while poor families must spend what they make, wealth differences are ten times larger than income differences. <u>Therefore</u> most poor and working-class families cannot accumulate the down payment required to buy a house, which in turn shuts them out from our most important tax shelter, the write-off of home mortgage interest. Working-class parents cannot afford to live in elite subdivisions or hire high-quality day care, so the process of educational inequality replicates itself in the next generation. <u>Finally</u>, affluent Americans also have longer life expectancies than lower- and working-class people, the largest single cause of which is better access to health care. . . .

Once Loewen establishes this causal relationship, he concludes ("Therefore," "Finally") with the argument that poverty persists from one generation to the next.

In paragraph 10, Loewen uses the transition word *ultimately* to make the point that social class matters, so much so that it limits the ways in which people see the world, that it even "determines how people think about social class."

Steps to Appealing to Logos

1 **State the premises of your argument.** Establish what you have found to be true and what you want readers to accept as well.

2 **Use credible evidence.** Lead your readers from one premise to the next, making sure your evidence is sufficient and convincing and your inferences are logical and correct.

3 **Demonstrate that the conclusion follows from the premises.** In particular, use the right words to signal to your readers how the evidence and inferences lead to your conclusion.

RECOGNIZING LOGICAL FALLACIES

We turn now to **logical fallacies,** flaws in the chain of reasoning that lead to a conclusion that does not necessarily follow from the premises, or evidence. Logical fallacies are common in inductive arguments for two reasons: Inductive arguments rely on reasoning about probability, not certainty; and they derive from human beliefs and values, not facts or laws of nature.

RECOGNIZING LOGICAL FALLACIES 271

Here we list fifteen logical fallacies. In examining them, think about how to guard against the sometimes-faulty logic behind statements you might hear from politicians, advertisers, and the like. That should help you examine the premises on which you base your own assumptions and the logic you use to help readers reach the same conclusions you do.

1. *Erroneous Appeal to Authority.* An authority is someone with expertise in a given subject. An *erroneous authority* is an author who claims to be an authority but is not, or someone an author cites as an authority who is not. In this type of fallacy, the claim might be true, but the fact that an unqualified person is making the claim means there is no reason for readers to accept the claim as true.

Because the issue here is the legitimacy of authority, your concern should be to prove to yourself and your readers that you or the people you are citing have expertise in the subject. An awareness of this type of fallacy has become increasingly important as celebrities offer support for candidates running for office or act as spokespeople for curbing global warming or some other cause. The candidate may be the best person for the office, and there may be very good reasons to control global warming; but we need to question the legitimacy of a nonexpert endorsement.

2. *Ad Hominem.* An ad hominem argument focuses on the person making a claim instead of on the claim itself. (*Ad hominem* is Latin for "to the person.") In most cases, an ad hominem argument does not have a bearing on the truth or the quality of a claim.

Keep in mind that it is always important to address the claim or the reasoning behind it, rather than the person making the claim. "Of course Senator Wiley supports oil drilling in Alaska—he's in the pocket of the oil companies!" is an example of an ad hominem argument. Senator Wiley may have good reasons for supporting oil drilling in Alaska that have nothing to do with his alleged attachment to the oil industry. However, if an individual's character is relevant to the argument, then an ad hominem argument can be valid. If Senator Wiley has been found guilty of accepting bribes from an oil company, it makes sense to question both his credibility and his claims.

3. *Shifting the Issue.* This type of fallacy occurs when an author draws attention away from the issue instead of offering evidence that will enable people to draw their own conclusions about the soundness of an argument. Consider this example:

> Affirmative action proponents accuse me of opposing equal opportunity in the workforce. I think my positions on military expenditures, education, and public health speak for themselves.

The author of this statement does not provide a chain of reasoning that would enable readers to judge his or her stance on the issue of affirmative action.

272 CHAPTER 13 | FROM ETHOS TO LOGOS: APPEALING TO YOUR READERS

4. *Either/Or Fallacy.* At times, an author will take two extreme positions to force readers to make a choice between two seemingly contradictory positions. For example:

> Either you support the war, or you are against it.

Although the author has set up an either/or condition, in reality one position does not exclude the other. People can support the troops involved in a war, for example, even if they don't support the reasons for starting the war.

5. *Sweeping Generalizations.* When an author attempts to draw a conclusion without providing sufficient evidence to support the conclusion or examining possible counterarguments, he or she may be making sweeping generalizations. Consider this example:

> Despite the women's movement in the 1960s and 1970s, women still do not receive equal pay for equal work. Obviously, any attempt to change the status quo for women is doomed to failure.

As is the case with many fallacies, the author's position may be reasonable, but we cannot accept the argument at face value. Reading critically entails testing assumptions like this one—that any attempt to create change is doomed to failure because women do not receive equal pay for equal work. We could ask, for example, whether inequities persist in the public sector. And we could point to other areas where the women's movement has had measurable success. Title IX, for example, has reduced the dropout rate among teenage girls; it has also increased the rate at which women earn college and graduate degrees.

6. *Bandwagon.* When an author urges readers to accept an idea because a significant number of people support it, he or she is making a bandwagon argument. This is a fairly common mode of argument in advertising; for example, a commercial might attempt to persuade us to buy a certain product because it's popular.

> Because Harvard, Stanford, and Berkeley have all added a multicultural component to their graduation requirements, other institutions should do so as well.

The growing popularity of an idea is not sufficient reason to accept that it is valid.

7. *Begging the Question.* This fallacy entails advancing a circular argument that asks readers to accept a premise that is also the conclusion readers are expected to draw:

> We could improve the undergraduate experience with coed dorms because both men and women benefit from living with members of the opposite gender.

Here readers are being asked to accept that the conclusion is true despite the fact that the premises—men benefit from living with women, and women benefit from living with men—are essentially the same as the conclusion. Without evidence that a shift in dorm policy could improve on the undergraduate experience, we cannot accept the conclusion as true. Indeed, the conclusion does not necessarily follow from the premise.

8. *False Analogy.* Authors (and others) often try to persuade us that something is true by using a comparison. This approach is not in and of itself a problem, as long as the comparison is reasonable. For example:

> It is ridiculous to have a Gay and Lesbian Program and a Department of African American Culture. We don't have a Straight Studies Program or a Department of Caucasian Culture.

Here the author is urging readers to rethink the need for two academic departments by saying that the school doesn't have two other departments. That, of course, is not a reason for or against the new departments. What's needed is an analysis that compares the costs (economic and otherwise) of starting up and operating the new departments versus the contributions (economic and otherwise) of the new departments.

9. *Technical Jargon.* If you've ever had a salesperson try to persuade you to purchase a television or an entertainment system with capabilities you absolutely *must* have—even if you didn't understand a word the salesperson was saying about alternating currents and circuit splicers—then you're familiar with this type of fallacy. We found this passage in a student's paper:

> You should use this drug because it has been clinically proven that it inhibits the reuptake of serotonin and enhances the dopamine levels of the body's neurotransmitters.

The student's argument may very well be true, but he hasn't presented any substantive evidence to demonstrate that the premises are true and that the conclusion follows from the premises.

10. *Confusing Cause and Effect.* It is challenging to establish that one factor causes another. For example, how can we know for certain that economic class predicts, or is a factor in, academic achievement? How do we know that a new president's policies are the cause of a country's economic well-being? Authors often assume cause and effect when two factors are simply associated with each other:

> The current recession came right after the president was elected.

This fallacy states a fact, but it does not prove that the president's election caused the recession.

11. *Appeal to Fear.* One type of logical fallacy makes an appeal to readers' irrational fears and prejudices, preventing them from dealing squarely with a given issue and often confusing cause and effect:

> We should use whatever means possible to avoid further attack.

274   CHAPTER 13 | FROM ETHOS TO LOGOS: APPEALING TO YOUR READERS

The reasoning here is something like this: "If we are soft on defense, we will never end the threat of terrorism." But we need to consider whether there is indeed a threat, and, if so, whether the presence of a threat should lead to action, and, if so, whether that action should include "whatever means possible." (Think of companies that sell alarm systems by pointing to people's vulnerability to harm and property damage.)

12. *Fallacy of Division.* A fallacy of division suggests that what is true of the whole must also be true of its parts:

> Conservatives have always voted against raising the minimum wage, against stem cell research, and for defense spending. Therefore, we can assume that conservative Senator Harrison will vote this way.

The author is urging readers to accept the premise without providing evidence of how the senator has actually voted on the three issues.

13. *Hasty Generalization.* This fallacy is committed when a person draws a conclusion about a group based on a sample that is too small to be representative. Consider this statement:

> Seventy-five percent of the seniors surveyed at the university study just
> 10 hours a week. We can conclude, then, that students at the university are
> not studying enough.

What you need to know is how many students were actually surveyed. Seventy-five percent may seem high, but not if the researcher surveyed just 400 of the 2,400 graduating seniors. This sample of students from a total population of 9,600 students at the university is too small to draw the conclusion that students in general are not studying enough.

14. *The Straw Man Argument.* A straw man fallacy makes a generalization about what a group believes without actually citing a specific writer or work:

> Democrats are more interested in running away than in trying to win the war
> on terrorism.

Here the fallacy is that the author simply ignores someone's actual position and substitutes a distorted, exaggerated, or misrepresented version of that position. This kind of fallacy often goes hand in hand with assuming that what is true of the group is true of the individual, what we call the fallacy of division.

15. *Fallacy of the Middle Ground.* The fallacy of the middle ground assumes that the middle position between two extreme positions must be correct. Although the middle ground may be true, the author must justify this position with evidence.

> E. D. Hirsch argues that cultural literacy is the only sure way to increase test
> scores, and Jonathan Kozol believes schools will improve only if state legisla-
> tors increase funding; but I would argue that school reform will occur if we
> change the curriculum and provide more funding.

This fallacy draws its power from the fact that a moderate or middle position is often the correct one. Again, however, the claim that the moderate or middle position is correct must be supported by legitimate reasoning.

ANALYZING THE APPEALS IN A RESEARCHED ARGUMENT

Now that you have studied the variety of appeals you can make to connect with your audience, we would like you to read an article on urban health problems by Meredith Minkler and analyze her strategies for appealing to her readers. The article is long and carefully argued, so we suggest you take detailed notes about her use of appeals to ethos, pathos, and logos as you read. You may want to refer to the Practice Sequence questions on page 289 to help focus your reading. Ideally, you should work through the text with your classmates, in groups of three or four, appointing one student to record and share each group's analysis of Minkler's argument.

MEREDITH MINKLER

Community-Based Research Partnerships: Challenges and Opportunities

Meredith Minkler is a professor of health and social behavior at the School of Public Health, University of California, Berkeley. She is an activist and researcher whose work explores community partnerships, community organizing, and community-based participatory research. With more than one hundred books and articles to her credit, she is coeditor of the influential *Community Based Participatory Research for Health* (2003). The following article appeared in *The Journal of Urban Health* in 2005.

■ ■ ■

Abstract
The complexity of many urban health problems often makes them ill suited to traditional research approaches and interventions. The resultant frustration, together with community calls for genuine partnership in the research process, has highlighted the importance of an alternative paradigm. Community-based participatory research (CBPR) is presented as a promising collaborative approach that combines systematic inquiry, participation, and action to address urban health problems. Following a brief review of its basic tenets and

276 CHAPTER 13 | FROM ETHOS TO LOGOS: APPEALING TO YOUR READERS

historical roots, key ways in which CBPR adds value to urban health research are introduced and illustrated. Case study examples from diverse international settings are used to illustrate some of the difficult ethical challenges that may arise in the course of CBPR partnership approaches. The concepts of partnership synergy and cultural humility, together with protocols such as Green et al.'s guidelines for appraising CBPR projects, are highlighted as useful tools for urban health researchers seeking to apply this collaborative approach and to deal effectively with the difficult ethical challenges it can present.

Keywords
Community-based participatory research, Ethical issues in research, Participatory action research, Partnership, Urban health.

Introduction

The complexity of urban health problems has often made them poorly suited to traditional "outside expert"–driven research and intervention approaches.[1] Together with community demands for authentic partnerships in research that are locally relevant and "community based" rather than merely "community placed," this frustration has led to a burgeoning of interest in an alternative research paradigm.[1,2] Community-based participatory research (CBPR) is an overarching term that increasingly is used to encompass a variety of approaches to research that have as their centerpiece three interrelated elements: participation, research, and action.[3] As defined by Green et al.[4] for the Royal Society of Canada, CBPR may concisely be described as "systematic investigation with the participation of those affected by an issue for purposes of education and action or affecting social change." The approach further has been characterized as

> [A] collaborative process that equitably involves all partners in the research process and recognizes the unique strengths that each brings. CBPR begins with a research topic of importance to the community with the aim of combining knowledge and action for social change to improve community health and eliminate health disparities.[5,6]

This article briefly describes CBPR's roots and core principles and summarizes the value added by this approach to urban health research. Drawing on examples from a variety of urban health settings nationally and internationally, it discusses and illustrates several of the key challenges faced in applying this partnership approach to inquiry and action. The article concludes by suggesting that despite such challenges and the labor-intensive nature of this approach, CBPR offers an exceptional opportunity for partnering with communities in ways that can enhance both the quality of research and its potential for helping address some of our most intractable urban health problems.

Historical Roots and Core Principles

The roots of CBPR may be traced in part to the action research school developed by the social psychologist Kurt Lewin[7] in the 1940s, with its emphasis on the active involvement in the research of those affected by the problem being studied through a cyclical process of fact finding, action, and reflection. But CBPR is most deeply grounded in the more revolutionary approaches to research that emerged, often independently from one another, from work with oppressed communities in South America, Asia, and Africa in the 1970s.[3,8,9] Brazilian adult educator Paulo Freire[9] provided critical grounding for CBPR in his development of a dialogical method accenting co-learning and action based on critical reflection. Freire,[9] Fals-Borda,[10] and other developing countries' scholars developed their alternative approaches to inquiry as a direct counter to the often "colonizing" nature of research to which oppressed communities were subjected, with feminist and postcolonialist scholars adding further conceptual richness.[11,12]

Among the tenets of participatory action approaches to research outlined by McTaggart[13] are that it is a political process, involves lay people in theory-making, is committed to improving social practice by changing it, and establishes "self-critical communities." As Israel et al.[6] adds, other core principles are that CBPR "involves systems development and local community capacity development," is "a co-learning process" to which community members and outside researchers contribute equally, and "achieves a balance between research and action." CBPR reflects a profound belief in "partnership synergy." As described by Lasker et al.[14]:

> [T]he synergy that partners seek to achieve through collaboration is more than a mere exchange of resources. By combining the individual perspectives, resources, and skills of the partners, the group creates something new and valuable together—something that is greater than the sum of its parts.

Moreover, CBPR embodies a deep commitment to what Tervalon and Murray-Garcia[15] have called cultural humility. As they point out, although we can never become truly competent in another's culture, we can demonstrate a "lifelong commitment to self evaluation and self-critique," to redress power imbalances and "develop and maintain mutually respectful and dynamic partnerships with communities."[15] Although the term *cultural humility* was coined primarily in reference to race and ethnicity, it also is of value in helping us understand and address the impacts of professional cultures (which tend to be highly influenced by white, western, patriarchal belief systems), as these help shape interactions between outside researchers and their community partners.[15]

278   CHAPTER 13 | FROM ETHOS TO LOGOS: APPEALING TO YOUR READERS

CBPR is not a method per se but an orientation to research that may   6
employ any of a number of qualitative and quantitative methodologies. As Cornwall and Jewkes[16] note, what is distinctive about CBPR is "the attitudes of researchers, which in turn determine how, by and for whom research is conceptualized and conducted [and] the corresponding location of power at every stage of the research process." The accent placed by CBPR on individual, organizational, and community empowerment also is a hallmark of this approach to research.

With the increasing emphasis on partnership approaches to improv-   7
ing urban health, CBPR is experiencing a rebirth of interest and unprecedented new opportunities for both scholarly recognition and financial support. In the United States, for example, the Institute of Medicine[17] recently named "community-based participatory research" as one of eight new areas in which all schools of public health should be offering training.

Although the renewed interest in CBPR provides a welcome contrast   8
to more traditional top-down research approaches, it also increases the dangers of co-optation as this label is loosely applied to include research and intervention efforts in search of funding that do not truly meet the criteria for this approach. The sections below illustrate some of the value added to urban research when authentic partnership approaches are taken seriously and then briefly highlight some of the ethical challenges such work may entail.

The Value Added to Urban Health Research by a CBPR Approach

CBPR can enrich and improve the quality and outcomes of urban health   9
research in a variety of ways. On the basis of the work of many scholars and institutions,[4,6,8,18] and as summarized by the National Institutes of Health (http://grants.nih.gov/grants/guide/pa-files/PAR-05-026.html), some of its primary contributions may be characterized and illustrated as follows.

CBPR Can Support the Development of Research Questions That Reflect Health Issues of Real Concern to Community Members

Ideally, CBPR begins with a research topic or question that comes   10
from the local community, as when the nongovernmental organization (NGO) Alternatives for Community and Environment (ACE) in the low-income Roxbury section of Boston, reached out to Harvard University's School of Public Health and other potential partners to

study and address the high rates of asthma in their neighborhood. Collaborative studies using air-monitoring and other approaches yielded data supporting the hypothesis that Roxbury was indeed a hot spot for pollution contributing to asthma. This in turn paved the way for a variety of policy and community education actions and outcomes.[19]

Although having a community partner such as ACE identify an issue and catalyze a research partnership may be the ideal, it is often the privileged outside researcher who initiates a CBPR project. In these instances too, however, a genuine commitment to high-level community involvement in issue selection, with NGOs and formal and informal community leaders engaged as equal partners, can help ensure that the research topic decided upon really is of major concern to the local population.

CBPR Can Improve Our Ability to Achieve Informed Consent, and to Address Issues of "Costs and Benefits" on the Community, and Not Simply the Individual Level[20]

With its accent on equitable community involvement in all stages of the research process,[6] CBPR often finds creative means of ensuring informed consent. The "One Hand, One Heart" study in urban and rural Tibet, which included a randomized controlled clinical trial of an indigenous medicine to prevent maternal hemorrhaging, actively involved local midwives and other community partners on the research team who played a key role in helping find locally translatable concepts to improve informed consent. Their help in early ethnographic work thus revealed that the concept of disclosing risk was highly problematic, because such disclosure was believed to disturb the wind element responsible for emotions, potentially leading to emotional upset and other adverse outcomes. By reframing risk disclosure as "safety issues," needed information could be conveyed in a far more culturally acceptable manner.[21]

CBPR also offers an important potential opening for extending the gaze of our ethical review processes such that we examine and address risks and benefits for the community. In Toronto, Travers and Flicker[20] have pioneered in developing such guidelines, pointing out the importance of having us ask such questions as "Will the methods used be sensitive and appropriate to various communities?" "What training or capacity building opportunities will you build in?" and "How will you balance scientific rigor and accessibility?" The strong philosophical fit between questions such as these and CBPR's commitments to equitable partnership and community capacity building reflect another source of value added to urban health research through this approach.

CBPR Can Improve Cultural Sensitivity and the Reliability and Validity of Measurement Tools through High-Quality Community Participation in Designing and Testing Study Instruments

Particularly in survey research, community advisory boards (CABs) and other partnership structures can improve measurement instruments by making sure that questions are worded in ways that will elicit valid and reliable responses. In a study of urban grandparents raising grandchildren due to the crack cocaine epidemic, the author and her colleagues used validated instruments, such as those for depressive symptomatology. However, they also learned from CAB members how to word other questions about sensitive topics. Rather than asking a standard (and disliked) question about income, for example, the CAB encouraged us to rephrase the question as "How much money is available to help you in raising this child?" When this alternate wording was used, a wealth of detailed income data was obtained, which improved our understanding of the challenges faced by this population.[22]

CBPR Can Uncover Lay Knowledge Critical to Enhancing Understanding of Sensitive Urban Health Problems

Through the cultural humility and partnership synergy involved in deeply valuing lay knowledge and working in partnership with community residents, CBPR can uncover hidden contributors to health and social problems. The high rates of HIV/AIDS in India and the often sensitive nature of this subject among young men led the Deepak Charitable Trust to develop a research committee for a study in the industrial area of Nandesari, in Gujarat, comprised of several male village health workers and other young men from the area. Working closely with a medical anthropologist, the research committee planned the research, including developing a sampling plan and the phrasing of culturally sensitive questions. Their insider knowledge helped reveal that AIDS itself was not perceived as a major problem by the young men in this area. Instead, men who were engaging in high-risk behaviors wanted to find sex partners at least partly to avoid "thinning of the semen" and sexual dysfunction and fatigue, which were believed to be long-term consequences of masturbation and nocturnal emissions. These fears appeared to be contributing to high rates of unprotected intercourse with sex workers at the area's many truck stops and with other sex partners.[23] This insider knowledge both strengthened the research and led to subsequent interventions to help dispel such misinformation.

By Increasing Community Trust and Ownership, CBPR Can Improve Recruitment and Retention Efforts

In a participatory epidemiology project on diabetes in an urban Aboriginal community in Melbourne, Australia, a marked increase in

recruitment was experienced following the hiring of a community codi-
rector and the changing of the project's name to one chosen by the local
community.[24] Similarly, a 69 percent response rate achieved in a CBPR
study of the health and working conditions of the largely immigrant
hotel room cleaner population (many of them undocumented) in several of San Francisco's major tourist hotels was heavily attributed to the
hiring and training of a core group of twenty-five room cleaners as key
project staff. That high response rate, together with the high quality of
data collected, made a substantial contribution when results later were
presented and used to help negotiate a new contract.[25]

CBPR Can Help Increase Accuracy and Cultural Sensitivity in the Interpretation of Findings

Even highly engaged community members of the research team may
not wish to be involved in the labor-intensive data analysis phase of a
research project,[26] nor do all methodological approaches lend themselves to such involvement. Yet when applicable and desired, community involvement in data analysis can make real contributions to our
understanding of the themes and findings that emerge. In a U.S. study
of and with people with disabilities on the contentious topic of death
with dignity legislation in their community, the author and an "insider/
outsider" member of the research team met on alternate Saturdays
with a subcommittee of the CAB to engage in joint data analysis. Using
redacted transcripts, and applying lessons learned in qualitative data
interpretation, the diverse CAB members came up with far richer codes
and themes than outside researchers could have achieved alone.[27]

CBPR Can Increase the Relevance of Intervention Approaches and Thus the Likelihood of Success

One of the strengths of CBPR is its commitment to action as part of
the research process. But without strong community input, researchers not infrequently design interventions that are ill suited to the local
context in which they are applied. In the Gujarat case study mentioned
above, partnership with local community members helped in the design
of culturally relevant interventions, such as street theater performed
by locally recruited youth at *melas* (or fairs), and the dissemination of
study findings through the fifteen local credit and savings groups that
often provided platforms for discussing reproductive health and related
issues. Both these approaches provided critical means of information
dissemination on this culturally and emotionally charged topic.[23]

Ethical and Other Challenges in Community-Based Participatory Research

Engaging in urban health research with diverse community partners
can indeed enrich both the quality and the outcomes of such studies.

At the same time, CBPR is fraught with ethical and related challenges, several of which are now highlighted.

"Community Driven" Issue Selection

A key feature of CBPR involves its commitment to ensuring that the research topic comes from the community. Yet many such projects "paradoxically . . . would not occur without the initiative of someone outside the community who has the time, skill, and commitment, and who almost inevitably is a member of a privileged and educated group."[28] In such instances, outside researchers must pay serious attention to community understandings of what the real issue or topic of concern is.

20

In South Africa, for example, high rates of cervical cancer in the Black and Colored populations led Mosavel et al.[29] to propose an investigation of this problem. In response to community feedback, however, they quickly broadened their initial topic to "cervical health," a concept which "acknowledged the fact that women's health in South Africa extends well beyond the risk of developing cervical cancer, and includes HIV-AIDS and STDs, sexual violence, and multiple other social problems." In other instances, the outside researcher as an initiator of a potential CBPR project needs to determine whether the topic he or she has identified really is of concern to the local community—and whether outsider involvement is welcome. The Oakland, California–based Grandmother Caregiver Study mentioned above grew out of the interests of my colleague and me in studying the strengths of as well as the health and social problems faced by the growing number of urban African American grandmothers who were raising grandchildren in the context of a major drug epidemic. As privileged white women, however, we had to determine first whether this was a topic of local concern and, if so, whether there might be a role for us in working with the community to help study and address it. We began by enlisting the support of an older African American colleague with deep ties in the community, who engaged with us in a frank discussion with two prominent African American NGOs. It was only after getting their strong support for proceeding that we wrote a grant, with funds for these organizations, which in turn helped us pull together an outstanding CAB that was actively involved in many stages of the project.[21,26]

21

We were lucky in this case that a topic we as outsiders identified turned out to represent a deep concern in the local community. Yet not infrequently "the community" is in fact deeply divided over an issue. Indeed, as Yoshihama and Carr[30] have argued, "communities are not places that researchers enter but are instead a set of negotiations that inherently entail multiple and often conflicting interests." In such situations, outside researchers can play a useful role in helping community partners think through who "the community" in fact is in relation to a proposed project and the pros and cons of undertaking the project to

22

begin with. The holding of town hall meetings and other forums may then be useful in helping achieve consensus on an issue that is truly of, by, and for the community, however it is defined.[26]

Insider–Outsider Tensions

Urban health researchers in many parts of the world have written poignantly about the power dynamics and other sources of insider–outsider tensions and misunderstandings in CBPR and related partnership efforts. Ugalde[31] points out how in Latin America participants may be exploited as cheap sources of labor or may become alienated from their communities because of their participation. In her work with Native American and other marginalized groups in New Mexico, Wallerstein[32] further illustrates how even outsiders who pride ourselves on being trusted community friends and allies often fail to appreciate the extent of the power that is embedded in our own, often multiple sources of privilege, and how it can affect both process and outcomes in such research.

One major source of insider–outsider tensions involves the differential reward structures for partners in CBPR. For although a major aim of such research is to benefit the local community, the outside researchers typically stand to gain the most from such collaborations, bringing in grants, getting new publications, and so forth. The common expectation that community partners will work for little or no pay and the fact that receipt of compensation may take months if the funds are coming through a ministry of health or a university are also sources of understandable resentment.[6,26]

To address these and other sources of insider–outsider tensions in work with indigenous communities in both urban and rural areas, researchers in New Zealand,[33] Australia,[34] the United States,[35] and Canada[36] have worked with their community partners to develop ethical guidelines for their collaborative work, including protocols that address

1. negotiating with political and spiritual leaders in the community to obtain their input and their approval for the proposed research,
2. ensuring equitable benefits to participants (e.g., appropriate training and hiring of community members) in return for their contributions and resources,
3. developing agreements about the ownership and publication of findings, and the early review of findings by key community leaders.

Although such protocols cannot begin to address all of the conflicts that may arise in CBPR, they can play a critical role in helping pave the way for the continued dialogue and negotiation that must be an integral part of the process.

Constraints on Community Involvement

Outside researchers committed to a CBPR approach not infrequently express frustration at the difficulty moving from the goal of heavy community partner involvement in the research process to the reality. As Diaz and Simmons[37] found in their Reproductive Health Project in Brazil, despite a strong commitment to involving the most marginalized and vulnerable classes (in this case, women who were users of the public sector services being studied), such individuals often "are least likely to be in a position to donate their time and energy." Further, and even when outside researchers are careful to provide child care and transportation, there are differential costs of participation by gender.[30]

Still another set of challenges may arise when community desires with respect to research design and methods clash with what outsider researchers consider to be "good science." In an oft-cited CBPR study with a local Mohawk community in Québec, Chataway[38] describes how community members at first strongly objected to the idea of using a questionnaire approach which they saw as "putting their thoughts in boxes." Through respectful listening on both sides, the value of such an approach was realized and a more qualitative methodology developed, through which community members would then be actively involved in helping analyze and interpret the quantitative findings that emerged. As such case studies illustrate, CBPR does not condone an abandonment of one's own scientific standards and knowledge base. But it does advocate a genuine co-learning process through which lay and professional ways of knowing both are valued and examined for what they can contribute.[26]

Dilemmas in the Sharing and Release of Findings

A crucial step in CBPR involves returning data to the community and enabling community leaders and participants to have an authentic role in deciding how that data will be used. As Travers and Flicker[20] suggest, ethical research review processes that ask questions such as "Are there built-in mechanisms for how unflattering results will be dealt with?" should be employed at the front end of our CBPR projects. In addition to the formal IRB process they propose, which offers a critical next step for the field, CBPR partners can look to a variety of formal or informal research protocols and particularly to the detailed guidelines for health promotion research developed by Green et al.,[4,39] which help partnerships decide in advance how potentially difficult issues concerning the sharing and release of findings and other matters will be handled.

Challenges in the Action Dimensions of CBPR

Numerous ethical challenges lastly may arise in relation to the critical action component of CBPR. In some instances, community partners may wish to move quickly into action, whereas academic and other outside research partners may want to "put the [brakes] on" until findings have been published or other steps brought to fruition. In other cases, the nature of funding (e.g., from a government body) may constrain action on the policy level that is prohibited or discouraged by the funder. And in still other instances, including the Brazilian Reproductive Health Project[37] cited above, community members may not wish to be associated with a CBPR project that appears connected to a broader political agenda.

Participation in the action phase of CBPR projects may sometimes present risks to community participants, as when immigrant hotel room cleaners in the San Francisco study took part in a Labor Day sit-in and in some cases faced arrest.[25] And for both professionally trained researchers and their community partners, actions that involve challenging powerful corporate or other entrenched interests may have negative consequences for those involved. At the same time, CBPR's fundamental commitment to action and to redressing power imbalances makes this aspect of the work a particularly important contributor to urban health improvement through research.

Conclusion

Difficult ethical challenges may confront urban health researchers who engage in CBPR. Yet this approach can greatly enrich the quality of our research, helping ensure that we address issues of genuine community concern and use methods and approaches that are culturally sensitive and that improve the validity and reliability of our findings. Moreover, through its commitment to action as an integral part of the research process, CBPR can help in translating findings as we work with community partners to help address some of our most intractable urban health problems.

Acknowledgement

Many current and former community and academic partners have contributed to my understanding of the advantages and pitfalls of collaborative urban health research and I am deeply grateful. Particular thanks are extended to Nina Wallerstein, Kathleen M. Roe, Barbara Israel, Lawrence W. Green, and Ronald Labonte, who have greatly stimulated my own thinking and scholarship in this area. I am grateful to former students, Rima Shaw and Caroline Bell, as well as other individuals who have shared some of the cases drawn upon in this paper. My gratitude is extended to Claire Murphy for assistance with manuscript preparation.

References

1. Minkler M, Wallerstein N. Community Based Participatory Research for Health. San Francisco, CA: Jossey-Bass; 2003.

2. Green LW, Mercer SL. Can public health researchers and agencies reconcile the push from funding bodies and the pull from communities? *Am J Public Health.* 2001;91:1926–1929.

3. Hall BL. From margins to center: the development and purpose of participatory action research. *Am Sociol.* 1992;23:15–28.

4. Green LW, George A, Daniel M, et al. *Study of Participatory Research in Health Promotion.* Ottawa, Ontario: Royal Society of Canada; 1995.

5. Community Health Scholars Program. *The Community Health Scholars Program: Stories of Impact.* Ann Arbor, MI; 2002.

6. Israel BA, Schulz AJ, Parker EA, Becker AB. Review of community-based research: assessing partnership approaches to improve public health. *Annu Rev Public Health.* 1998;19:173–202.

7. Lewin K. Action research and minority problems. *J Soc Issues.* 1946;2:34–46.

8. Brown LD, Tandon R. Ideology and political economy in inquiry: action research and participatory research. *J Appl Behav Sci.* 1983;19:277–294.

9. Freire P. *Pedagogy of the Oppressed.* New York, NY: Seabury Press; 1970.

10. Fals-Borda O. The application of participatory action-research in Latin America. *Int Sociol.* 1987;2:329–347.

11. Maguire P. *Doing Participatory Research: A Feminist Approach.* Amherst, MA: Center for International Education; 1987.

12. Duran E, Duran B. *Native American Postcolonial Psychology.* Albany, NY: State University of New York Press; 1995.

13. McTaggart R. Sixteen tenets of participatory action research. In: Wadsworth Y, ed. *Everyday Evaluation on the Run.* Sydney, Australia: Allen & Unwin; 1997:79.

14. Lasker RD, Weiss ES, Miller R. Partnership synergy: a practical framework for studying and strengthening the collaborative advantage. *Milbank Q.* 2001;79:179–205, III–IV.

15. Tervalon M, Murray-Garcia J. Cultural humility vs. cultural competence: a critical distinction in defining physician training outcomes in medical education. *J Health Care Poor Underserved.* 1998;9:117–125.

16. Cornwall A, Jewkes R. What is participatory research? *Soc Sci Med.* 1995;41:1667–1676.

17. Gebbie K, Rosenstock L, Hernandez LM. *Who Will Keep the Public Healthy? Educating Public Health Professionals for the 21st Century.* Washington, DC: Institute of Medicine; 2002.

18. O'Fallon LR, Dearry A. Community-based participatory research as a tool to advance environmental health sciences. *Environ Health Perspect.* 2002;110:155–159.

19. Loh P, Sugerman-Brozan J. Environmental justice organizing for environmental health: case study on asthma and diesel exhaust in Roxbury, Massachusetts. *Environ Health Perspect.* 2002;584: 110–124.

20. Travers R, Flicker S. Ethical issues in community based research. In: *Urban Health Community-Based Research Series Workshop.* Wellesley, MA; 2004.

21. Bell C. *One HEART (Health Education and Research in Tibet) Community Based Participatory Research on Top of the World.* Unpublished manuscript, University of California, Berkeley, School of Public Health; 2004.

22. Roe KM, Minkler M, Saunders FF. Combining research, advocacy and education: the methods of the Grandparent Caregiving Study. *Health Educ Q.* 1995;22:458–475.

23. Shah R. *A Retrospective Analysis of an HIV Prevention Program for Men in Gujarat, India.* Unpublished manuscript, University of California, Berkeley, School of Public Health; 2004.

24. Thompson SJ. Participatory epidemiology: methods of the Living With Diabetes Project. *Intl Q Community Health Educ.* 2000;19: 3–18.

25. Lee P, Krause N, Goetchius C. Participatory action research with hotel room cleaners: from collaborative study to the bargaining table. In: Minkler M, Wallerstein N, eds. *Community Based Participatory Research for Health.* San Francisco, CA: Jossey-Bass; 2003: 390–404.

26. Minkler M. Ethical challenges for the "outside" researcher in community based participatory research. *Health Educ Behav.* 2004;31: 684–701.

27. Fadem P, Minkler M, Perry M, et al. Ethical challenges in community based participatory research: a case study from the San Francisco Bay Area disability community. In: Minkler M, Wallerstein N, eds. *Community Based Participatory Research for Health.* San Francisco, CA: Jossey-Bass; 2003.

288 CHAPTER 13 | FROM ETHOS TO LOGOS: APPEALING TO YOUR READERS

28. Reason P. *Participation in Human Inquiry.* London, UK: Sage; 1994.

29. Mosavel M, Simon C, van Stade D, Buchbinder M. *Community Based Participatory Research (CBPR) in South Africa: Engaging Multiple Constituents to Shape the Research Question.* Unpublished manuscript; 2004.

30. Yoshihama M, Carr ES. Community participation reconsidered: feminist participatory action research with Hmong women. *J Community Pract.* 2002;10:85–103.

31. Ugalde A. Ideological dimensions of community participation in Latin American health programs. *Soc Sci Med.* 1985;21:41–53.

32. Wallerstein N. Power between evaluator and community: research relationships within New Mexico's healthier communities. *Soc Sci Med.* 1999;49:39–53.

33. Cram F. Rangahau Maori: Tona tika, tona pono: The validity and integrity of Maori research. In: Tolich M, ed. *Research Ethics in Aotearoa New Zealand.* Longman, Auckland: Pearson Education; 2001:35–52.

34. Anderson I. Ethics and health research in Aboriginal communities. In: Daly J, ed. *Ethical Intersections: Health Research, Methods and Researcher Responsibility.* St. Leonards, New South Wales: Allen & Unwin; 1996:153–165.

35. Turning Point, National Association of County and City Health Officials. Thirteen policy principles for advancing collaborative activity among and between tribal communities and surrounding jurisdictions. In: Minkler M, Wallerstein N, eds. *Community Based Participatory Research for Health.* San Francisco, CA: Jossey-Bass; 2003:436, Appendix E.

36. Stuart CA. Care and concern: an ethical journey in participatory action research. *Can J Couns.* 1998;32:298–314.

37. Diaz M, Simmons R. When is research participatory? Reflections on a Reproductive Health Project in Brazil. *J Women's Health.* 1999;8:175–184.

38. Chataway CJ. Examination of the constraints of mutual inquiry in a participatory action research project. *J Soc Issues.* 1997;53: 747–765.

39. Green LW, George MA, Daniel M, et al. Guidelines for participatory research in health promotion. In: Minkler M, Wallerstein N, eds. *Community Based Participatory Research for Health.* San Francisco, CA: Jossey-Bass; 2003:419, Appendix C.

A Practice Sequence: Analyzing the Appeals in a Researched Argument

1 Make a list of the major premises that inform Minkler's argument, and examine the evidence she uses to support them. To what extent do you find her evidence credible? Do you generally agree or disagree with the conclusions she draws? Be prepared to explain your responses to your class or peer group.

2 Note instances where Minkler appeals to ethos, pathos, and logos. How would you describe the ways she makes these three types of appeals? How does she present herself? What does she seem to assume? How does she help you understand the chain of reasoning by which she moves from premises to conclusion?

3 Working in groups of three or four, compose a letter to Minkler in which you take issue with her argument. This does not mean your group has to disagree with her entire argument, although of course you may. Rather, present your group's own contribution to the conversation in which she is participating. You may want to ask her to further explain one or more of her points, or suggest what she might be leaving out, or add your own take or evidence to her argument. As a group, you will have to agree on your focus. In the letter, include a summary of Minkler's argument or the part of it on which your group is focusing. Pay close attention to your own strategies for appealing to her—how you present yourselves, how you appeal to her values and emotions, and how you present your reasons for your own premises and conclusion.

APPENDIX:
Citing and Documenting Sources

You must provide a brief citation in the text of your paper for every quotation or idea taken from another writer, and you must list complete information at the end of your paper for the sources you use. This information is essential for readers who want to read the source to understand a quotation or an idea in its original context. How you cite sources in the body of your paper and document them at the end of your paper varies from discipline to discipline, so it is important to ask your instructor what documentation style he or she requires.

Even within academic disciplines, documentation styles can vary. Specific academic journals within disciplines will sometimes have their own set of style guidelines. The important thing is to adhere faithfully to your chosen (or assigned) style throughout your paper, observing all the rules prescribed by the style. You may have noticed small citation style differences among the examples in this text. That's because the examples are taken from the work of a variety of writers, both professionals and students, who had to conform to the documentation requirements of their publication venues or of their teachers.

Here we briefly introduce two common documentation styles that may be useful in your college career: the Modern Language Association (MLA) style, frequently used in the humanities, and the American Psychological Association (APA) style, often used in the social sciences. The information is basic, for use when you begin drafting your paper. In the final stages of writing, you should consult either the *MLA Handbook*, Eighth Edition, or the *Publication Manual of the American Psychological Association*, Sixth Edition.

291

292   APPENDIX | CITING AND DOCUMENTING SOURCES

Although you'll need the manuals or a handbook for complete style information, both the MLA (style.mla.org) and the APA (http://www.apastyle.org/learn/faqs/) maintain Web sites for frequently asked questions. Again, before you start your research, check with your instructor to find out whether you should use either of these styles or if there's another style he or she requires.

MLA and APA styles have many similarities. For example, both require short citations in the body of an essay linked to a list of sources at the end of the essay. But it is their differences, though subtle, that are crucial. To a great extent, these differences reflect the assumptions writers in the humanities and in the social sciences bring to working with sources. In particular, you should understand each style's treatment of the source's author, publication date, and page numbers in in-text citations, as well as verb use in referring to sources.

Author.   MLA style prefers that you give the author's full name on first mention in your paper; APA style uses last names throughout. The humanities emphasize "the human element"—the individual as creative force—so MLA style uses the complete name at first mention to imply the author's importance. Because the social sciences emphasize the primacy of data in studies of human activity, in APA style last names are deemed sufficient for identifying the source.

Publication date.   In-text citations using MLA style leave out the date of publication. The assumption is that the insights of the past may be as useful as those of the present. By contrast, APA in-text citations include the date of the study after the author's name, reflecting a belief in the progress of research, that recent findings may supersede earlier ones.

Verb use.   MLA style uses the present tense of verbs ("the author claims") to introduce cited material, assuming the cited text's timelessness, whether written last week or centuries ago. By contrast, APA style acknowledges the "pastness" of research by requiring past-tense verbs for introducing cited material ("the author claimed" or "the author has claimed"); the underlying assumption is that new data may emerge to challenge older research.

Although it is useful to understand that different citation styles reflect different attitudes toward inquiry and research in different disciplines, for the purposes of your writing, it is mainly important to know the style you have to follow in your paper and to apply it consistently. Whenever you consult a source—even if you don't end up using it in your paper—write down complete citation information so that you can cite it fully and accurately if you need to. Doing so will help you be a responsible researcher and save you the trouble of having to hunt down citation information later. Table A.1 shows the basic information needed to cite books, chapters in books, journal articles, and online sources. You also should note any other

THE BASICS OF MLA STYLE   **293**

TABLE A.1   Basic Information Needed for Citing Sources

BOOKS	CHAPTERS IN BOOKS	JOURNAL ARTICLES	ONLINE SOURCES
Author(s) or editor(s)	Author(s)	Author(s)	Author(s)
Title and subtitle	Chapter title and subtitle	Article title and subtitle	Document title and subtitle
Edition information	Book editor(s)	Journal title	Print publication information, if any
Place of publication (APA only)	Book title	Volume and issue number	Site publisher or sponsor
Publisher	Edition information	Date of publication	Site title
Year of publication	Place of publication (APA only)	Page numbers	Date of publication or most recent update
	Publisher		URL or DOI
	Year of publication		Date accessed
	Page numbers		

information that could be relevant—a translator's name, for example, or a series title and editor. Being able to cite a source fully without having to go back to it to get more information saves you time.

THE BASICS OF MLA STYLE

In-text citations.   In MLA style, you must provide a brief citation in the body of your essay (1) when you quote directly from a source, (2) when you paraphrase or summarize what someone else has written, and (3) when you use an idea or a concept that originated with someone else.

In the excerpt that follows, the citation tells readers that the student writer's argument about the evolution of Ebonics is rooted in a well-established source of information. Because the writer does not mention the author in the paraphrase of her source in the text, she gives the author's name in the citation:

> The evolution of U.S. Ebonics can be traced from the year 1557 to the present day. In times of great oppression, such as the beginning of the slave codes in 1661, the language of the black community was at its most "ebonified" levels, whereas in times of racial progress, for example during the abolitionist movement, the language as a source of community identity was forsaken for greater assimilation (Smitherman 119).

The parenthetical citation refers to page 119 of Geneva Smitherman's book *Talkin and Testifyin: The Language of Black America* (1977). Smitherman is a recognized authority on Ebonics. Had the student mentioned Smitherman's name in her introduction to the paraphrase, she would not have had to repeat it in the citation. Notice that there is no punctuation within the parentheses and no *p.* before the page number. Also notice that the citation is considered part of the sentence in which it appears, so the period ending the sentence follows the closing parenthesis.

294 APPENDIX | CITING AND DOCUMENTING SOURCES

By contrast, in the example that follows, the student quotes directly from Richard Rodriguez's book *Hunger of Memory: The Education of Richard Rodriguez* (1982):

> Many minority cultures in today's society feel that it is more important to maintain cultural bonds than to extend themselves into the larger community. People who do not speak English may feel a similar sense of community and consequently lose some of the individuality and cultural ties that come with speaking their native or home language. This shared language within a home or community also adds to the unity of the community. Richard Rodriguez attests to this fact in his essay "Aria." He then goes on to say that "it is not healthy to distinguish public words from private sounds so easily" (183).

Because the student mentions Rodriguez in her text right before the quotation ("Richard Rodriguez attests"), she does not need to include his name in the parenthetical citation; the page number is sufficient.

Works cited. At the end of your researched essay and starting on a new page, you must provide a list of works cited, a list of all the sources you have used (leaving out sources you consulted but decided not to use). Entries should be listed alphabetically by author's last name or by title if no author is identified. Figure A.1 (p. 296) is a sample Works Cited page in MLA style that illustrates a few of the basic types of documentation.

Steps to Compiling an MLA List of Works Cited

1 Begin your list of works cited on a new page at the end of your paper.

2 Put your last name and page number in the upper-right corner.

3 Double-space throughout.

4 Center the heading ("Works Cited") on the page.

5 Arrange the list of sources alphabetically by author's last name or by title if no author is identified.

6 Begin the first line of each source flush left; second and subsequent lines should be indented ½ inch.

7 Invert the author's name, last name first. In the case of multiple authors, only the first author's name is inverted.

8 Italicize the titles of books, journals, magazines, and newspapers. Put the titles of book chapters and articles in quotation marks. Capitalize each word in all titles except for articles (*a, an, the*), short prepositions (*in, at, of,* for example), and coordinating conjunctions (*and, but, for, so,* for example).

THE BASICS OF MLA STYLE   **295**

> **9** For books, list the name of the publisher and the year of publication. For chapters, list the editors of the book, the book title, and the publication information. For articles, list the title of the journal, magazine, or newspaper; the volume and issue numbers (for a journal); and the date of publication.
>
> **10** List the relevant page numbers for articles and selections from longer works.

The steps outlined here for compiling a list of works cited apply to printed sources. MLA formats for citing online sources vary, but this is an example of the basic format:

Author. "Title of Work." *Name of Site*, Publisher or Sponsor, publication date/most recent update date, DOI or URL.

Things to remember:

- Invert the author's name (or the first author's name only, when there are multiple authors).
- Italicize the name of the site.
- If the site publisher or sponsor — usually an institution or organization — isn't clear, check the copyright notice at the bottom of the Web page. If the name of the publisher or sponsor is identical to the name of the site, include only the Web site name in your citation.
- Give the publication date or the most recent update date. Use the day-month-year format for dates in the Works Cited list. Abbreviate all months except May, June, and July.
- Notice that there's a comma between the sponsor and the publication date.
- Include the DOI (if available) or URL for the source.
- If a source has no date, give the date of access at the end of the entry.

In addition to books, articles, and Web sites, you may need to cite sources such as films, recordings, television and radio programs, paintings, and photographs. For details on how to format these sources, consult a handbook (if your instructor has assigned one) or the *MLA Handbook*, Eighth Edition, or go to the MLA Style Center (style.mla.org).

296 APPENDIX | CITING AND DOCUMENTING SOURCES

Eck 10

Works Cited

For three or more authors, list the first author's name, followed by "et al."

Gutiérrez, Kris D., et al. "English for the Children: The New Literacy of the Old World Order." *Bilingual Review Journal*, vol. 24, no. 1/2, Fall/Winter 2000, pp. 87-112.

Article in an online journal, no author

"History of Bilingual Education." *Rethinking Schools*, vol. 12, no. 3, Spring 1998, www.rethinkingschools.org/restrict .asp?path=archive/12_03/langhst.shtml.

Article in a print journal

Lanehart, Sonja L. "African American Vernacular English and Education." *Journal of English Linguistics*, vol. 26, no. 2, June 1998, pp. 122-36.

Article from a Web site

Pompa, Delia. "Bilingual Success: Why Two-Language Education Is Critical for Latinos." *English for the Children*, One Nation/ One California, 1 Nov. 2000, www.onenation.org/article/ bilingual-success/.

Rawls, John. *Political Liberalism*. Columbia UP, 1993.

Essay in an edited collection; second source by same writer

---. "Social Unity and Primary Goods." *Utilitarianism and Beyond*, edited by Amartya Sen and Bernard Williams, Cambridge UP, 1982, pp. 159-85.

Rodriguez, Richard. "Aria." *Hunger of Memory: The Education of Richard Rodriguez*, Bantam Books, 1982, pp. 11-40.

Article in a magazine

Schrag, Peter. "Language Barrier." *New Republic*, 9 Mar. 1998, pp. 14-15.

A book

Smitherman, Geneva. *Talkin and Testifyin: The Language of Black America*. Wayne State UP, 1977.

Willis, Arlette Ingram. "Reading the World of School Literacy: Contextualizing the Experience of a Young American Male." *Harvard Educational Review*, vol. 65, no. 1, Spring 1995, pp. 30-49.

FIGURE A.1 Sample List of Works Cited, MLA Format

THE BASICS OF APA STYLE

In-text citations. In APA style, in-text citations identify the author or authors of a source, page or paragraph numbers for the information cited, and the publication date. If the author or authors are mentioned in the text, provide the publication date immediately following the author's name:

> Feingold (1992) documented the fact that males perform much better than females in math and science and other stereotypically masculine areas (p. 92).

APA style does not explicitly require page or paragraph numbers to be included with paraphrased material. It does, however, recommend page or paragraph numbers for all in-text citations, particularly when readers might have trouble finding the material in the original source without that information. If the source is quoted directly, a page number must be included in parentheses following the quotation:

> Feingold (1992) argued that "men scored significantly higher than women in situations designed to test aptitude in mathematics and hard sciences" (p. 92).

APA style uses the abbreviation *p.* or *pp.* before page numbers, which MLA style does not. If the author is not introduced with a signal phrase, the name, year, and page number would be noted parenthetically after the quotation:

> One study found that "men scored significantly higher than women in situations designed to test aptitude in mathematics and hard sciences" (Feingold, 1992, p. 92).

Many studies in the social sciences have multiple authors. In a work with two authors, cite both authors every time:

> Dlugos and Friedlander (2000) wrote that "sustaining passionate commitment to work as a psychotherapist reflects passionate commitment in other areas of life" (p. 298).

Here, too, if you do not identify the authors in a signal phrase, include their names, the year the source was published, and the relevant page number parenthetically after the quotation—but use an ampersand (&) instead of the word *and* between the authors' names:

> Some believe that "sustaining passionate commitment to work as a psychotherapist reflects passionate commitment in other areas of life" (Dlugos & Friedlander, 2000, p. 298).

Use the same principles the first time you cite a work with three to five authors:

> Booth-Butterfield, Anderson, and Williams (2000) tested . . .
>
> (Booth-Butterfield, Anderson, & Williams, 2000, p. 5)

298   APPENDIX | CITING AND DOCUMENTING SOURCES

Thereafter, you can use the name of the first author followed by the abbreviation *et al.* (Latin for "and others") in roman type:

> Booth-Butterfield et al. (2000) tested . . .
> (Booth-Butterfield et al., 2000, p. 5)

For a work with six or more authors, use *et al.* from the first mention.

These are only some of the most basic examples of APA in-text citation. Consult the APA manual for other guidelines.

References.   APA style, like MLA style, requires a separate list of sources at the end of a research paper. In APA style, this list is called "References," not "Works Cited." The list of references starts on a new page at the end of your paper and lists sources alphabetically by author (or title if no author is identified). Figure A.2 shows a sample list of references with sources cited in APA style.

Steps to Compiling an APA List of References

1. Begin your list of references on a new page at the end of your paper.

2. Put a shortened version of the paper's title (not your last name) in all caps in the upper-left corner; put the page number in the upper-right corner.

3. Double-space throughout.

4. Center the heading ("References") on the page.

5. Arrange the list of sources alphabetically by author's last name or by title if no author is identified.

6. Begin the first line of each source flush left; second and subsequent lines should be indented ½ inch.

7. Invert all authors' names. If a source has more than one author, use an ampersand (not *and*) before the last name.

8. Insert the date in parentheses after the last author's name.

9. Italicize the titles of books, capitalizing only the first letter of the title and subtitle and proper nouns.

10. Follow the same capitalization for the titles of book chapters and articles. Do not use quotation marks around chapter and article titles.

11. Italicize the titles of journals, magazines, and newspapers, capitalizing the initial letters of all key words.

THE BASICS OF APA STYLE **299**

12 For books, list the place of publication and the name of the publisher. For chapters, list the book editor(s), the book title, the relevant page numbers, and the place of publication and the name of the publisher. For articles, list the journal title, the volume number, the issue number if each issue of the volume begins on page 1, the relevant pages, and the DOI (digital object identifier) if available. If you retrieve a journal article online and there is no DOI, include the URL of the journal's home page.

GENDER AND TEACHING   15

References

Journal article with no DOI
Campbell, R. J. (1969). Co-education: Attitudes and self-concepts of girls at three schools. *British Journal of Educational Psychology, 39,* 87.

Report, seven authors
Coleman, J., Campbell, E., Hobson, C., McPartland, J., Mood, A., Weinfeld, F., & York, R. (1966). *Equality of educational opportunity (The Coleman Report).* Washington, DC: U.S. Government Printing Office.

Journal article with a DOI
Feingold, A. (1992). Sex differences in variability in intellectual abilities: A new look at an old controversy. *Review of Educational Research, 62,* 61–84. doi:10.3102/00346543062001061

Online source
Haag, P. (2003). *K–12 single-sex education: What does the research say?* Retrieved from http://www.ericdigests .org/2001-2/sex.html

Journal article retrieved online with no DOI
Hallinan, M. T. (1994). Tracking: From theory to practice. *Sociology of Education, 67,* 79–84. Retrieved from http:// www.asanet.org/journals/soe/

Hanson, S. L. (1994). Lost talent: Unrealized educational aspirations and expectations among U.S. youth. *Sociology of Education, 67,* 159–183. Retrieved from http://www .asanet.org/journals/soe/

Jovanovic, J., & King, S. S. (1998). Boys and girls in the performance-based science classroom: Who's doing the performing? *American Educational Research Journal, 35,* 477–496. doi:10.3102/00028312035003477

FIGURE A.2   Sample List of References, APA Format

300 APPENDIX | CITING AND DOCUMENTING SOURCES

Lee, V. E., & Marks, H. M. (1990). Sustained effects of the single-sex secondary school experience on attitudes, behaviors, and values in college. *Journal of Educational Psychology, 82,* 578–592.

Mickelson, R. A. (1989). Why does Jane read and write so well? The anomaly of women's achievement. *Sociology of Education, 62,* 47–63. Retrieved from http://www.asanet.org/journals/soe/

Scholarly book

Rosenberg, M. (1965). *Society and the adolescent self-image.* Princeton, NJ: Princeton University Press.

Schneider, F. W., & Coutts, L. M. (1982). The high school environment: A comparison of coeducational and single-sex schools. *Journal of Educational Psychology, 74,* 898–906.

Essay in an edited collection

Spade, J. Z. (2001). Gender education in the United States. In J. H. Ballantine & J. Z. Spade (Eds.), *Schools and society: A sociological approach to education* (pp. 270–278). Belmont, CA: Wadsworth/Thomson Learning.

Streitmatter, J. L. (1999). *For girls ONLY: Making a case for single-sex schooling.* Albany, NY: State University of New York Press.

Dissertation from a database

Winslow, M. A. (1995). *Where the boys are: The educational aspirations and future expectations of working-class girls in an all-female high school* (Doctoral dissertation). University of Arizona. Retrieved from ProQuest Dissertations and Theses database. (AAT 9622975)

The *APA Manual* is your best resource for formatting online sources, but here is an example of a basic reference to an online source:

Author. (Date posted/revised). *Document title.* Retrieved from URL

- Provide the author's name in inverted order: last name first. If no author is identified, alphabetize the entry by its title.
- Capitalize an online document title like an article title and italicize it; don't enclose it in quotation marks.
- Include a retrieval date after the word "Retrieved" only if the content is likely to change.

THE BASICS OF APA STYLE   **301**

- Notice that there is no end punctuation after the **DOI** or **URL**.
- **APA** style asks you to break lengthy **DOIs** or **URLs** after a slash or before a period, being sure that your composing software doesn't insert a hyphen at the line break.

You should know that some sources you may rely on in your research in the social sciences—interviews and focus groups, for example—do not have to be included in your list of references. Instead, you would cite the person you interviewed or the focus group you conducted in the text of your paper. For example:

(J. Long, personal interview, April 7, 2017)

ACKNOWLEDGMENTS

Susan D. Blum. "The United States of (Non)Reading: The End of Civilization or a New Era?" From *HuffPost College*, October 8, 2013. Copyright © 2013 by Susan Blum. Reprinted with permission.

Anne Colby and Thomas Ehrlich, with Elizabeth Beaumont and Jason Stephens (the Carnegie Foundation for the Advancement of Teaching). Excerpt from "Undergraduate Education and the Development of Moral and Civic Responsibility." From *The Communitarian Network*, www2.gwu.edu/~ccps/Colby.html. Reprinted by permission of the Institute for Communitarian Policy Studies.

William Deresiewicz. "The End of Solitude." From the *Chronicle of Higher Education*, January 2009. Used with the permission of the *Chronicle of Higher Education*. Copyright © 2009. All rights reserved.

John Dickerson. "Don't Fear Twitter." From Nieman Reports, Summer 2008. Nieman Foundation for Journalism at Harvard. Reprinted by permission.

Steve Grove. "YouTube: The Flattening of Politics." From Nieman Reports, Summer 2008. Nieman Foundation for Journalism at Harvard. Reprinted by permission.

Kris Gutiérrez. Excerpt from "Teaching Toward Possibility: Building Cultural Supports for Robust Learning." From *PowerPlay: A Journal of Educational Justice* 3.1 (2011), pp. 22–37. Reprinted by permission.

E. D. Hirsch Jr. "Preface to *Cultural Literacy*." From *Cultural Literacy: What Every American Needs to Know* by E. D. Hirsch Jr. Copyright © 1987 by Houghton Mifflin Harcourt Publishing Company. Reprinted by permission of Houghton Mifflin Harcourt Publishing Company. All rights reserved.

Dan Kennedy. "Political Blogs: Teaching Us Lessons about Community." From Nieman Reports, Summer 2008. Nieman Foundation for Journalism at Harvard. Reprinted by permission.

Paul Rogat Loeb. "Making Our Lives Count." From *Soul of a Citizen: Living with Conviction in Challenging Times* by Paul Rogat Loeb. Copyright © 1999 by Paul Rogat Loeb. Reprinted by permission of St. Martin's Griffin, an imprint of St. Martin's Press. All Rights Reserved.

James W. Loewen. "The Land of Opportunity." Excerpt from *Lies My Teacher Told Me: Everything Your American History Textbook Got Wrong* by James W. Loewen. Copyright © 1995, 2007 by James W. Loewen. Reprinted by permission of The New Press. www.thenewpress.com.

Meredith Minkler. "Community-Based Research Partnerships: Challenges and Opportunities." From *Journal of Urban Health: Bulletin of the New York Academy of Medicine* 82.2, Supplement 2. Copyright © 2005 by Meredith Minkler. Reprinted with permission.

Laurie Ouellette. Excerpt from "Citizen Brand: ABC and the Do Good Turn in US Television." From *Commodity Activism: Cultural Resistance in Neoliberal Times*, edited by Roopali Mukherjee and Sarah Banet-Weiser. Copyright © 2012 New York University. Reprinted by permission.

Phil Primack. "Doesn't Anybody Get a C Anymore?" From the *Boston Globe*, October 5, 2008. Reprinted by permission.

Eugene F. Provenzo Jr. "Hirsch's Desire for a National Curriculum." Excerpt from *Critical Literacy: What Every American Ought to Know* by Eugene F. Provenzo Jr., pp. 53–55. Copyright © 2005 by Paradigm Publishers. Republished with permission of Taylor & Francis Group LLC Books; permission conveyed through Copyright Clearance Center, Inc.

304 ACKNOWLEDGMENTS

Anna Quindlen. "Doing Nothing Is Something." From *Newsweek*, May 12, 2002. Copyright © 2002 by Anna Quindlen. Used by permission. All rights reserved.

Dana Radcliffe. "Dashed Hopes: Why Aren't Social Media Delivering Democracy?" From the *Huffington Post*, October 21, 2015, http://www.huffingtonpost.com/dana-radcliffe/dashed-hopes-why-arent-so_b_8343082.html. Copyright © 2015. Reprinted by permission of the author.

Stuart Rojstaczer. "Grade Inflation Gone Wild." From the *Christian Science Monitor*, March 24, 2009. Copyright © 2009 by Stuart Rojstaczer. Reprinted with permission.

Tom Standage. Excerpt from "History Retweets Itself," the epilogue to *Writing on the Wall: Social Media—The First 2,000 Years* by Tom Standage. Copyright © 2013. Reprinted by permission of Bloomsbury Publishing Inc.

Clive Thompson. "On the New Literacy." From *WIRED Magazine*, August 24, 2009. Copyright © 2009 Condé Nast. Reprinted with permission.

Sherry Turkle. "The Flight from Conversation." From the *New York Times Magazine*, April 22, 2012. Copyright © 2012 The New York Times. All rights reserved. Used by permission and protected by the Copyright Laws of the United States. The printing, copying, redistribution, or retransmission of this Content without express written permission is prohibited.

David Tyack. "Whither History Textbooks?" From *Seeking Common Ground: Public Schools in a Diverse Society* by David Tyack, Cambridge, Mass.: Harvard University Press. Copyright © 2003 by the President and Fellows of Harvard College. Reprinted by permission of the publisher.